Building the Post-War World

Building the Post-War World

Modern architecture and reconstruction in Britain

Nicholas Bullock

Routledge
Taylor & Francis Group

LONDON AND NEW YORK

First published 2002 by Routledge
11 New Fetter Lane, London EC4P 4EE

Simultaneously published in the USA and Canada
by Routledge
29 West 35th Street, New York, NY 10001

Routledge is an imprint of the Taylor & Francis Group

Typeset in Galliard by Bookcraft Ltd, Stroud,
Gloucestershire
Printed and bound in Great Britain by
St Edmundsbury Press, Bury St Edmunds, Suffolk

British Library Cataloguing in Publication Data
A catalogue record for this book is available from the
British Library

Library of Congress Cataloging in Publication Data
A catalog record for this book has been requested

ISBN 0–415–22178–1 (hb)
ISBN 0–415–22179–X (pb)

Contents

Figures

Illustration credits

The authors and the publishers would like to thank the following individuals and institutions for giving permissions to reproduce illustrations. We have made every effort to contact copyright holders, but if any errors have been made we would be happy to correct them at a later printing.

Aerofilms   4.17i; 4.19†

Architectural Design and Construction (John Wiley and Sons)   8.4ii; 8.5ii; 8.7

Architectural Press   2.2ii, iii, iv; 2.8; 3.1; 3.2; 3.3i, ii; 3.4i; 3.7i, ii, iii, iv; 4.1†; 4.2; 4.3; 4.4; 4.5i, ii; 4.6ii; 4.7; 4.8i, ii; 4.9i, ii†, iii, iv; 4.14i, ii; 4.16i†, ii; 4.17ii†; 4.18i, ii; 4.20ii; 5.2i†, ii, iii, iv; 5.4; 5.11i, ii; 5.13i; 5.14i; 6.2i, ii, iii; 6.3; 6.8i, ii; 8.2; 8.8ii†; 8.10i, ii; 8.11; 8.13i, ii; 8.14i, ii, iii, iv, v, vi†; 9.3i; 10.2iii; 10.4ii; 10.5ii; 10.9ii; 10.10i, ii; 11.2i, ii, iii†; 11.3; 11.4i, ii; 11.5i, ii; 11.6ii; 11.9i; 11.10i†, ii; 11.12i, ii, iii, iv; 11.13ii; 11.14ii, iv

The Builder Group   4.6i; 11.1i, ii; 11.6i; 11.8†; 11.9ii, iii

James Stirling Archive, Centre Canadien d'Architecture/Canadian Center for Architecture, Montreal   5.13ii

Coventry Cathedral Archive   4.11i, ii

Crown Copyright   1.3i, ii; 4.20i; 7.2i, ii, iii; 7.6; 8.1; 8.3i, ii; 8.4i; 8.5i; 8.6i, ii; 8.8i, iii; 8.9i, ii; 8.12; 10.1i, ii; 10.2i, ii; 10.3i, ii; 10.5i; 10.6; 10.7i, ii; 10.9i; 11.11i, ii, iii

© DACS 2002   5.1

Richard Einzig/ARCAID.co.uk   5.15

Emberton, Kathleen   2.1iv

Ezra Stoller © Esto   2.3; 3.5

© FLC/ADAGP, Paris and DACS, London, 2002   5.3i†, ii; 5.6ii

Forum   4.10ii; 6.6

Getty Images   9.5i

Lady Patricia Gibberd   6.1

© Richard Hamilton 2002. All Rights Reserved, DACS   5.8

Mrs Janet Henderson   6.5

Simon Houfe   11.7

Mrs Dorothea Kidder-Smith   2.5; 2.6; 2.7†; 3.4ii

Lady Susan Lasdun   6.9i, ii

Leeds Library and Information Service   7.4iv

London Metropolitan Archive   7.1ii; 9.1i, ii; 9.2; 9.4i, ii, iii; 9.5ii; 9.6; 10.8ii

Macmillan   1.1; 1.5; 7.3i, ii; 7.5

The Roger Sturtevant Collection, Oakland Museum of California   2.4

Peter Smithson   4.13iii, iv; 5.12i, ii; 5.13iii; 5.14ii; 6.7

Sandy Wilson and Peter Carter   4.13i, ii

Tower Hamlets Library   10.11ii

Mrs Jocelyn Underwood   2.1iv

† denotes a figure which has also been used on the cover.

Acknowledgements

This book has taken a long time to write and many people have helped, though I alone am responsible for any failings. It began as a series of open lectures at Kettle's Yard Gallery in the Michaelmas Term 1990 with lectures by architects of the time: Bill Allen, Oliver Cox, Bruce Martin, Peter Moro, Peter Smithson and Sandy Wilson. I have often found that research benefits from teaching and from 1993 to 2001 I taught this topic as a course of lectures to the Department of Architecture's second-year students. I am grateful to them for their questions, confusions and perceptions, from which I have profited handsomely. I have also benefited from the work of Cambridge students, amongst them Nick Bethune, Mark Davies, Matt Dearlove and Laura Giordani, whose third- and fifth-year dissertations have explored different aspects of the subject in a variety of different ways. Many people who were active at the time have been willing to talk to me about their views of this period and to read my typescript, amongst them I am particularly grateful to Bill Allen, Colin Boyne, Jean and Oliver Cox, Trevor Dannatt, Leslie Martin, Peter Moro and Sandy Wilson. My contemporaries, my colleagues, research students and friends have been generous with their time: Peter Carolin, Catharine Cooke, Dean Hawkes, Hugo Hinsley, Elizabeth Lebas, Nick Ray, Andrew Saint, Koichi Watanabe. Taina Rikala offered unstinting editorial assistance which was as invaluable as it was creative and constructive. I have relied heavily on the staff at a number of libraries and archives, particularly those at the Department of Architecture Library, Cambridge, the London Metropolitan Archive and the Public Record Office. The illustrations form an important part of the book and I am grateful for the help Philippa Lewis gave in securing copyright permissions and to Tom Houston and Myke Clifford for scanning the seemingly endless images for the illustrations. Caroline Mallinder, Helen Ibbotson and the team at Routledge, Karl Sharrock at Northwood Editorial Services and Joan Hodsdon at Bookcraft Ltd have all been unfailingly patient and helpful. I owe a special debt of gratitude to my wife for her encouragement, her sympathy and her patience. The book is dedicated to my parents who were bringing up a young family through this first post-war decade. I hope it brings to life the architecture of a period that they have always described with such enthusiasm.

Introduction

By 1955 modern architecture had become established in Britain. This was new. In the 1930s modern architecture, although increasingly familiar in one form or another, the 'jazz moderne' of the new cinemas, the stripped brick classicism of the London underground stations or the bright white render of the occasional flat-roofed villa, was still the exception rather than the rule. The number of architects who denied any allegiance to the styles of the past and could thus claim to be active modernists was small. Smaller still was the number whose buildings directly reflected the values of the Modern Movement, of Le Corbusier, Walter Gropius and the continental avant-garde.[1] After the war this changed. By 1955 modern architecture was no longer a minority interest confined largely to London. It was now the style of choice for local authorities, industry, business, and private clients. Modern schools, modern flats and modern public buildings were being built up and down the country.[2]

This book examines the way in which World War II and the ten years of reconstruction that followed did much to bring about this change. It charts the opportunities created by post-war rebuilding. It shows how the spirit of innovation and experimentation necessary to winning the war found new applications in post-war reconstruction. Above all it shows how hopes for a new and better society became linked to the fortunes of the new architecture.

The impact of the war is central to this study. Across Europe war broke the continuity of architectural activity. It scattered the avant-garde, isolating some under Nazi rule or German occupation, encouraging others to flee to the United States. In Britain architects were conscripted or called upon to contribute to the war effort. The continuity with the old peace-time world of the 1930s was lost. From September 1939 until the middle of 1942 architectural interests were overtaken by the debate on post-war reconstruction. Pressures of war and mounting destruction fostered the national determination to build a 'better tomorrow'. People from every quarter of society began to speculate with a new freedom about the nature of the post-war world. Architects of all persuasions, from Royal Academicians to young radicals, prepared designs and debated ideas for post-war rebuilding.

When in 1942 it was at last ready to start actively planning for post-war reconstruction, the government initiated a new wave of architectural activity. True, discussion of the nature of the new architecture, driven by the preoccupations of the avant-garde, revived as the prospect of rebuilding drew closer. But other areas of architectural activity were transformed. The war opened up an unparalleled demand for experimentation and innovation. The war both forced innovation on general practice and incorporated the avant-garde into the new order of production. On the one hand, the building industry, habitually resistant to change, was coerced into experimenting with new forms of construction. On the other, young architects entered the service of the state to plan reconstruction during the war and to design and build housing, schools and new towns when the war was over.

Most importantly, World War II and the changes it ushered in transformed the nature of the Modern Movement. The war set modern architects in the service of society and encouraged them to look forward to the bright prospect of reconstruction. As reconstruction finally began in the summer of 1945 architects and their skills were much in demand. They were thrown into the task of designing and building the New Britain for which the nation had been waiting. By the mid-1950s, modern architecture was no longer the exclusive interest of a small elite group of pioneers. The values of the Modern Movement had been widely adopted by the profession, forcing the avant-garde to rethink its role.

The change in the relationship between the elite and the mainstream of architectural practice demands a new and broader approach to the writing of history. Histories of modern architecture of the 1920s and 1930s – the 'heroic period' – tend to focus on the role of a small pioneering elite.[3] From Nikolaus Pevsner and Sigfried Giedion to Kenneth Frampton and William Curtis, historians have privileged the actions of an architectural avant-garde committed to a radical break with the past.[4] The assumption has been that the ideas of the vanguard are then adapted, disseminated and diluted in their use by general practice. It is the fascination with the vanguard that, with few exceptions, has led historians to concentrate largely on the Modern Movement, that clustering of pioneering groups and individuals which acquires a collective identity between 1925 and the foundation of the Congrès Internationaux d'Architecture Moderne (CIAM) in 1928. These historians have for the most part played down the role of technical invention and belittled the kinds of innovation and advances that have taken place in general practice.[5]

These conventions are too narrow to write a history of modern architecture in this post-war period that is broad enough to capture the activities of the avant-garde as well as their interplay with the mainstream of modern architecture. What is called for is an account that can bring together these different histories: the significance of the Smithsons' Hunstanton School for the avant-garde, the importance of the Hertfordshire schools for new ways of building and education,

and the value of both for the development of modern architecture in Britain at the time. The intense, sometimes introverted world of the avant-garde is best served by an account that follows the flash and exchange of ideas, focusing on the activities of individuals, small groups and their international connections. The world of post-war practice demands, by contrast, a history that tells of the way in which the special social, economic and political events of the time determined what could be built and when. This history necessarily fastens on what is particular to the conjunction of events in a country, for example on the frustrations of hopes for post-war housing, in the case of Britain, or the success of post-war school building. The mainstream acceptance of modern architecture was not unique to Britain. In one form or another it was becoming the established architecture of reconstruction, as much at home in Italy as in Scandinavia, in Berlin as in Paris. But the way in which this was happening in Britain differed from the course of events in France, and events in both countries took a different course again from those in Germany.

In a reversal of the position before the war, social, political and economic developments in Britain during and after the war are important to our general understanding of the architecture of this period. This is as true of mainstream modern architecture as it is of the avant-garde. Ravaged though the British economy was by the war, rebuilding began immediately the war ended. Progress was faster than in France and under way long before the start of rebuilding in Germany.[6] After 1945, the mainstream of modern architecture in Britain provided the clear opportunity to test in practice new ideas – formal, social and technical – earlier than anywhere else in Europe. Foreign deputations came to visit the English New Towns, foreign periodicals published articles on the housing being built by the London boroughs and the London County Council, and European festival juries awarded prizes for British school design.

Nor was it just the general practice of reconstruction in Britain that attracted attention. In contrast to the situation before the war, the British debate on architecture during the 1940s and 1950s attracted widespread interest. As debate on the new architecture took off again after the war, the British contribution was to emerge as a potent force in shaping the international debate on the new architecture: two of the four CIAM conferences of the first post-war decade were held in Britain, and British architects played a central role in the founding of Team X, the key international forum for the younger generation of the architectural avant-garde.

Focusing on the first post-war decade, 1945–55, this book contrasts and brings together two forms of history. The first part of the book offers an account of the debates and the key buildings of the new architecture that featured in the leading journals of the period, the *Architectural Review*, the *Architects' Yearbook* and, after 1954 with a change of editor, *Architectural Design*. This is the domain of the architectural elite. The second part examines the engagement of modern architecture with post-war reconstruction and the way that this then led to new forms of modern practice. In a number of ways this differentiation between architectural debate and practice is artificial: the ideas that were being debated were being tested in practice; current building did raise questions that sparked debate. Nevertheless this separation is of value because it acknowledges the essential autonomy of the architectural debate at the time. Much of the debate is self-referential, concentrated on formal architectural rather than social or technical issues, and needs to be followed in its own, often limited, terms. With these limitations accepted, it is possible to trace the evolution of core ideas that shaped avant-garde attitudes to architectural form and to follow the exchanges and disagreements between the key groups engaged in these debates. Equally important, by telling the story of reconstruction as it was shaped by economic, social and political considerations, it is possible to understand what was actually built and how modern architecture won widespread acceptance in Britain. Reconstruction changed architecture

and its practice and the terms in which mainstream practice and the architectural elite viewed and addressed each other.

The account of both the vanguard and the mainstream of modern architecture necessarily begins with the war. The Prologue to both parts of the book opens with the impact of the war and the start of the debate on reconstruction. For Britain, it is the shock of the Blitz that marks the break between the world of the 1930s and the war years, that encourages people to look forward to the future, to start debating the form reconstruction should take, and to begin imagining the new post-war world.

Notes

The following abbreviations have been used in the chapter notes throughout the book.

ABN	The *Architect and Building News*
AD	*Architectural Design*
AJ	The *Architects' Journal*
AR	The *Architectural Review*
AYB	The *Architects' Yearbook*
JRIBA	*Journal of the Royal Institute of British Architects*
GLRO	The Greater London Record Office (now the London Metropolitan Archive)
PRO	The Public Record Office, Kew

1 The term 'modern architecture' is used throughout this book in the broadest sense to convey the range of architectural interests which claimed no allegiance to the architectural styles of the past. By contrast, the Modern Movement is identified as that more exclusive group which had become identified after 1928 with CIAM; see e.g. G. Ciucci, 'The Invention of the Modern Movement', *Oppositions*, 24 (Spring), 1981.
2 The scale of this change can be gauged by comparing the list of modern buildings in Britain in the first edition of J.M. Richards' *Introduction to Modern Architecture*, Harmondsworth, Penguin, 1940, with the range of entries in T. Dannatt (ed.) *Modern Architecture in Britain*, London, Batsford, 1959.
3 The use of the term avant-garde to characterise the leaders of the Modern Movement, the pioneering elite, is problematic. In his classic study of the avant-garde, *The Theory of the Avant-Garde*, with its focus on groups like the Futurists and its emphasis on the visual arts and literature, Renato Poggioli offers a definition of the avant-garde that is conceived in terms of a limited number of key attributes: activism, antagonism, nihilism and agonism. The extension of this

usage to architecture has attracted criticism, and a number of writers – notably Hilde Heynen in *Architecture and Modernity, a Critique*, Cambridge, MIT Press, 1999 – have recently challenged the use of the term avant-garde as a way of characterising the leaders of the Modern Movement. Heynen argues that Sigfried Giedion's canonical text *Space, Time and Architecture: The Birth of a New Aesthetic* (Cambridge, Mass., Harvard University Press, 1941), which was critical to establishing the identity of the Modern Movement, fails to qualify for inclusion under Poggioli's definition. By this test, it is clear that many figures who are central to the development of the Modern Movement, such as Le Corbusier, Gropius and Mies van der Rohe, to name only the most obvious, cannot be counted as members of the avant-garde in these narrow terms. Their exclusion suggests the need for a more inclusive definition of the architectural avant-garde. This book follows Reyner Banham's *Theory and Design in the First Machine Age* (London, Architectural Press, 1960), an extended homage to the architectural avant-garde of the 1920s, in describing the pioneering elite of the Modern Movement as the architectural avant-garde.

4   This is as true for the pioneering histories of the Modern Movement as it is for recent surveys: N. Pevsner, *Pioneers of the Modern Movement: From William Morris to Walter Gropius*, London, Faber & Faber, 1936, and Giedion, *Space, Time and Architecture*; K. Frampton, *A Critical History of Modern Architecture*, London, Thames & Hudson, 1980; W. Curtis, *Modern Architecture since 1900*, Oxford, Phaidon, 1982. The term heroic period is a reference to the title of Alison and Peter Smithson's article 'The Heroic Period of Modern Architecture 1917-37', *Architectural Design*, Dec. 1965, which eulogised the work of the leaders of the Modern Movement before World War II.

5   Exceptions to this general rule are Reyner Banham's *The Architecture of the Well-Tempered Environment*, London, Architectural Press, 1969, and, more recently, Kenneth Frampton's *Studies in Tectonic Culture: The Poetics of Construction in Nineteenth and Twentieth Century Architecture*, Cambridge, Mass., MIT Press, 1996.

6   On reconstruction in France see A. Kopp, F. Boucher and D. Pauly, *L'Architecture de la Reconstruction en France 1945–1953*, Paris, ARDJ, 1980, and D. Voldman, *La Reconstruction des Villes Françaises de 1940 à 1954*, Paris, Harmattan, 1997. For Germany see K. von Beyme, *Der Wiederaufbau, Architektur und Städtebaupolitik in beiden Deutschen Staaten*, Munich, Prestel, 1987, and J. Dieffendorf, *In the Wake of War: The Reconstruction of German Cities after World War II*, Oxford and New York, Oxford University Press, 1993. For a comparative survey of European reconstruction see J. Dieffendorf (ed.), *Rebuilding Europe's Bombed Cities*, London, Macmillan, 1990.

Prologue

1 The war-time debate on reconstruction

An air-raid warden watched in disbelief as the first wave of bombers droned overhead. Miniature silver planes circled 'round and round the target area in such perfect formation that they looked like a child's toy model of flying boats or chair-o-planes at a fair'.[1] There had of course been air-raids during that first year of war but the number of casualties and the scale of destruction was much smaller than had been earlier envisaged.[2] The first raid had been in Canterbury in May 1940, with few casualties. People who had been evacuated from cities like London began gradually to drift back. The fear of air attack seemed somehow remote, particularly when set beside the immediate difficulties of evacuation for both 'guests' and 'hosts'.[3] Air attacks during June and July had been heavier, but civilian casualties were limited to fewer than 100 deaths in June and 300 in July, and still the predicted onslaught did not come.

But the raid launched on 7 September 1940 marked a change in the scale of the air war. With nearly half the strength of the Luftwaffe organised in two great waves, the impact of the attack was shattering. Over 400 civilians lost their lives, 1600 people were severely injured, and the scale of destruction was unparalleled.[4] One 18-year-old observer in Poplar described the attack:

> Around five o'clock I went outside the house, I'd heard the aircraft, and it was very exciting, because the first formations were coming over without any bombs dropping, but very majestic; terrific. And I

had no thought that they were actually bombers. Then from that point on I was well aware, because the bombs began to fall, and shrapnel was going along King Street, dancing off the cobbles. The real impetus came, in so far as the suction and the compression from the high explosive blasts just pushed and pulled you, and the whole atmosphere turbulating so hard that, after an explosion of a nearby bomb, you could actually feel your eye-balls being sucked out. I was holding my eyes to try to stop them going. And the suction was so vast, it ripped my shirt away, and ripped my trousers. Then I couldn't get my breath, the smoke was like acid and everything around me was black and yellow. And these bombers just kept on and on, the whole road was moving, rising and falling.[5]

The next morning people gazed over the wreckage in areas that had been badly hit, like Stepney and Silvertown in the East End (Figure 1.1). There was astonishment at the sheer level of destruction. Whole streets were destroyed, tens of thousands of people had been made homeless. The plight of those left without homes was pitiful: bombed-out families desperate for food, clothing and shelter were further disoriented to find that local authorities had made practically no provision for them. What was to be done with the daily mounting number of families who no longer had a home to go to? How were local services to cope with the problems of feeding, clothing and supporting people who were dependent for even

1.1 The morning after a raid on the East End. By the middle of October 1940 bomb damage forced over 25,000 people to seek housing from the local authorities

their most basic needs? Difficult enough questions at any time, the task was enormously complicated by the war. The raids left a field of destruction that had to be cleared each day for the life of the city to continue. The day after that first heavy raid the bombers returned again, and they continued to do so, with one brief respite – 2 November – for the next 76 nights.

As the bombing continued people began to adapt to the extraordinary rhythms of a city under prolonged attack from the air. They still felt a pervading sense of vulnerability, but the panic subsided and families no longer trekked out of the East End in search of the safety of Epping Forest or the Kent hop fields. Attacks on the East End continued until the end of September, when German strategy directed the raids further west to Belgravia and Kensington, then further out still in all directions to the suburbs of Croydon, Wandsworth, Plumstead and Ilford. In one heavy raid on 15 October, the whole of London was under attack. Bombs fell from East Ham to Fulham, from Lewisham to Tottenham. Destruction in the East End was most intense. By early November 40 per cent of all dwellings in Stepney had been destroyed or badly damaged. Stepney suffered more than most areas, but even in western boroughs like Paddington and Hammersmith the end of 1940 saw the level of

damage and casualties fast approaching the average for all London's inner boroughs. By mid-October 1940, 25,000 Londoners had been made homeless by the bombing.[6]

The destruction wrought by the war opened the agenda for reconstruction. The first priority, however, was to meet the needs of those whose homes had been bombed. This duty fell to the local authorities, who at the beginning of the war were woefully equipped to meet their obligations, not least because of the inadequate Poor Law regulations that governed provision for the homeless. The first haven for homeless people was the 'rest centre' run by the local borough. But that assistance was quickly overrun by the number of people seeking shelter: nineteen days after the first raid on London, occupancy in the rest centres reached 25,000.[7] The Charity Organisation Society reported on the despair that reigned in most of these centres:

> Dim figures in dejected heaps on unwashed floors in total darkness: harassed, bustling, but determinedly cheerful helpers distributing eternal corned beef sandwiches and tea – the London County Council panacea for hunger, shock, loss, misery and illness … Dishevelled, half-dressed people wandering between the bombed house and the rest centre salvaging bits and pieces, or trying to keep in touch with the scattered family … A clergyman appeared and wandered about aimlessly, and someone played the piano.[8]

With the backing of the newly appointed Home Secretary, Herbert Morrison, and with funding for the homeless from the Treasury, provision rapidly improved. The immediate shortage of camp beds and blankets was overcome. The Londoners' Meals Service run by the London County Council (LCC) provided cheap and nutritious food. Information on accommodation, education and welfare was centralised by the local authorities, while voluntary organisations like the Women's Voluntary Service established advice centres.

Collaboration between the LCC and the Entertainments National Service Association and the Council for the Encouragement of Music and the Arts established informal entertainment. By the end of 1941 conditions had been transformed: 'The bleak, inhospitable poor law standards of the centres of September 1940 had given way to good and kindly board and lodging, available without charge to the homeless victims of air attack.'[9]

Improving the rest centres addressed the immediate post-raid needs of the homeless but the most difficult problem was to find long-term accommodation.[10] During the first six weeks of the Blitz, councils in the region had housed barely 7,000 of London's homeless. In East End boroughs the problems were particularly acute. Stepney had suffered more damage than any other borough and faced large numbers of homeless for the first two months of the Blitz without a billeting or rehousing department. The task of the billeting departments was never an easy one. Families rehoused by the local authority were often unwelcome. Householders forced to accept an East End family could be frankly hostile:

When we arrived we all looked a bit dirty and dishevelled and the lady of the house decided that she didn't want us in and she wouldn't open the door. The billeting officer said, 'You've got to open the door by law and let them in,' and eventually she did. We felt awful. We were put in the attic, there were two rooms. Me and my sister had to share a bed with mum and my brothers went in the other room. There was nowhere to cook and the lady wouldn't let us bring food into the house. She didn't like us in the house in day-time and so we spent most of the day in the park. We'd eat some sandwiches, sit on benches or walk around to keep warm. We would have gone back to the East End if we could, but our home was totally uninhabitable.[11]

Shared arrangements with relatives or neighbours might be more convivial but living conditions were often primitive:

We all went to 32 Wrythe Lane to my sister's little maisonette. There were eighteen of us there in two rooms because we were all bombed out. My father fixed up scaffold boards along the walls and at night ten of us would sleep in one room, all in line, and eight in the other little room. Of course we didn't get much sleep. Outside my father fixed up some buckets for the men and built a latrine. In the garden there was a bit of a grass patch and my brother-in-law fixed up a ridge tent, so I used to sleep in that with three or four of the other men.[12]

Public recognition of the suffering and difficulties of the homeless fuelled the debate on reconstruction (Figure 1.2). People who were bombed out would have been too busy coping with day-to-day survival to take part in the debate, but as destruction became more widespread and people elsewhere came to recognise what was happening in the East End, demands that government start making plans for rebuilding grew more insistent. As middle-class discovery of the poverty and condition of many evacuees was to reinforce demands for social reforms, so the plight of the homeless forced the issue of post-war housing to the top of the agenda for reconstruction.

Reconstruction and continuity: linking the past and future

From the start it was clear that reconstruction would involve much more than simply rebuilding what had been before. The bombing and the war offered a chance for radical change. The experience of Dunkirk – the prospect of defeat followed by the unexpected success of escape – heightened the feeling that it was not enough simply to avoid defeat. It was important for people to believe that they were fighting to

1.2. War-damaged housing. Though most houses damaged during the Blitz had received first-aid repairs, the damage caused by flying bombs and rocket attacks of 1944–45 was to be a serious drain on the resources available for reconstruction

achieve something positive. J.B. Priestley's 20 minute radio broadcasts *Postscripts*, broadcast after the 9 p.m. news on Sundays, reflected this popular feeling. His words spoke for the mood of the country:

> Now there are two ways of looking at this war. The first way, which, on the whole, we are officially encouraged to adopt, is to see this war as a terrible interruption. As soon as we can decently do it, we must return to peace … and go back to where we started from, the day before war was declared. This brings us to the second, and more truthful, way of looking at this war. That is to regard this war as a chapter in a tremendous history, the history of a changing world, the breakdown of one vast system and the building up of a new and better one … There's nothing that really worked that we can go back to. But we can go forward … and really plan and build a nobler world in which ordinary, decent folk can not only find justice and security but also beauty and delight.[13]

But reconstruction was not just about building 'a nobler' new world. Planning for the future was inseparably mingled with a desire for continuity with the past. True, the changes, often brutal, created by the war offered unique opportunities to sweep away what was bad, unjust, worn out and inadequate, but the same process of change also created a longing to return to what was familiar, to the happier images of a pre-war world fondly remembered (Figure 1.3). Writing in 1943, G.D.H. Cole acknowledged the conflicting responses to the promise of reconstruction:

Even if [people] have in them the spark of idealism and are ready to play their part in making the world a better place than it used to be … they are still apt to keep their private and their public aspirations in separate compartments, so as to speak to you one minute about the new world they hope to see, and the next about how nice it will be to get back to their old jobs and their old homes, or to something as like them as can be managed.[14]

In Priestley's *Postscripts* this sense of continuity was linked to the feeling for community, to 'the ploughman and parson, shepherd and clerk, turning out at night, as our forefathers had often done before us, to keep watch and ward over the sleeping English hills and fields and homesteads'.[15] This sense of continuity enabled the country to know what to defend and how to rebuild. For Priestley reconstruction would have to secure and preserve the qualities of the English – and the Welsh and the Scots – that made them so different from the Nazis. The humour, courage, modesty, the decency and imagination, the determination when roused, sketched in affectionate detail by Dickens, were the qualities he admired. These were the qualities worth fighting for and that would emerge in the New Britain

after the sufferings of war. This tradition of Englishness, this benign myth of national identity, was celebrated across the arts, in the paintings of Paul Nash and John Piper, in the photographs of Bill Brandt, in the writings of John Betjeman, and in the music of Benjamin Britten.[16]

This revaluation of national tradition was also to find a powerful response in the struggle to preserve the country's physical heritage so obviously threatened by war. This new sense of the value of Britain's landscapes, buildings and monuments brought renewed animation to pre-war campaigns;[17] new vigour to the Council for the Protection of Rural England's battles to preserve the countryside; urgency to organisations like the Georgian Group that championed the upkeep of buildings not sufficiently ancient to catch the tweedy interests of the Society for the Protection of Ancient Buildings; and conviction to writers and artists like Betjeman and Piper, at once avant-garde enthusiasts and popularisers, who through the *Shell Guides* wished to preserve the local culture of villages and market towns, unassuming architectural graces recently rendered accessible to (and threatened by) a motorised middle class.

These interests, galvanised by the war, were to find a practical expression in the documentation from 1941 by the National Buildings Record of buildings of architectural distinction, so that

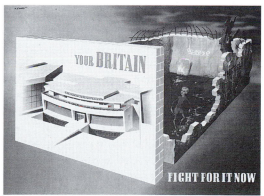

i   ii

1.3 Posters produced in 1942 by the Army Bureau of Current Affairs: (i) 'Your Britain. Fight for It Now', Frank Newbould's view of the South Downs; (ii) Abram Games' depiction of the contrast between the ill health of the past and modern health care symbolised by Tecton's Finsbury Health Centre

rebuilding after the war would not be at odds
with preserving the best of the past. Indeed, for
John Summerson – a member of both the
Modern Architectural Research (MARS) Group
and the Georgian Group, and engaged day to
day with listing of the nation's buildings – preservation and reconstruction were not in conflict.
The strength of the link between preservation
and reconstruction was reflected too in the provisions of the first legislation for post-war
rebuilding, the 1944 Town and Country
Planning Act, which offered statutory protection
for 'listed' buildings and other monuments as
plans for reconstruction were prepared.[18]

**Preparing the agenda for reconstruction,
1940–42**

The war set the agenda for reconstruction
(Figure 1.4). The inescapable need to consider
the problems of physical rebuilding was imposed
by the course of destruction which continued
into the New Year and through into the spring of
1941. Surveying the rubble of the East End or
the devastation of Coventry, Hull or Plymouth,
it was clear that a massive programme of peace-
time rebuilding lay ahead. To talk about the way
Britain should be built after the war was natural,
if only as an act of defiance against a seemingly
hostile fate, and as a way of bolstering morale.
Here was the occasion not just to build but to
improve what had been. Reformers who had
campaigned for social change in the pre-war
years, advocates of slum clearance and garden
cities alike, were determined that this opportunity for change should not be allowed to slip by.

The heavy raids of October and November
1940 spurred discussion in the press, and for the
next two years reconstruction was to become the
subject of innumerable newspaper articles, pamphlets, books, exhibitions and films. Newspapers
not only reported speeches at length, but ran
special articles or series on different aspects of
reconstruction. Papers sympathetic to the left,
the *News Chronicle*, the *Observer* and *Picture
Post*, focused interest on reconstruction issues. In

1.4 Cover to the catalogue of the 'Rebuilding Britain'
exhibition, July 1943

articles like 'A Ministry for the Future', the *News
Chronicle* under the editorship of Gerald Barry
called on the government to set about the task of
reconstruction without delay.[19] *Picture Post*, champion of the new photo-journalism, ran frequent
articles like 'Readers Work on a Plan for Britain'
or 'Plan Britain Now' that called for a government lead in planning and reconstruction.[20] The
more progressive elements of the popular press,
the *Herald*, the *Mirror* and the *London Standard*, called on government to 'set the ball rolling'.[21] Interest in reconstruction was not confined to papers that were sympathetic to the left.
Under the editorial direction of both R.M.
Barrington-Ward and E.H. Carr, *The Times* took
an equally progressive line calling for decisive
governmental action. Even conservative dailies
like the *Daily Telegraph* urged government to
take the lead.

Radio gave considerable time to reconstruction issues. In early October 1940, the art critic

Herbert Read invited BBC listeners to speculate on the way in which London might be rebuilt after the war. Encouraging them to think expansively, he cited the example of Le Corbusier's 1925 Voisin plan for the rebuilding of the centre of Paris.[22] In a series of programmes called *Making Plans*, broadcast from the start of 1941, listeners could hear 'ordinary people giving their views' on the form of post-war Britain. These talks were complemented by ideas expressed by various experts. Elizabeth Denby, a well-known figure in the pre-war housing reform movement interviewed young architects like Leslie Martin and Richard Llewelyn Davies on 'The New Houses'. Frederic Osborn, secretary to the Town and Country Planning Association, could be heard talking to Harding Thompson on 'Making New Towns for the People', and William Holford discussed 'The Reconstruction of Old Towns' with Frank Mears and Lancelot Keay.[23]

Picture Post's special number on reconstruction may have conveyed a sense of excitement at the prospect of what might be built after the war but remained understandably vague about how the proposals it illustrated were to be achieved.[24] The prospect of reconstruction seemed to promise the opportunity of sweeping away all the ills of pre-war society, and reformers of all hues and convictions hurried to proffer their views on the shape of the post-war world. But for all this talk, the debate remained inchoate. By the end of 1940, it was no longer a question of making the case for reconstruction, that was agreed. The task was now to settle how this was to be done.

The role of the state

Despite the variety of groups, each with its own proposals, there was common to all – sometimes implicit, more often explicit – the assumption that only government could direct the programme of reconstruction. When required to improvise, to meet the challenge of completely unknown circumstances, government may have faltered, but it had shown resource, it had not failed. Inevi-tably it had been forced to intervene in order to prosecute the war. It commanded in the field. Civilian life too was more regulated than it had been during the First World War. The government ran the economy, taking charge of industry, mobilising women as well as men, and introducing rationing for food, clothing and other scarce resources. Public acceptance of widespread intervention by the government in the day-to-day details of the lives of ordinary British citizens, evident for example, in the popular support for rationing, did much to advance the case for the role of the state in planning.

If government could persuasively secure equality of sacrifice and a fair sharing of scarce resources during the war, could it not be trusted to determine the terms of post-war reconstruction? Hancock and Gowing's official history of the war economy underlines the central role that people felt the government should play and the importance of it doing so:

> There existed, so to speak, an implied contract between Government and people; the people refused none of the sacrifices that the Government demanded from them for the winning of the war; in return, they expected that the Government should show imagination and seriousness in preparing for the restoration and improvement of the nation's well-being when the war was won. The plans for reconstruction were, therefore, a real part of the war effort.[25]

During the 1930s conventional wisdom had favoured market forces and laissez-faire; the case for government intervention had been predominantly the cause of the left.[26] Now, across the broad centre of politics it was increasingly acceptable to argue that only government should regulate priorities, allocate resources and ensure some measure of social justice between different groups. The left naturally supported these views, which represented a continuation of the policies that Labour had been urging before the war. But now there were conservatives too who found these views acceptable. Churchill remained as opposed as ever to involvement in post-war social reform, but other conservative politicians like R.A. Butler, Harold Macmillan, Quentin Hogg and Lord Hinchingbroke were prepared to press for a central role for government in planning post-war reconstruction and the social and economic changes that this would bring.

Despite this shift in the political consensus government was slow to respond to the clamour for reconstruction. The sheer pressure of fighting the war and meeting the succession of challenges to daily survival left little enough time for thinking about the present, let alone for looking into the future. But with Dunkirk and the fall of France, the government came grudgingly to recognise, and with no encouragement from Churchill, that it was not enough simply to urge sacrifice. It was necessary to say what the country was fighting for. Senior figures in the Ministry of Information pressed the view that it was important for the sake of raising morale to announce promises of a better post-war Britain.[27] The year 1941 would see the emergence, with the active assistance of government, of proposals that were to lay the foundations for the post-war welfare state.[28] John Maynard Keynes's unpublished paper on British war aims is generally identified as the starting point for rethinking the tangle of issues associated with social security and unemployment. The resulting formation of an inter-departmental committee in May 1941 to examine the existing provision of social insurance and 'allied services' was to lead directly to the publication of the Beveridge Report in December 1942. In this report William Beveridge, then Master of University College, Oxford, and chairman of the Unemployment Insurance Statutory Committee, set out to remedy the evident defects of pre-war health care, unemployment benefits, pensions and similar social services. In place of the means-tested patchwork of pre-war provision, Beveridge proposed to unify social services and make them available to everyone in return for a single weekly, flat-rate contribution. A minimum standard of living would be guaranteed to all. More than any other set of proposals, the Beveridge Report gave specific shape to plans for reconstruction. Despite government hostility, his proposals won public support as the real promise of a fairer and better post-war society. An arrogant academic to some, Beveridge became a popular hero, 'the people's William', trusted by the nation to slay the pre-war giant evils of want, ignorance, disease, squalor and idleness.[29]

Ideas for reconstruction were developing in other areas too. In 1941 proposals emerged for managing the economy that would eventually make it possible to address the problem of mass unemployment. Incorporated into the Budget of April 1941 were the first official statistics of national income and expenditure, transforming the Budget into the key regulator of the economy. Central to economic management for the war effort, the methods of forecasting and regulating national demand would also offer for the post-war years a way of eradicating mass unemployment. The 1944 White Paper on the planning of employment was one of the first results of these developments in economic management and an attempt to attack one of the most damaging social problems of the 1930s.

In education and health 1941 was a decisive year in establishing blueprints for post-war reconstruction. Appointed to the Board of Education in June 1941, R.A. Butler used his diplomatic skills to advance the proposals drawn up by the board for the expansion of the education system. Developing the recommendations of the Hadow Report of 1926 and the Spens Report of 1938, the Board of Education proposed the creation of separate primary, secondary and further education sectors. Butler, James Chuter Ede and their team were to encounter formidable obstacles to these plans. Negotiations with the churches over the way in which state support for church schools would affect denominational control, and the discussion of the position of the public schools within the expanded school system, were only the most obvious difficulties. But by the end of 1942 the proposals for the White Paper on education were proceeding through the government machine.

In health too, Dunkirk provided an important impetus to confronting the failings of the 1930s. The programme of reforms first sketched out during the course of 1941 was eventually to lead to the establishment of the National Health Service in 1946. The programme was shaped by two separate developments. The first started with the establishment of the Emergency Medical Service, originally launched to provide medical treatment for air-raid victims and soon extended to provide for sick servicemen, unaccompanied evacuees, and others in need of medical care. Working alongside the old health services the Emergency Medical Service achieved limited integration of the public and the voluntary hospitals, suggesting to Whitehall the basis for a single national health service. The second development grew from the pre-war conviction of the medical profession that the existing system of national health insurance was inadequate and should be extended and that the existing hospital system, divided between local authority and voluntary sectors, should be integrated administratively. These critical steps led to the formation in August 1940 of the Medical Planning Commission, which brought together the British Medical Association, the Royal Colleges, the Royal Scottish Corporations and the Medical Officers of Health, to prepare plans for post-war health care. In May 1941 the commission published its interim findings recommending the creation after the war of a national health service that would be freely available to all. The nation would have to wait until after the war for a true national health service, but the progress made in 1940–41 was important and a measure of how professional attitudes were changing with the war.

But 1941 was also an important year for preparing plans for physical reconstruction after the war. Destruction caused by bombing gave the word reconstruction an immediate and practical meaning. The press and the succession of experts speaking on the radio held high hopes of what might be achieved by government action on housing and town planning. Though the government wished to be seen to respond to this agitation for reconstruction – what Churchill

sardonically called the 'continual buzz of ardent discussion' – its response was cautious. For Churchill plans for reconstruction could be little more than 'false hopes and airy visions of Utopia and Eldorado', at least until war was won.[30] An opportunity for government to set out its views was provided in response to the publication in January 1940 of the report of the Barlow Commission on the Geographical Distribution of the Industrial Population, which had been established by Neville Chamberlain in 1937 to consider a variety of planning issues, from the containment of suburban sprawl to addressing the problems of depressed areas like the North East and south Wales. A majority of the fourteen commissioners had pressed for the creation of a central planning authority with a wide range of national planning powers. A minority report had gone further, demanding that these powers be taken over by government itself. The report and its recommendations attracted little attention at the time of publication, but with the beginning of the Blitz public interest in town planning had risen sharply. Spurred by the evident need for rebuilding and by the propaganda in support of planning by pressure groups like the Town and Country Planning Association (TCPA), government conceded the need to initiate a system of planning. Mindful of the new popular appeal of planning, the government responded to the Barlow Report's recommendations by appointing John Reith, former Director General of the BBC, as Minister of Works and Buildings not just to take charge of the newly created Ministry of Works but with an additional, if limited, brief to consult government departments and other organisations about the post-war rebuilding of cities.[31]

Whom was Reith to consult? In November 1940 and again in July 1941, the period of the most intense – and least focused – debate on reconstruction, the *Architectural Review* summarised proposals and activities of nearly twenty groups concentrating on physical reconstruction alone.[32] These groups, although similar to others debating reconstruction, were the focus of gentle teasing for their earnest activities. H.G. Wells caricatured the 1941 Committee, a ginger group set up to collect informed criticism and communicate it to government and typical of many reconstruction committees, as a 'well-meaning (but otherwise meaningless) miscellany of people … earnestly and obstinately going in every direction under vehement professions of unity'.[33] The *Architectural Review* described groups as diverse in their aims as those debating social insurance, where 'a common language of visionary patriotism and a common sense of national unity continued to mask an immense diversity of value and goals'.[34] Notwithstanding their diversity, the groups had much in common. Members tended to be drawn from professional circles, academic life, the voluntary sector and central and local government. Interests frequently overlapped. The same faces were visible in different combinations at different committee meetings discussing the many aspects of reconstruction. As plans for reconstruction advanced, members of these groups would be drawn into the orbit of government. Some sat on government committees, some ended up working, occasionally without pay, in governmental departments: some rose to high office. It was the ready absorption of these people into government that linked the 1940–42 debate on reconstruction with the plans for postwar Britain set out by the government between 1942 and 1945.

These groups can be classified in a number of ways: by political bias, by the balance of their interests between planning and housing, or by the character of their membership. A first distinction can be drawn between those groups campaigning for a particular issue and those content to coordinate and focus the approaches of others. Typical of the latter, with their concern to coordinate research and bring the debate to bear on government action, were the Royal Institute of British Architects (RIBA) and the Town Planning Institute (TPI), organisations that sought to convey the consensus of the professions. The contrast with the stance of campaigning pressure groups like the TCPA[35] or the Association of Architects, Surveyors and Technical Assistants (AASTA)[36] could hardly be greater. While the TCPA represented the views of

believers in Ebenezer Howard's vision, such as Frederic Osborn, Richard Reiss and C.B. Purdom, the RIBA was expected to reflect the diversity within the architectural profession. This was apparent from the careful balance maintained in the choice of thirty-four members for the RIBA's Reconstruction Committee established in March 1941.[37] Radical younger architects like Godfrey Samuel, Maxwell Fry, Jane Drew and Leslie Martin were matched with older or more conservative figures like Banister Fletcher, A.E. Richardson, Giles Gilbert Scott and Frederick Hiorns. Howard Robertson and Charles Reilly, who retained the confidence of the older generation while being known for their sympathy for the Modern Movement, held the centre ground. Members of the committee were assigned, according to their interests, to eight subcommittees, with many members serving on more than one. The subjects covered by these subcommittees went well beyond a narrow perspective of professional interest and duty to consider the professional status of the architect, professional qualifications for town planning and for architecture, planning and amenity, housing, building legislation, the building industry, building techniques, and publicity.

Similar to the RIBA Reconstruction Committee were organisations such as the 1941 Committee, the 1940 Council and the Nuffield College Social Reconstruction Survey, established specifically to look at the problems created by the war. The 1940 Council was set up under the aegis of the Housing Centre, with close links to the RIBA and the TPI, to sponsor research on 'the environmental needs of the community and the study of the means by which these [could] be fulfilled'.[38] In contrast to bodies like the TCPA, the 1940 Council stressed that it had no special theory or proposal to promote and likened its impartial role in encouraging research to that of the Medical Research Council. Typical of these committees was the Architectural Science Group, started at the urging of Dr Stradling, director of the Building Research Station, to bring together representatives of the building industry, the architectural profession and building scientists to pool ideas on the technical questions of rebuilding.[39]

Reconstruction and the campaign for planning, 1940–42

In contrast to the first group of organisations were those campaigning on a single issue, such as the TCPA. More than any other single issue, planning came to be seen as the test of the government's willingness to address the challenge of reconstruction in radical terms. The prospect of what might be done with a national system of planning captured the imagination of those pressing for a new and better post-war Britain. By the time the RIBA's Reconstruction Committee presented the first interim reports of its Planning and Amenities Sub-Committee in September 1940, even a cautious professional body like the RIBA was putting forward recommendations that would have seemed inflammatory before the war began.[40] That this was possible was a measure of the movement in 'middle opinion' and the acceptance of the idea of planning brought about by the activities of a range of campaigning organisations.

The activities of the TCPA illustrate better than the work of any similar body both the effort of the campaigning organisations and the way that they were able to form links with government.[41] Founded in 1898 to spread the Garden City gospel, the TCPA had concentrated on winning public support for Howard's ideas and for further application in practice of the principles first demonstrated at Letchworth. After World War I the TCPA had benefited from the interest in housing and town planning generated by government plans for housing, and its prestige had been boosted by the establishment in 1920 of a second Garden City at Welwyn. But by the end of the 1920s, both the membership and momentum of the TCPA were in decline. In the mid-1930s this was to change. The appointment of Gilbert McAllister as Secretary – as well as editor for the association's journal, *Town and Country Planning* – and the arrival of Frederic Osborn as Honorary Secretary brought new

direction to the association.[42] Under new leadership the TCPA lost no time in moving beyond merely extolling the virtues of life at Letchworth and Welwyn to enter the debate on the central physical planning issues of the day – the containment of urban sprawl and the location of industry – and the growing concern over the economic imbalance between North and South.

In 1937 Osborn armed the TCPA with a new seven-point statement of policy that emphasised the need for national planning on decentralist lines and demanded a clear distinction between town and country. The same summer the TCPA mounted a major exhibition, 'The Satellite Towns Exhibition', to promote its policy of satellite cities and decentralisation and to win more members. Equally important in winning a high profile was its engagement with the debate on the 'Special Areas' and the problems of the deprived regions, a debate that led to the establishment in 1937 of the Royal Commission on the Distribution of the Industrial Population under Sir Montague Barlow. Not only did Osborn's statement of evidence to the Royal Commission win widespread support from other groups that were in agreement with the idea of some form of national planning, but – through members of the commission who were sympathetic to the TCPA's ideas, particularly Patrick Abercrombie, a long-standing member of the TCPA – Osborn's views were reflected in the Barlow Report, when it was finally published in January 1940. By the summer of 1939 the TCPA was calling for a 'National Planning Front' to unite the various bodies campaigning for legislation to provide a system of nationwide town and country planning.

The war created fresh opportunities for the TCPA. The publication of the Barlow Report gave new impetus for action. Although the report's commissioners were not unanimous in their recommendations, they were all agreed in demanding the establishment of a national agency for planning and the administrative machinery for drawing up a national system of planning. With the onset of the Blitz in the autumn of 1940, the TCPA was able to add to the arguments for national planning the necessity of rebuilding after the war. As the debate on reconstruction gathered pace, the TCPA's seven-point programme was adopted as the rallying point by many of the organisations campaigning for a system of national physical planning, including the RIBA, the TPI, the National Trust, the Council for the Protection of Rural England and the 1940 Council.[43]

The campaign for planning, and the eventual establishment of the Ministry of Town and Country Planning, is well documented but bears summarising if only to emphasise the mechanisms by which the agenda for post-war reconstruction came to be set. During 1940 Frederic Osborn, while remaining the Honorary Secretary of a voluntary organisation, the TCPA, also became an unpaid under-secretary in the newly established Ministry of Works and Planning.[44] By December 1940 Osborn was working directly for Reith on the task of establishing the machinery for national planning, while the panel of twenty-one expert advisers to Reith, the Consultative Panel on Physical Reconstruction, contained nine members of the TCPA, including Montague Barlow himself, who had joined the TCPA.[45] Contributions from Osborn and Barlow to Reith's panel illustrate the way in which the debate on reconstruction was to shape post-war developments and the way in which government was to incorporate the ideas of those pressing for change into the official committees and other governmental bodies charged with responsibility for carrying proposals for change through into action.

Osborn's involvement in government did nothing to limit the activities of the TCPA. If anything the propaganda activities of the TCPA gathered pace. From 1941 the association began to run a series of well-attended lunchtime meetings in central London to discuss different aspects of planning. In 1941 the TCPA published Osborn's essay 'Overture to Planning', the first of a series of widely read pamphlets under the series title *Rebuilding Britain* that set out ways in which the TCPA's ideas should be incorporated into government plans for reconstruction.[46] In March 1941

the first in a series of influential annual conferences on planning was held.[47] Scheduled originally for June 1940, the 'Replanning Britain' conference took place in Oxford, with papers delivered by key advocates in the campaign for planning like Barlow, Abercrombie and W. Harding Thompson, as well as those like Lord Justice Scott and George Pepler who were concerned with creating the actual machinery of planning.

Despite these advances, the TCPA's hopes for a central planning authority remained caught up in the government's equivocation over reconstruction. For much of 1941 there was little progress in official plans for a new planning ministry as these plans lay 'becalmed in the Sargasso Sea of Anthony Greenwood's Reconstruction Committee'.[48] But in February 1942, Reith was eventually able to win Cabinet approval for the setting up of a separate Ministry of Town and Country Planning, hailed by the TCPA as 'a landmark in our campaign – our Battle of Egypt'.[49] Reith's dismissal from ministerial office shortly afterwards and Lord Portal's subsequent appointment as minister dramatically reduced Osborn's influence on the ministry's policy and slowed the drive for planning legislation. But the cause for which the TCPA fought, the first priority of the early years of the debate on reconstruction, had been adopted by government as a central element of national post-war policy.

By the close of 1942 progress towards a national system of planning may have slowed but there were nevertheless grounds for optimism. Arthur Greenwood's replacement by Sir William Jowitt as Minister of Reconstruction in February was seen to favour reconstruction, and before Reith was dismissed he had taken a number of important initiatives.[50] Reith had already established two committees to address problems that would inevitably arise from introducing a national planning system: the Scott Committee on the countryside and the Uthwatt Committee set up to examine the technically complicated and politically difficult issues of compensation and betterment.[51] But Reith had done more than advance the cause of national planning, he had also encouraged a number of war-damaged cities to take the lead in thinking about how to rebuild when the new planning powers became available.

In 1941 Reith had told a deputation from Coventry that in their position he 'would plan boldly and comprehensively' without worrying about the niceties of finance, the details of local boundaries or the long-promised planning powers which were to be tailored to their needs.[52] Similar advice encouraged the cities of Southampton, Plymouth and Hull to start thinking about their post-war requirements and to begin actively preparing plans. The most important step in the direction of encouraging the preparation of local plans was Reith's success in persuading Lord Latham and the LCC to agree that Patrick Abercrombie, in collaboration with the County Architect, John Forshaw, should draw up a plan for the post-war development of the County of London. Here was a real promise of planning for a post-war future.[53]

Reconstruction and the campaign for housing, 1940–42

By the end of the war government was to give housing high priority, but in the early debate on reconstruction housing figured less prominently than planning, and the housing cause was to be championed in very different terms. Those campaigning for a national system of town and country planning were seeking to expand the role of government to do what it had not done, or had barely done, before the war. By contrast, the provision of housing had already long been accepted as a duty of government. There was, moreover, the need to do something in the short term to meet the pressing needs of the homeless. Implementing a national system of planning would inevitably have to wait until the war was over and could, as a result, be discussed with certain idealism. Housing problems demanded both long-term planning and immediate action. Yet by the autumn of 1940, as the Blitz became more intensive and spread to other cities besides London, many local authorities who might have been prepared to think about the problems of housing in the long term were being inundated

with the day-to-day problems of constructing air-raid shelters, feeding, clothing and relocating people left homeless, and the thorny issues of billeting or requisitioning housing.[54]

A number of campaigning groups, particularly those like AASTA with left-wing affiliations, dismissed talk of the long-term benefits of planning after the war as window-dressing, as procrastination by those keen to defend the status quo. They argued that it was necessary to address the immediate problems of the homeless:

> It is of no avail for planners to hope that 'after the war' all the present obstacles to decent planning will miraculously disappear. Whatever organisation takes place now will be the basis of post-war organisation, present building will not all disappear … AASTA's work on reconstruction is thus concentrated on vital immediate problems which are in danger of being left unsolved while attention is given to a more distant future.[55]

In contrast to the prevailing view in which questions of housing were naturally subsumed in any discussion of town and country planning, AASTA argued that preparation for reconstruction should begin with the immediate problems of the construction of shelter and provision for the homeless. Only when these immediate issues had been addressed could debate move forward to consider the long term; and then, AASTA argued, it should do so in terms of a radical programme that envisaged the nationalisation of land and the building industry.

AASTA represented the views of an outspoken minority. For the majority of organisations engaged in debating housing and reconstruction – the Housing Centre, the Leverhulme Trust, the 1940 Council – these unrealistic aspirations were less important than the strategic battle to advance the cause of reconstruction, and to counter the view that plans for reconstruction could be made only when the war was over. If the mistakes that were made after World War I were to be avoided, planning the building of post-war housing had to begin immediately. The post-World War I 'Homes for Heroes' programme had failed for a variety of reasons, two of which were of special importance to a government preparing plans for a post-war housing drive: first, a failure to ration the scarce supply of manpower and materials to the building industry had done much to fuel the inflation in costs and thus forced the cancellation of the programme,[56] and second, the failure to plan the new housing in relation to transport, employment and public services such as shops and schools had led to criticism that the new estates lacked any vestige of community.[57]

One central theme of the campaign for better post-war housing was to use the opportunity created by reconstruction to carry on the task of clearing the slums that had been interrupted by the war. The anti-slum campaign of the late 1920s and early 1930s had focused attention on the condition of housing in the heart of cities like Manchester, Liverpool, Leeds and London.[58] Local authorities were at last prepared to tackle the problems of the slums by sweeping away the verminous, dilapidated and insanitary housing conditions documented in books such as H. Barnes's *The Slum* or H. Marshall and A. Trevelyan's *Slum* or in Frederick Anstey's film *Housing Problems*.[59] With a shift to the left on local councils – Labour captured the LCC in 1934 and Leeds in 1933 – London, Manchester, Leeds and Liverpool initiated slum clearance programmes under the Housing Acts of 1930 and 1935, programmes that were to run until the Munich Crisis in 1938, and were only to be abandoned with the outbreak of war.[60]

Issues that slum clearance campaigns had forced into the open remained in the public eye. A study by Margery Spring-Rice for the Women's Health Enquiry Committee, *Working Class Wives*, published just before the outbreak of war as a Penguin Special, provided further documentation of the fact that the conditions for the majority of working-class women remained as degrading and damaging as ever.[61] Her pre-war research was further corroborated by the evidence produced by evacuation. Children from the inner cities, evacuated to what were generally larger houses in safer areas, forced a shocked middle class to acknowledge the effect on children's behaviour and family life of the conditions reported by the anti-slum campaign.[62] With the deterioration of housing conditions during wartime, housing campaigners argued that improving housing conditions was one of the most effective ways of defending the interests of children, women and the family. War-time studies of the family under the strain of evacuation such as *Our Towns* drew the same conclusions as pre-war campaigners like Spring-Rice:

> Poverty leads to bad housing without the space, water supply, food storage and private sanitation essential to good home-making. Ill found accommodation encourages bad feeding. Slum conditions – noisy streets, crowded beds, the irritation of bugs, lice and skin disease – murder sleep.[63]

Those, like Elizabeth Denby or Judith Ledeboer, campaigning to improve the architecture of housing emphasised the same points. To defend the family, housing conditions had to be improved.

Government responsibility for housing was long recognised. A campaign for better housing as part of the programme of reconstruction could be conducted through established institutions. Pressure groups like the Housing Centre and women's organisations like the Women's Advisory Housing Council and the National Federation of Women's Institutes demanded action by central government at meetings of the Central Housing Advisory Council, which was established in 1935 to offer advice directly to the Minister of Health.[64] Local government too was urged to act. Members of local authority housing committees and others with an interest in housing affairs, called for action and the preparation of plans for post-war housing.[65]

In April 1942, the Minister of Health initiated action. The Dudley Committee was established to report on post-war housing standards, housing layout and housing densities, and on the relationship between housing and town planning – an issue of growing importance with the prospect of a system of national planning.[66] In effect the minister was calling on the committee to write a new edition for post-war Britain of the Tudor Walters Report, which had launched the government's housing programme in 1919.

Equally important for the preparation of plans for the post-war housing programme was the establishment of an inter-departmental committee by the ministries of Health and Works to consider the use of non-traditional forms of construction as a way of escaping the shortages of traditional skills and materials that had held back the housing programme after World War I. The committee, chaired by Sir George Burt, the chairman of the building contractors Mowlem, brought together expertise from a variety of sources: from different parts of the building industry, government departments and the Building Research Station.[67] By October 1942, the committee had established 'performance standards' for comparing different forms of housing construction and had already started reviewing the experiments in non-traditional forms of construction tried after World War I.

Local authorities too were taking steps to tackle the devastation caused by bombing. Recognising that they would be called upon to play a key role in rebuilding after the war, many authorities were keen to prepare for post-war housing. Faced with the destruction of so much housing, particularly in the East End, the LCC was already preparing for a post-war 'housing drive' before the end of 1940.[68] Thomas Dawson, chairman of the LCC's Housing Committee, requested the county's officers, the Valuer, the Architect and the Engineer, to make plans for house building immediately after the war. The LCC was faced with the need to build housing on an exceptional scale, but it was not alone in starting to make plans for post-war house building at this early stage. Coventry, short of housing even before the war began, was

planning new housing along with the rebuilding of the city centre. So great was the need for housing for workers in the munitions factories that Coventry was one of the few cities where house building was allowed to continue after the start of the war.[69] In other cities making plans for post-war housing – Hull, Plymouth and Bristol – housing featured as an integral part of the plans being prepared for the day when post-war reconstruction would at last begin.[70]

Reconstruction: from debate to action

By the end of 1942, the early days of talking about reconstruction and the rebuilding of cities after the war had given way to a number of initiatives by central and local government. A variety of independent committees, departmental and inter-departmental, had been set up to look at different aspects of housing and planning. Campaigns by pressure groups for action on housing and planning remained important in spurring government forward. The campaign for reconstruction was at last leading to action. The prospect of legislation to establish a national system of town and country planning no longer seemed remote; the demands of labour and materials for a post-war housing drive were being considered as part of the infinitely complex task of converting the economy from war to peace.

Perhaps the preparation of the County of London Plan by Forshaw and Abercrombie captures best the uneven mixture of idealism and hard-headed realism of this period (Figure 1.5). In its conception, an advisory document with no legislative powers for its implementation, the plan was very much a product of the early debate on reconstruction, a vision of the way the world should be changed but with no clear view of how these changes should be put into practice. After its presentation in 1943, it was to prove enormously influential. Forshaw and Abercrombie's plan not only provided a model for proposals being prepared for other cities in Britain and further afield. It also came to shape the practice of reconstruction –

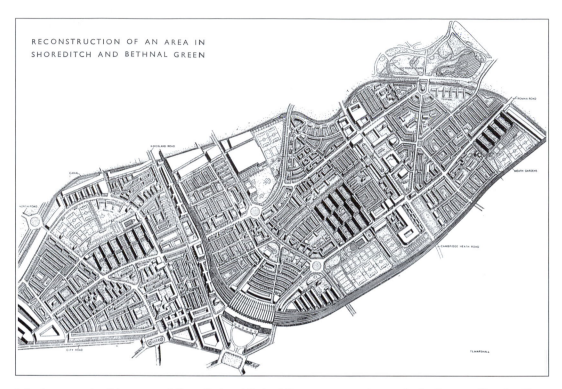

RECONSTRUCTION OF AN AREA IN
SHOREDITCH AND BETHNAL GREEN

1.5. Axonometric of the proposed Shoreditch and Bethnal Green reconstruction area in the County of London Plan

when the plan was eventually adopted, in modified form – as the basis for planning in the LCC area carried out with the powers created by the 1947 Town and Country Planning Act.

Presenting Forshaw and Abercrombie's plan to the press in the summer of 1943, Lord Latham, leader of the LCC, used the language of the early debate on reconstruction. Echoing Beveridge's call for an attack on the five giants standing in the path to the reform of social security, Latham contrasted the difficulties that stood in the way of rebuilding London – 'conflicting interests, private rights, an outworn and different scale of values, and lack of vision' – with the faith and the vision needed to realise the plan. Praising the planners for being 'practical visionaries', he commended the plan 'to the people of London … for their thought, their criticism, but, above all, for their enthusiasm, not necessarily for the particular projects in the Plan, but for the faith it embodies and the hope it inspires.'[71]

Reconstruction promised the vision of a new and better Britain, but at the end of 1942, like so many images of a bright future, this vision still lacked specificity. Nowhere was this more obviously true than of the physical forms of reconstruction. Forshaw and Abercrombie had offered only schematic images of a rebuilt London: their proposals for the redevelopment of Stepney or Hackney were curiously anodyne and wooden. The suggestive watercolour renderings of London's new flats and terraces are tantalising, but lack substance. Their images of reconstruction had no single architectural style. They were not alone in leaving unresolved the choice of architectural style for reconstruction. Different proposals favoured different styles: the Bourneville Trust's vision of post-war reconstruction as a Garden City[72] was no less valid than the modernist vision set out in the exhibition 'Living in Cities' organised by Ralph Tubbs for the 1940 Council (Figure 1.6).[73] The need to build a

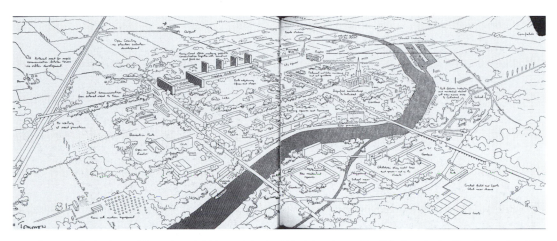

1.6 The city rebuilt. A panel from the exhibition 'Living in Cities' showing an English city rebuilt after the war in a form reflecting the general link between reconstruction and modernism

shared vision of the future, to create a unified front to demand change, appeared to require either a deliberate avoidance of specificity or a bland catholic vision that allowed for all tastes and enthusiasms.

The architecture of reconstruction thus remained to be defined. But the prospect of the extraordinary opportunities that rebuilding would create were certain. Architects looked forward to post-war rebuilding. For the advocates of the new architecture here was the unrivalled chance to build the New Britain. Yet ideas on modern architecture were also changing. Those who urged reconstruction acknowledged that the certainties and simple forms of the 1930s were part of the pre-war world that had been overtaken. By 1943 some of the best known advocates of modern architecture, like J.M. Richards, were arguing that it was necessary to rethink the very nature of the new architecture.

Notes

1 Quoted in A. Calder, *The People's War: Britain 1939–45*, London, Literary Guild, 1969, p. 154.
2 There is an extensive literature on the Blitz and the problems of the home front; see especially *ibid.* and N. Longmate, *How We Lived Then: A History of Everyday Life During the Second World War*, London, Hutchinson, 1971.
3 On evacuation see especially R. Titmus, *The Problems of Social Policy*, London, HMSO, 1950, part II, and Calder, *People's War*, ch. 2.
4 Titmus, *Problems of Social Policy*, part III, ch. IV; J. Mack and S. Humphries, *The Making of Modern London 1939–45, London at War*, London, Sidgwick & Jackson, 1985, ch. 2, Calder, *People's War*, ch. 4.
5 Quoted in Mack and Humphries, *London at War*, p. 4. The experience of individual boroughs was frequently recorded, e.g. J. Golden, *Hackney at War*, London, Alan Sutton, 1995; L. Blake, *How we Went to War: Deptford and Lewisham 1939–1945*, London, London Borough of Lewisham, 1996. For a survey of this material see H. Creaton, *Sources of the History of London 1939–45*, London, British Records Associations, 1998, ch. 6
6 Titmus, *Problems of Social Policy*, part III, ch. XIV.
7 *Ibid.*, p. 277.
8 *Ibid.*, p. 261.
9 *Ibid.*, p. 267.
10 *Ibid.*, pp. 272–96.
11 Quoted in Mack and Humphries, *London at War*, p. 79.
12 *Ibid.*, p. 77.
13 J.B. Priestley, *Postscripts*, London, Heinemann, 1940, pp. 35–6.
14 G.D.H. Cole *et al.*, *Plan for Britain: A Collection of Fabian Essays*, London, George Routledge & Sons, 1943, pp. 1–2.
15 Priestley, *Postscripts*, p. 12.
16 The celebration of Englishness during the war is discussed in A. Calder, *The Myth of the Blitz*, London, Jonathan Cape, 1991, ch. 9, and D. Mellor (ed.), *A Paradise Lost: The Neo-Romantic Imagination in Britain 1935–55*, London, Lund Humphries, 1987.

17 The renewal of interest in the protection of the nation's physical heritage is reflected, for example, in the Reconstruction supplement published in the *Architectural Review* from July 1941.

18 For a discussion of the development of the war-time campaign for the preservation of the nation's physical heritage see M. Hunter (ed.), *Preserving the Past: The Rise of Heritage in Modern Britain*, Stroud, Alan Sutton Publishing, 1996, especially chs 5 and 7.

19 *News Chronicle*, 27.9.1940, p. 4. The paper, owned by the Cadbury family, reflected the views of progressive Liberals and Fabians.

20 *Picture Post*, 8.3.1941, pp. 14–18. *Picture Post* was the most progressive of the British illustrated magazines. Owned by Edward Hulton, a radical Liberal, it was launched with Stefan Lorant as editor in 1938 and was edited by Tom Hopkinson from the summer of 1940.

21 For a general characterisation of the political allegiances of the war-time press see P. Addison, *The Road to 1945: British Politics and the Second World War*, London, Jonathan Cape, 1975, ch. 5.

22 *Listener*, 24.10.1940, pp. 586–7. For a discussion of broadcasting, reconstruction and morale see I.M. McLaine, *The Ministry of Morale*, London, George Allen & Unwin, 1979.

23 *Listener*, 9.10.1941, pp. 497; 4.12.1941, pp. 751–2; 11.12.1941, pp. 784–6.

24 'A Plan for Britain, The Britain we Hope to Build When the War is Over', *Picture Post*, 4.1.1941, pp. 7–49. This number had articles on different aspects of the Plan for Britain: by Thomas Balogh on economics, by Owen on social security, by Elizabeth Denby on housing, by Huxley on health, by Lindsay on education, by Newfield on medicine, by Maxwell Fry on town planning and by Priestley on the New Britain after the war.

25 W.K. Hancock and M.M. Gowing, *The British War Economy*, London, HMSO, 1950, p. 541.

26 For a discussion of the development of British party politics see Addison, *Road to 1945*, chs IV–VI.

27 McLaine, *Ministry of Morale*, pp. 100–7.

28 The most comprehensive review of plans for physical reconstruction is J.B. Cullingworth, *Environmental Planning*, vol. I: *Reconstruction and Land Planning 1937–1947*, London, HMSO, 1975.

29 J. Harris, *William Beveridge*, Oxford, Clarendon Press, 1997.

30 *Ibid.*, p. 422.

31 Reith recorded his own view of his appointment in his autobiography, J.C.W. Reith, *Into the Wind*, London, Hodder & Stoughton, 1949, pp. 407–8.

32 'Reconstruction: Research Activities', *AR*, Jul. 1941, pp. 40–4.

33 Quoted in Addison, *Road to 1945*, p. 189.

34 Harris, *Beveridge*, p. 368.

35 For an account of the TCPA see D. Hardy, *From Garden Cities to New Towns: Campaigning for Town and Country Planning 1896–1946*, London, E. and F.N. Spon, 1991. For an account of Osborn's activities during the war see M. Hebbert, 'Frederic Osborn 1885–1978', in G. Cherry (ed.), *Pioneers in British Planning*, London, Architectural Press, 1981.

36 AASTA's position is summarised in *AR*, Jul. 1941, p. 42. The group's views are set out fully in the February, March and April 1941 issues of *Keystone*, the AASTA journal. The association was by the early 1940s strongly influenced by the group of radical architects who had links with *Focus*, the little magazine whose four numbers had been published in 1938–39 at the Architectural Association. The members of this group on the AASTA Council and Technical Council included J. Blanco-White, B. Haward, E.E. Hollamby, A.G. Ling and C. Penn.

37 The establishment of the Reconstruction Committee, and its full membership, is reported in *JRIBA*, Mar. 1941, p. 75.

38 The establishment of the 1940 Council at the Housing Centre conference on 'Problems of the Social Environment' was announced in *JRIBA*, Feb. 1940, p. 76; its views are summarised in *AR*, Jul. 1941, pp. 40–1. The membership was drawn from education, industry, agriculture, housing, health and recreation and included Frederic Osborn, Elizabeth Denby, Eugen Kauffmann and Henry Morris. The convenor of the first meeting was R. Furneaux Jordan.

39 *Ibid.*, p. 42–3.

40 'A National Planning Authority is Essential', *JRIBA*, Sep. 1941, pp. 187–90.

41 The TCPA journal *Town and Country Planning* provides a record of the association's activities. For a recent assessment see Hardy, *From Garden Cities*, chs 4 and 5.

42 Osborn's activities have received considerable attention and his views publicised in various ways, notably through the publication of his correspondence with Lewis Mumford in M.R. Hughes (ed.), *The Letters of Lewis Mumford and Frederic J. Osborn, a Transatlantic Dialogue*, Bath, Adam & Dart, 1971. See also Hebbert, 'Frederic Osborn'. Gilbert McAllister is also remembered as the author (with Elizabeth Glen McAllister) of *Town and Country Planning, a Study of Physical Environment: The Prelude to Post-war Reconstruction*, London, Faber & Faber, 1941.

43 The programme is set out in 'The Seven Point Planning Policy, a Useful Discussion', *Town and Country Planning*, 8, 1940, pp. 31–4.

44 Hardy, *From Garden Cities*, pp. 248–9.

45 Reith's Consultative Panel on Physical Reconstruction included most of the people who were most actively involved in debating or campaigning for

different aspects of reconstruction: Patrick Abercrombie; W.H. Ansell, President of the RIBA; Lord Balfour of Buleigh, Chairman of the 1940 Committee; Sir Montague Barlow, Chairman of the Royal Commission on the Distribution of the Industrial Population; Sir Walter Citrine, General Secretary to the TUC; F.R. Hiorns, Architect to the LCC; L.H. Leay, Architect to the City of Liverpool; F.J. Osborn; L. Dudley Stamp, Director of the Land Utilisation Society; *Town and Country Planning*, 9, 1941.

46 F. Osborn, *Overture to Planning*, Rebuilding Britain 1, London, Faber & Faber, 1941. Other titles in the series were No. 4, W.A. Robson, *The War and the Planning Outlook*, 1941; No. 5, C. Williams-Ellis, *Plan for Living: The Architect's Part*, 1941; and No. 9, L. Mumford, *Social Foundations of Post-War Building*, 1943. By the end of 1941 many publishers were publishing a series of pamphlets and books on reconstruction, such as the Target for Tomorrow series published by the Pilot Press, The Democratic Order series published by Kegan Paul, and the Building and Society series published by J.M. Dent & Son for the Co-operative Permanent Building Society.

47 The proceedings of these conferences were published by Faber & Faber: F.E. Towndrow (ed.), *Replanning Britain*, London, 1941; H. Bryant Newbold (ed.), *Industry and Rural Life*, London, 1942.

48 Addison, *Road to 1945*, p. 177.

49 'A Victory and a Challenge', *Town and Country Planning*, 10, 1942, p. 115.

50 Cullingworth, *Reconstruction and Land Planning*, ch. 1.

51 The Scott Committee, appointed in October 1941, was asked to consider questions of the allocation of land for agriculture, industry and other uses. The Uthwatt Committee was appointed in January 1941 to examine the payment of compensation and the recovery of betterment 'in respect of the public control of the use of land'. For a contemporary summary see the Penguin Special prepared by G.M. Young, *Country and Town*, Harmondsworth, Penguin, 1943.

52 Reith's account of the meeting is to be found in Reith, *Into the Wind*, p. 421–4. See also below, ch. 11.

53 J. Forshaw and P. Abercrombie, *The County of London Plan 1943*, London, Macmillan, 1943. For an account of the preparation, the contents and the reception of the plan, see K. Young and P.L. Garside, *Metropolitan London: Politics and Urban Change 1837–1981*, London, Edward Arnold, 1982, ch. 8. See also J. Gold, *The Experience of Modernism: Modern Architects and the Future City 1928–53*, London, E. and F.N. Spon, 1997, ch. 7.

54 Titmus, *Problems of Social Policy*, ch. XIV.

55 *AR*, Jul. 1941, p. 42.

56 For a discussion of the difficulties facing the government's housing programme in 1919–23 see M. Bowley, *Housing and the State 1919–44*, London, George Allen & Unwin, 1945, ch. II.

57 These criticisms had been voiced by the Council for Social Service and by a number of sociologists, e.g. R. Durant, *Watling: A Survey of Social Life on a New Estate*, London, S. King & Son, 1939, and T. Young, *Becontree and Dagenham*, London, Pilgrim Trust and Becontree Social Survey Committee, 1934. See also below, ch. 7.

58 For a discussion of the anti-slum campaign see Bowley, *Housing and the State*, ch. VII, and J. Stevenson, *Social Conditions in Britain between the Wars*, Harmondsworth, Penguin, 1977. The position in London is reported in *London Housing*, London, London County Council, 1937.

59 H. Barnes, *The Slum: Its Story and its Evolution*, London, P.S. King, 1931; H. Marshall and A. Trevelyan, *Slum*, London, Heinemann, 1933; H. Quigley and I. Goldie, *Housing and Slum Clearance*, London, Methuen, 1934. Arthur Elton and Frederick Anstey's *Housing Problems*, 1935, was just one of a number of films, sponsored by the London Gas, Light and Coke Company, to investigate social problems such as housing.

60 Bowley, *Housing and the State*, ch. VII; J.A. Yelling, *Slums and Redevelopment: Policy and Practice in England, 1918–45*, London, UCL Press, 1992.

61 M. Spring-Rice, *Working Class Wives*, Harmondsworth, Penguin, 1939.

62 Calder, *People's War*, pp. 35–50.

63 Women's Group on Public Welfare, *Our Towns: A Close-Up*, Oxford, Oxford University Press, 1943, p. 103.

64 The Central Housing Advisory Council was established under Section 24 of the Housing Act 1935 to advise the Minister of Health on housing matters. Its subcommittees were made up of experts drawn from the housing reform movement, the professions, the building industry and related fields and staffed by a secretariat drawn from the Housing Division of the Ministry of Health.

65 Typical of the literature urging government to prepare for the anticipated housing drive were *Municipal and Private Enterprise Housing*, London, Dent & Sons, 1945, by Captain R.L. Reiss, a member of the Central Housing Advisory Council, the LCC Housing Committee, active in Garden City circles and a director of Welwyn Garden City and Hampstead Garden Suburb, and *Who Shall Rebuild Britain?*, London, Dent & Sons, 1945, by Lancelot Keay, City Architect for Liverpool, member of both

the Burt and the Dudley Committees and a senior figure on the RIBA Reconstruction Committee.

66 For a discussion of the background to the Dudley Report see below, ch. 7.

67 For a discussion of the work of the Burt Committee see below, ch. 8.

68 For an account of the development of the LCC's wartime housing policy see below, ch. 9.

69 See below, ch. 10.

70 See e.g. J. Paton Watson and L.P. Abercrombie, *A Plan for Plymouth*, Plymouth, Underhill, 1943; E. Lutyens and L.P. Abercrombie, *A Plan for the City of Kingston-upon-Hull*, Hull, Brown, 1945; R. Nicholas, *City of Manchester Plan*, Manchester, Jarrold, 1945; and M. Lock, *Middlesbrough Survey and Plan*, Middlesbrough, Middlesbrough Corporation, 1946.

71 Forshaw and Abercrombie, *County of London Plan*, p. iv.

72 The Bournville Village Trust, *When We Build Again*, London, George Allen & Unwin, 1941.

73 R. Tubbs, *Living in Cities*, Harmondsworth, Penguin, 1942. The book was assembled from material for the exhibition of the same name designed for the 1940 Council and the British Institute of Adult Education and circulated by the Council for the Encouragement of Music and the Arts.

PART I

Rethinking the new architecture

2   The war-time debate

During 1942 the flow of architectural debate was beginning to shift its course. Utilitarian problems shaped the working lives of architects, who continued to design temporary housing, temporary hospitals, airfields, and military buildings necessary to the war effort and the invasion of Europe.[1] But by the end of 1942 architects were thinking more adventurously about the kind of buildings that they would design after the war. Campaigns for planning and housing, and the formation of the various committees on reconstruction had fostered new alliances linking architects with non-architects and had forged affiliations between practitioners of different generations and varying approaches. The public might be persuaded that there was a broad connection between modern architecture and reconstruction, but how were the architects themselves to determine what modern architecture now was? When the war ended, would modern architecture simply carry on from where it had left off in 1939?

Even in the late 1930s, to declare support for modern architecture was to speak in favour of something that might be interpreted in a number of ways.[2] Indeed, it was easier to say what it was not than to secure agreement on what it was: as a lowest common denominator, modernists of every persuasion could make common cause in their rejection of the architectural styles of the past. But beyond this, modernists of different generations might agree on little else.

The older generation, born in the 1880s and trained before World War I, drew inspiration for their views of a modern architecture from a variety of sources (Figure 2.1). For some the route to modernism might be a reaction against the literal use of period styles: Grey Wornum's Royal Institute of British Architecture building, with its simplified classical detailing represented one approach to modernism; Charles Holden's University of London Senate House was a compromise between classicism and modernism that inclined more towards classicism than the simple modern charm of his Underground stations. A number of architects of this generation, for example Oliver Bernard, architect of the foyer of the Strand Palace Hotel, drew ideas from the buildings of the 1925 Paris Exposition des Arts Décoratifs, the origins of Art Deco. Yet another route to modernism was to demonstrate the possibilities of new materials. At the Empire Pool in Wembley and at the Boots Factory in Nottingham, Owen Williams might create an authoritative architecture of reinforced concrete, steel, glass and chromium. But the use of these new materials was no guarantee of architectural purity. Wallis Gilbert and Partners, exploiting in Britain the approach developed by Albert Kahn – including Kahncrete – concealed the structural sophistication of their buildings behind facades with brightly coloured tiles and the 'speed whiskers' of streamlined styling, such as in the Hoover Factory at Perivale.

Many older-generation architects regarded modernism like any other style to be deployed as occasion warranted, working in a number of styles for commissions where modernism and its connotations were not appropriate. Oliver Hill was designing Tudor, classical and modern houses at

i

iii

ii

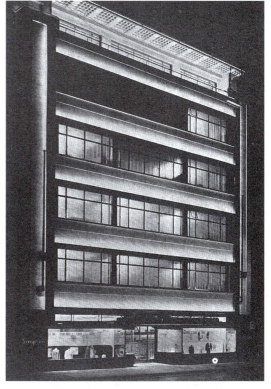

iv

2.1 Different approaches to modern architecture during the 1930s: (i) the lobby of the Strand Palace Hotel by Oliver Bernard (1930); (ii) the RIBA Building by Grey Wornum (1932–34); (iii) Arnos Grove Underground Station by Charles Holden (1931–34); (iv) Simpson's of Piccadilly by Joseph Emberton (1934–35)

the same time. Howard Robertson, an architect with active links to Europe and the United States and considered as a possible leader of an English delegation to CIAM, was happy to design classical villas for his friends while putting up buildings with the structural clarity of the Royal Horticultural Society's exhibition hall or elegant 'machine age' tube stations like the one at Loughton (Figure 11.2).[3] The work of Joseph Emberton serves as a reminder of the blurred border between different modernist camps. The style of some of Emberton's early shop fronts were straight 'jazz modern'. The Midland Hotel, Morecambe, or the Empire Hall, Olympia, were passable exercises in contemporary modern styling. But some of his work, notably Simpson's of Piccadilly and the Royal Corinthian Yacht Club at Burnham-on-Crouch, shows a clarity of form that makes Emberton's membership of the avant-garde Modern Architectural Research (MARS) Group less surprising than it might seem at first sight.[4]

The younger, hard-line modernists, born around the turn of the century and trained in the 1920s, championed ideas derived from the continental avant-garde, from Gropius and Le Corbusier. They expressed a general disdain for the modernist fellow travellers of the previous generation. To committed modernists, for example to the members of the MARS Group, it was critical to differentiate between the purity of the new architecture and the much larger number of buildings which they characterised disparagingly as 'moderne', 'modernistic' or merely 'contemporary' and which threatened to discredit the true values of modernism (Figure 2.2).

Leslie Martin, one of the editors of *Circle*, a British voice for international Constructivism, sought to distance the work illustrated in the magazine from what he regarded as less rigorous interpretations of modernism:

> The modern movement in architecture has developed rapidly in this country during the last few years. By this I do not refer to the increase of *modernistic* garages, or the *moderne* dance halls and amusement palaces of our seaside resorts. Whilst at first glance these 'imitations' may seem to point to a growing interest in contemporary design, on closer observation it becomes clear that they are not only misguided effort but even a positive danger.[5]

i

iii

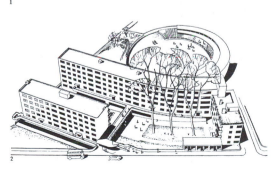

ii

iv

2.2 A selection of work by leading hard-line modernists: (i) High and Over by Amyas Connell and Basil Ward (1929–30); (ii) Kensal House by Maxwell Fry and others (1934–36); (iii) the De La Warr Pavillion, Bexhill, by Mendelsohn and Chermayeff (1934–35); the Penguin Pool, London Zoo, Tecton (1933–34)

This combative sense of identity amongst the younger modernists was further heightened by the formation of various groups such as the Twentieth Century Group and Unit One who sought to champion the role of modernism in architecture. The most important was the MARS Group.[6] Founded in 1933, the MARS Group was affiliated to CIAM and formed a direct link to the Continental avant-garde. With Wells Coates as chairman and F.R.S. Yorke as secretary, the group provided a rallying point for leading young architects like Amyas Connell, Colin Lucas, Basil Ward and Francis Skinner, for foreign émigrés like Gropius, Serge Chermayeff, Eric Mendelsohn and Kauffmann,[7] and for writers like Philip Morton Shand, Hubert de Chronin Hastings, John Gloag, John Summerson and Herbert Read, who were to act as persuasive advocates of the group's ideas. MARS Group members sat on the editorial staff of journals like the *Architectural Review*, *Architect and Building News* and the *Architects' Journal* and could be counted on to provide a sympathetic hearing for modernism in the architectural press.

Even for this group, agreement on the nature of the new architecture was not straightforward. However, the sense of unity, of belonging to a Modern Movement in Britain, did grow from shared responses to a number of critical contemporary issues. Thus the young modernists were generally 'for' the machine, industrial production and standardisation and 'against' the crafts and hand production, even if their interiors used furniture and finishings produced in craft workshops. For many hard-line modernists, though not all, engagement with social issues like housing and living conditions was important and a spur to both architectural and political activity. Their most important shared convictions were that the new architecture should demonstrate, if only symbolically rather than literally, a rational response to the demands of the brief, to construction and to the use of materials old and new.

This younger generation first attracted public attention at the start of the 1930s. Amyas Connell's High and Over at Amersham, finished in 1930 and the first example in Britain of fully fledged continental modernism, created a shock of interest and a buzz of hostility.[8] It was followed by a number of houses designed in the same uncompromisingly modern manner by Colin Lucas, Basil Ward, Maxwell Fry, F.R.S. Yorke and Christopher Nicholson.[9] By the end of the decade examples of private houses in the new modern style were plentiful. In addition there were larger buildings. In London the Highpoint flats at Highgate, designed by Tecton, were followed by Pulman Court at Streatham by Frederick Gibberd, Lawn Road Flats in Hampstead by Wells Coates and Kensal House by Fry, Drake and Lasdun. Buildings like Tecton's Finsbury Health Centre, Mendelsohn and Chermayeff's Bexhill pavilion, Emberton's Royal Corinthian Yacht Club and Gropius and Fry's Impington Village College established a recognisable identity for public architecture. Tecton's Penguin Pool at London Zoo was one of the few modern buildings to win true popular affection. It offered a rare combination of formal invention, structural ingenuity, and the gentle amusement of watching the penguins, who might be imagined to be bankers or City gents, parading endlessly up the stairs, down the ramp and into the water.[10]

By the end of the 1930s, buildings of the younger modern architects working in Britain had won international recognition. In 1937 the New York Museum of Modern Art devoted its spring exhibition to modern architecture in England, and Henry-Russell Hitchcock, a leading US interpreter of modern architecture, praised the pace with which the 'English school of modern architecture' had developed in two or three years. Hitchcock argued that it was 'evident that England was not only accepting modern architecture as the logical contemporary way of building, but was providing opportunities for architectural talent of the highest technical and esthetic ingenuity'.[11] By 1939 Britain had ceased to be the architectural backwater that it would have seemed to a modernist only ten years before. But now, in 1943, after four years of war and an unbridgeable break in continuity with the 1930s, were the pre-war identities for modern architecture still meaningful? Would it still be possible to present stripped classicism as a modern style? Would the old certitudes of the MARS Group still seem credible?

The war limited discussion of these questions. There was no shortage of books on the promise of modern architecture for the building of a New Britain: Howard Robertson's *Architecture Arising* may be taken to represent the views of the older generation, whereas *Fine Building* by Maxwell Fry states the position of a MARS modernist.[12] But neither book, nor others in the same vein, offered a vision of the architectural way forward. Meetings of those who had led the pre-war debate were hampered by the absence of members serving in the forces or otherwise occupied with the war effort. The MARS Group met only occasionally after the summer of 1940.[13] From 1940 to 1944 its activities were confined to the work of the unrepresentative Town Planning Committee on the replanning of London. To many MARS members the abstract and ambitious proposals for the replanning of the entire centre of London, which might have seemed acceptably radical in the late 1930s, were now painfully unrealistic and out of tune with the need for constructive engagement with the problems of reconstruction.[14] Nor were the architecture schools or the architectural press any more successful in sustaining the part they had played in promoting the new architecture in the 1930s. Relocated out of London and short of staff, the schools of architecture were quiet. They scrambled to cram one year's teaching into the six short months available to students before joining the forces.[15] Architectural journals did little to promote discussion of specifically architectural questions. Most journals continued to concentrate on the dominant issues of the day: housing, new forms of construction and prefabrication, and planning. They ran lengthy commentary on publications like the *Dudley Report*, Forshaw and Abercrombie's County of London Plan or the Ministry of Health's *Housing Manual 1944*.[16] They had little to say about architecture.

But new ideas were beginning to stir. In 1943 the *Architectural Review* started to identify a new set of interests and to question the terms in which modern architecture might develop after the war.[17] Other journals might run the occasional article on modernism in Sweden or the United States, but the *Review* played the most important role in urging forward the debate on the future of architecture after the war. It had always addressed a wide range of readers and had used its position to discuss architecture in terms that went beyond the narrow interests of the profession. From the late 1920s it shifted towards support for the new architecture, publishing and reviewing the work of leading modernists in Britain and on the Continent. In 1934 the *Review* had published a series of articles, 'Scenario for a Human Drama', providing an early and sympathetic history of the development of modern architecture. Hubert de Chronin Hastings, the journal's reclusive owner, and other members of the editorial board were members of the MARS Group.[18] This advocacy of modernism was balanced by other interests: an enthusiasm for the Gothic Revival style, an admiration for the architecture of Edwin Lutyens, publication of cartoons by Osbert Lancaster and a commitment to documenting the history of the English house. But its support for modernism had not wavered.

In 1943 the *Review* started to publish regularly a series of special numbers that raised important questions about the nature of the new architecture. Throughout the war it continued to publish a wide range of articles on architectural history, popular taste, the nineteenth-century tradition of engineering and utilitarian building, and a range of architectural developments taking place in countries untouched by war. But the special numbers encouraged readers to look forward actively to the promise of rebuilding. In 1942 there was only one special number, on Canada; in 1943 there were three, devoted to reconstruction, to the work of the Tennessee Valley Authority (TVA) and to

Swedish modern architecture; in 1944 special numbers highlighted Brazil, wartime housing in the USA, and South Africa.[19]

The *Review* also looked across the Atlantic for ideas. In war-time Britain, which was dependent on the United States and its resources and increasingly familiar with the US way of life through films and contact with US servicemen, this reliance on transatlantic ideas seemed more natural than it would have done five years before. In addition to the regular illustration of American architecture, the *Review* featured key points of interest – such as *Brazil Builds*, an exhibition of Brazilian architecture – that figured prominently in the debate fostered in the United States by high-profile institutions like the Museum of Modern Art and professional journals like *Architectural Forum*, *Pencil Points* and *Architectural Record*.[20] This focus on America reflected the fact that building was possible in the United States on a scale not possible elsewhere. Where better to find examples of current practice unconstrained by the rationing and limitations that dominated building in Britain? American achievement seemed to hold a particular significance for the British debate on reconstruction. The *Review* was now as keen to hold up for its readership the example of American achievements such as the TVA and US housing for war workers as US reformers like Catharine Bauer and other members of the Regional Planning Association of America had been before the war to present European examples of housing and planning to Americans.[21] The *Review*'s message was simple: if reconstruction was to succeed, planning and production would need to be carried out on a scale already achieved in the United States.

This bias reflected the growing importance of America for the whole direction of the debate in England on modern architecture. Key pre-war European modernists were now in America: Gropius, Martin Wagner and Marcel Breuer were at Harvard; Sigfried Giedion and José Luis Sert were in New York; László Moholy-Nagy, now director of the Institute of Design in Chicago, and Josef Albers, teaching at Black Mountain College in North Carolina, were carrying on and extending the work of the Bauhaus. Notwithstanding Le Corbusier's publication of the Athens Charter in France in 1943, CIAM was now based in the United States and continuing its activities: *Can Our Cities Survive?* was edited by Sert while teaching at Harvard in 1943 and published by Harvard University Press.[22] This concentration of talent naturally led to new developments reflected in symposia, conferences and, most influentially, in the exhibitions and publications of the Museum of Modern Art.

The issues discussed in New York, Chicago and Cambridge, Massachusetts carried a resonance for British readers that the architectural debate in America had not enjoyed before. The *Review* followed US developments in its special numbers. It published American buildings and reviewed American books. It was interested to report what Americans thought about developments in Sweden, in Brazil and elsewhere. Of course the *Review* looked beyond America. The articles in the *Review* and other journals, especially the *Architects' Journal* and *Architectural Design*, are a reminder of the strength of British interest in Sweden throughout this period. But what should not be forgotten is the way that the continuing architectural debate in the United States coloured the terms in which the young English modernists came to rethink the direction of the new architecture.

Regionalism and alternatives to the certitudes of the 1930s

One of the issues that was to attract attention in Britain from 1943 onwards was the growing American interest in the 'regional' rather than the 'international' qualities of the work of modern architects. From 1933 the Museum of Modern Art, which had first proclaimed the new 'International Style' at the architectural exhibition of European modernism the year before, had hung exhibitions that emphasised instead the strength of regional traditions in American architecture.[23] These exhibitions explored the emergence over the last three centuries of a specifically American tradition separate from that of Europe, as well as the different regional traditions of building and design within the United States. To British observers, the new interests of the Museum of Modern Art might appear at first sight to be heretical, but they soon agreed with the museum that the sheer scale of the United States and the range of its climates and local traditions demanded differentiation in this way.

Equally important for British interest in regionalism was the attention paid by Americans to the new Scandinavian architecture (Figure 2.3). The Museum of Modern Art's 1937 exhibition of the architecture and furniture of Alvar Aalto was the museum's first one-man show.[24] Many Americans had been impressed by the Swedish and the Finnish pavilions at the 1939 New York World's Fair, designed by Sven Markelius and Aalto respectively, as representing a specifically Scandinavian interpretation of modernism.[25] Aalto's pavilion, with its free-flowing forms, its unconventional moulding of interior space and the arresting exploitation of the qualities of natural timber, attracted widespread attention as being rooted in a different tradition from that normally associated with modern architecture in Europe.

In 1940 the Museum of Modern Art maintained this interest in Scandinavian architecture with an exhibition of the work of young Swedish architects, 'Stockholm Builds'.[26] Assembled largely with photographs by G.E. Kidder-Smith, the exhibition conveyed with striking success how Markelius, Backström and other young Swedes were designing houses, blocks of flats and even modest public buildings in a way that was at once unmistakably modern and yet maintained the elements of a Swedish tradition in the use of materials and the sense of landscape.

Summarising the development of modern architecture in the United States in *Built in USA, 1932–1944*, Elizabeth Mock, then acting director of the Architectural Section of the Museum of Modern Art, stressed the importance of this interest in the regional qualities of architecture as a new point of departure:

> Americans looked again at the stone and wood barns of Pennsylvania, the white clapboard walls of New England, the low, rambling ranch houses of the West, and found them good. They were not interested in the picturesque detailing of these buildings, but in their straightforward use of material and their subtle adaptation to climate and topography. Here was a local encouragement for the growing international movement towards a friendlier, more differentiated contemporary architecture.[27]

2.3 The Finnish pavilion at the New York World's Fair, 1939

Acknowledging Scandinavian influence, and Aalto in particular, as a source of inspiration for this new interest in the regional, Mock identified California in particular as a region that had developed from the local tradition of building its own brand of modernism, exemplified by the work of William Wurster (Figure 2.4).[28]

For architects in Britain who were beginning to think again about the nature of modern architecture, these ideas were particularly suggestive. England had been the subject of the Museum of

2.4 The Jensen House Berkeley, California (1937) by William Wurster

Modern Art's exhibition 'Modern Architecture in England' in 1937, but this architecture was very much a product of Continental inspiration. The support of the *Architectural Review* and the arrival as émigrés in England of some of the leaders of the new style – Berthold Lubetkin, Gropius, Mendelsohn, Breuer and others – had produced a sudden burst of achievement exemplified by the work of Tecton, of Gropius and Fry, and of the other modernists championed by J.M. Richards' popular Penguin book, *Introduction to Modern Architecture*.[29] But now, in 1943, many architects welcomed the prospect of advancing beyond the simple dogmatic certitudes of the pre-war years. As people in America discussed the need to 'humanise' modern architecture, to develop an architecture that might symbolise or express society's ideals and aspirations, architects in Britain took up these ideas with interest.

In Britain, one of the first presentations of a modern architecture that seemed to depart from the International Style canon of the 1930s was the *Review*'s treatment of Sweden in September 1943 under the title 'Swedish Peace in War'.[30] The editors presented Sweden as a country that Britain might emulate to advantage when setting about the task of reconstruction. Led by informed and sensitive government patronage, Sweden was building, despite the war-time hardships imposed even on a neutral country, just the

kind of housing, schools and other essential buildings that would be so urgently needed in Britain after the war:

> Swedish housing is the most progressive in Europe in its social organisation. The Co-operatives build better than anywhere else, and building societies don't lag behind. Prefabrication is used more widely and sensibly than anywhere else. Most public buildings, especially the smaller accessory ones, are pleasant, light-hearted, almost playful, and yet strictly contemporary.[31]

For William Holford, author of the *Review*'s main article, Sweden was exciting because here the forms of a possible post-war Britain were already become reality. Holford encouraged English architects to refresh their ideas from Swedish examples: 'It is not good for architects to live too long in shadow; and it is hoped that at the end of the war, if not before it, English representatives will go and see for themselves what beacons have been kept alight in Sweden.'[32]

Looking through the photographs by Kidder-Smith of Swedish buildings and reading an interpretation of the new Swedish architecture by Sven Backström, one of the leaders of the younger generation of Swedish architects, readers of the *Review* would have had the chance to see, perhaps for the first time, the way in which architectural ideas were developing since 1939 (Figure 2.5). In place of the fondly remembered Stockholm Exhibition in 1930 (Figure 4.10), 'the victorious *debut* of functionalist architecture in Sweden', Backström introduced an architecture which was softer and, in his terms, better suited to the real needs of the people. Instead of the architectural arrogance of the 1930s, he described how

> architects began to develop an ear for the shifting values and phases of actual life. Man was once more to become the point of departure and the criterion. And it was discovered that man is a highly complicated phenomenon that is not to be satisfied or understood with the help of any

2.5 Torviks flats at Lidingoe, Stockholm

2.6 The South Cemetery, Stockholm (1915–49), by Gunnar Asplund. For older and younger generations alike Asplund's cemetery was one of the most potent images of a particularly Swedish combination of buildings and landscape

new epoch-making formulae. And one result of this growing insight was a reaction against the all too schematic architecture of the 1930s. Today we have reached the point where all the elusive psychological factors have again begun to engage our attention. Man and his habits, reactions and needs are the focus of interest as never before. One tries to understand them, and to adapt the building in such a way that it really serves. And there is the desire to enrich it and beautify it in a living way, so that it may be a source of joy.[33]

Though Holford owned that much of this architecture was excellent if not 'spectacularly good', he did single out Asplund and Lewerentz's Woodland Cemetery as an outstanding example of the way in which the 'Funki' style of the 1930s had been tempered by an understanding of tradition to produce 'the most considerable recent monument in Sweden, and a superb composite design of landscape and buildings' (Figure 2.6).[34] Here in Sweden, the best of

architecture offered a real alternative to the modernist certitudes of the 1930s.

Sweden illustrated one way in which the modernism of the 1930s might be given a regional flavour and adapt to the qualities of a particular country. Brazil illustrated another. The Museum of Modern Art's exhibition 'Brazil Builds', assembled by Philip Goodwin, head of the museum's architectural division, with photographs by Kidder-Smith and a catalogue written by Elizabeth Mock, opened in May 1943. In March 1944 the exhibition travelled to London, and the *Review* devoted a special number to Brazil and its architecture (Figure 2.7).[35] More forcefully than with Sweden, the architecture of Brazil was presented as an example of the way in which the International Style of the 1930s was already giving way to a series of regionally determined variants of modernism. To the readers of the *Review* and the visitors to the exhibition, what was important was not that Brazil might plausibly serve – as might Sweden – as a paradigm for British reconstruction, but that the emergence of new regional variants, determined by

2.7 The Ministry of Education building (1937–44) by Costa, Niemeyer, Reidy. With its sun screens and its azuleijo tiles this building was interpreted by the Museum of Modern Art and by the *Architectural Review* as exemplifying a particularly Brazilian variant of modern architecture

local culture and climate, marked the next stage in the evolution of the Modern Movement.

In the leading article on Brazil's new architecture, Kidder-Smith argued that Brazil was fundamentally different from both Europe, the original source of modern architecture, and the United States. The extraordinary climate and the absence of readily available steel or timber combined to demand an architecture in concrete which shielded buildings from the sun by using elements like the brise-soleil to shape the facade in a way unknown elsewhere. Just as Brazil had absorbed and shaped its own interpretation of the European Baroque tradition, the Museum of Modern Art set out to demonstrate the way in which Brazil had made its own version of modern architecture. Even faced with somebody whose work was as self-consciously European as

Le Corbusier's, Brazil was able to absorb and transform his ideas: 'Le Corbusier's influence has been strong ... but it has been an inspiration of ideals, not of cliches thrown together in the accepted manner. The product has always been distinctly Brazilian.'[36] Comfort in the climate of Rio de Janeiro demanded design ideas that had no precedent in modern architecture: 'To control sunshine and heat there was nothing which could be done except to start afresh with common sense, fortified by an exploration into technical requirements.'[37] The resulting rippling rhythm of the elevations of buildings like the Ministry of Education building were hailed as being as specifically Brazilian as, say, the rhythm of Samba:

> Le Corbusier was asked to advise a group of Brazilian architects on the new building for the ministries of education and health. He may even have been the first to suggest the extensive use of the *brise-soleil* or sun-blind. But the use made of it by the Brazilian achieves surfaces within the limitations of the twentieth century idiom just as flickeringly alive as the stucco and woodwork of Salvador.[38]

The lesson urged by the *Review* was clear: the new architecture had moved on since the 1930s, and even a country as young as Brazil was developing its own distinctive form of modernism.

Towards a British identity in architecture

If Brazil and Sweden were already transforming the ideas of the 1930s to define an architecture attuned to their particular characteristics, what form of architecture would be appropriate to Britain: to England, to Wales and to Scotland? As early as January 1944 the *Review* was already preparing an answer. Having examined the history of English architecture and design, the editors of the *Review* pronounced that there was indeed, however inexplicably overlooked, a unique English contribution to the visual arts: 'We propound a simple thesis. That England has

2.8 Aerial view of Lansdown Terrace, Bath. English developments such as Bath or Regent's Park exemplified the application of Picturesque principles to the layout of the town, as demanded by the *Architectural Review*

a traditional way of seeing things which was brought into full consciousness, and raised to an art, in Picturesque theory and practice, known to the eighteenth century as the Modern Manner.'[39] (Figure 2.8)

During 1944 and 1945 the editors, particularly Pevsner, devoted a number of articles to the history of the Picturesque. Three articles, on Sir Uvedale Price, on 'Lord Burlington's Bijou, or Sharawaggi at Chiswick', and on 'The Genesis of the Picturesque', set out for readers what the editors understood by the Picturesque and its appropriateness not just for the English character but for the modern design as well.[40]

The application of Picturesque principles of composition to the opportunities presented by reconstruction would lead naturally, claimed the *Review*, to a revival in modern form of an older English tradition and thus to an English (rather than a British) identity in architecture and town planning:

> The opportunity has come. The technique reveals itself on inspection as having exactly the elastic qualities demanded by the occasion. Whether we call it Exterior Furnishing or landscape architecture, whether we call it the Picturesque, or the Romantic Movement – or whether we just call it Sharawaggi – it is found to be, in

essence, an aesthetic method which is designed to reconcile by various means – contrast, concealment, surprise, balance – the surface antagonisms of shape which a vital democracy is liable to go on pushing up in its architecture in token of its own liveliness.[41]

The argument advanced in the *Review* was presented in terms of groups of buildings and landscape, but readers would have been left in no doubt that the editors saw Picturesque principles applying in the widest terms to a continuum of tasks from town planning to the design of groups of buildings and even to the individual building. The editors recognised that the design of the individual monument or monumental building would always be subject to individual invention, but how this was woven into the urban (or rural) landscape was a matter for Picturesque treatment. So too was the way in which everyday architecture, the houses, schools, shops and pubs of the ordinary English town, combined to produce the typical urban landscape of the pre-industrial age. As in the making and planting of a rural landscape, so the planning and 'planting' of buildings would shape the landscape of reconstruction. It was the relationship between the aggregate of buildings rather than the detail of the individual building that did much to determine the quality of architecture both in the English Picturesque tradition and, argued the editors, in much of contemporary Swedish architecture.

The most important statement of how the Picturesque might be applied to contemporary affairs appeared as the central article in the special number of the *Review* devoted to the reconstruction of London. Faced with the task of rebuilding London in all its diversity, the *Review* argued that the formal tradition of Beaux Arts planning associated with the making of Paris was inappropriate and simply unworkable for London. In place of Haussmannisation and Beaux Arts attitudes symptomatic of control and constraint, English planners were now to learn from Picturesque theory and Whig principles to develop an approach to rebuilding London that would acknowledge diversity and difference, in a manner fitting to democracy, to make a virtue of London's existing contrasts:

> The modern spirit is but a natural enlargement of the 18th-century spirit which in its turn was a rationalisation of the traditional vernacular English way of looking at the world, the characteristic common to all three being that tendency to take the functional approach to build up the human background in those visual terms the layman calls the Picturesque ... Thus it is precisely *because of their functional approach* that modern architects have rediscovered picturesque theory. It is precisely *because of their functional approach* that they appreciate, unlike most academic architects, that London is a product of the picturesque impulse.[42]

Pressing Le Corbusier into service as a surprising champion of the Picturesque and 'one of the first to introduce English landscape principles into the urban scene', the editors called on London's planners to marry modernism with local traditions in architecture and planning by rebuilding according to Picturesque principles.

The challenge of peace

The immediate impact of the *Review*'s hopes for the revival of Picturesque principles was minimal. But it is of interest as an illustration, far-fetched and eccentric perhaps, of the impatience already felt in the United States, Sweden and elsewhere with the old certitudes of the 1930s, and the growing determination to address again the aesthetic dimension of architecture when reconstruction began.

As the prospect of peace edged closer, preparations for post-war rebuilding gathered pace. The Parliamentary debate of the White Paper on the housing programme in March 1945, the publication of Abercrombie's proposals for planning in the London region and the presentation of government-sponsored prototypes for the temporary housing drive were all pointers to the long-awaited day when reconstruction would begin in earnest. By the end of 1944 a number of architects were being asked by local authorities to start preparing designs for rebuilding. After five years of farming in Gloucestershire, Lubetkin was starting the design of blocks of flats for a site on Busaco Street in Finsbury (later named Priory Green). New opportunities encouraged a new realistic approach. The MARS Group's Town Planning Committee abandoned its proposals for the radical rebuilding of the entire centre of London to welcome the County of London Plan (1943) as the first scheme 'in which modern planning principles are applied to our established social organism'.[43]

Far from submerging interest in the debate on new directions for modern architecture, the prospect of a resumption of architectural activity served as a spur to new activity. Alongside the MARS Group's interests in reconstruction and planning of London, the group staged its first major architectural discussion since 1940. The meeting, held in December 1944, addressed the question 'What is Modern Architecture?' and attracted an audience of 200 people to a debate chaired by Professor Charles Reilly, with contributions from William Holford, Mark Hartland Thomas, John Summerson, Erno Goldfinger and Anthony Chitty. The views of the speakers and the comments from the floor reflected the hopes for a new direction in architecture. Summing up the discussion, Hartland Thomas signalled the MARS Group's collective determination to go beyond the position reached at the end of the 1930s and to expand 'the theory of Functionalism in design'. In its place he called for a 'New Architecture of Humanism', a less dogmatic approach to architecture, and one that would recognise the full range of human needs.[44] As 1945 dawned it was apparent that modern architecture after the war might look distinctly different from that of the 1930s.

Notes

1 Bolero, the massive programme of construction necessary to house the US forces in preparation for the invasion, alone involved the building in little more than 18 months of accommodation for 1,446,000 men, together with other facilities such as hospitals and warehousing and storage for munitions for the invasion force; see C.M. Kohan, *Works and Buildings*, London, HMSO, 1952, part III, especially pp. 260–77.

2 For a general discussion of modern architecture in the 1930s see A. Jackson, *The Politics of Architecture: A History of Modern Architecture in Britain*, London, Architectural Press, 1970; C. and T. Benton, 'Architecture: Contrasts of a Decade', in J. Hawkins and M. Hollis (eds), *The Thirties: British Art and Design before the War*, London, Arts Council, 1979; G. Stamp (ed.) 'Britain in the Thirties', *Architectural Design*, Oct/Nov, 1979; J. Gold, *The Experience of Modernism: Modern Architects and the Future City 1928–1953*, London, E. & F.N. Spon, 1997; and D. Dean, *The Thirties: Recalling the Architectural Scene*, London, Trefoil, 1983.

3 Howard Robertson's standing as a modernist is reviewed in ch. 11.

4 R. Ind, *Emberton*, London, Scholar Press, 1983. Significantly, Emberton's Royal Corinthian Yacht Club was selected, along with Amyas Connell's High and Over, as the representative British buildings for the Museum of Modern Art's 'International Style' exhibition in 1932.

5 L. Martin, 'The State of Transition', in J.L. Martin, B. Nicholson and N. Gabo (eds), *Circle: International Survey of Constructive Art*, London, Faber & Faber, 1937, p. 215.

6 Despite its central role in championing the ideas of the Continental avant-garde in Britain, there is still no comprehensive account of the MARS Group. Material on the group is held in the Architectural Association library and in various sets of papers, the Arup papers and the Skinner papers, in the British Architectural Library. For a summary of the group's work see J. Summerson (himself a member of the group), 'The MARS Group in the Thirties', in J. Bold and E. Chaney (eds), *English Architecture, Public and Private*, London, Hambledon Press, 1993, pp. 303–10; L. Campbell, 'The MARS Group 1933–39', *RIBA Transactions,* vol. 4, no. 2, 1984–5, pp. 69–79.

7 For an account of the foreign emigrés see C. Benton, *A Different World: Emigré Architects 1928–58*, London, RIBA Heinz Gallery, 1955.

8 D. Sharp (ed.), *Connell, Ward and Lucas: Modern Movement Architects in England 1929–1939*, London, Book Art, 1994, pp. 26–7.

9 F.R.S. Yorke, *The Modern House*, London, Architectural Press, 1934.

10 J. Allen, *Berthold Lubetkin: Architecture and the Tradition of Social Progress*, London, RIBA, 1992, ch. 6.

11 H.-R. Hitchcock, *Modern Architecture in England*, New York, Museum of Modern Art, p. 41.

12 H. Robertson, *Architecture Arising*, London, Faber & Faber, 1944; M. Fry, *Fine Building*, London, Faber & Faber, 1944.

13 In 1941 there were only four poorly attended meetings; a further four were held in 1942 and seven in 1943. However, from 1944 the group's activities began to revive with 15 generally better-attended meetings in 1944 and a similar number in 1945.

14 With so many members of the MARS Group away from London, the London plan was largely the work of Arthur Korn and Felix Samuely. Some members, like Ralph Tubbs, argued that its unrealistic ambitions would damage the credibility of the MARS Group when it came to reconstruction; others, like Fry, saw it as a radical and realistic response to the destruction of London at the time; Gold, *Experience of Modernism*, ch. 6.

15 M. Crinson and J. Lubbock, *Architecture: Art or Profession? Three Hundred Years of Architectural Education in Britain*, Manchester, Manchester University Press, 1994. See the biography of A.E. Richardson for an account of Richardson's agreeable war-time sojourn in Cambridge: S. Houfe, *Sir Arthur Richardson, the Professor*, Luton, White Concert Press, 1980.

16 The *Architects' Journal* was typical of the weeklies in its focus on the day-to-day problems of architecture during the war, reporting the changing regulations, the results of government speeches and the personalities in the news. *Architectural Design* similarly addressed many of the day-to-day issues facing architects and ran frequent articles on issues associated with reconstruction such as 'Housing Notes', a regular feature. But it also devoted space to discussion on architectural issues, such as the editors' enthusiasm for Swedish architecture.

17 Until June 1941, the *Architectural Review* had adopted a policy of not commenting on the war, thereafter its monthly Reconstruction Supplement focused on current issues such as the campaign for town-planning and the documentation of buildings of architectural value damaged by bombing.

18 In 1943 the editors were Chronin de Hastings, Nikolaus Pevsner, John Betjeman, Osbert Lancaster and J.M. Richards. Richards gives some impression of the atmosphere at the *Review* in his autobiography: *Memoirs of an Unjust Fella*, London, Weidenfeld & Nicholson, 1980.

19 The war-time special issues were 'Canada' (Apr. 1942), 'Rebuilding Britain' (Apr. 1943), 'TVA, an Achievement of Democratic Planning' (Jun. 1943), 'Sweden Past and Present' (Sep. 1943), 'Brazil' (Mar. 1944), 'US War-time Housing' (Aug. 1944), 'South Africa' (Oct. 1944), 'Electricity in its Regional Setting' (Apr. 1945).

20 The Museum of Modern Art's exhibition 'Brazil Builds' was held in September 1943; *Brazil Builds: Architecture Old and New 1652–1942*, New York, Museum of Modern Art, 1943.

21 The pre-war interest of US reformers in European achievements is best illustrated by Catharine Bauer's *Modern Housing*, Boston, Houghton Mifflin, 1934.

22 J.L. Sert, *Can Our Cities Survive?*, Cambridge, Mass., Harvard University Press, 1944.

23 The museum's architectural exhibitions are listed in E. Mock, *Built in USA, 1932–1944*, New York, Museum of Modern Art, 1944.

24 The 1937 Aalto exhibition at the Museum of Modern Art showed his recent architectural works, the Viipuri Library, the Turku Sanomat and the Paimio Sanatorium, as well as displays of his bent-plywood furniture.

25 These two pavilions attracted considerable interest in contemporary US journals: *Architectural Forum*, Jun. 1939, pp. 442–5; *Architectural Record*, Aug. 1936, p. 46. The more general interest in Scandinavian architecture is evident in articles such as T.F. Hamlin, 'Sven Markelius', *Pencil Points*, Jun. 1939, pp. 357–66.

26 This exhibition focused on the work of the younger Swedish architects like Backström and Markelius.

27 Mock, *Built in USA*, p. 14.

28 *Ibid*.

29 J.M. Richards, *Introduction to Modern Architecture*, Harmondsworth, Penguin Books, 1940.

30 *AR*, Sep. 1943: 'Swedish Peace in War, a Special Number on Sweden'.

31 W. Holford, 'The Swedish Scene: An English Architect in War-time Sweden', *AR*, Sep. 1943, p. 59.

32 *Ibid*., p. 79.

33 S. Backström, 'A Swede looks at Sweden', *AR*, Sep. 1943, p. 80.

34 Holford, 'Swedish Scene', p. 62.

35 *AR*, Mar. 1944: 'Brazil, a Special Number'.

36 G.E. Kidder-Smith, 'The Architects and the Modern Scene', *AR*, Mar. 1944, p. 84.

37 *Ibid*.

38 J. Summerson, 'The Brazilian Contribution', *AR*, May 1943, p. 134

39 'Exterior Furniture or Sharawaggi: The Art of Making an Urban Landscape', *AR*, Jan. 1944, p. 8.

40 'Price on Picturesque Planning', *AR*, Feb. 1944, pp. 47–50; H.F. Clark, 'Lord Burlington's Bijou, or Sharawaggi at Chiswick', *AR*, May 1944, pp. 125–30; N. Pevsner, 'The Genesis of the Picturesque' *AR*, Nov. 1944, pp. 139–46.

41 'Exterior Furniture or Sharawaggi', p. 8.

42 'The English Planning Tradition in the City', *AR*, Jun. 1945, p. 170.

43 'Observations on the County of London Plan', *MARS Report No. 2*, 1945, p. 1.

44 M. Hartland Thomas, 'Report of the Discussion of 13th December: What is Modern Architecture', *MARS Report No. 1*, 1945, p. 32.

3 The search for new directions after 1945

With the ending of the war the terms of the architectural debate expanded. Now there was the prospect of travel and meeting up again with friends and others who had been cut off by war. There was the promise of beginning the tasks of reconstruction, rather than merely talking about ideas and ideals. There was a fresh opportunity now for action, not just debate. Yet because of the shortages of manpower and materials, reconstruction was restricted to the most immediate utilitarian needs, housing and schools. The first years of rebuilding offered only limited opportunities to test in practice ideas that had been discussed since 1943. Limited opportunities, however, did not inhibit theoretical debate. New journals were started. Old journals offered more material. The men and women returning from the war to architectural practice or to schools of architecture made up a keen audience for discussion who contributed a wider range of voices than had been heard during the war. The central issue was the extent to which post-war architecture should continue the developments of the 1930s or should reflect the demands for a more humanistic architecture and, indeed, whether these two positions were necessarily opposed.

The faces of the participants in this debate – architects, critics, journalists and students, nearly all male, generally tweed-jacketed, often with pipe in hand – look out of the pages of the contemporary journals. They make an unlikely avant-garde. But in their contribution to the debate on the new architecture, in their designs and their words, they were to recast the new direction of modern architecture just as their predecessors had first shaped it in the 1930s. Who were they and where did debate take place?

Joining the debate: the MARS Group, the journals and the schools of architecture

The MARS Group, which during the war had spoken more authoritatively than any other group for modern architecture, now in 1945 began to meet almost monthly. In contrast to the occasional, rather poorly attended sessions of earlier war years, meetings began to attract a mixed and growing membership.[1] Reconstruction dominated the conversations, particularly the progress of planning in London. The group also found time to debate the future of the new architecture, often in the terms set out by the *Architectural Review*: Sharawaggi and the Picturesque ideal were topics of recurring interest. MARS now operated as an effective sounding board for ideas originating elsewhere; it was no longer at the forefront of debate. Yet this role, it continued as an important forum for discussion and remained throughout the late 1940s the principal British conduit for international contacts with modern architecture abroad. Through MARS, links were re-established with the leaders of CIAM, with Cornelius van Eesteren and later with Sigfried Giedion. The possibility of a liaison with the Polish branch of

CIAM and Russian architects was explored. MARS helped host the first post-war international conference, the International Union of Architects Conference held in London in September 1946. More importantly, MARS offered to host CIAM's first post-war conference, CIAM 6, scheduled for the summer of 1947. Working closely with Giedion and the Swiss branch of CIAM at the CIRPAC (Comité Internationale pour la Résolution des Problèmes de l'Architecture Contemporaine) meetings held to plan the event, J.M. Richards and Arthur Ling, as representatives of MARS, played a central role in proposing the agenda for debate.[2]

The expansion of the MARS Group and its desire to represent the diverse voices speaking for the new architecture made it inevitable that its former role as a forcing ground for new ideas should pass elsewhere. In its place, a number of key journals now took the lead in promoting the debate on architectural rather than reconstruction issues. The major architectural weeklies, the *Architects' Journal*, the *Builder* and the *Architect and Building News*, continued as they had done during the war. As before, the greater part of the architectural press devoted itself to the day-to-day priorities of reconstruction: assisting architects in understanding the complexities of claiming for war-damage repairs, wrestling with the licensing system and documenting the inflation of building costs. With the prospect of action, war-time issues like planning and prefabrication became more, not less, important.

The monthlies took a different line. *Architectural Design*, the *Architectural Review* and, from 1945, the *Architects' Yearbook* looked beyond immediate war-related concerns. Geared to the interests of a wider readership than the weeklies, these journals created the forum for the debate. *Architectural Design* reflected the terms in which the modern movement was to engage with a range of different reconstruction issues and provided a general coverage of planning, school building and housing.[3] The variety of articles about developments in America, Sweden and further afield are a reminder too of the journal's links with CIAM and with the terms in which

MARS was discussing the future of modern architecture. But *Architectural Design*'s openness to different points of view robbed the journal of a well-defined editorial point of view. More clearly identifiable were the positions of the *Architectural Review* and the *Architects' Yearbook*.[4] The *Review*, its editorial team strengthened from the end of 1946 by the return from Egypt of Jim Richards, developed further the position it had taken up in 1943–44.

By contrast, the *Architects' Yearbook* was a new venture. Edited by Jane Drew and supported by an editorial board of pre-war champions of the Modern Movement – Maxwell Fry, Herbert Read and Charles Reilly – *Architects' Yearbook* was published by Paul Elek. He had published books with a left-wing bias on social issues, reconstruction and architecture, and launched the *Architects' Yearbook* in the hope of establishing a journal that would take up where *Circle* had left off.[5] Early editorials conveyed the strength of commitment to pre-war values and the possibility of adapting them to the needs of the moment.[6]

Though few British buildings built immediately after the war answered the journal's expectations, the *Architects' Yearbook* set out examples of buildings from abroad, particularly America and Scandinavia, to illustrate how the ideals of the 1930s could be adapted to post-war conditions at home. To this end Drew published the work of Gropius, Sert, Alfred Roth, Richard Neutra, Ernst May and others associated with CIAM, providing British readers with early articles on Le Corbusier's post-war work, and on Aalto.

For all the differences in emphasis, the monthly journals had much in common – their editorial teams shared links with MARS and beyond to CIAM – not least of which was a shared basic sympathy for modern architecture. With little architecture of note being built, coverage from one magazine to another tended to focus on the same projects. By contrast, the schools of architecture differed sharply. Not only was modern architecture interpreted differently from school to school, in some there was still outright hostility toward modern architecture in any form. In the 1930s students at the Architectural Association (AA) had given modern architecture an enthusiastic welcome. At Liverpool too, lecturers like Gordon Stephenson were, under Reilly's benign leadership, beginning to change the way architecture was taught.[7] Now in 1945 architecture schools faced new concerns. Crammed with students, short of staff, shorter still of resources, what was the contribution of the schools to the debate on the new architecture? Students' attitudes varied. Some returning from the war were eager to get on, finish their education, move into the profession and make up for lost time. Others returned to architectural education with a keen sense of idealism and were determined to build a better and, generally, a new and modern Britain.

In contrast to the radical hopes of many students, the pace of change in most schools was leisurely. Despite a number of pre-war victories for modernism, most famously at the AA in 1938,[8] many schools taught in an Arts and Crafts or Beaux Arts manner. At the Bartlett, Albert Richardson, who had enjoyed a comfortable war at St Catharine's College, Cambridge, still held sway, only to be followed in the same Neo-Georgian mould by Hector Corfiato in 1947.[9] The Bartlett was exceptional in the vigour of its resistance to modernism, but in most schools studios with explicitly modernist interests had to cohabit with older traditions of teaching. The architecture school at Cambridge continued on a small scale its pre-war provincial conservatism, despite the best efforts of a few younger staff to speed the pace of change. Elsewhere committed modernists like Peter Moro (who had worked for Tecton) at the Regent Street Polytechnic or Gordon Stephenson at Liverpool, who had worked for Le Corbusier in the 1930s, were the exception, not the rule. At the AA under the directorship of Raymond Brown, some studios were taught by young modernists like Anthony Chitty and or Anthony Cox and Kenneth Capon from the Architects' Co-Partnership. Others continued to be taught by representatives of the Arts and Crafts tradition, such as Brandon Jones, until R. Furneaux Jordan became director in

February 1949.[10] The pages of the *Architectural Association Journal*, devoted to the life of the school, suggest the diversity of interests in a community rather like that of a contemporary Oxford or Cambridge junior common room, with talk of the social responsibilities of architecture alongside preparations for the annual pantomime and descriptions of jolly outings to buildings of historical importance.[11]

Yet the schools were beginning to change. A new spirit was evident in *Plan*, the student magazine taken over by AA students in 1948.[12] In contrast to the tweedy enthusiasms of the *Architectural Association Journal*, *Plan* discussed the efforts of CIAM, problems of housing, group work – now allowed for the first time – and the Unité d'Habitation. By 1947 student work illustrated in the architectural journals was predominantly modernist. At the AA, students' projects appeared more adventurous than before the war in handling issues of construction, structure and servicing. Students seemed to develop an extraordinary facility for picking up ideas from publications and foreign travel. Immediately after the war, despite the high cost and difficulty of securing foreign currency, AA students began travelling to Scandinavia, Holland, Italy, Germany and France. Hundreds made the long trip south to visit the site of Le Corbusier's Unité d'Habitation, which was just beginning, in 1949, to rise above the southern suburbs of Marseilles.[13] Discussion and designs in schools like the AA reflected the preoccupations of the journals. Random rubble walls, the extensive use of natural materials like timber, even the return to traditional pitched roofs featured in the work of AA students quite as regularly as in the published work of the younger Swedish architects. But in one important respect the interests of the students appeared to differ from those of the immediately preceding generation. Students continued to be fascinated by the work of the leading 1930s modernists, especially Le Corbusier. They not only knew Le Corbusier's pre-war writings like *Vers une architecture* and his key pre-war buildings, the Pavillon de l'Esprit Nouveau, Villa Stein and the Villa Savoie, but they were excited by his post-war buildings too, above all by the attempts to address problems of housing and reconstruction in the Unité d'Habitation. This admiration was evident from the invitation to speak at the celebrations of the Architectural Association's centenary, issued by the students, rather than by the association.[14] To students everywhere, Le Corbusier appeared to offer a radical if simplified view of architecture, uncompromised and unqualified by the limitations of austerity and the regulations that the war brought in its wake. His passionate appeal to architectural principle, a sharp contrast with the pragmatic tenor of the English debate, caught the students' imagination and encouraged further the enthusiastic response to the avant-garde of the 1920s and 1930s.

The search for the Englishness of English architecture

The terms of the debate expanded after the war, but the central themes from before 1945, shared on both sides of the Atlantic, continued to figure as actively as ever. One response to the widespread demand for the humanising of modern architecture was to encourage the development of a 'monumental' modern architecture. This was not to follow the pattern of the architectural monumentality of totalitarian states, but was to be an architecture that would go beyond utilitarian issues to address the spiritual and cultural needs of society. A second and not necessarily mutually exclusive way forward was to pursue still further the war-time interest in a regional architecture in which form and materials would answer to local circumstances and conditions, and not just the abstract requirements of some international style. Over the next five years, the *Architectural Review* was to play a prominent part in debating these two themes. Its survey of the current state of architecture, published in 1947 to celebrate the journal's 'Second Half Century', summarised the agenda:

> After the Act of Revolution comes the act of building anew ... A short-term objective

must involve new richness and differentiation of character, the pursuit of differences rather than sameness, the re-emergence of monumentality, the cultivation of idiosyncrasy, and the development of those regional dissimilarities that people have always taken pride in. In fact architecture must find a way of humanising itself as regards expression without in any way abandoning the principles of the Revolution on which it was founded.[15]

For the editors of the *Review*, more than for any other participant in the debate, the idea of regional dissimilarities was easily equated with an interest in England. During the war Pevsner had already started collecting the material that was eventually to make up the 1955 Reith Lectures, 'The Englishness of English Art'.[16] Richards likewise shared this interest, although in very different terms. While stationed in the heat and dust of cities in the Middle East, in Cairo, Jerusalem and Aleppo, Richards had written *Castles on the Ground*, an affectionate appreciation of the English suburbs that discomfited those who saw him only as the champion of modern architecture. In this essay, Richards extolled the way in which the suburban neighbourhood, house and garden – 'Ewban'd inside and Atco'd out'– so perfectly matched the aspirations of the English middle classes. Derided perhaps by those with taste, but hugely popular, he saw the architecture of the suburbs as the new English vernacular and a triumph of regionalism.[17]

Offering practical advice on how ideas of Englishness might be reflected in modern architecture, the *Review* continued to urge the case for Picturesque theory:

> Take as but one example the Picturesque tradition. This is England's one great contribution to the art of landscape and it has been an important part of the *Review*'s policy to show that it can now profitably be studied in relation to the new problems of landscape which have been clarified by sociological research.[18]

Serving the wider causes of 'visual re-education' and the policies of Picturesque theory, the *Review* explored different visual dimensions of Englishness in a succession of special issues. In numbers devoted to subjects like 'Canals', 'The Functional Tradition' and 'Townscape', illustrated with photographs by Eric de Mare, the *Review* set out to capture elements of an unselfconscious tradition that had informed the form of the rural and urban English landscape for over a century:

> Today we are attempting consciously to design things in terms of the most suitable materials, processes and performance standards to satisfy one or several specific functions. These same principles, unexpressed, have unconsciously controlled the forms evolved by countless generations of blacksmiths, masons, wheelwrights, millwrights and shipwrights. This is the Functional Tradition. This is the living tradition from which each successive generation can learn and has learned, and our generation is no exception.[19]

In the sympathetic recording of paving, quays, bridges, lock gates, walls, entrances, railings, steps and the other elements that made up the traditional visual qualities of English market towns, of canals, of seaside towns like Lyme Regis or university cities like Oxford and Cambridge, the *Review* illustrated the ingredients of an English vernacular tradition, time established elements of a visual vocabulary that might be combined as part of the new application of Picturesque theory (Figure 3.1):

> The Picturesque Movement has a significance far transcending its local position in landscape-gardening history, for acknowledgement in our own day of the existence of a perennially English visual philosophy could revolutionise our national contribution to architecture and town-planning by making possible our own regional development of the International Style, as a

3.1 'The Functional Tradition: the Canals': Eric de Mare's photographic essay brought to life the world of nineteenth-century engineering, the canals, shipbuilding and the mills

result of our own self-knowledge – technics given in marriage to psychology.[20]

Presenting this new Picturesque as a radical alternative to both the classicism of Le Corbusier and to the romanticism of Frank Lloyd Wright, de Chronin Hastings proposed that the 'operation' of the new aesthetic could be understood, by analogy with the development of the common law, in pragmatic and truly British terms as determined by precedent, as a 'casebook' of English examples:

> Taking the phrase *casebook* in the lowest and most literal sense the true radical would set out to begin the long business of establishing visual planning precedents (not principles), by the collection of individual examples of civic design. How

significant and idiosyncratic – how radical – this simple act is, is seen when we remind ourselves that that is exactly the method that has been followed in the creation of this country's greatest contribution to civil organisation – the common law ... I submit that the moment the thing is put in that way it becomes clear to any English mind that that is the only way an English visual tradition could be reborn. A mass of precedents gone over creatively to make a living idiom.[21]

To match de Chronin Hasting's puff of liberal theory, Gordon Cullen presented a series of individual visual 'cases', characterising them in a way in which the eye might enjoy them – 'the eye as exterior decorator', 'the eye as sculptor', 'the eye as movie camera' – to form the 'Townscape Casebook' (Figure 3.2).[22]

The *Review* was equally concerned to identify the elements of an English vernacular tradition. The design of the pub exemplifies *in parvo* the way in which the *Review* posed the question of finding an appropriate architecture for a distinctly English institution:

> The church and the pub have proved to be two the of knottiest architectural problems of our age. Perhaps in the interior of the pub the problem that wrecks contemporary architecture is posed more vividly than anywhere else. That problem is how to establish an architecture which is modern in the sense of belonging to our time – which takes full advantage of contemporary techniques and materials – but is yet fully rooted in the needs and responses of ordinary people, giving them what they have a right to demand of their environment – an architecture progressive without being inhuman and popular without being silly.[23]

The *Review*'s approach emphasised the importance of tradition and an understanding of history. It documented the evolution of the

3.2 'Townscape Casebook': Gordon Cullen's drawings and articles drew attention to the picturesque qualities of seaside towns and traditional English towns like Ludlow (pictured above), Woodstock and Ross-on-Wye

alehouse, the inn and the tavern, from the kitchen of the wayside house, to the urban 'public bar' and the 'Rococo Saloon Bar', and their demi-monde contemporaries 'the Road House' and the 'Cocktail Bar'.[24] This documentation was proposed as the basis for recovering the sense of tradition applicable in the design of new pubs: '[W]hat can be learnt from the pub tradition ... in order that the atmosphere so effectively created in the past can be re-created in a modern way?'[25] Sketches by Gordon Cullen suggested, in 'The Tradition Reborn', how the lessons of the past might be used as a basis for the design of the modern pub interior. The *Review*'s special number on pubs invited its readers to take part in a competition for the design of interiors for different pub types sponsored by the *Review* and a number of brewers.

The competition was lively. The *Review* and the *Architects' Journal* went on to publish the

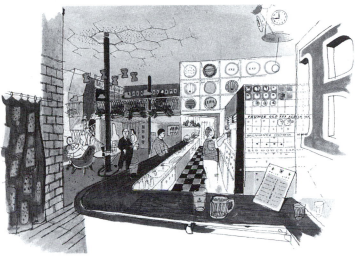

i   ii

3.3 The competition for the design of the new English pub, 1950: (i) one of the *Architectural Review*'s examples of the traditional English pub; (ii) the interior of the winning entry by Pollak, Prus, Hasler, Sharland and Negus

winning designs and the judges pronounced the competition a successful answer to the editors' expectations (Figure 3.3).[26] But looking back on these designs today they seem to lack those very qualities of atmosphere, of 'Englishness' and 'pubness', that the competition sought to inspire. The winning designs have neither the exuberance of the nineteenth-century gin palace nor the robust simplicity of the country pub. Established details – beer barrels, jugs of spirits, beer handles and the brewers' lettering – all speak of tradition, but the designs lack conviction and authority. With modern lamp fittings and hexagonal patterning, the winning design looks more like an exhibition of international contemporary furnishings than a design for a uniquely English form of interior. The step from well-articulated theory to the practice of design was to prove difficult.

From the New Empiricism to 'organic architecture'

Even the *Review* recognised that this pursuit of the regional, of the Picturesque and Whigishness, of the fascination with 'Victorian merry-go-rounds and rustic railway stations, lighthouses, gin-palaces and non-conformist chapels, exotic villadom, cemeteries and monkey-puzzles',[27] could easily be dismissed as self-indulgent, frivolous and downright quirky. And by 1947 the *Review*, sensitive to ideas from the US and elsewhere, was beginning to use the term 'regionalism' to convey more than just the association with any region. By a process of association which was far from rigorous, regionalism was now linked increasingly with the architecture of a number of specific regions, particularly with Scandinavia and the West Coast of the United States.

The interest in regionalism had been linked from the start with an implicit, and occasionally explicit, rejection of the values of the 'International Style' and the 'creed of functionalism' that had been assumed to provide its underpinning. Now in the late 1940s the *Review* and other journals, such as *Architectural Design*, continuing their war-time enthusiasm for Swedish architecture, came to present it not just as one regional style amongst many, but as a paradigm for an architectural alternative to functionalism (Figure 3.4). This was the central theme in articles

i ii

3.4 The New Empiricism in Sweden: (i) flats at Danviksklippan, Stockholm, by Backström and Reinius; (ii) Markelius's own house at Kevinge

written by Eric de Mare, an architect, photographer and an editor of the *Architects' Journal*, and himself half Swedish.

De Mare's first article, 'The New Empiricism: Sweden's Latest Style', opened with the contrast between the passing revolutionary phase of 'functionalism' and the growing interest of the younger generation of Swedish architects in humanising the new architecture. De Mare saw no absolute reaction against functionalism in their work but instead a determination to recast the way that functional principles were interpreted: 'The tendency is ... both to humanise the theory on its aesthetic side and to get back to the earlier rationalism on its technical side.'[28] Under the banner of the New Empiricism, the young Swedish architects wished to be 'more objective than the functionalists, and to bring back another science, that of psychology, into the picture'. The New Empiricism was the response to what Sven Backström, one of their leaders, diagnosed as the failure of the 'objective' or functionalist architecture of the 1930s:

The years passed and one 'objective' house after the other stood ready for use. It was then that people gradually began to discover that the 'new objectivity' was not always so objective, and the houses did not always function as well as had been expected. They also felt the lack of many of the aesthetic values and the little contributions to cosiness that we human beings are so dependent upon, and that our architectural and domestic tradition had nevertheless developed. It was difficult to settle down in the new houses because the 'new' human beings were not so different from the older ones ... One result of this growing insight was a reaction against all the too-schematic architecture of the 1930s.[29]

Looking through the plans and photographs of the buildings by Sven Markelius, Uno Ahren, Sture Frolen, Backström and the other members of this generation, readers of the *Review* were encouraged to see how the programmatic forms of the 1930s could be adapted and developed without abandoning the 'positive achievements of the modernist revolution'.[30] De Mare described modern architecture in Sweden in terms calculated to touch the imagination of English architects labouring to build despite the constraints of austerity:

> In general it is a reaction against a too rigid formalism. The first excitement of structural experiment has gone and there is a return to workaday common sense. There is a feeling that buildings are made for the sake of human beings rather than for the cold logic of theory. The word *spontanietet*, so often on the lips of the young Swedish architect today, perhaps gives the key to the new approach ... Why, they ask, make windows larger than necessary just to show that we can create a wall entirely of glass? Why flat roofs when they start to leak in the spring? Why avoid traditional materials when they do their job well and provide pleasant texture and colour at the same time? Why eschew fantasy and decoration for which, in our hearts, we long?[31]

Markelius's own house, set amidst birch trees in the outskirts of Stockholm at Kevinge, exemplified what de Mare valued in the work of this generation:

> [P]lanning has become much freer and far less concerned with the pattern on paper than with the final reality. Fenestration, too, is freer and windows occur at the places and of the sizes which needs dictate and as the pattern pleases. Indigenous traditional materials are used both inside and out, especially brick and timber. In domestic work cosiness is coming back and there is a tendency among the more sophisticated at any rate to fix furniture in different styles in the Sharawag manner. Buildings are married carefully to the sites and to the landscape, and flowers and plants are made an integral part of the whole design.[32]

But even as he applauded the work of this younger generation, de Mare sounded a note of caution, warning against the dangers of an uncritical return to tradition and thus allowing the architectural revolution to slip 'quietly into reverse'. Looking forward to ways in which the New Empiricism might develop, de Mare suggested that Frank Lloyd Wright's work, though little known in Sweden, might provide a source of future inspiration.[33]

The connection between the New Empiricism and Wright's self-proclaimed 'organic architecture' would not have struck the readers of the *Review* as far-fetched. Wright would have appeared as a natural precursor to the younger Swedes in their reaction against the modern architecture of the 1930s. Despite Wright's status as one the pioneers of the modern movement and the inclusion of his work in the International Style exhibition in 1932, his position as an architect with strong feelings for the regional nature of architecture and his disparaging of 1930s European modernism would have been clearly remembered during the 1940s by those familiar with the development of American architecture.[34] Wright was already known in England from the 1939 RIBA lecture series 'An Organic Architecture, the Architecture of Democracy', at which he had shown films of his recent work, including the construction of Taliesin West.[35] The lectures, delivered in a theatrical preaching style, confirmed his reputation as an idiosyncratic prophet of a non-European and 'organic' architecture for America. This he presented as the antithesis of the universal classical ideal, as an architecture that claimed the unique conditions of the individual programme, Nature and 'Life itself', as sources of inspiration:

> So modern architecture rejects the major axis and the minor axis of classic architecture. It rejects all grandomania, every building that would stand in military

fashion heels together, eyes front, something on the right hand and something on the left hand. Architecture already favours the reflex, the natural easy attitude, the occult symmetry of grace and rhythm affirming the ease grace and naturalness of natural life. Modern architecture – let us now say *organic* architecture – is a natural architecture – the architecture of nature, for Nature[36]

The claim for a link between Wright's work and recent European developments was made at greater length in a book, *Towards an Organic Architecture*, written at this time by Bruno Zevi, a young Italian who had fled Fascism to Britain and finished his architectural training at Harvard.[37] Zevi cast Wright as the hero in the emergence of a new American architecture freed of the stylistic constraints of Europe. It was this American 'organic' tradition, argued Zevi, which had liberated Europeans like Neutra, Gropius and Breuer from the narrow corset of functionalism on their arrival in the United States and would now liberate European architecture generally.[38]

The widespread use of the word 'organic' described the kind of developments that both Zevi and the *Review* wished to encourage, an architectural alternative to the International Style. But Zevi's book lacked substance, offering at best a definition of 'organic' architecture by what it was not: thus organic architecture was not classical, not academic, not constrained by arbitrarily imposed rules, not linked to established traditions of composition. But Zevi's linking of the work of the young Scandinavians and Aalto with Wright was indicative of the growing interest in the idea of an organic architecture as an alternative to the International Style of the 1930s.

A more important step in establishing a new and widely accepted – if no more rigorous – usage for the word 'organic' was Sigfried Giedion's study of Alvar Aalto, published as an article in the *Architectural Review*, and included as a new chapter to the 1949 edition of *Space,*

Time and Architecture, the first authoritative post-war history of modern architecture widely available in Britain.[39] Giedion's study was the first major presentation of Aalto's work to British readers and, as such, a powerful spur to thinking about an alternative approach to architecture.[40] Giedion lionised Aalto as one of those few architects 'to dare to leap from the rational-functional to the irrational-organic'[41] and to move forward from his own interpretation of the International Style, represented by the Viipuri Library and the Paimio Sanatorium, to the 'organic' forms of Villa Mairea, the Finnish Pavilion at the 1939 New York World's Fair, the planning of Kautta and the recently finished Baker dormitory building at Massachusetts Institute of Technology (Figure 3.5).

What was the source of inspiration for Aalto's organic forms? Giedion allowed that Aalto's architecture might be based on a response to the lakes, forests and granite landscape, to the

3.5 Baker House, Massachusetts Institute of Technology (1945–48) by Alvar Aalto. Giedion's article in the *Architectural Review* presented Aalto as the leading proponent of an 'organic' architecture

curious fusion of East and West, found only in Finland. But in Giedion's view Aalto's work was not just an extension of post-war Scandinavian regionalism. Indeed, Giedion was emphatic in differentiating the use of the word 'organic', as applied to Aalto's buildings, from any association with the New Empiricism:

> To avoid misunderstanding, let it be stated that this development towards the organic in no way approximates to the German reaction of the thirties, nor to certain Nordic evasions of the real problem, curiously labelled *New Empiricism* which means that 'cosiness is coming back into domestic work'.[42]

Despite the evident differences between the work of Aalto and the younger Swedes, the theoretical distinctions between Giedion's use of the word organic and de Mare's, Backström's or even Zevi's were slight. By 1949, Giedion's protestations notwithstanding, terms such as 'organic architecture', the 'New Empiricism' and 'regionalism' had come to be widely and loosely used to categorise one branch of architectural alternatives to the supposedly rational and functional architecture of the 1930s.

The New Monumentality

The idea that modern architecture should address more than merely utilitarian needs in a functional manner and should seek to meet society's cultural expectations, as had the monumental architecture of the past, was central to the architectural debate from 1943 onwards. But the use of the term 'monumentality' was problematic. To many the absence of monumentality was viewed as one of the strengths of modern architecture; indeed, the very idea of monumentality had negative associations, most immediately with the architecture of the Nazi regime. But the term 'New Monumentality' was coined to convey something very different, a set of new architectural aspirations.[43] The first British encounter with this term occurred in September 1946 during the meeting in London of the International Reunion of Architects (later to become the IUA), at which Giedion gave a lecture by this title at the RIBA to a well-attended session hosted by the MARS Group.[44] This was a subject that lay close to the interests of CIAM members in the United States, and the subsequent British discussion of the New Monumentality did much to atune the British to issues being debated elsewhere.

In the United States the idea of a New Monumentality had been first discussed in 1944 at a symposium whose proceedings were published as *The New Architecture and City Planning*.[45] In a section entitled 'The Problems of a New Monumentality', Giedion presented the keynote paper along with papers by other figures from East Coast architectural circles: George Nelson, editor of *Architectural Forum* and a member of the steering committee for the Museum of Modern Art's architectural division; Louis Kahn; Philip Goodwin, director of the Museum of Modern Art's architectural division; and the artist Ernest Fiene.[46]

Giedion's paper was the most explicit statement of the issues addressed in this section; it grew out of discussions with Fernand Leger and José Sert at the Abstract Artists Association of New York the year before, but all the contributors were convinced of the need to go beyond purely functional or utilitarian considerations to explore the visual and the expressive qualities of modern architecture. Anticipating the prospect of reconstruction in Europe, Giedion and Sert recognised that simply building new housing, new schools and new roads or returning to the 'four functions' of CIAM's pre-war analysis of the city would not be enough. If, after the war, Europe's cities were to continue to play the central role that they had played in shaping Western civilisation, then it would be necessary to make physical, architectural provision for the social, political and spiritual life of the city. European cities would have to be rebuilt in the image of Lewis Mumford's *Culture of Cities*, rather than as the CIAM city of *Can Our Cities Survive?* To give architectural expression to these hopes, a New Monumentality was necessary, CIAM's values would have to change.

Even from the perspective of the British, reliant on publications and the reports of those few architects able to visit the United States, it was possible to recognise the significance of the New Monumentality and the way it cut across contemporary discussion in the architectural press of war memorials and monuments.[47] Looking over what had been built in the United States since the 1932 International Exhibition on Modern Architecture, and celebrating the twelfth year of the museum's Department of Architecture, Elizabeth Mock, exhibition curator and editor of the museum's survey *Built in the USA, 1932–1944*, focused on the New Monumentality as one of the few topical questions 'fervently discussed by everyone who believes in the art of architecture'.[48] For Mock, too, the question was, 'Can Modern Architecture answer the need for buildings which will symbolise our social ideals and aspirations?' Acknowledging the confusion caused by the 'shifty word monumentality', she argued that

> Democracy needs monuments, even though its requirements are not those of a dictatorship. There must be occasional buildings which raise the every-day casualness of living to a higher and more ceremonial plane, buildings which give dignified and coherent form to that interdependence of the individual and the social group which is the very nature of our democracy. ... The need is apparent, but the answer is still nebulous. The question of suitable scale is a delicate one ... can the desired effect be achieved solely through the drama of bold and imaginative structure and the richness of revealed material? ... The monumental possibilities of the city square, for example, have scarcely yet been considered in modern terms. Endless discussion is possible, and healthy, but the solution will be found only in the actual trial of creation.[49]

Assessing *Built in the USA* and Zucker's 1945 publication of the proceedings of the previous year's New Monumentality symposium, British reviewers acknowledged the importance of the question of monumentality; but in a country beset by the most acute shortages of the resources needed for even the most utilitarian buildings, this issue was not easily addressed. In post-war Britain utilitarian not monumental building was the first priority.[50] During the war, as part of the reaction against the dogmatic certitudes of the International Style, there had been a general agreement that architecture after the war would have to be based on a wider range of considerations than functionalism alone, that social and psychological values would need to be taken into account. But before the end of the war these very general aspirations had not yet been linked in the British debate with the specific idea of a New Monumentality.

With Giedion's RIBA lecture in 1946, this was to change. His starting point was the conviction that the Modern Movement in the pre-war years had focused too narrowly on functional issues and had defined modernity too specifically in terms of the machine. In *Mechanisation Takes Command* (1948) Giedion saw the machine and mechanisation as means to an end: 'Mechanisation is an agent, like water, fire, light. It is blind and without direction of its own. It must be canalised.'[51] As in the nineteenth century, the task for the mid-twentieth century was to re-establish that unity of feeling and thought, that balance of art and technique, that had distinguished all the great epochs of the past. The revolutionary architects of the 1920s had broken with the past by purging architecture of all but its most basic elements. Now, Giedion urged, modern architecture should recover its lyrical and expressive powers. To do this it was necessary to find a new mode of monumental expression, remote from the exploitation of the styles. Giedion anticipated that the task would be difficult:

> In view of what had happened in the last century, it is not only *the most dangerous but also the most difficult step* ... The people

want buildings representing their social, ceremonial and community life. They want their buildings to be more than a functional fulfilment. They seek the expression of their aspirations for joy, for luxury and for excitement.

The need for architecture to reflect these emotions was universal and necessary to the modern age too:

> Every period has the impulse to create symbols in the form of monuments, which according to the Latin meaning, is 'something that reminds', something to be transmitted to later generations. This demand for monumentality cannot in the long run, be suppressed. It tries to find an outlet at all costs.[52]

With Leger and Sert, Giedion believed this universal need was also a key link between the past and the present, the currency of a vital tradition:

> Monuments are human landmarks which men have created as symbols for their ideals, for their aims, and for their actions. They are intended to outlive the period which originated them, and constitute a heritage for future generations. As such they form a link between the past and the future.[53]

Giedion's lecture put the issue of monumentality firmly on the agenda for the British avant-garde. The term monumentality, charged with the particular meaning assigned to it by Giedion, was to occur regularly in the *Review*.[54] This growing interest in monumentality and in the aesthetics of architecture was to prepare the British avant-garde for a discussion of the future of the Modern Movement that was to take place at the first post-war meeting of CIAM in Bridgwater, Somerset, the following summer. The debate on the new architecture was regaining its international character, and the role now played by the British was crucial.

CIAM 6 at Bridgwater

With CIAM struggling to recover its sense of purpose, and wrestling with the task of agreeing a new constitution, the meeting at Bridgwater lacked the flourish of success of the pre-war events. Giedion, secretary to CIAM, and CIRPAC had set quite limited goals for the meeting: the resumption of contacts between the different groups for the first time since the war and the reconstitution of some kind of international collaboration. The results were positive. The delegates' pleasure at meeting old friends was real (Figure 3.6). A number of procedural decisions were made, for example the institution of an organising council, a new committee structure and the adoption of the CIAM *grille* ('grid'), developed by Le Corbusier and his research collective ASCORAL as the basis for collective analysis and presentation. But, more significant for the future of CIAM, the sixth congress at Bridgwater also marked the broadening of CIAM's interests and saw the first interventions by members of the younger generation.

CIAM 6 saw the first discussion of architectural aesthetics: 'To work for the creation of a physical environment that will satisfy man's emotional and material needs and stimulate his spiritual growth.'[55] The meeting's final communiqué went still further to emphasise the new centrality of aesthetics, the New Monumentality, to CIAM's work:

> To achieve an environment of this quality, we must combine social idealism, scientific planning and the fullest use of available building techniques. In doing so we must enlarge and enrich the aesthetic language of architecture in order to provide a contemporary means whereby people's emotional needs can find expression in the design of their environment. We believe that thus a more balanced life can be produced for the individual and for the community.[56]

TOP-ROW 1. (Left to right).
1. Milton (England).
2. Browne (England).
3. Rogers (Italy).
4. Cedercreutz (Finland).
5. Grannasztoi (Hungary).
6. Hruska (Czechoslovakia).
7. Neumann (Czechoslovakia).
8. Marshall (England).
9. Kadleigh (England).
10. van Bodegraven (Holland).
11. Entwistle (England).
12. Richards (England).
13. Elte (Holland).

14. Samuel (England).
15. Roth (Switzerland).
16. Emery (Algeria).
17. Bijhouwer (Holland).
18. de Vries (Holland).
19. van den Broek.
20. Kloos (Holland).
21. Kleykamp (Holland).
22. Michel (Belgium).

ROW 2.
23. Cadbury-Brown (England).
24. Shepheard (England).
25. De Syllas (England).

26. Cox (England).
27. Moffett (Ireland).
28. Batista (Cuba).
29. Arroyo (Cuba).
30. Fuchs (Czechoslovakia).
31. Honnegger (Switzerland).
32. Fischer (Hungary).
33. Steiger (Switzerland).
34. Mrs. Stam Beese (Holland).
35. Katona (England).
36. Pritchard (England).
37. Bakema (Holland).
38. Hogan (England).
39. Singer (Czechoslovakia).

ROW 3.
40. Papadaki (U.S.A.).
41. Morton Shand (England).
42. Rosenberg (England).
43. Martin (England).
44. Goldfinger (England).
45. Jensen (England).
46. Ling (England).
47. Ferrari Hardoy (Argentine).
48. Mrs. Wiener (U.S.A.).
49. Wiener (U.S.A.).
50. Maxwell Fry (England).
51. Wells Coates (England).

52. Townsend (England).
53. Krejcar (Czechoslovakia).
54. Oberlander (Canada).
55. Schutte (Austria).
56. Merkelbach (Holland).

ROW 4. (Front row).
57. Le Corbusier (France).
58. Vivanco (Argentine).
59. Sadie Speight (England).
60. Susan Cox (England).
61. Malnai (Hungary).
62. Mrs. Malnai (Hungary).
63. Barbara Randell (England).

64. Monica Pidgeon (England).
65. Sert (U.S.A.).
66. Giedion (Switzerland).
67. Jane Drew (England).
68. van Eesteren (Holland).
69. M. de Silva (India).
70. Gropius (U.S.A.).
71. Mrs. Fischer (Hungary).
72. Blanche Lemco (Canada).
73. Kalivoda (Czechoslovakia).
74. Mrs. Sert (U.S.A.).
75. Mrs. Schutte (Austria).
76. van Tijen (Holland).

3.6 The delegates at CIAM 6 at Bridgwater, photographed on an outing to the BAC factory, which was producing aluminium housing. Copyright untraceable

This question of architectural aesthetics surfaced in two quite different forms. First was the issue, pressed by J.M. Richards and members of the MARS Group, of the response of the 'common man' to the appearance of modern architecture and the extent to which architects should be 'accountable' to the public for the form of their buildings, an interest inspired perhaps by the egalitarian ideal fostered by wartime experiences.[57] Second, and more important, was the extent to which a new architectural aesthetic might be generated by collaboration between the arts, painting, sculpture and architecture, a return to the theme of the New Monumentality. It was this topic that was to spark the most spirited discussion. Even Le Corbusier, slightly aloof from the mainstream of the congress, was moved to 'intervene' from the floor to applaud the congress's willingness to debate at last questions of imagination and poetry: 'I experienced a profound happiness when I heard Giedion demanding that we should place art at the summit of our preoccupations.'[58]

The issues raised at Bridgwater opened up a new agenda for CIAM and for the avant-garde debate internationally. Again, the *Architectural Review* was to play a central role in promoting discussion. Over the next eighteen months, it returned to these themes a number of times in anticipation of a resumption of the debate at the Bergamo meeting of CIAM, planned for the summer of 1949. In September 1948 the *Review* organised a symposium, 'In Search of New Monumentality', with a varied cast of art historians and architects from both sides of the Atlantic.[59] Introducing the results of the symposium, the editors reiterated the now familiar call for an expansion of the expressive powers of modern architecture:

Modern Architecture has now won its battle against period revivalism and against the denial of the technical revolution that the use of reminiscent styles implies. But in doing so it has only achieved the first negative stage of the struggle for a contemporary architectural language. The second positive stage has still to be undertaken, the development of an idiom rich and flexible enough to express all the ideas that architecture – especially representative architecture – ought to be capable of expressing …

In its next phase modern architecture will blossom in several new directions, none of which need represent a retreat from functionalism but rather a broadening of the term to include a building's moral and emotional functions in addition to its material functions.[60]

The outcome of the symposium was not unexpected: while there was some dissent on what the term monumentality might mean, there was widespread agreement that the development of a more expressive architecture was critical for the future of the Modern Movement. But, as at Bridgwater, there was little sense of how this might be achieved. Developments such as the Ministry of Education building in Rio de Janeiro and Le Corbusier's League of Nations project of 1927 were cited by Giedion as examples of modern developments that conveyed some of the qualities to be expected from the New Monumentality.[61] Hopes were expressed that painters and sculptors working alongside architects on the design of projects such as the design of the United Nations building in New York, on new civic centres as part of the reconstruction of Europe or on the building of new towns in the United States might point the way forward. But there was tacit agreement, as at Bridgwater the summer before, that the debate could be carried no further without action, and that the only way to establish the New Monumentality was to do so through design.

The Bergamo meeting of CIAM in July 1949, far from advancing the issues raised at Bridgwater, only served to exacerbate the divisions within the Modern Movement. Helena Syrkus attacked the Western delegates for their capitulation to capitalism and their surrender of the cultural values of the past, thus leaving modern architecture remote from popular appeal and locked in sterile formalism. Her view, forthrightly expressed, was a reminder of the measure of disagreement between East and West on the forms that a New Monumentality might take.[62] As delegates voted to focus on the challenge of designing the 'core of the city' for the next CIAM meeting, hopes of establishing in theoretical debate a common approach for modern architecture seemed as elusive as ever. But there was at least general agreement that the new architecture of the post-war years would need to be more expressive of spiritual values than CIAM had ever allowed before the war. In asking the British representatives to prepare plans for the next meeting (CIAM 8) in Hoddesdon, the leaders of CIAM were recognising the importance of the British contribution to the debate and signalling their hopes that in Britain at least there would, by 1951, be an opportunity to see the first architectural fruits of reconstruction.

Revaluing the pre-war pioneers

Agreement on the terms of the debate might be difficult, and the linking of these with practice more problematic still, but the buildings of one or two key architects were already coming to be recognised as addressing the issues that CIAM had been debating and that architects faced as reconstruction got under way not just in Britain but across Europe. Giedion had elevated Aalto to the role of standard-bearer for organic architecture. Now after nearly ten years of neglect, Le Corbusier too was again beginning to attract attention in a way that the other pre-war leaders of the modern movement were not. Mies van der Rohe's post-war work was barely known: his first buildings for the Illinois Institute of Technology, designed and built between 1938 and 1942, were published in Britain only in 1949.[63] Gropius's work, though better known, failed to command interest. His position as elder statesman of modernism and his ideas on the role of the architect and on architectural education had kept him in the public eye. But his recent work, the Graduate Housing in Harvard Yard and his own house in Lincoln, Massachusetts, simply lacked the assurance of his pre-war buildings in Germany.

As the post-war debate gathered momentum, interest in Le Corbusier's achievements quickened, and not just among students. The *Architects' Yearbook*, for example, presented Le

Corbusier as the champion of reconstruction in France and stressed the continuity of his current work with his pre-war ideas and the values of CIAM.[64] His proposals for rebuilding St Dié exemplified the promise of reconstruction, and the grouping of public buildings and open spaces at the heart of its administrative and cultural centre seemed to offer a physical setting for the public life of the community that reflected a vision of the New Monumentality. More important still, Le Corbusier was revered across Europe as the designer of the Unité d'Habitation, hailed as the grand summation of at least thirty years of patient research on housing and a central architectural contribution to the debate on reconstruction (Figure 5.3).[65]

But in other quarters Le Corbusier's work was being interpreted in very different terms from the way that he had been seen in Britain before the war. John Summerson's essay 'Architecture, Painting and Le Corbusier', first given as a lecture at Bristol in 1947 and published as one of the collection of essays entitled *Heavenly Mansions*, presents Le Corbusier not as the humourless champion of pre-war functionalist theory but as sublimely nonsensical, as an architect of wit and of poetry:

> It was generally supposed that his kind of architecture must be an expression of sheer utilitarianism … the word 'functionalism' freely used to express this point of view. But it was impossible, at the same time, to deny these buildings a certain artistry – a perverse poetry of their own; it was impossible to deny that the designs were *felt*; to deny, in fact, that they possessed 'style'.[66]

Colin Rowe was equally impatient with the narrow 'functionalist' characterisation of Le Corbusier. In Rowe's 1947 article 'The Mathematics of the Ideal Villa: Palladio and Le Corbusier compared', Le Corbusier is recast, not as the brash revolutionary of the 1920s but as someone more to the taste of the late 1940s, as someone whose work should be seen as sensitive to the lessons of history and the gravitational pull

of the architecture of the past. Pressing the comparison between Palladio and Le Corbusier, Rowe introduces the Villa Savoye as a reinterpretation of an older Virgilian vision of the villa in the countryside:

> The Savoye House has been given a fair number of interpretations: it may be a machine for living in, an arrangement of interpenetrating volume and external space, another emanation of space, time and architecture. It is probably all these things; but the suggestive reference to the dreams of Virgil, and a certain similarity of site, solution and feeling put one in mind of the passage in Palladio which describes the Rotunda. The landscape there is more agrarian and bucolic, there is less of the untamed pastoral, the scale is larger, but the effect is somehow the same.[67]

Rowe goes on to argue that it is Le Corbusier's ordering of spaces and elevations through a geometric system of proportion that lifts Le Corbusier, like Palladio, above the transient. It is the sense of order and the feeling for rules that marks Le Corbusier's work as being exemplary, the difference between 'the universal and the decorative or merely competent', and which point the way to the possibility of establishing a new modern canon of customary beauty.

But despite this willingness by some to see the importance of Le Corbusier's work to the direction in which debate was moving, this view was not shared by all. The stance of the *Review* remained one of general indifference tempered with occasional hostility. Lionel Brett, a regular contributor to the journal, was scathing in his review of Le Corbusier's recent work. Le Corbusier was dismissed as a propagandist and self-promoting publicist, with the 'arrogance reminiscent of Leonardo' and little relevance to the current condition of architecture:

> Le Corbusier is a painter, a poet, only accidentally an architect. An intimate sympathy with the nature of materials, an easy felicity

of structure and a sense of scale, these three vital attributes of the born constructor are not specially prominent in him.[68]

Speaking of the recently published volume of the *Oeuvre Complète 1938–46*, Brett questioned its status:

It remains a puzzle (which the latest volume does nothing to solve) how these carelessly assembled picture books, with their impudent doodlings, their pretentious but half-baked *esquisses*, and their tantalising omissions, have leapt the barriers of language (including the English translation) and become the students' bible from Helsinki to Rio.[69]

Brett concluded that it was Le Corbusier's skill as a propagandist and manipulator of images that had won over the new generation of students. Even Le Corbusier's Unité d'Habitation at Marseilles, hailed by many of the younger generation of architects as one of the most potent contributions to the debate on housing and reconstruction, was dismissed by Brett and the *Review* as a failure:

It is ... significant that Le Corbusier, outstanding inventor of modern architectural symbols, has failed with the block of flats. The residential quarters of *La Ville Radieuse* were as inhumane as the frightening Unité d'Habitation de grandeur conforme now rising at Marseilles.[70]

Whatever the interest of the younger generation in Le Corbusier and the pre-war pioneers, the *Review* continued to look on the organic and pragmatic architecture of Finland and Sweden as the way forward. But could this approach, well suited to housing and schools, be adapted for the design of a major public building in an urban setting?

The TUC headquarters competition

Until the end of 1947 there were no real opportunities to put the ideas that were being debated to the test of design. But the announcement of the competition for the Trades Union Congress Memorial building answered this need. Here was the first opportunity since the war to explore what the New Monumentality might mean in practice, to design a building which would celebrate the status of the trade unions in post-war Britain and serve as a memorial to the trade union members who had died during the war. The building was to be sited in central London, on the corner of Great Russell Street and Dyott Street, and was to accommodate the memorial, the administrative offices of the TUC and a training college for the trade unions.

The competition attracted a record number of entries, more than any since the competition for the design of the RIBA building in 1932 (Figure 3.7).[71] Though the *Review* remained largely indifferent to the competition, the results attracted widespread interest. For the editor of the *Architect and Building News*, the competition marked a watershed in the acceptance of modern architecture for a major public commission. He wrote, 'The judgement of Sir Percy Thomas, the assessor, reveals it as a milestone competition in which suddenly, and clearly, it becomes evident that competitors can henceforward design in any contemporary manner, without fear of elimination through overstepping the limits of providence.'[72]

With so many entries, every possible stylistic approach was represented. Raymond Erith's carefully detailed symmetrical study showing a Doric order ground floor surmounted by an Ionic order *piano nobile* was held by the *Architects' Journal* to be the most distinguished exercise in the classical manner.[73] Stripped classicism appeared across many entries, from the taut designs of Gollins Melvin Ward to the anodyne elevations of Sir John Brown, A.E. Henson and Partners, and to designs which the *Architect and Building News* ridiculed as 'that bloated and disagreeable compromise for which there is no better label than

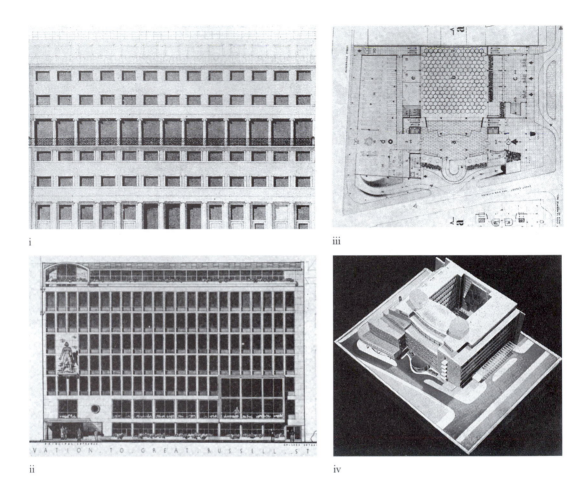

3.7 Entries for the TUC headquarters competition, 1948: (i) elevation of Raymond Erith's design; (ii) design by E.D. Lyons and C. Israel; (iii) ground floor plan of the winning entry by David Aberdeen; (iv) model of David Aberdeen's entry

"Midlands provincial"'.[74] Modern classicism was exemplified by George Grenfell Baines's entry, whose elevations seemed to catch an echo of the restrained rhythms of pre-war Sweden.

Modernists were well represented and the simple glazed frame design submitted by E.D. Lyon and C. Israel was awarded second prize. For a tight urban site adjoining Lutyens's YWCA building, there was no New Empiricist design worthy of note, but a number bore the influence of Le Corbusier: 'The Corbusier influence is the most pervading, recalling old numbers of *L'Architecture Vivante* and projects for Geneva or the Moscow of pre-reaction days. There is also the later Corbusier, with the sudden jerky

insertion of elements and changes of scale.'[75] Le Corbusier's ideas were as evident in the work of architects trained before the war as in that of current students.[76]

The influence was clearly visible in the winning scheme by David Aberdeen. This illustrated a familiarity with Le Corbusier's pre-war buildings like the Centrosoyus, as well as his ability not only to handle large elements of accommodation, lecture space and restaurant in plan and section independently of the office space above, but to express this distribution of elements clearly on the elevations. Aberdeen adapted Le Corbusier's ideas to interpret the brief in such a way as to leave the ground floor of his design free for circulation. Unlike other competitors, who followed the competition guidelines and retained the Memorial Hall as an entrance hall, Aberdeen placed the Memorial to British Workers, in sombre Genoa green marble, against the western side of the court and relegated the large lecture room, the largest single element in the brief, to the basement. With the entrance floor opened up, Aberdeen was able to create the effect of spaciousness to be seen on the ground floor of the Centrosoyus, and to use the pilotis, the stairs and other elements to direct the movement of conference delegates or visitors to the offices above with a fluidity and generosity normally associated with successful planning in the grand Beaux Arts tradition.

Equally successful was Aberdeen's treatment of the facades. The *Architect and Building News* had commented scathingly on the general low standard of elevations when set against the sophistication of most plans:

> In architecture the plan is only one projection of the design – throughout the exhibition at the Imperial Institute of these TUC designs stalked the spectre of uncertainty and eclecticism in the matter of elevations. … The architect, and the assessor in particular, is apt to place the plan first, but the public knowing little and caring less for functional contrivance, will ultimately assess achievement in design by the composition, the mass, and the appeal of the architectural envelope.[77]

By comparison with the offerings of most competitors, many of whom felt upstaged by the elevations of Lutyens's building next door, Aberdeen's elevations were a success. He was able to play off the Centrosoyus-like simplicity of the Great Russell Street facade against the animation of the project along Dyott Street. This elevation, while reflecting the essential symmetry of the major office elements on either side of the court, acknowledged the irregularity of the site, the jut of the library and the extension of the southern office floors above it.

Whatever the objections voiced against the diagrammatic and dogmatic qualities of the architecture of the 1930s, Aberdeen's winning entry marked the continuing strength of pre-war ideas. Against the flow of debate, Aberdeen had returned to the 1930s for inspiration: Le Corbusier's pre-war approach to making the elevations of a major public building still seemed serviceable in post-war building. Despite the best efforts of the *Review* to promote other approaches, there seemed to be no viable modern alternatives. In the practice of design at least, the ideas of the 1930s seemed more durable than was suggested by the debate in the journals. Hopes for an architecture which might be at once more humane and fitting for a central London site were still frustrated.

The opportunities to explore these questions in practice seemed as remote as ever. Even a project as prestigious as the TUC Memorial Building had no real chance of being built until the resources necessary for its construction were less urgently needed for housing, schools and other forms of priority building.[78] Of necessity, the architectural debate would have to proceed still further without the benefit of testing in practice.

'The Next Step?' The limits of debate

The sympathetic interest in the work of the pre-war pioneers was not shared by the *Review*. In 1950, in an important article, 'The Next Step?' – published in the *Review* along with a photographic essay on the development of modern architecture – Richards picked out three possible ways in which modern architecture might develop. The first, characterised as a product of mechanisation, standardisation and prefabrication and represented most obviously for British readers by the Hertfordshire schools, he welcomed with caution.[79] Recognising its value for utilitarian purposes, he discounted the architectural value of this approach for its failure to address the concerns about human and aesthetic values which had figured so centrally in the debate in avant-garde circles since the war. The second alternative he categorised as the 'social-realist approach'. This he disparaged for its treatment of architecture as a mere by-product of social circumstances, rather than as an agent for change in its own right.[80]

The third alternative, the one that he viewed with greatest sympathy, he defined as the 'organic approach', which he claimed was concerned with the 'conscious humanisation' of architecture and with 're-establishing the human appeal of architecture so that it can perform its traditional cultural role'. This approach favoured basing architectural form on local conditions and looked to the coming of a new regional architecture informed by climate, materials and the particular qualities of the *genius loci*. For Richards this direction built on the tradition of pragmatism, which treats each situation in its own terms, searching for 'particular characteristics of every problem, admitting only one rule: the right of every occasion to be a law unto itself'.[81] In the photographic survey accompanying the article, the majority of buildings labelled 'Empiric Organic' are the work of Scandinavian architects, by Aalto and the younger generation of Swedish architects, though Frederick Gibberd's Somerford Grove is allowed as a representative English building (Figure 4.14).

Predictably, Richards says little about the work of the pre-war pioneers. The work of Mies van der Rohe and Le Corbusier is covered in cursory fashion. Mies's post-war work at the Illinois Institute of Technology was pigeonholed along with the 'Mechanistic'. Le Corbusier's post-war work was firmly ignored and his pre-war achievements safely relegated to the section 'The Pioneers', along with those no longer capable of contributing to the current debate. In his view of the future, Richards could find no place for the pre-war masters. But for the younger generation it was the work of Mies and Le Corbusier which appeared to point the way ahead. The battle lines in the conflict between an older generation, centred on the *Review*, and the younger generation just entering practice, were already being drawn.

Notes

1   From 1945 to 1947, the MARS Group was meeting about once a month. The topics discussed were diverse and ranged across non-traditional housing, the County of London Plan, neighbourhood planning and aesthetic issues like the Picturesque and Sharawaggi. From late 1946 many of the meetings were focused on the preparations for CIAM meetings at Bridgwater, Bergamo and Hoddesdon. After CIAM 8 at Hoddesdon MARS meetings were less frequent and devoted largely to the planning of the next CIAM meeting at Aix. Thereafter the group was less active, and after the 'Turn Again' exhibition at the Royal Exchange in July 1955 the group met only sporadically. In January 1957 the group formally disbanded.

2   In the immediate post-war period, when travel was difficult, MARS provided welcome opportunities for contact with modernists elsewhere. A Foreign Relations Committee was set up in January 1946 and links established with CIAM, the IUA and architects in Russia, Poland and Switzerland.

3   In 1946 the editorial board of *Architectural Design* consisted of only Monica Pidgeon, the secretive 'NRD' and Barbara Randell, with F.E. Towndrow as consulting editor. Over the next five years the board was to grow by the addition of more consultants: in 1950 there were three, David Aberdeen, Edward Mills and Gordon Tait; in 1951 these three consultants were joined by Gontran Goulden and Mark Hartland Thomas. In 1954 the changes were more far-reaching: Theo Crosby replaced Barbara Randell, and Dargan Bullivant and Erno Goldfinger joined the consultant committee.

4   The editorial board of the *Architects' Yearbook* consisted in 1945 of Jane Drew as editor, Trevor Dannatt as assistant editor and Maxwell Fry, Herbert Read and Sir Charles Reilly as the editorial board; Ove Arup joined the board in 1952 on Reilly's death.

5   Trevor Dannatt's recollections in J. Gold, *The Experience of Modernism: Modern Architects and the Future City*, London, E. & F.N. Spon, 1997, p. 175.

6   M. Fry, 'The Architect and his Time', *AYB*, 3, 1949, p. 9.

7   M. Crinson and J. Lubbock, *Architecture: Art or Profession? 300 Years of Architectural Education in Britain*, Manchester, Manchester University Press, 1994, ch. 3.

8   For a characterisation of developments at the AA just before the war, see A. Saint, *Towards a Social Architecture: The Role of School Building in Post-War England*, London, Yale University Press, 1987, ch. 1.

9   S. Houfe, *Sir Albert Richardson, the Professor*, Luton, White Concert Press, 1980.

10 J. Summerson, *The Architectural Association 1847–1947*, London, Pleiades Books, 1947.

11 The flavour of life at the AA is conveyed by the August-September 1949 issue of the *Architectural Association Journal*, to use one random example, which covered the annual prize giving, examples of the school's work, a review of Vanbrugh's 'The Provok'd Wife' (the Dramatic Society's summer production) and an account of the annual cricket match against the RIBA.

12 *Plan* was first published in 1943 by the Architectural Students Association in Cheadle, Cheshire. It resumed publication in 1948, with an editorial committee that was increasingly dominated by AA students and was published from the AA's address, 34 Bedford Square. By *Plan* 9, however, editorial control had shifted to the Birmingham School of Architecture.

13 S. Macfarlane's article on the Unité, 'Unité d'Habitation', *Plan*, 4, 1949, pp. 23–8, was only the first of a series of articles on the Unité.

14 'Students Centenary Celebrations 5th–19th December', *Architectural Association Journal*, Jan. 1948, pp. 140–8.

15 'The Second Half Century', *AR*, Jan. 1947, p. 36.

16 Pevsner's Reith Lectures were later published as N. Pevsner, *The Englishness of English Art*, London, Architectural Press, 1956.

17 J.M. Richards, *Castles on the Ground*, London, Architectural Press, 1946.

18 'The First Half Century', *AR*, Jan. 1947, p. 36.

19 *Ibid*.

20 I. de Wolfe (pseudonym of H. de Chronin Hastings), 'Townscape', *AR*, Dec. 1949, p. 355.

21 *Ibid*., p. 362.

22 G. Cullen, 'Townscape Casebook', *AR*, Dec. 1949, pp. 363–74.

23 'Inside the Pub: Introduction', *AR*, Oct. 1949, p. 207.

24 'Inside the Pub: The Tradition', *AR*, Oct. 1949, pp. 223–58.

25 'Inside the Pub: The Tradition Reborn', *AR*, Oct. 1949, p. 259.

26 The results of the competition were published in *AR*, Jun. 1950, pp. 366, 383–96.

27 'Second Half Century', p. 22.

28 E. de Mare, 'The New Empiricism: Sweden's Latest Style', *AR*, Jun. 1947, p. 199.

29 S. Backström, 'A Swede looks at Sweden', *AR*, September 1943, p. 80.

30 De Mare, 'The New Empiricism', pp. 199–204.

31 E. de Mare, 'The Antecedents and Origins of Sweden's Latest Style', *AR*, Jan. 1948, p. 9.

32 *Ibid*.

33 *Ibid*., p. 10.

34 Wright's work would have been familiar through the section on his work in Sigfried Giedion's *Space, Time and Architecture*, Cambridge, Mass., Harvard University Press, 1941, and through H.-R. Hitchcock, *In the Nature of Materials: The Buildings of Frank Lloyd Wright 1887–1941*, New York, Meredith Press, 1942.

35 Wright's lectures, the Sir George Watson Lectures of the Sulgrave Manor Board for 1939, were published as F. Lloyd Wright, *An Organic Architecture: The Architecture of Democracy*, London, Lund Humphries, 1939.

36 *Ibid*., p. 3.

37 B. Zevi, *Towards an Organic Architecture*, London, Faber & Faber, 1950. Zevi, opposed to the Fascists, left Italy just before the war to continue his studies first at the Architectural Association and then at Harvard. He returned to Italy after military service with the Americans in Britain, and his book was first published in Italy in 1945.

38 *Ibid*., pp. 10–11.

39 S. Giedion, 'Alvar Aalto', *AR*, Feb. 1950, pp. 77–84.

40 In Britain, Aalto might have been remembered for his pre-war exhibition pavilions at Paris in 1937 and New York in 1939, for articles on him in the *Architectural Review* by Chermayeff and Morton Shand. The first post-war article on him in a British journal appeared in 1952, 'Rovaniemi: a Finnish Reconstruction Project, Alvar Aalto', *AYB*, 2, 1952, pp. 51–8. By contrast Aalto was already known on the East Coast of the United States, both through his teaching at the Massachusetts Institute of Technology and through the Baker dormitory building for MIT, completed in 1948.

41 Giedion, 'Alvar Aalto', p. 77.

42 *Ibid*.

43 Lewis Mumford's article 'Monumentalism, Symbolism and Style', *AR*, Apr. 1949, pp. 173–80, explores the changing meaning of the term 'monumentality' and his own misgivings at Giedion's usage of the term. For a more recent discussion see C.C. and G.R. Collins, 'Monumentality: a Critical Matter in Modern Architecture', *Harvard Architecture Review*, Spring 1984, pp. 15–35.

44 Giedion's lecture, at what was one of the first international conferences of architects after the war, was reported in summary form in the *Architects' Journal*: 'In Search of a Word', *AJ*, 17.10.1946, p. 274.

45 The proceedings of the symposium arranged by Cooper Union and the New School for Social Research were published as P. Zucker, *The New Architecture and City Planning*, New York, Philosophical Library, 1944.

46 S. Giedion, 'The Need for Monumentality', in *New Architecture and City Planning*, pp. 549–68.

47 Memorials and monumentality were discussed in a variety of terms in the US architectural press during 1944–45; typical were 'Memorials? Yes, but no Monuments', *Pencil Points*, May 1944, p. 35, and articles such as 'Living Memorials', *Architectural Forum*, Sep. 1944, pp. 106–12; Aug. 1945, p. 141.

48 E. Mock, *Built in the USA, 1934–1944*, New York, Museum of Modern Art, 1944, p. 25.

49 *Ibid.*

50 G.M. Kallann, 'New Uncertainty', *AR*, Mar. 1946, p. 95.

51 S. Giedion, *Mechanisation Takes Command*, Oxford, Oxford University Press, 1948, p. 714.

52 'In Search of a New Monumentality', *AR*, Sep. 1948, p. 126.

53 *Ibid.*

54 See e.g. 'New Building in Switzerland: Public Buildings', *AR*, Sep. 1946, pp. 77–8.

55 In Giedion's account of the Bridgwater conference: S. Giedion, *A Decade of Contemporary Architecture*, Zurich, Editions Girsberger, 1954, p. 12.

56 *Ibid.*, p. 23.

57 It is useful to contrast Giedion's selective report on the Bridgwater congress with other accounts, e.g.: M. Hartland Thomas, 'CIAM 6, Bridgwater', *AD*, Oct. 1947, pp. 269–71; 'After Fourteen Years', *AJ*, 18.9.1947, pp. 246–9; 276–9; and H.T. Cadbury-Brown, 'The CIAM Conference', *JRIBA*, Oct. 1947, p. 612.

58 *Ibid.*, p. 279.

59 'The New Monumentality', *AR*, Sep. 1948, pp. 117–28.

60 *Ibid.*, p. 117.

61 *Ibid.*, p. 126, though the editors' summary of the discussion of 'how to achieve monumentality' was even less specific, *ibid.*, p. 121.

62 Unlike the other CIAM conferences, CIAM 7 at Bergamo was not well documented, though *Metron* (33 & 34, 1949) and *L'Architecture d'Aujourd'hui* (16, 1948) published full reports. The most widely read account was that by Giedion, published as 'Architects and Politics: an East-West Discussion', in *Architecture You and Me: The Diary of a Development*, Cambridge, Mass., Harvard University Press, 1958, p. 79–90. For a recent discussion see E. Mumford, *The CIAM Discourse on Urbanism, 1928–1960*, Cambridge, Mass., MIT Press, 2000, pp. 179–200.

63 Mies's work at the Illinois Institute of Technology was first published in Britain in *AJ*, 3.1.1946, pp. 7–14.

64 'Ascoral; a French Reconstruction Group', *AYB*, 2, 1947, p. 74.

65 In addition to the generally positive comments on the Unité to be found in editorials and articles, the *Architects' Yearbook* published Le Corbusier's article 'Housing Equipment for a Machinist Society', *AYB*, 2, 1947, pp. 76–8, and a review of the Unité in 1952, O. and C. Carey, 'Unité d'Habitation', *AYB*, 4, 1952, pp. 130–5.

66 J. Summerson, *Heavenly Mansions*, London, Cresset Press, 1949, p. 189.

67 C. Rowe, 'The Mathematics of the Ideal Villa', *AR*, Mar. 1947, p. 101.

68 L. Brett, 'The Space Machine: An Evaluation of the Recent Work of Le Corbusier', *AR*, Nov. 1947, p. 147.

69 *Ibid.*

70 L. Brett, 'Towards a New Architecture: Post-War Flats in Britain', *AR*, Nov. 1949, p. 315.

71 The weekly journals gave generous coverage to the results. See e.g. 'The TUC Competition', *AJ*, 22.7.1948, pp. 93–8.

72 'Architecture and the TUC', *ABN*, 30.7.1948, pp. 85–6. It is tempting to think that the editorial voice was that of John Summerson.

73 'The Resurrection of a Style', *AJ*, 19.8.1948, p. 176.

74 'Architecture and the TUC', p. 86.

75 *Ibid.*

76 A number of schemes by AA students are illustrated in J. Gowan (ed.), *Projects: Architectural Association 1946–71*, London, Architectural Association, 1974, p. 16.

77 'Architecture and the TUC', p. 85.

78 Although Aberdeen won the competition in 1948, construction did not start until 1953 and was not finished until 1957.

79 J.M. Richards, 'The Next Step?', *AR*, Mar. 1950, p. 179.

80 *Ibid.*, p. 180.

81 *Ibid.*

4   1951

From debate to practice

In 1950, five years after the end of the war, architects in Britain were still being denied the opportunity to test in any but utilitarian terms the ideas that they were actively debating. Even the construction of Aberdeen's winning scheme for the TUC building had been postponed for want of steel and the labour to build it. But during the next eighteen months, British architects would at last be presented with the opportunity to design buildings other than houses, schools and factories. In the design of the Royal Festival Hall, the layout of the Festival of Britain, and the competition for the design for Coventry Cathedral, architects would be called to give architectural form to very different tasks from those that had occupied them in the first five years after the war.

The Royal Festival Hall

The Royal Festival Hall, the first public building of significance built in Britain after the war, provides an opportunity to examine the response of the Modern Movement at the end of the 1940s to the challenge of designing a building that went beyond merely utilitarian concerns (Figure 4.1). Here at last was the chance to design a major modern building. Planned for one of the most prominent of riverside sites in London as the first step in the cultural centre on the South Bank envisaged in the County of London Plan, the Royal Festival Hall brought together just the

kind of issues debated during the meetings of CIAM at Bridgwater and Bergamo and championed by the *Architectural Review*.

If the project provided an opportunity to explore the nature of a non-utilitarian architecture, it was also a project that demanded the solution of a host of technical problems and this within a very tight timetable. As the design team and consultants struggled to find a way of meeting the extraordinary challenge of building a concert hall next to a railway bridge, or wrestled with the resolution of the design of the elevations, they were all conscious of the overriding need for the building to be ready for the opening of the Festival of Britain by George VI at eleven

4.1 The river front of the Royal Festival Hall, rigged for the Festival of Britain

o'clock in the morning on 3 May 1951, in conscious emulation of Victoria's opening of the Great Exhibition 100 years before.[1]

The story of the design and construction of the building, set against the inflexible timetable of the opening of the festival in May 1951, brings home the scale of the challenge that faced Robert Matthew and his team.[2] This team was created specially, brought in from outside to by-pass the senior establishment architect Edwin Williams, who had already worked with Charles Holden on the development of a concert hall in a stripped classical manner for the South Bank site.[3] As leader of the team, Robert Matthew was able to recruit Leslie Martin, who had been working at the research and development division of the LMS railway. Martin not only had the reputation, as editor of *Circle*, of a pre-war leader of rational modernism, but had established for himself, through his work on prefabrication with Richard Llewelyn Davies at LMS and through articles such as 'A Note on Science and Art', a reputation as somebody who could bridge the divide between art and science, between design and the technical challenges that the hall and its acoustics presented.[4] Matthew also recruited Peter Moro, who had worked for Tecton before the war, knew Llewelyn Davies, and who brought with him eight talented students from the Regent Street Polytechnic. Matthew, as the London County Council's architect, smoothed the administrative way for the team with the LCC committees. Edwin Williams, with his experience of the LCC Architect's Department's procedures, took on the crucial task of overseeing the implementation of the design team's ideas and the construction of the project.[5]

The task was daunting and time was short. The team was asked to fit a complex brief onto a small and difficult site. They had to be ready to start on site in six months. The project called for a number of major public spaces: a large hall for over 3,000 people; a small hall for 700–800 people which was to be used for chamber music, theatre and ballet; a restaurant facing the river; an extension gallery, and foyer space which would enable the building

to be used in a number of different ways. Sometimes each of these spaces might have to function independently, while on other occasions, such as a music festival, it was envisaged that the building should work as a whole. In addition to these public spaces, the building needed to provide facilities for performers and artists, rehearsal rooms, dressing rooms and other ancillary spaces, as well as the administrative offices, kitchens and service areas.

The team considered four different configurations for this accommodation (Figure 4.2). Given the restricted size of the site, Leslie Martin argued that there would be obvious advantages to placing the major concert hall above the foyer space that would give access to the auditoria. Given the need to isolate the concert hall from Hungerford Bridge, Martin recognised the advantages of enclosing the hall with an envelope containing the smaller public and ancillary spaces, the idea of the 'solid egg in the transparent box', the concert hall

4.2 Sketch by Leslie Martin showing the basic alternative configurations possible for the Royal Festival Hall and (right) the final 'egg in the box' solution

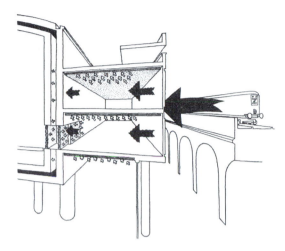

4.3 A diagrammatic representation of the solution to the acoustic problem posed by Hungerford railway bridge, showing the outer skin, the absorbent foyers and the double walls and double doors of the auditorium itself

surrounded by ancillary and circulation space.[6] Speaking on 'Science and the Design of the Festival Hall' at the RIBA not long after the hall's opening, Martin described the evolution of the design:

> Whilst this conception undoubtedly met the scientific requirements, I cannot say that it was achieved by logic. It came, like all ideas, out of the blue, as an arrangement which suddenly seem to fit and to bring into order all the requirements.[7]

The originality of this solution, now widely accepted as an established type, is easily forgotten. Within the modern canon there were precedents for this arrangement.[8] But in comparison with the form of large-scale halls like the Queen's Hall, which served London in the pre-war years, the solution arrived at by Martin and his team was ingenious and novel.

The advantages of this solution for the acoustic problems created by the site were obvious (Figure 4.3). The hall could be treated as an acoustically isolated space, protected by its envelope from the noise of the nearby passing trains. Following the advice of the acoustic consultant Hope Bagenal, the team recognised that the only way to achieve acoustic isolation of the hall was through sufficient structural mass.[9] This was to be obtained by treating the hall as a self-contained structure, an 'inner fortress', a hard core of resistance to sound whose entrances would be screened by the surrounding foyers but would be visible above this surrounding screen. Thus the 'egg' was treated formally as a self-contained and clearly identifiable form independent of its box (Figure 4.4).

The 'egg in the box' solution that elegantly answered the planning and the acoustic requirements did create other problems, notably a structural challenge of considerable complexity. How was the mass of the auditorium to be supported above the foyer in such a way that this public space would be obstructed as little as possible? To exclude external noise, the acoustic consultants

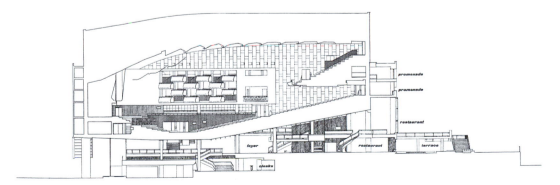

4.4 Section through the Royal Festival Hall showing the inner 'egg' and the surrounding 'box'

recommended that the auditorium should be built of two independent shells separated by a void. In practice this was to be achieved by building the walls of the auditorium as two independent concrete walls 10 inches thick, separated by a void of 12 inches.[10] Similarly the roof and the floor were to be of double skin construction, though the roof construction was lighter, in recognition of the fact that protection against external sound was less critical here. The resulting structure, weighing 25,000 tons – about the equivalent of a contemporary battle-cruiser – had to be supported in such a way as to maintain the spaciousness of the main foyers and allow the flow of space between this and the surrounding circulation areas. To support this very solid egg, the enveloping box was to be built from reinforced concrete. This had the practical advantage of providing a way of avoiding the restrictions imposed by the post-war steel shortage. Moreover, it had the formal advantage of making it possible to treat the side galleries and staircases of the surrounding envelope as a series of flat or cranked planes cantilevered off the reinforced concrete frame, emphasising both formally and structurally the distinction between box and auditorium. In the foyers the columns supporting the auditorium pierce but do not dominate the space; indeed they bring a sense of order to the space of the foyers that is reminiscent, at a smaller scale, of Le Corbusier's design for the Palace of the Soviets, where the two principal auditoria are supported on columns which order the enclosed landscape of the foyers beneath.

Contemporary responses to the
Royal Festival Hall

The project was first published barely seven months after the design team had been assembled, as construction began at the end of April 1949. The sense of anticipation in the *RIBA Journal* was palpable:

> The new London County Council Concert Hall is Britain's first post-war non-austerity and non-essential building. Inspection of

the drawings and a visit to the already busy site … reveals a monumental building in the course of erection, a fact that is stimulating to an austerity-ridden architectural profession. Here is the first effort at that large-scale, fine public building for which British architects have been longing since the end of the war.[11]

The acoustic problems created by the site and the way that these were addressed by both the consultants and the design team, and then incorporated into the design, attracted special attention. But naturally, the critics withheld judgement until they could see the building for themselves.

The opening of the building in May 1951, linked to the excitement of the start of the festival of Britain, was greeted warmly by the architectural press. The July 1951 issue of the *Architectural Review*, devoted to the Royal Festival Hall, caught the mood of enthusiasm: '[The planning] can be described, without exaggeration, as masterly.'[12] Aspects of the design were to attract criticism, but, all in all, the judgement of the press was positive. The solution of the acoustic problems, both of sound exclusion and finding an appropriate acoustic balance for the hall, was praised. Hope Bagenal, with Peter Parkin and William Allen of the Building Research Station, were lauded for having carried off what had seemed impossible, though a number of commentators wrote of the need to reserve judgement on the acoustics until the process of fine-tuning had been completed.[13] With the hall built to time and budget under the control of Edwin Williams, the scale of the constructional achievement on a difficult and constricted site attracted a succession of equally positive comments.

The reviews of the major journals, which were remarkably similar given their differences in other respects, can best be summarised by considering the reactions to the building at three different levels: at the strategic level of the 'egg in the box' approach, at the tactical level of the architectural treatment of this initial *parti*, and at the handling of the detailed design of the building, its fittings and furnishings. At the strategic level, there was widespread agreement on the success of the initial design concept as a solution to a complex problem, one which broke with tradition. Martin and his team were congratulated for having solved the functional problems of the hall in a manner that was uncompromisingly modern. At a time when the inspiration for other major projects, like the rebuilding of the House of Commons or the new cathedral at Coventry, seemed tied to the past, the architectural press hailed the design of the Royal Festival Hall for its bold modernity.

The elaboration of the basic design concept and the exploitation of the contrast between the auditorium and the surrounding envelope were widely applauded. Richards judged it an 'architectural *tour de force*':

> It was the masterly handling of the flow of the internal spaces and the views out of the building across London from such a favoured site that created this success: the familiar London landscape takes on a magical quality when seen from these airy platforms of glass and metal and polished wood and Derbyshire marble.[14]

This estimation was widely shared. Whatever reservations *Architectural Design* may have felt about the design of the interior of the auditorium, it appreciated the architectural skill in leading the audience through the building:

> Once inside, the egg is immediately felt. Powerful columns with a primitive Doric stoutness, which contrasts with the lightness of the glazing, convey the feeling of weight. The huge chamber is held aloft uncluttered and without comment, and the stairs reach forward, inviting us to climb up into inner vastness, and there above it, separate from teeming London, to be in communion with others and with music. One is primed for a major architectural experience.[15]

There was also admiration for the detailed design of the building. After years of austerity, the colours and quality of the materials – leather, hardwoods, bronze, plate glass, polished marble – were in themselves exciting. So too were the feel of the bronze and wooden door handles and the reassuring solidity of the balustrades, comfortably wide enough to lean on as one looked across the foyers. This was dramatically different from so much building since the war. Suddenly here was quality to match the best pre-war work but set in the service of modern design. Contemporaries generally agreed that the hall evoked that elusive feeling of occasion: 'a concert hall stands or falls by its atmosphere or personality. In this respect the Royal Festival Hall is a triumphant success.'[16] The detailed design of the entrance, the stairs and the foyers sweeps the visitor up to the auditorium. The continuity between outside and inside emphasises the flow from arrival terrace to entrance foyer, the gentle ripple of the garde-robe counter encourages the crowd onwards and upward, while the sense of expectation is heightened by the contrast between the cool whites of the foyers and the polished Devonshire marble of the exterior of the egg and the darker, warmer tones of the interior of the auditorium (Figure 4.5). *The Architect and Building News* commented on the way in which the lighting reinforced architectural intention:

> Lighting, colour and materials are used throughout the building to emphasise this contrast (between 'egg and box') and to dramatise its effect. The lighting near the main entrance is concentrated on special areas such as doors, steps, cloak counters, leaving the intervening space in subdued light. As the stairs rise to the main foyer, lighting intensity builds up to a powerful concentration. Here the entire underside of the auditorium, which forms the foyer ceiling, has been made into a giant light source.[17]

Most journals were willing to devote page after page to photographs and descriptions of

i   ii

4.5 Interiors of the Royal Festival Hall: (i) the upper entrance hall lobby, promenade and bar; (ii) the auditorium, showing the boxes breaking through the interior elevation of the hall

the fittings, the furnishings and detailed aspects of the design. Technical information was available in profusion, from 1:5 sections through the glazing to the way to keep the plants alive without soil in the planters. Yet the journals add little insight by way of comment on the architectural significance of this level of design. How were the novel details of the building viewed by contemporaries in relation to the architectural issues that were being discussed in journals like the *Architectural Review*? Though the journals did not say so, those familiar with the work of Scandinavian architects like Aalto or Gunnar Asplund might have seen the parallels between their approach and the detailed design of the Royal Festival Hall. Asplund's work, for example the interior of the addition to the Gothenburg Law Courts, well publicised in the architectural press and already familiar at first hand to the limited number of English architects with the resources or the determination to visit it, might have appeared as one source of inspiration for the Festival Hall.[18] Equally, Asplund's willingness to consider every detail afresh, evident for example in the light fittings and the interior furnishings of the offices at the State Bacteriological Institute, might have suggested a way of approaching the design, for

example, of the aluminium music stands for the orchestras in the hall. Closer to home, were contemporaries conscious of the parallels between Tecton's pre-war interiors and the Royal Festival Hall? Did they see the entrance foyer of Highpoint I as a starting point for the design of the foyers and circulation spaces of the Festival Hall?

Looking back at the fittings, furniture and the detailed design, it is difficult now to set aside entirely the attacks by Reyner Banham and others on the 'Festival Style'. The Royal Festival Hall was not their main target. But even in the hall the insistent pattern of the carpet, the choice of colours and the design of the boxes along the auditorium walls have a restlessness that attracted comment: its interiors lack the restraint of the best Scandinavian work of the time. *Architectural Design* voiced regret at the 'lack of formal unity' in the auditorium, citing the 'uncomfortable' relationship of the boxes to the rest of the interior, the lack of formal discipline necessary to control 'the dazzling pattern' and 'the exuberance of the complex chequerboard' of the auditorium elevations.[19] Yet for the most part contemporaries simply recorded pleasure at what they saw: 'A splendid interior this – a place for the eye as well as the ear.'[20]

But for all the enthusiasm for the overall conception of the building and the arrangement of the interiors, the critics were troubled by the handling of the exterior of the building and the way in which the elevations reflected the building's organisation. Richards allowed that 'the general modelling of the exterior of the Royal Festival Hall is both logical and stately, with each structural element, as in the contemporary fashion, clearly articulated and the structure differentiated from infilling by changes of material and colour', but nevertheless argued that 'the complex and highly stylised modelling of the river front' contradicted the overall conception of the auditorium surrounded by a transparent envelope. According to Richards, the viewer should have been encouraged to 'penetrate beyond the river facade and apprehend the significance of the three dimensional conception'.[21] Other commentators were highly critical of the facade for failing to reveal enough of the interior, for being 'cardboardy', for failing to find the right balance between solid and void – a difficulty compounded by the apparent weight of the large area of stonework on the upper storey above a thin horizontal strip of glazing.[22]

Richards raised the level of critical discussion by insisting that the handling of elevations of a non-utilitarian building was problematic to the current condition of modern architecture: 'To give a building of this kind sufficient robustness of modelling and richness of architecture to produce an effect of monumentality is extremely difficult in view of the absence of a recognised modern decorative idiom'. He understood this as a challenge to the avant-garde as a whole and recognised that if the designers of the Royal Festival Hall had not been wholly successful, this was because of the sheer difficulty of the task and the dangers of settling for some formulaic solution: 'an attempt to contrive such an idiom is liable to appear mannered and is soon dated'.[23]

In retrospect, the difficulties facing Martin and Moro were not unique. The team had not adopted a direct functional translation of the organisation of the building as the basis for understanding the elevations (Figure 4.1). To

have done so would have undermined the visual logic of the scheme because, with the need to place the escape stairs and the lavatories on the facade to achieve direct ventilation to the outside air, the masonry elements housing them would have read too heavily on the two side facades. To maintain the transparency of the envelope needed for an understanding of the contrast between the 'egg' and the 'box', it was necessary to do more than just project onto the elevations the nature of the construction: it was important to design a facade that would read in these terms.

These difficulties were shared by other architects who were attempting to meet the challenge to go beyond the utilitarian and to create a richer formal vocabulary for modern architecture. Lubetkin's handling of the facades of the Spa Green, Priory Green and Hallfield estates had raised similar issues, and attracted similar criticisms.[24] Lubetkin had abandoned a literal treatment of the repetitive elements of these blocks of flats in favour of an approach which emphasised the visual coherence of the facade as a formal composition. In 'Facade', an article on Tecton's treatment of the facades at the Hallfield estate, Banham pointed to the difficulties the Modern Movement now experienced with the design of facades in general:

Facade treatments do not form part of the common theory of the Modern Movement as our elders and betters have left it. In the pure theory the problem of the facade does not exist – form follows function, and when the problems of the interior have been correctly resolved the exterior form will be found to have crystallised into an unarguable solution. Or, if this be too sanguine a manner of phrasing a widely held idea, one may use the alternative formulation – the modern architect is not interested in facades, but allows his elevations to express the inner workings of his building.[25]

Banham declared that the time had come for architects to abandon the belief that the exterior

4.6 Views of the north elevation of the Royal Festival Hall: (i) the apparent solidity of the stone and tile cladding belies the frame structure of the 'box' around the hall; (ii) the view at night emphasises the contrast between the transparency of the river elevation, with views through to the 'egg' inside, and the solidity of the corners

treatment of a building could be somehow objectively determined, 'forced upon the designer by structural, technical considerations which were almost beyond his control – climate, column-loadings, privacy, for instance'.[26] Modern architects had to accept publicly the responsibility for design that Banham believed they had always exercised in reality:

> The ultimate factor deciding the appearance of a building's elevations is apt to be an aesthetic decision pure and simple – but an aesthetic decision which cuts deeper into the philosophy of architecture than any other architect may be called upon to make.[27]

The architectural idiom of the Royal Festival Hall sought to address symbolic issues of formal clarity and legibility, not simply utilitarian questions of efficiency and economy. Given the architectural background of Martin and Moro, the architectural language used for the Royal Festival Hall should have come as no surprise. The forms of the Royal Festival Hall, the use of the reinforced concrete frame, the separation between structure and infill, the clear articulation of the different elements of the building, are based, like much of Tecton's contemporary work, on the ideas of the pre-war avant-garde and derived largely from Le Corbusier's work of the late 1920s. The distinction between the massiveness of the egg and the lightweight skin of the

surrounding box must be understood in these terms. The view – best at night – through the glazing of the river front to the columns of the box is intended to remind the viewer that one is looking at a stone-skinned, not a stone-built, building (Figure 4.6). The reservations expressed by the critics about the side elevations arise from a confusion in the use of this vocabulary: from the appearance of a predominantly stone-built wall – apparently resting on glazing – instead of a stone-skinned wall supported by a frame. The tiling used at the rear of the side facades and the handling of the elevations that project beyond the frame on both the north and the south facades, to house the bars and side galleries, are clearly expressed as elements supported by the frame. However, the stone skin at the river end of these facades continues in the same plane and the material of the frame, blurring the all-important distinction between structure and infill. To the taste of the younger generation, the use of so many different materials to differentiate and articulate the different elements of the facade appeared fussy or even pretty, but at least the use of materials in this way was an attempt to maintain the underlying coherence of the building's formal logic.

As early as 1943 Giedion had argued that people 'want their buildings to be more than a functional fulfilment. They seek the expression of their aspirations for joy, luxury and for excitement.'[28] Contemporary impressions from concert-goers and musicians suggest that the

Royal Festival Hall answered these needs and that it was viewed with enthusiasm, even affection. But despite CIAM's passing preoccupation with the views of the general public voiced at the Bridgwater conference, contemporary architectural enthusiasm for the Royal Festival Hall was nearly always qualified: reservations about the elevations remained and eventually led to the remodelling of the exterior in 1962. In its use and adaptation of the elements of the architectural vocabulary of the 1930s to create so successful a modern setting for orchestral music, the Royal Festival Hall is a reminder of how much the avant-garde was still looking back to the formal experiments of the pre-war years as it struggled to expand the vocabulary of modern architecture to handle the design of monumental public buildings.

The Festival of Britain

While Martin and Moro were wrestling with the problems of placing the bulk of the Royal Festival Hall on the restricted South Bank site, another team of architects was assembled to start work on the major national exhibition, the Festival of Britain, planned for the area surrounding the

proposed concert hall. The exhibition was to celebrate British achievement, 'the British contribution to civilization, past, present and future, in arts, in science and technology, and in industrial design'. It was also, as Gerald Barry, one of the original proponents of the idea of a Festival of Britain in 1951, succinctly put it, to serve as a 'tonic to the nation'.[29]

The designers of the Festival of Britain faced the same tight timetable as the Festival Hall team. Progress was brisk, and by the end of the summer of 1948 Gerald Barry and Ian Cox, responsible for the presentation of science at the festival, had drawn up an organising schema for the exhibition as a whole. In response to the questions 'What is it that gives the British character and British achievement such diversity? What is the link between the past and the present that gives us such faith in the future? What provides the spark for British initiative?'[30] Barry and Cox argued that it was the variety and resources of Britain and the mixed races of the people, their 'innate curiosity', that led to British achievement and discovery in every sphere. These were the central themes to be celebrated at the festival. To achieve this, two principal sequences were created, one focusing on the land and the

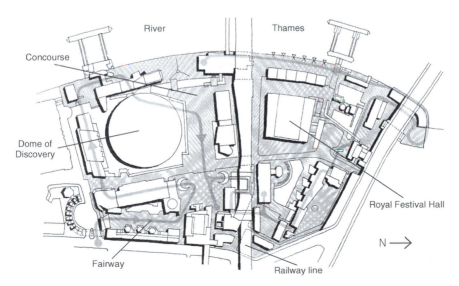

4.7 Overall layout of the Festival of Britain exhibition. The 'upstream circuit' lies to the south of the railway line, the 'downstream circuit' to the north. The Fairway described in Figure 4.9 is at the bottom left-hand corner of the site plan

development of its resources, the other present-ing the people and the ways in which they had resolved the diversity of their characteristics and adapted to their environment. These two central themes were to be exhibited in narrative terms, with the individual 'chapters' of each story treated as separate displays to celebrate British exploration and discovery, both intellectual and geographical (Figure 4.7).

This schema was the starting point for the architects and designers of the festival's design group. Chaired by Hugh Casson, the group con-sisted of four young designers, Misha Black, Ralph Tubbs, James Holland and James Gardner.[31] All had some experience of exhibition design – a valuable preparation for the task of organising such a large exhibition with such limited resources in so little time – gained either during the war or immediately after.

The South Bank, the site chosen for the festi-val, was far from ideal. The site was small, 27 acres, smaller still than the site on which Asplund had created the Stockholm Exhibition in 1930. It was encumbered with contractors working on the construction of a new river wall, and others feverishly piling for the foundations of the Festi-val Hall. It was divided in half by Charing Cross railway bridge and other rights of way. Near its centre stood a late eighteenth-century shot tower. It was littered with rubble from the Blitz. It was already occupied by tenants with unex-pired leases. More positively, however, the site was central and would offer, when completed, magnificent views across the river into the very heart of London.[32]

From the start, the design group decided to concentrate on establishing a number of general organising principles rather than on an explicit design. Unlike the 1930 Stockholm Exhibition, where the overall design of the major buildings and external spaces had been conceived as a whole by one architect, and unlike the 'Britain Can Make It' exhibition, where the designer had been able to determine the layout of the exhibi-tion as well as the individual displays, Casson and Black recognised that they would be able to exer-cise little control over the design of the festival.

Like a team of town planners, the design group were able to do little more than establish four guiding principles for a layout which would only come to life when animated by the individual pavilions. First, the site would be divided in half: upstream was given to the Land of Britain; downstream to the People of Britain. Second, the site on the South Bank would be linked visu-ally and physically with the north bank. Third, the great saucer dome of over 300 feet in diame-ter would be the dominating structure. And finally, because the site was so small, an informal approach to planning the festival's exhibits and outside spaces would replace the traditional axial exhibition layout. Casson described with engag-ing simplicity the way the different buildings of the exhibition, the 'chapters' of the overall narra-tive, were set within the guiding principles:

> Gradually it began to fall into place: the Origins of the Land, Agriculture, Mining, Industry all grouped around the shining cranium – as we saw it – of invention (Hence the Dome of Discovery.) The Origins of the People through and under the bridge to Education, the English at Home, their character and recreations, the Arts and the Seaside (again naturally by the river) all grouped around the Festival Hall, still to be built.[33]

By December 1948 the first draft of the masterplan was ready for presentation to the fes-tival Council. By February, the design group moved to appoint architects and designers for the individual pavilions or zones. A few of the zones were put out to competition. Powell and Moya, fresh from the competition success with their Pimlico housing scheme, won the competi-tion for the exhibition's vertical feature, the Skylon. Leonard Manasseh won the competition for the design of the '51 Bar. But the majority of the festival buildings were designed by architects appointed by the design group. The list of names drew together, through personal contacts and recommendation, a group of thirty architects who were similar in background, and age:

i   ii

4.8 Pavilions or 'Zones' at the Festival of Britain: (i) the Dome of Discovery by Ralph Tubbs; (ii) the Lion and the Unicorn Pavilion by R.D. Russell and R.Y. Goodden

Maxwell Fry, under 50, was the oldest, most others were under the age of 40, and a number were in their twenties. Most of the architects had little or no experience of building on their own account, though the majority had seen some kind of practice before the war, generally in an office sympathetic to modern architecture. A further bond between them was their architectural education. Of those trained in Britain all had attended schools where modern architecture was, if not dominant, at least seriously discussed; over half came from the Architectural Association, with a scattering from the Regent Street Polytechnic, Liverpool and Cambridge. Here was a group who would have been familiar with the ideas of pre-war modernism and would have been well aware of the direction the post-war debate was taking. As champions of modern architecture, what can their designs tell us of the state of architecture and the way in which architects were seeking to go beyond the vocabulary of the 1920s and 1930s?

Assessing their designs is not straightforward. Shortages of labour and material, and the all-pervading pressure of time constraints, affected what could be built. More important, the design of the individual pavilions could not be used for unfettered experimentation. Each had to be treated as part of an overall sequence both to sustain the narrative of the exhibition and, in terms of design, to shape the landscape of the South Bank. Thus a number of pavilions, for example the Architects' Co-Partnership's 'Minerals of the Island' building, were conceived almost entirely in terms of the theme, abandoning any claim to an independent architectural identity. Others, like the section on Sport, or the Harbour Bar, were conceived not as separate buildings but as displays within the exhibition.

In contrast, a number of buildings were treated as identifiably separate architectural exercises (Figure 4.8). Most obvious was the Dome of Discovery. But there were others too: the Power and Production Building, the Lion and the Unicorn Pavilion and the Transport Building opposite the Dome on the main concourse. Some of these, however visible, seem to have attracted no comment or only disparagement from contemporaries. Gordon Tait's design for the Waterloo Gate entrance, with its laminated timber arches dominating the view south down the Concourse, was widely criticised for the lack of connection between these grandiose arches to the design either of the entrances beneath or of the administration building which they abutted. Most critics passed it by in silence. Richards, again one of the few willing to speak his mind, could find nothing good to say about it, describing its detailing as coarse, and dismissing the York Road elevation as reminiscent of the primitive modernism of the 1930s and 'an encouraging reminder of the warmth and sensitivity that the modern movement has acquired since then'.[34] But if buildings like this or Grenfell Baines and Reifenberg's Power and Production Building were not the face of authentic modern architecture, what was?

The Dome of Discovery, the largest building on the festival site (and, as patriotic commentators never tired of noting, the 'largest dome in the world'), invariably attracted interest, although not all of it flattering. Most critics shared the view of the *Builder* that the Dome was 'brave and adventurous' in its construction even if the potential impact of the size of the interior was robbed by the crowding of the exhibits. Richards was sharper in his judgement. He argued that the promise of the Dome's construction, 'the wonderful effect of dramatically enclosed space', owed much to the contrast, so evident during construction, between 'the fragile lattice-work of the interior dome structure, lightly resting on its slender struts' and the smooth outer surface of the dome. But this effect was thrown away with the clumsy handling of the external walling and the raking ribs supporting the soffit of the dome.[35] Far from being handled as the lightweight infilling that it was, the enclosing wall was treated as if it was supporting the weight of the dome, confusing the clarity of the whole design.

Richard Russell and Richard Goodden's Lion and Unicorn Building also attracted critical attention. Exceptional in that both the building and display were designed by the same team, the Lion and Unicorn Building seems to have won general approval principally because its simplicity contrasted effectively with the elaboration and richness of the display – the corn-dolly Lion and Unicorn, the flock of doves and the statue of the White Knight – which caught the public's imagination. The *Builder* and the *Review* found it the most successful building on the South Bank: 'The

lightly constructed envelope, with two walls wholly of glass and an arched timber roof, is essentially simple; it is elegantly proportioned and beautifully finished.'[36] Richards judged it 'somewhat Scandinavian' in style, high praise from one of the champions of the New Empiricism.

What is striking about contemporary reaction to the South Bank is less the reaction to the individual pavilions and more the response to the effect of the exhibition as a whole. What seems to have caught the imagination of the critics and the public alike was the opportunity to experience for the first time an urban landscape that was self-consciously modern. *Architectural Design* and the *Builder* may have crabbed about the details but they applauded the impact of the overall effect. The most enthusiastic reception to the South Bank exhibition was from the *Review*. The *Review* argued that, following on from Stockholm, the festival broke with the old Beaux Arts conventions to provide an opportunity to explore new ideas as applicable to the layout of an individual site as to the planning of a New Town:

> how to give a feeling of space while economizing in the use of space; how to achieve a compact urban character while avoiding congestion – visual or real; how to wield the ideas of many architects into a whole without stifling originality or imposing uniformity; how to marry the new with the old so that one does not harm the other but, on the contrary, so that the qualities of each enhance the other.[37]

The lessons that the South Bank offered would have come as no surprise to readers of the *Review*. The planning principles on which the layout was based were presented as a modern application of the principles of Picturesque theory. What excited the editors of the *Review* was now, at last, to have a successful demonstration of these principles in practice. To demonstrate their conviction the August 1951 issue set out, first, to examine the exhibition as an exercise in the design of landscape and, second, to generalise this understanding in the form of a 'Town

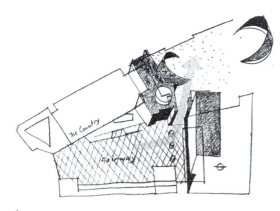

i

ii

4.9 The route through the Fairway to the Concourse: (i) diagrammatic axonometric of the Fairway, with its narrow exit to the Concourse; (ii) the view out of the enclosed Fairway into the contrasting spaciousness of the Concourse; (iii) the view to the left on leaving the Fairway, the first view of the largest building on the site, the Dome of Discovery; (iv) the view down the Concourse to the river promenade and the Skylon, with the picturesque outline of Whitehall Court behind

iii

Builder's Pattern Book', along the lines already used in the *Review*'s discussion of the Townscape Casebook two years earlier.

The article, 'The Exhibition as Landscape', provides the clearest exposition of the *Review*'s ideas on the way that Picturesque theory might be applied to modern architecture and planning in terms of the progress from the Fairway to the Concourse (Figure 4.9):

iv

> As in a well-planned town, the exhibition makes the most of the space available by not disclosing itself all at once glance. By breaking it up into a sequence of enclosures the planners have greatly increased its apparent size. This particular enclosure, the Fairway, is planned with a fine sense of drama, because only as you approach the far end corner do you become aware of the relatively narrow exit. You turn the corner of the wall occupying the foreground, the sense of enclosure being retained to the last. Then with a shock of surprise, you find yourself on the brink of a vast territory. It

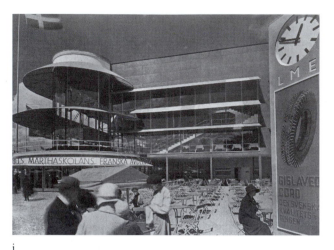

i

ii

4.10 Precursors to the Festival of Britain: (i) the Stockholm Exhibition 1930, designed by Gunnar Asplund; (ii) the 'Rotterdam Ahoy' exhibition, 1950, layout by van den Broek and Bakema

extends away before you, drops to a lower level, takes in the white plumes of the fountains and proceeds uninterrupted to the romantic outline of Whitehall Court, which is in fact on the far side of the river, but so skilfully are the levels managed that the river itself is not yet seen and its whole width is brought into the apparent area of the exhibition. You are now at the head of the main concourse, the limits of which are defined on either flank by the long glass facade of the Transport building and the rising curve of the Dome of Discovery. Above the entire scene the Skylon is poised as a dramatic punctuation mark.[38]

From this dense analysis of the exhibition layout and its spatial mechanics, the *Review* proceeded to offer a catalogue of the detailed elements of the exhibition under the title of 'Town Builder's Pattern Book'. This examination returned to themes such as the Functional Tradition or the Nautical Style that the *Review* had been exploring in a succession of issues as part of the search for the essential ingredients of a specifically British identity in design. In place of pictures of pubs or

long-boats, Eric de Mare's black and white photographs capture elements of the exhibition, canvas and metal screens, canopies, light metal platforms over water, flowerpots, rubble walls from Yorkshire, lamp-standards, signposts, so that even in long retrospect the exhibition comes to convey a concentrated vitality and a sense of novelty. Through these photographs one can just recover a suggestion of the promise that modern architecture seemed to hold for so many of the festival's visitors.

The British architectural press, led by the *Review*, congratulated the exhibition as a great British achievement: 'a triumphant demonstration of the vitality of contemporary British architecture'.[39] The *Builder* declared that 'the buildings show that we have architects and display designers in Britain as talented as any nation in the world'.[40] Given the circumstances, this hyperbole might be forgiven, but how did the festival appear to those from abroad? What did the delegates to the 1951 CIAM summer congress think of the South Bank as they arrived in London en route to Hoddesdon?

Those who remembered the 1930 Stockholm exhibition (Figure 4.10) or had visited Le

Corbusier's Pavillon des Temps Nouveaux at the 1937 Paris International Exhibition would have recognised in the forms of the festival ideas carried over from pre-war exhibitions. Stockholm had offered Asplund's lightweight metal structures, the advertising mast with its flags, the canvas awnings and screens, the exploitation of the water's edge. In Paris Le Corbusier's pavilion had contrasted the delicate filigree of the metal pylons and the all-enveloping tent with the lightweight internal display structures within.

The festival had much in common with contemporary post-war exhibitions too. Those who had seen Rotterdam Ahoy,[41] an exhibition to celebrate the reconstruction of the port of Rotterdam after war-time destruction, would have been struck by the similarities with the South Bank. Yes, there were differences: most of the Rotterdam pavilions were designed and built as permanent structures to be used by the port after the exhibition; the park section of the exhibition must have seemed more like a combination of the South Bank with Battersea Gardens than either one or the other; the new quays were not displays but newly constructed working quays thrown open to the public for the duration of the exhibition. But the parallels were clear: the blending of display and architecture; the liberation of typography from the flat plane of the display panel to create, along with sculptural statistical displays and spaces enclosed and shaped by photographic panels, a three-dimensional vitality to the exhibition that would have prepared those (like Casson and Black) who saw it for much of what was to happen on the South Bank. Like Stockholm, and like the treatment of the riverfront in London, Bakema and van den Broek's Rotterdam exhibition made much of water and forms of ships: rigging, derricks, lightweight steel platforms. The repetition of these exhibition effects, not only at Rotterdam and London, but in Milan in 1948 and across postwar Europe, was to establish a common vocabulary of forms and motifs.[42]

The CIAM delegates attending the congress at Hoddesdon to discuss 'the heart of the city' may have been politely enthusiastic to their British hosts about what they saw on the South Bank. They may have been bemused by the Lion and the Unicorn, or baffled by 'Black Eyes and Lemonade' at the Whitechapel Gallery, which sought to depict in visual terms the elusive qualities of the British national character. Perhaps the particularly English form of humour represented by Rowland Emett's fantastical Far Tottering and Oyster Creek Railway in the Festival Gardens was forgiven as a necessary by-product of a national imagination that could cultivate both Shakespeare and Lewis Carroll.[43] But in judging the achievement on the South Bank, CIAM delegates would hardly have been surprised. It would have been a curiously British version of something already encountered, but familiar none the less.

Familiar too would have been the arguments made by the British journals, that the exhibition on the South Bank, with its combination of the arts and architecture, was in some special way a paradigm for laying out the core of the city or the non-residential centre of a New Town or rebuilding the war-damaged centre of an existing town or city. The CIAM conference included a bus trip to the South Bank, to Battersea Gardens and to Lansbury, and it appeared that the delegates welcomed an opportunity to see the British interpretation of the theme that they were discussing at the congress. But in contrast with the illustrious historical examples like the Roman fora, Venice's Piazza San Marco or the range of proposals assembled by the national delegates to exemplify the best of current practice, the lessons of the South Bank were easily overshadowed. Set beside Le Corbusier's plans for the centre of Chandigarh, Kenzo Tange's plans for the reconstruction of the centre of Hiroshima or, locally, the proposals for the rebuilding of Coventry's centre or the new town centre at Stevenage, the South Bank exhibition must have appeared to lack the general significance claimed for it and to offer at best only a particularly English contribution to this theme of general interest.

The Coventry Cathedral competition

Before the Festival of Britain had closed its gates, modern architecture was again in the news. At the end of August the results of the Coventry Cathedral competition were announced. The scheme by Basil Spence was declared the winner (Figure 4.11). Widely illustrated in the press, the results were greeted with qualified enthusiasm. Spence's design, generally judged to have deserved its first prize, troubled the traditionalists because of its modernity and frustrated the modernists by its deference to tradition. Together with the other schemes illustrated in the press it raised again the larger question of a monumental architecture, of the ability of modern architecture to create the devotional atmosphere required of a cathedral in terms that would be recognised by the general public.

The competition for the design of Coventry Cathedral, launched early in 1951, was a product of ten years of debate on the way in which the cathedral might be rebuilt after its destruction during the raid in November 1940 that had devastated the centre of the city.[44] An initial attempt to secure a design for the rebuilding of the cathedral had not been successful. In March 1942 Provost Richard Howard, the person responsible for the fabric of the cathedral, appointed Giles Gilbert Scott to prepare a 'modern Gothic design' along broadly traditional lines. This attracted criticism from modernists and conservatives alike. On the one hand Bishop Gorton, who had arrived in Coventry in February 1943, held strong links to the liturgical movement and had high hopes for a modern building. On the other hand the representatives of the city on the cathedral council favoured the restoration of St Michael's, or something very similar. Despite a succession of revisions to his design, Scott could please neither camp nor the Royal Fine Arts Commission, and he resigned the appointment at the end of 1945. Following Scott's resignation, a commission chaired by Lord Harlech was established to advise on the new cathedral. The commission's recommendations, published nearly two years later, on the character of the building were bland, stating that it favoured a building sympathetic to the ruins of St Michael's. But the commission did take the unusual step of recommending that the design of the new cathedral be selected by competition.

Preparations for the competition were put in the hands of a Reconstruction Committee, composed of both traditionalists and modernisers, which was to draw up the brief and act as a client for the new building throughout the competition

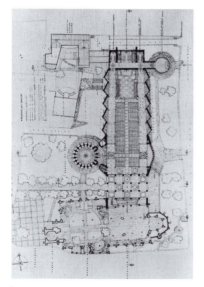

i

ii

4.11 Basil Spence's winning entry for the Coventry Cathedral competition, 1951: (i) plan of the new cathedral showing the north–south orientation of the nave and the relationship to the ruins of St Michael's; (ii) view of the modified scheme from the east

period. Finally, in the summer of 1950, after delays caused by shortages in funding and the need to buy additional land to enlarge the site, the Reconstruction Committee was in a position to discuss the details of the competition with three assessors appointed by the RIBA: Percy Thomas, Edward Maufe and Howard Robertson. They had been selected with a careful view to an even-handed balance between modernism and tradition: Thomas, President of the RIBA from 1943 to 1946, had served with the Harlech Commission; Maufe, most obviously the representative of tradition, was a member of the Royal Fine Arts Commission, the architect of Guildford Cathedral and had considerable experience as a church architect; Robertson, head of the Architectural Association, had already shown himself sympathetic to the modernist cause before the war. The Reconstruction Committee and assessors agreed a competition brief which was intended as a compromise between the different interests. Overall the design of the new building and the treatment of the remaining cathedral ruins was to be conceived in terms of the theme of sacrifice and resurrection, which was to be symbolised by the linking of the new building with the ruins. The layout of the building was to be traditional: while there was no statement limiting the style of the new building, the brief favoured a long building with an altar at the east end clearly visible from the nave. The altar was to be flanked by a Bishop's throne and clergy stalls. Provision was

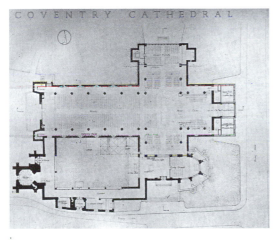

i

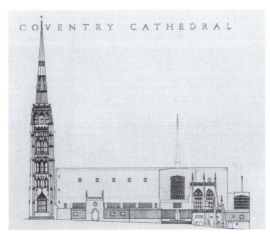

ii

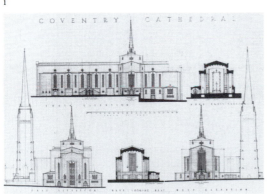

iii

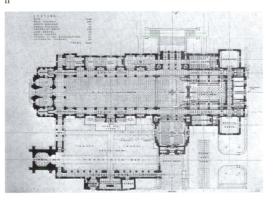

iv

4.12 Second and third placed entries for the Coventry Cathedral competition: (i–ii) the scheme by W.P. Hunt; (iii–iv) the entry by A.D. Kirby

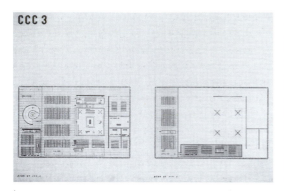

i

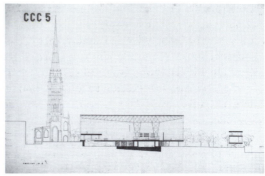

ii

iii

iv

4.13 Coventry Cathedral competition. Unplaced entries by young modernists: (i–ii) the scheme by C.A. St John Wilson and P. Carter; (iii–iv) the entry submitted by A. and P. Smithson

to be made for a choir in a chancel at the head of the nave. In addition there were to be eight 'hallowing places', or shrines, to represent the work of the city, together with a lady chapel, a guild chapel, children's chapel and a chapel of resurrection. To help them understand the form and the significance of the ruins, the competitors were sent information about the site, photographs and drawings of the ruins, and photographs of war-time services held among the ruins. In addition to details of the other historic buildings surrounding the site – Holy Trinity, the Georgian terrace Priory Row and the existing cathedral tower – the competitors received an

artist's impression of the cathedral tower seen from the proposed new shopping centre. With the emphasis on respect for the past, the competition brief was weighted towards the traditionalists rather than those like Gorton who hoped that the competition would lead to something radically new.

The competition was announced in January 1951. It not only attracted a large number of entries, but encouraged submissions of very different character. The traditionalists regarded the competition as an opportunity to demonstrate their ability to address the grand themes in architecture in a way that they believed the modernists could not. For the modernists, here at last was a chance to explore in practice the ideas on the New Monumentality that CIAM had debated at each of the three post-war meetings. Finally, for those fresh out of architectural school here was the occasion to look beyond the debates of the last five years to a revaluation of the tenets of the Modern Movement.

The results of the competition were at best a qualified success (Figures 4.11 to 4.13). Commenting on the results, Maufe noted that the assessors were troubled by the quality of the majority of the entries and had reservations about the most successful schemes, including Spence's design. The press recorded widespread relief that it had been possible to find a clear winner but did not disguise impatience with the limitations of many of the schemes. *Architectural Design* attacked most competitors for having side-stepped the central issue, how to design a building which would evoke the qualities of the great cathedrals of the past:

> the bulk of the field jibbed or refused. Many obviously had no belief that cathedral and contemporary could be reconciled architecturally at all – they sought their inspiration in the past. Others, in their anxiety to eschew past forms floundered in meaningless new ones. The result, therefore, was largely a parade of sterile, dreary, vulgar or stunt designs with, of course, the odd pipe dream or so.[45]

The assessors' comments also convey disappointment at the way in which most entries, while able to solve the problems of planning and organisation, had simply failed to develop a coherent architectural form for the building: 'Many were able to produce satisfactory plans but few were able to build these up to form satisfactory cathedrals.'[46]

As in most other competitions at the time, the majority of designs failed to reach a satisfactory standard, but there were at least twenty or so entries that were thought to have done well enough to be chosen for illustration in the journals, and it was these schemes that formed the basis for contemporary judgement of the results of the competition. With the exception of Richardson's design, which was included as the most promising of the large number of traditional entries, most of the schemes chosen for illustration could be loosely described as modern, as Summerson's jaunty assessment of the results for the *New Statesman* suggests:

> In general there appear to be two ways of designing a modern church. The obvious, elementary way is to grab at the disappearing tail of the Gothic Revival ... This means leaving out all the expensive and technically difficult parts of Gothic, streamlining the silhouette, keeping everything plain (say two cusps for every twenty in a 14th century equivalent) and relying on charming materials and a little sculpture on the safe side of Eric Gill. That way has the very substantial merit of being instantly acceptable to the majority of church-goers. Well done, it is completely unobjectionable; modesty and orthodoxy commend it.
>
> The other way is to venture everything on some really striking originality of conception, to work this out as decoratively as possible, with gaps hopefully left for equally striking originalities in sculpture and stained glass, and let the root idea speak for itself. That is, in principle, the way of the exhibition designer, and there is the risk of a church designed on these lines coming out like a Pavilion of Religious Art. Thousands of church-goers will hate it and call it a biscuit-factory, but the others will retort that it is 'contemporary', the 20th century counterpart of the bold adventuring of the creators of Gothic.[47]

It is a measure of the difficulty of successfully designing a scheme of 'really striking originality of conception' to suit the essentially traditional brief of the competition that the majority of the projects illustrated in the magazines, including the winning scheme by Basil Spence, fell into

Summerson's first category. The strengths and weaknesses of W.P. Hunt's entry are typical of the schemes that exemplify this first approach (Figure 4.12). It was judged the most successful of the plans in which the new cathedral was arranged parallel to the ruins of St Michael and praised by the assessors as a 'very convincing solution to the problems of layout and the grouping of the various elements of the design'.[48] The disposition of the chapels and of the accommodation at the east end to take advantage of the fall in the land has an ease and rightness about it that contrasts with the elaboration of rival schemes with this plan form. Equally accomplished is the handling of the building on its site. The small footprint of the scheme, easier to achieve with the parallel plan, creates a number of advantages: more generous spaces between the proposed building and the existing buildings on the site, and the approach from Broadgate leads very naturally to a cathedral yard in front of the main entrance of the cathedral.

Hunt's design, both externally and internally, fails however to match the assurance of the planning. The overall architectural effect is of a bloodless simplicity. It was judged to have failed to 'fully develop the basic potentialities of the scheme'.[49] Yet by comparison with the other schemes chosen for illustration it is possible to see why the assessors judged it as they did. Major A.D. Kirby's entry, placed third, also adopted the parallel plan, arranging the different elements of the brief in similar fashion but with a heavier hand (Figure 4.12). Where Hunt had hesitated to commit himself architecturally, Kirby did so only to create a prickly, ersatz Gothic. Understandably the assessors found that the quality of the layout could not make up for 'the lack of distinction in the quality of architectural detail'.[50]

By comparison with the other premiated schemes, Basil Spence's entry had an authority and a completeness that was widely recognised (Figure 4.11). The architectural press was united in supporting the assessors' decision to offer it the first prize: 'The outcome of the competition for Coventry Cathedral is a happy one thanks to Mr Basil Spence. His design had pleased nearly everybody, which is quite a feat.'[51]

On the qualities of the planning of Spence's scheme all were agreed. With the new building at right angles to the axis of St Michael's the layout was praised for its simplicity, directness and the dramatic effect to be won from the progression from old to new. It seemed almost effortlessly easy by comparison with the elaboration of most other schemes. In planning the main body of the new building as a long aisled basilica, focusing on the altar at the east end, with the main ancillary spaces such as the Chapel of Unity as separate elements, Spence produced a design that functioned in a traditional fashion. The 'right-angled plan' offered pronounced advantages in the placing of the building on the site: the view from Broadgate leads naturally to the new porch between the new building and the ruins. The space around the new building is also sufficiently generous both to enable elements like the Chapel of Unity or the Guild Chapel to read as pavilions set in their own space, and to leave ample and usable outdoor areas between the new and the existing buildings on the site.

But if there was widespread admiration for Spence's scheme, there were also hard questions about the form and the general character of the building raised from his plan. Richards in the *Review* was quick to pick out the two obvious faults of the design: the weakness of the porch and the confused nature of the building's structure. The first was more easily remedied. Caught between the mass of the new building with its blank west wall and the ruins of St Michael's, the porch as originally proposed seemed inadequate, too small to mark the turn from the axis of St Michael's to the long dramatic view down the length of the new building to the new altar. Spence redesigned a taller and more substantial porch before the end of the year. But the confusion in the structure of the new building remained. To critics familiar with the critical importance for modern architecture since the late 1920s of the distinction between a masonry architecture of walls and a frame architecture of columns, Spence's attempt to marry these two forms of structure was a mistake. The zig-zag walls, with their impression of massive strength and associations running back to a tough northern Gothic, appeared quite capable of supporting the roof without help from the spindly concrete columns proposed for the interior. In an exhibition pavilion this might have been forgivable. But in a building of this kind it was emphatically not.

There was also a more fundamental debate about the way Spence had struck the balance between tradition and modernity in his effort to achieve an atmosphere appropriate to a cathedral. The issue had divided all those involved in the rebuilding of the cathedral from the start, from those responsible for preparing the brief, through to the critics commenting on the results. To many critics Spence's entry was successful because of the way in which his interpretation of modern architecture could also accommodate references to traditional forms. *Architectural Design* praised it in just these terms:

> Fundamentally, the winning design is traditional in concept and form; it is in direct descent from the Christian basilica and the Gothic cathedrals: elongated nave with side aisles. The roof structure is a vaulted masonry design translated, with elegance, into contemporary building material – reinforced concrete … In the handling of space, within and without, in treatment of solid and void, in massing and contrast of forms, in the texturing of planes, the design follows a tried, safe path.[52]

To the more conservative, Spence's design was offensive for leaning too far towards modernity, for abandoning the traditional qualities of cathedral architecture still to be found at Liverpool or even Guildford. But to the *Architectural Review*, which had been urging architects to think in the most general terms about the relationship between modernity and tradition, Spence's scheme came as a disappointment. In place of some principled answer to this issue, Richards found Spence at once too literal in his use of

tradition and too romantic, too woolly, too much the exhibition architect:

> Religious architecture is a matter of feeling rather than logic, and Mr Spence has made brave efforts to arouse feelings, to stimulate an emotional response, in the somewhat bewildered public with which modern architecture has to come to fresh terms … Yet in trying to assess Mr Spence's winning designs one can only repeat that there are limits to the extent to which the arbitrary and capricious, however skilfully handled, can establish emotional communication with its public because it has no single artistic principle to communicate.[53]

If Spence's scheme relied too obviously on tradition, what of those entries that fitted Summerson's second category, those that had opted for 'originality of conception' unfettered by the past? Most were ignored.[54] However, two schemes attracted attention for the way the designers attempted to create a cathedral through an understanding of the principles rather than the forms of tradition; one by Sandy Wilson and Peter Carter, and the other by Alison and Peter Smithson (Figure 4.13).[55] The first was conceived as a single great space, roofed by a huge steel trussed structure, within which the spaces for the subsidiary chapels are differentiated by simple planes in the manner of Mies van der Rohe's projects of the 1940s. The space of the main altar was defined by the four pylons supporting the main trusses and the platform on which they stand. Spurning any reference to the ruins of St Michael's or the other historic buildings surrounding the site, Wilson and Carter's scheme offered an interpretation of a modern cathedral as a grand space shaped by new structural possibilities, a parallel to the central role of the structural and constructional innovations of the twelfth and thirteenth centuries in shaping the Gothic cathedral.

Alison and Peter Smithson were even more explicit in the way they set out to invoke the principles of tradition. Their project too was conceived as a great single space housing all the different elements of the brief, clearly related to the route from Broadgate and bringing order to the seemingly random grouping of buildings on the site. The great space was created by the use of a parabolic concrete shell tilted to open the space out towards the east end and reaching a climax over the altar, an interpretation of traditional layout. The Smithsons claimed to have retained 'the ancient symbolism of eastern orientation, cruciform plan, and trinitical arrangements' but to have given them 'new vigour'.[56]

Equally important to the Smithsons as a link to tradition was the use of geometry and proportion as a basis for form in the manner of Renaissance architects like Alberti and Palladio, a tradition described by Rudolf Wittkower in *Architectural Principles in the Age of Humanism*, just published in 1949. Thus they claimed that the positions of the altar, the organ and the other elements within the square were determined by a triangular grid generated by the base of the tower of St Michael's. The resulting sense of order would appear, argued the Smithsons, like that of the churches of the Renaissance, 'absolute, immutable, static and entirely lucid'. In the report accompanying their submission, they set out with engaging arrogance the way in which they saw the strength of the connection between their design and tradition:

> It is hoped ... that the building of this cathedral will fully explode the fallacy that Modern Architecture is incapable of expressing abstract ideas and will prove that *only* Modern Architecture is capable of creating a symbol of the dogmatic truths of the Christian faith ... Modern Architecture is the heir to this great tradition and has at its disposal means of expression which would have sent Brunelleschi wild with joy. For the first time it is possible for architects to be completely aware of the forces at work in their structures and to find their exact plastic expression without arbitrariness or fear.[57]

For the modernists, represented by Richards and the *Review*, the results of the Coventry competition were troubling. They demonstrated the scale of the difficulty of finding an accommodation between the expression of traditional values and modernism. Spence's cathedral, though recognisably 'modern', was sufficiently traditional in inspiration to stand on the frontier of what the public found to be acceptable, even in Coventry. But what rendered it acceptable to the public was a source of misgiving to modernists. Equally, Richards was no more enthusiastic about attempts to develop a design for the cathedral that seemed, like the Smithsons', to set tradition aside. Their engagement with tradition was too abstract, too remote from the terms in which the issues of the New Monumentality were being discussed. But in their scheme and in the explanation of their intentions, the Smithsons could claim that they were addressing these very same issues and doing so in a way, both radical and direct, that did not involve a return to the forms of the past.

These three projects, the Royal Festival Hall, the layout of the Festival of Britain and the competition for Coventry Cathedral, had provided welcome opportunities for experimentation. The Royal Festival Hall and the Festival of Britain at least had generally won public and critical approval. But how far do these three projects represent a realisation of the hopes for a new direction in architecture? The *Review*'s hopes for a revival of the Picturesque and of Englishness had proved an uncertain guide to design: in practice the results might too easily be mistaken for whimsy and formal eccentricity. Equally, calls for a new humanity and expressiveness in architecture may have encouraged a freer approach to design, though hopes for an 'organic' English style remained unrealised. But, if the promise of theory still remained unfulfilled in practice, experimentation was not limited to headline projects alone – housing was soon to provide important opportunities for architectural advance.

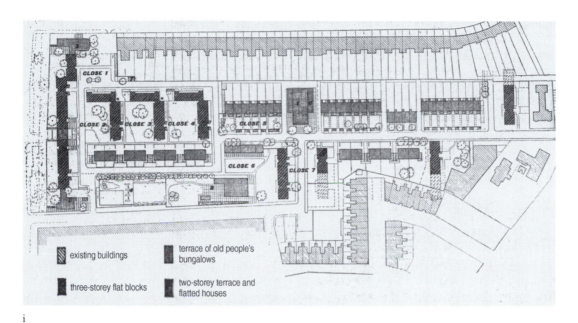

existing buildings	terrace of old people's bungalows
three-storey flat blocks	two-storey terrace and flatted houses

i

ii

4.14 Somerford Grove estate, Hackney, by Frederick Gibberd (1947–49): (i) site plan; (ii) view east from Close 4 towards the single-storey terrace in Close 6

The new architecture of housing

For most architects, practice during the late 1940s focused on utilitarian tasks, on repairing war damage, on rebuilding factories, schools and above all else, housing. Despite the volume of housing being designed (if not actually built) at the time, few housing projects, and even fewer schools, were used to illustrate the architectural issues that were being debated.[58] The most interesting schools, the primary schools being built by Hertfordshire County Council, were published but were sidelined either as school building or as developments in construction, rather than

presented as a central contribution to the current architectural debate.[59] From 1948 housing schemes appear in the architectural press with growing regularity, though for the most part they too are treated as an autonomous area of architectural activity, as housing rather than as architecture.[60] There are well-known exceptions, the most important being Le Corbusier's Unité d'Habitation, built from 1947 to 1952 in Marseilles. But there are also a small number of British schemes of the late 1940s and the beginning of the 1950s that illustrate the way in which the central themes of the architectural debate might be reflected in the design of housing.

Somerford Grove, Hackney

One of the first post-war housing developments to be featured in the *Architectural Review* was Frederick Gibberd's scheme for mixed development at Somerford Grove, Hackney, offering houses and gardens for families with children and flats for people without children (Figure 4.14).[61]

4.15 Woodyard Square, Woodton, by Tayler and Green (1950–51)

Built to a density of 100 people per acre, as recommended by the County of London Plan, the project matched the density of the surrounding area and combined the traditional English terrace with low-rise flats in a sequence of closes or courts. Somerford Grove is both clearly English and clearly modern: it takes the terrace and the square, traditional elements of London housing, and combines these with a vocabulary of modern forms to answer the hopes of the *Review* for a modern architecture rooted in a regional identity.

The scheme is laid out as a number of closes composed of three-storey flat-roofed blocks of flats, two-storey pitched-roof flats, and a number of conventional two-storey terraces with pitched roofs. The *Review* described the Picturesque quality of the layout, complemented by mature trees and a sympathetic approach to the creation of a small-scale urban landscape, as 'brilliant'. It applauded the linking of the courts and closes to offer a sequence of vistas ranging from the intimate views and the sense of enclosure within the individual close to the contrasting long view down the terrace street.

In the design of the individual blocks Gibberd combined and contrasted elements of the English tradition of housing with forms of obvious modernity. Thus the three-storey blocks which enclose the space of the closes are 'modern', with their flat roofs, though this modernity is softened by the use of brick, the framing of the windows and the decorative detailing of the projecting balconies. They are set opposite the traditional qualities of the terraces, two-storey flats and housing for the elderly, all of which share the same pitched roofs, the same brick and much of the detailing of the windows and balconies of the three-storey blocks. The terraces too combine modernity with a feeling for tradition: the porches and the rhythm of brick structure set against the infill of windows and rendered spandrel panels animate the elevations, avoiding the monotony of the traditional terrace.

This modern revaluing of traditional English housing types was equally successful in a number of rural housing projects. The housing built by Tayler and Green for Loddon Rural District Council just north of the Norfolk–Suffolk border in villages like Woodton, Hedenham and Geldeston fit into the landscape with rare tact (Figure 4.15).[62] The design of the individual dwellings combines a feeling for traditional building with a modern simplicity, exemplifying that quality of being 'of the region' that many had admired in Swedish architecture. Ian Nairn praised the evolution of Tayler and Green's work from 'International Good Taste' to 'East Anglian' and the growing use of local materials like glossy black tiles and colour-washed lime render in just these terms, and called for the wider application of the same approach:

Loddon RDC have got, for their original adventurousness, a set of council housing unequalled in the whole country … It is vital if this sort of achievement is to happen elsewhere to understand just how the architects interpreted the local spirit. They did so in purely 20th century terms … In doing so they have been faithful to the *genius loci* in a deeper sense than that implied by a few design cliches; it would be quite possible, starting from these basic terrace units, to produce a mid-Devon solution, soft and shaggy, or a rough gritty West Riding solution or a large-scale easy-going East Sussex solution.[63]

In the design of terraces, cottages and courts, the kind of housing typified by Gibberd's Somerford Grove or Tayler and Green's Smith's Mill, Hedenham, architects could turn to tradition, but what of the design of flats? Lionel Brett, commenting in the *Review* in 1949 on the first post-war blocks of flats, set out the central and intractable issue facing designers. With no national tradition on which to rely, English architects had to learn to reconcile the domestic scale of the individual dwelling with an appropriate monumentality for the block:

It is difficult to think of an architectural problem so compounded of contradictory elements. Domesticity, yes, we understand that; and we have traditional ways of expressing it. Monumentality, too, we respect at a distance. But can domesticity be expressed in ten storeys, or should the Little Man have to live in a monument?[64]

Unsurprisingly, Brett dismissed the designs still being built in London by the LCC and the majority of the boroughs. Significantly, too, in a judgement that serves as a reminder of the suspicion with which Le Corbusier was greeted by a number of those around the *Review*, Brett condemned the Unité d'Habitation still under construction in Marseilles as 'inhumane' and 'frightening'.[65] Despite the range of experimentation in Britain, Brett concluded that 'the large group of flats … has not yet developed a characteristic contemporary form'.[66] Against the mediocre quality of design of most flats being built in London, he did allow that a number of projects

could be said to demonstrate a new and appropriate form for the block of flats. Two developments in particular, Churchill Gardens in Pimlico and the Spa Green Estate in Finsbury, were singled out repeatedly by the architectural press as exemplifying this new approach.

Churchill Gardens, Pimlico, Westminster

Churchill Gardens in Pimlico, designed by Powell and Moya in 1946 and ready for occupation in the summer of 1950, was planned as the initial phase of a 'neighbourhood unit' of the kind that the County of London Plan had proposed as the basic building block for the redevelopment of London after the war (Figure 4.16).[67] In place of the monotonous repetition of the individual flat in the relentless pre-war White City Estate, Churchill Gardens was to be a mixed development combining ten-storey blocks of flats, four-storey maisonettes and a few three-storey terraced houses for large families. In response to the criticism of pre-war LCC estates like Watling or Becontree, Powell and Moya designed a community that was to be served by a wealth of facilities: two primary schools, one secondary school, shops along Lupus Street, a community centre and a well-equipped play area for children. To round off this list of amenities, an existing church was to be retained, its spire being incorporated into the composition of blocks along Grosvenor Road.

The layout of the site contrasts sharply with the semi-enclosed courts of the pre-war tenement tradition. The parallel blocks of the neighbourhood are reminiscent of the pre-war *Zeilenbau* ('single aspect housing') site planning favoured by the German avant-garde but adapted and softened for English use. Here, in place of the programmatically correct orientation of the housing estates of Otto Haesler or Gropius, is a softer, pragmatic response to layout. The alignment of the blocks at Churchill Gardens is varied to create a feeling of enclosure around the site and to take advantage of the view: the neighbourhood is closed to the north

i

ii

4.16 The first phase of Churchill Gardens, Pimlico, by Powell and Moya (1946–51) (i) axonometric of site; (ii) view along the west facade of Chaucer House towards the heat exchanger

by the blocks along Lupus Street and opens out towards the south to give sunlight to all and a view, albeit at an angle, of the Thames for many. The monotony of the constant rooflines of the LCC's pre-war estates is avoided by the contrast between the different types of blocks: from the riverfront the composition rises from three-storey terrace houses to four-storey maisonette blocks to the taller ten-storey blocks of flats behind, which in turn are complemented by elements such as the spire of the church and the simple glazed cylinder of the heat accumulator.

The impression of bold simplicity caught the eye of contemporaries. On the east facade of the main blocks the straightforward organisation of the block is clearly expressed in the direct handling of the staircases and the entries to them. On the west front, too, this organisation is signalled by the vertical grouping of the balconies and the simple geometric forms of the service towers on the roof above each staircase. The brick cladding of the reinforced concrete frame, expressed as a floor slab at each storey, is handled cleanly and without fuss. The rhythm of windows and balconies identifies the individual flats without disturbing the impact of the block as a whole.

Some details may detract from this overall impression of clarity: why does the block break forward half-way along its length? Is the slight angle of the balcony for each flat, absent on blocks in later phases, a concession to New Empiricist whimsy? But for contemporaries the simple clarity of Churchill Gardens was refreshing and welcome. Writing in the *Observer* Sandy Wilson praised the scheme as one of the best examples of the new approach:

> In view of the size of the large blocks, the impression of lightness and gaiety is astonishing. Light yellow brick contrasted with pungent red and blue paintwork, and the sleekness of glass balcony fronts and staircase towers, give them a quality of weightlessness, fresh and sharp as a liner.[68]

J.M. Richards included in his first revised edition of *Introduction to Modern Architecture* (1953) photographs of the first phase of blocks as being among the few British buildings capable of standing international comparison. Here was an important and, on this riverside site, a very visible demonstration of the successful use of modern architecture for housing.

Spa Green, Rosebery Avenue, Finsbury

Like Churchill Gardens, Tecton's design for flats at Spa Green for Finsbury Borough Council starts from the principles of the County of London Plan and shows how, even at 136 people per acre, it was possible to create a mixed development of 129 dwellings, allocating small families to flats in the two main blocks and larger families to maisonettes in the third block.[69] Like Quarry Hill in Leeds and Kensal House in west London (Figure 2.2), the design for Spa Green follows the example of Continental estates like the large municipal developments in Vienna in seeking to provide more than housing alone (Figure 4.17). Though the scheme was too small to generate the range of services to be found at Pimlico, Tecton planned a nursery school at the centre of the estate between the two main blocks as an asset for families with children and as a benefit to the local community. The provision of open space around the estate, including the creation of Spa Gardens, was another contribution to the community and a welcome contrast with the monotony of the surrounding streets of bye-law housing.

More so than Norman and Dawbarn's flats at St Pancras Way or Churchill Gardens, Spa Green conveys an understanding of the work of the pre-war avant-garde and how this could be used to provide a vocabulary for the flat. Although the other two developments have layouts which no longer depend on the corridor street or on the pre-war tenement type, Lubetkin goes further to treat the blocks at Rosebery Avenue as 'objects in space'. The two main blocks, treated as separate entities, supported on columns and apparently lifted clear of the ground, refer back to Le Corbusier's work of the 1920s and 1930s. The use of ramps and other architectural elements to control movement and to define the space of the court formed by the three blocks looks to the 1930s and to Tecton's earlier work, particularly to the treatment of the ground floor of Highpoint I. Equally, the estate looks forward to developments in the mid-1950s. In its revaluation of the architectural vocabulary of the 1920s and 1930s it anticipates the way in which a younger generation of architects would turn to the work of Le Corbusier.

As important were Tecton's ideas on the development of an architectural language for the block of flats. In an article which accompanied the publication of the scheme in the *Architectural Review*, Lubetkin described the way in which the form of Spa Green and his designs for Priory Green and Paddington could be seen as the continuation of a series of explorations begun before the war into ways of relating structural form to architectural expression. Functionalism, or form bred of rigour in planning and construction, was not enough; this, he argued,

i

ii

4.17 Spa Green, Finsbury, by Tecton (1946–50); (i) aerial view of the whole estate; (ii) view of the flats across Spa Gardens

had to be balanced by a concern for the emotional impact of architecture:

> For too long modern architectural solutions were regarded in terms of abstract principles, with formal expression left to itself as a functional resultant. The principles of composition, the emotional impact of the visual, were brushed aside as irrelevant. Yet this is the material with which the architect operates; it is in this sphere that he is the sole master, by virtue of his training and tradition.[70]

Spa Green was intended as an illustration of the way in which the architect should combine 'uncompromising clarity of plan, articulation of volumes, and causal interrelation between structure and design' with 'solicitude for the human being, the reflection of the human scale, in the modelling of the whole composition and in the treatment of details'.[71]

The starting point for the design was the box frame structure, developed by Ove Arup, and used here for the first time in Britain. Lubetkin praised this form of structure for its economy, its simplicity and the freedom that it allowed the designer. Exploiting this freedom Lubetkin sets out to design elevations that are expressive both of the way the block is planned and built and of the identity of the individual flat and the way this is combined into the composition of the block as a whole. In contrast to an approach where elevations are treated as 'part of a continuous band of indeterminate limits, which could be snipped off at any point',[72] the elevations on the two facades of the blocks at Rosebery Avenue are clearly different: on the bedroom elevation, the regular rhythm of the bedroom windows is contrasted with the small-scale windows of the stairs. On the living room elevation, with six flats across each floor, the identity of the individual flat is clearly marked, with brick-clad living room, and the kitchen and bathroom behind the balconies.

While the individual flat is identifiable in these terms, Lubetkin does not neglect the effect of the whole block. On the bedroom facade, the elevation is surrounded by a frame, a reminder of the whole rather than the repetitive pattern of the windows of the individual dwelling. On the living room side, a similar device is used to give a tripartite reading of the facade, with greater emphasis on the central element, which is strengthened further by the drying floor at roof level and the central placing of the entrance canopy at ground level. Within this composition are a number of variations, such as the alternating position of the balcony parapets on each floor, creating a rippling effect across the facade and animating the elevation as a whole.

To the younger generation, Lubetkin's concern with formal issues gave cause for concern, especially where this involved falsifying the apparent logic of construction or planning. And at Rosebery Avenue there were elements of playfulness and a pursuit of formal exploration at the expense of strict logic: the checkerboard game played on the elevations of the maisonette block, and the alternation of the balcony elements on the living room facade of the main blocks. More wilful still to young purists was the artful framing of the central section on the living room facades in a way that confuses the reading of the relationship of living room to kitchen and bathroom and thus obscures the identity of the individual flats. This formal exuberance might be allowed, but Lubetkin's later designs at Priory Green and Paddington attracted a more hostile reaction. Contrasting Le Corbusier's Unité d'Habitation with Tecton's Spa Green and Priory Green, Julius Posener praised the Unité for being 'a frank statement of what it is: a honeycomb for human living', but cautioned against Tecton's over-elaboration of design: 'The architect plays around a sober and elementary structure. He refrains from playing *with* it, from changing the whole thing into an ornament'.[73] Sandy Wilson, contrasting Priory Green with Churchill Gardens, also found Tecton's pattern-making difficult. He welcomed Tecton's use of the checkerboard pattern as a way of reducing the scale of the block, but then went on to criticise the mismatch between formal expression and the logic of planning: 'the unit accommodation does not correspond organically with the single dwelling'.[74]

But notwithstanding the puritanical reservations of a younger generation, Tecton created at Spa Green an architecture which was expressive of the formal order of housing, of the balance between the identity of the individual dwelling and the character of the block as a whole. Here was a rejoinder to Lionel Brett's assertion only two years before that the English had yet to find a way to design blocks of flats. Extending the vocabulary with which Lubetkin had been working before the war, Tecton was developing a vital new architecture for housing.

LCC estates: Ackroydon and Alton East

A comparison of these post-war schemes with pre-war developments like Kensal House by Fry, Drake, Lasdun and others or Gibberd's Pulman Court underlines the way in which the work of the post-war modernists was indeed less programmatic, more sensitive to regional differences and traditions, as well as more pragmatic and responsive to demands of the particular situation. Even in Tecton's post-war work there is a new interest in materials and composition and a new fullness of effect that distinguish Spa Green from Highpoint I. Spa Green does represent a continuation of much of the formal language of Tecton's pre-war buildings, yet it is unmistakably a building of the post-war years. These three housing projects reflect different ways in which the direction of the new architecture was changing, both in the debts to the 1930s and in the search for new directions. But more than any other housing development of the time it was the work of the newly re-established Housing Division of the LCC Architect's Department, first at the Ackroydon Estate in Wimbledon (Figure 4.18) and then at Alton East (Figure 4.19), the first phase of the Roehampton Estate, that has come to stand as the exemplar of the dominant strands in the architectural debate and to represent best the condition of the new architecture at the end of the 1940s and the start of the 1950s.[75]

i   ii

4.18 The first 'point blocks' in Britain: (i) one of the 10-storey tower blocks on the Ackroydon Estate, Wimbledon (1950–53), by the newly re-established Housing Division of the LCC Architect's Department; (ii) the Lawn, Mark Hall, Harlow, by Frederick Gibberd (1948–51)

4.19 Aerial view of the LCC's Alton East Estate, Roehampton (1951–54)

In December 1949, with the Architect's Department once again responsible for the design of housing, Robert Matthew and his housing team under H.J. Whitfield Lewis were able to develop in prototype form on the Ackroydon Estate[76] an approach to mixed-development, medium-density housing that was to be applied in the following year at the Alton East section of the Roehampton Estate, the largest post-war development planned by the LCC. The key innovation at Ackroydon was the use of point or tower blocks for flats, in combination with lower maisonette blocks and houses with gardens, to provide the different types of dwellings needed in a mixed-development scheme. Frederick Gibberd had built the first point block, the Lawn,[77] at Harlow, an application of a form of housing widely used in Sweden and known to English architects through projects such as Backström and Reinius's Danviksklippan flats in Stockholm (Figure 4.18).[78] But in contrast to Gibberd's free if idiosyncratic plan, Whitfield Lewis and his team produced an economical T-shaped plan type, fitting three flats to a floor with two lifts serving alternate floors. As a result the LCC team were able to break down the scale of their towers to give a slimmer silhouette. When seen from different points of view, it offered a greater variety of modelling than by either the Lawn at Harlow or their shared Swedish prototypes. The design is not without shortcomings: there should, for example, have been a special solution to the arrangement of the flats on the ground floor. Nor is the structure treated as clearly as it might have been: the reinforced concrete frame is not made visible, except at the rear on the ground floor, so that it is easy to assume that the brick flank walls are part of a load-bearing structure in brickwork. But overall the design was judged a success. Set amongst mature trees, and simply detailed with a reinforced concrete frame turned up and rendered to form the wall under the strip windows, the Ackroydon blocks have a light, almost delicate quality. On the Ackroydon Estate the architects of the Housing Division showed how Swedish housing ideas could be adapted and naturalised for

English use and how even housing, previously treated in the most utilitarian way, could be approached using ideas currently debated in the *Review*.

What Gibberd had suggested at Mark Hall and Whitfield Lewis and his team experimented with at Ackroydon was employed on a larger scale at the Alton East (or Portsmouth Road) Estate, the first stage of the LCC's huge development at Roehampton.[79] Here, on a site that combined large mature nineteenth-century gardens with mature trees and views across parkland, the LCC architects were able to realise one of the most successful applications of the ideas explored in the *Review*. In a much publicised model of 1951, the architects presented a design that was the antithesis of the blocks that the Valuer had been building for the LCC only two years before. Working with a mix of different house types and at a density of 100 people per acre, Whitfield Lewis and his team were able to concentrate over half the dwellings planned for the site in ten eleven-storey towers placed along the eastern edge of the site to give magnificent views across to Richmond Park and Wimbledon Common. To place this number of dwellings in these towers and at the same to minimise their bulk, the team had to develop a new floor plan with four flats per floor, internal bathrooms and two lifts serving alternate floors. This was only made possible by ingenious juggling of the fire regulations and by the LCC's willingness to change the building regulations to allow internal ventilation for the bathrooms for the first time.[80] The result is a set of eleven-storey towers that are simpler in outline than their predecessors at Ackroydon.

At Roehampton these towers stand informally among the 60 ft trees, defining the edge of but not enclosing the site, and allowing views through to Wimbledon Common from the lower blocks to the west. Related to these towers, in the best Picturesque fashion, are the four- and five-storey maisonette blocks and the two-storey houses. The contrast between the eleven-storey towers and the pitched roofs of the maisonette blocks or the stepped pairs of houses reads like an illustration from the Ministry of

i   ii

4.20 Roehampton as an exemplar of the English Picturesque tradition: (i) Coxwold, Yorkshire; (ii) the combination of two-storey houses and eleven-storey flats at Alton East, Roehampton

Housing and Local Government's pamphlet *Good Design in Town and Village*, in which architects were urged to learn how to compose housing layouts from the lessons of the past (Figure 4.20). In place of the domineering effect typical of the juxtaposition of high and low blocks, this informal layout links the houses and the terraces visually to the towers beyond in a composition that leads the eye from one to another in the tradition of the best English landscapes.

Contemporary critics saluted the success of the LCC's new estates. In the Reith Lectures of 1955, 'The Englishness of English Art', Nikolaus Pevsner singled out the Ackroydon and Roehampton estates as especially successful examples of the urban application of the principles of Picturesque planning.[81] Returning to the same theme in an article in the *Review* in 1959, 'Roehampton, LCC Housing and the Picturesque Tradition', Pevsner looked back enthusiastically over the estate's two phases of development since 1950, hailing the combination of architecture and landscape as a return to a grand tradition:

> The setting of a cubic type of building in landscape is an eighteenth century tradition and has once before made a deep impression everywhere abroad ... Benefitting from this Georgian tradition the architects of the Roehampton Estate

succeeded in combining human scale with vast extent ... The effect accomplished at Roehampton ranges from the cosy to the violently startling.[82]

Pevsner hailed the estate as a successful application of the approach that the *Review* had championed since the war. He spoke for Richards and others at the *Review* by asserting that at Alton East modern architecture had been both humanised and made 'English'. Here at last was a triumphant realisation of the values of the New Humanism:

> Standing securely in a modern European tradition of town planning that reaches back into the early twenties, and equally secure in an English landscape tradition that goes back almost two centuries further, the LCC's Roehampton Estate is one of the masterpieces of post-war residential design.[83]

He praised particularly the 'humanism and variety' of the whole and lingered affectionately on the qualities of the first phase, with its faintly Swedish intonation of colours and forms:

> The earlier point-blocks are faced with pale cream brick and have lively projections and recessions in outline. The earlier maisonettes and cottages have roofs of gentle

pitch. The whole combines perfectly with the picturesque plan, the winding streets and informally placed trees. It is architecture at ease.[84]

But architectural attitudes were already changing. The team responsible for designing the next phase of Roehampton, the Alton West Estate off Roehampton Lane, adopted a very different approach. Generally younger and trained after World War II, they were no longer suspicious of the avant-garde pioneers of the 1920s. They admired the current work of Mies van der Rohe and Le Corbusier, passing over the Swedish models of the first phase of Roehampton for Le Corbusier's Unité d'Habitation. They were impatient with the predictable values of the *Review*, with the nostalgia of the New Humanism and the cosy romanticism of Organic Regionalism. Above all they wished to re-establish the Modern Movement on a basis of principle and rigour.

Notes

1 For the background to the design and building of the Festival, see M. Banham and A. Forty, *A Tonic to the Nation*, London, Thames & Hudson, 1976, especially chs 3 and 6.
2 The background to the design of the Royal Festival Hall is discussed in J. McKean, 'Royal Festival Hall: Masters of Building', *AJ*, 9.10.1991, pp. 24–47, and J. McKean, *The Royal Festival Hall*, London, Phaidon, 1992.
3 Holden's proposals for the development of the South Bank are illustrated in *AJ*, 9.2.1950, p. 190.
4 L. Martin, 'A Note on Science and Art', *AYB*, 2, 1947, pp. 9–11. Leslie Martin's achievements by the late 1940s are summarised in P. Carolin and T. Dannatt (eds), *Architecture, Education and Research, the Work of Leslie Martin: Papers and Selected Articles*, London, Academy Editions, 1996.
5 Edwin Williams, a senior architect in the Architect's Department under Forshaw, was passed over when Martin and Moro were brought in to lead the design team. Williams, a Rome Scholar, had been responsible for working up elements of the design proposed by Holden. His role under Martin was to provide a link between the technical services of the LCC and the design team, and the completion of the building on time owed much to his understanding of the council and its workings.
6 J.L. Martin, 'The Conception', *AYB*, 4, 1952, pp. 189–90. The sketch of the four alternatives appeared first in 'Royal Festival Hall', *AR*, Jun. 1951, p. 345.
7 J.L. Martin, 'Science and the Design of the Royal Festival Hall', *JRIBA*, Apr. 1952, p. 197.
8 E.g. Le Corbusier's design for the Palace of the Soviets and, though perhaps unknown to the design team, a design for a concert hall by Bruce Martin, then a student at the AA.
9 The acoustic issues are discussed in W.A. Allen and P. Parkin, 'Acoustics and Sound Exclusion', *AR*, Jun. 1951, pp. 377–84.
10 The structural problems are discussed in 'Royal Festival Hall: Technical', *AR*, Jun. 1951, pp. 389–94.
11 'The London County Council Concert Hall', *JRIBA*, Aug. 1949, p. 431.
12 J. Richards, 'Royal Festival Hall: Criticism', *AR*, Jun. 1951, p. 358.
13 'Musical Quality in Concert Halls', *JRIBA*, Dec. 1951, pp. 47–51.
14 Richards, 'Royal Festival Hall: Criticism', p. 356.
15 'The Royal Festival Hall', *AD*, Jun. 1951, p. 155.
16 Richards 'Criticism', p. 357.
17 'Royal Festival Hall', *ABN*, Jun. 1951, p. 636.
18 Asplund's Law Courts would have been familiar to readers of the *Review* through articles such as 'The Growth of Modern Architecture in Sweden', *AR*, Aug. 1938, p. 61, through P. Morton Shand's illustrated memorial to Asplund, 'Gunnar Asplund', *AR*, May 1941, pp. 99–102, and more immediately through G.E. Kidder Smith, *Sweden Builds*, London, Architectural Press, 1950.
19 'Have you Boys ever Built a Concert Hall Before?', *AD*, Jun. 1951, p. 155.
20 'The Royal Festival Hall', *Builder*, 25.5.1951, p. 730.
21 Richards, 'Royal Festival Hall: Criticism', p. 357.
22 'The Royal Festival Hall', *Builder*, 25.5.1951, p. 730.
23 Richards 'Royal Festival Hall: Criticism', p. 357.
24 J. Posener, 'Knots in the Master's Carpet', *AD*, Dec. 1951, pp. 354–6.
25 R. Banham, 'Facade', *AR*, Nov. 1954, p. 303.
26 *Ibid.*, p. 303.
27 *Ibid.*, p. 304.
28 S. Giedion, 'In Search of a New Monumentality', *AR*, Sep. 1948, p. 126.
29 Banham and Forty, *Tonic to the Nation*, p. 27.
30 *Ibid.*, p. 63.
31 The architects working on the festival were profiled in the architectural press: 'Marginalia', *AR*, Aug. 1951, pp. 139–41.
32 The choice of the site and the early days of the project are described in H. Casson, 'Period Piece', in Banham and Forty, *Tonic to the Nation*, pp. 76–81,

and the files on the Festival of Britain held in the Public Record Office.

33 Banham and Forty, *Tonic to the Nation*, p. 78; see also H. Casson, 'The 1951 Exhibition' *JRIBA*, Apr. 1950, pp. 207–15.

34 J. Richards, 'The Exhibition Buildings', *AR*, Aug. 1951, p. 151.

35 *Ibid.*, p. 123.

36 *Ibid.*, p. 124.

37 *Ibid.*, p. 74.

38 'The Exhibition as Landscape', *AR*, Aug. 1951, p. 83–5.

39 'The South Bank Exhibition: Foreword', *AR*, Aug. 1951, p. 73.

40 'Festival of Britain, the South Bank Exhibition', *Builder*, May 1951, p. 686.

41 Casson later described the impression left on him by the Rotterdam exhibition in 'Rotterdam Ahoy', *Forum*, 6 (June), 1950, pp. 190–237.

42 The Milan exhibition was reported in *AR*, Mar. 1949, pp. 147–8.

43 See the section 'Pleasure Gardens, Battersea Park', in Banham and Forty, *Tonic to the Nation*, pp. 118–37. This particular form of humour was evident too in the Schweppes advertisements of the time and in *Punch*, to which Emett was a regular contributor.

44 The background to the competition is discussed in L. Campbell, *Coventry Cathedral: Art and Architecture in Post-War Britain*, Oxford, Oxford University Press, 1996, especially chs 1–3.

45 'Coventry Cathedral Competition', *AD*, Sep. 1951, p. 258.

46 'Coventry Cathedral Competition', *Builder*, Aug. 1951, p. 239.

47 J. Summerson, 'Coventry Cathedral', *New Statesman*, Sep. 1951, pp. 253–4.

48 'Coventry Cathedral Competition', *AJ*, 30.8.1951, p. 250.

49 *Ibid.*, p. 250.

50 *Ibid.*, p. 252.

51 'The New Zig-Zag Structure', *A&BN*, 30.8.1951, p. 217. Similar views were expressed in the other journals.

52 'Coventry Cathedral Competition', *AD*, September, 1951, p. 258; *A&BN* applauded the design in similar terms.

53 J. Richards, 'Coventry', *AR*, Jan. 1952, p. 7.

54 Some of the schemes that fitted into Summerson's second category were very far-fetched, e.g. the entries by Verity, Cotton, Bramhill and Cotton. Others were more worthily modern: Aberdeen, Harper and Harvey. Some were interesting for their attempt to adapt the forms of the pre-war avant-garde to the design of a cathedral: Pelley and Subiotto, Percy Thomas of ARCON.

55 Wilson and Carter's entry was published in *AJ*, 30.8.1951, p. 259; the Smithsons' entry was more widely published, appearing in *AJ*, 30.8.1951, pp. 260–1, and *AD*, Sep. 1951, p. 262.

56 P. Smithson, 'Coventry Cathedral Competition Entry', *Church Building*, Jan. 1963, p. 8.

57 *Ibid.*

58 In his survey article 'The Next Step?' Richards pigeon-holes the Hertfordshire schools as 'Mechanistic', and in their article for the *AR* on the Hertfordshire schools Llewelyn-Davies and Weeks characterised their architecture as 'other' and outside the bounds of normal architectural conventions, see also ch. 8, note 85.

59 This view was not at odds with the attitudes of the leading architects of the group at the time like David Medd who appeared more concerned with questions of education and architectural production than with mere questions of architectural style or fashion.

60 There are occasional articles on housing schemes of architectural merit, notably on the Pimlico Housing Competition, *AJ*, 30.3.1946, pp. 411–16, and Tecton's block of flats on Rosebery Avenue, Finsbury, London, *AJ*, 12.9.1946, pp. 191–5, but most are concerned with the provision rather than the architecture of housing. Both the easing of the housing crisis and the attack on the architectural standards of LCC housing encouraged more active debate of the architecture of housing. The change is evident in Richards' 'Building in Britain: 1948', *AJ*, 20.1.1949, p. 54.

61 Gibberd's Somerford Grove attracted considerable comment, e.g. 'Housing at Hackney', *AR*, Sep. 1949, pp. 146–50.

62 Tayler and Green's work was widely illustrated as a model for rural and low density housing, e.g. 'Towards an Architecture: Post-war Housing Estates', *AR*, Jul. 1951, pp. 16–26. See also E. Harwood and A. Powers, *The Work of Tayler and Green*, London, Prince of Wales Institute, 1998.

63 I. Nairn, 'Rural Housing: Post-war Work by Tayler and Green', *AR*, Oct. 1958, p. 226.

64 L. Brett, 'Towards a New Architecture: Post-war Flats in Britain', *AR*, Nov. 1949, p. 315–22.

65 *Ibid.*, p. 315.

66 *Ibid.*

67 Churchill Gardens was published in 'Flats in Pimlico', *AR*, Feb. 1951, pp. 70–80.

68 C.A. St John Wilson, 'Patterns of Living', *Observer*, 20.7.1952, p. 8.

69 B. Lubetkin, 'Flats in Rosebery Avenue, Finsbury', *AR*, Mar. 1951, pp. 138–49; *ABN*, 20.5.49, pp. 442–6; *Builder*, 13.5.49, pp. 589–93; *AD*, Nov. 1948, pp. 237–8; *AJ*, 26.4.51, pp. 517–22. The flats at Rosebery Avenue are also discussed at length in J. Allen, *Lubetkin: Architecture and the Tradition of Progress*, London, RIBA, 1992, especially ch. 9.

70 Lubetkin, 'Flats in Rosebery Ave', p. 140.

71 *Ibid.*

72 *Ibid.*

73 Posener, 'Knots in the Master's Carpet', pp. 354–6.

74 Wilson, 'Patterns of Living', p. 8.

75 The work of the Housing Division of the LCC Architect's Department is well documented: R. Furneaux Jordan, 'LCC: New Standards in Official Architecture', *AR*, Nov. 1956; N. Pevsner, 'Roehampton: LCC Housing and the Picturesque Tradition', *AR*, Jul. 1959, pp. 21–35; N.M. Day, *The Role of the Architect in State Housing*, Warwick, PhD dissertation, 1988; R.S. Haynes, *Design and Image in English Urban Housing 1945–1957*, University College London, MPhil dissertation, 1976.

76 *AR*, Oct. 1954, pp. 222–5; *AD*, Jan. 1952, pp. 13–16; *Builder*, 16.7. 1954, pp. 92–4; for the responsibility for the design of housing, see below, ch. 9.

77 'Flats in Harlow', *AR*, Sep. 1951, pp. 154–9.

78 'Flat Scheme at Danviksklippan, Stockholm', *AJ*, 5.8.1946, pp. 121–4.

79 There is an extensive literature on the Alton East Estate, Roehampton, e.g. *AD*, Sep. 1955, pp. 50–1; Jan. 1959, pp. 7–21; *AR*, Jan. 1954, pp. 52–6; Nov. 1956, pp. 307–9; *JRIBA*, Jul. 1960, pp. 328–9.

80 A.W.C. Barr, *Public Authority Housing*, London, Batsford, 1958.

81 N. Pevsner, *The Englishness of English Art*, Harmondsworth, Penguin Books, 1993, p. 192.

82 Pevsner, 'Roehampton', p. 35.

83 *Ibid.*, p. 21.

84 *Ibid.*, p. 35.

5 Old masters and young Turks
The formation of a new avant-garde

Architectural Design published a statement on the 'New Brutalism' by Alison and Peter Smithson, in January 1955, with an introductory paragraph written by the newly appointed editor, Theo Crosby. Couched in the heroic language of the manifestos of the 1920s, their collective statement signalled the forceful rejection by a new avant-garde of what had become the values of mainstream modern architecture:

> In 1954, a new and long overdue explosion took place in architectural theory. For many years since the war we have continued in our habit of debasing the coinage of M. le Corbusier, and had created a style – 'Contemporary' – easily recognisable by its misuse of traditional materials and its veneer of 'modern' details, frames, recessed plinths, decorative piloti.[1]

The statement simultaneously honours the Modern Movement and demands a rereading of its tradition. It starts by placing the New Brutalism in direct line of descent from the pre-war masters and offers homage to the Le Corbusier of *béton brut* and the Unité. But then it breaks with all conventions by insisting on the importance of Japanese architecture for an understanding of both the Modern Movement and New Brutalism; Frank Lloyd Wright, Le Corbusier and Mies van der Rohe are presented

as having been seduced by the open plans, the continuous space, the simplicity of structure and screens of Japan.[2] Central to the qualities of the architecture admired by the modern masters, argue the Smithsons, is the reverence for materials shared with the Japanese: 'It is this reverence for materials – a realisation of the affinity that can be established between building and man – which is at the root of the New Brutalism.' Their statement ends with an assertion of freedom from the recent past of the Modern Movement:

> What *is* new about the New Brutalism is that it finds its closest affinities, not in a past architectural style, but in peasant dwelling forms. It has nothing to do with craft. We see architecture as the direct expression of a way of life.[3]

A final editorial paragraph provided a list of key Brutalist images and preoccupations:

> 1954 had been a key year. It has seen American advertising equal Dada in its impact of overlaid imagery; that automotive masterpiece, the Cadillac convertible, parallel-with-the-ground (four elevations) classic box on wheels; the start of a new way of thinking by CIAM; the revaluation of the work of Gropius; the repainting of the Villa at Garches?[4]

Self-important, provocative, this enigmatic statement created a stir but said very little about the Brutalist identity. This was first interpreted for public consumption in Reyner Banham's article 'The New Brutalism', published in the *Architectural Review* in December 1955.[5] Seeking to explain the activities of the group, of these architectural young Turks, Banham offered an account of the way in which a number of developments, starting in the early 1950s, had come together as the New Brutalism. The unifying power of his interpretation has tended to obscure any cross-currents and disagreements between the separate developments that he claimed for the movement.[6] But common to these different strands were a number of shared interests: an admiration for the pre-war masters, especially Mies van der Rohe and Le Corbusier, and a distaste for the architecture of the late 1940s and the early 1950s that had been advanced by the *Architectural Review* and had been triumphantly displayed at the Festival of Britain. The editors of *Architectural Design*, by 1955 the journal of the new avant-garde, were attacking the previous generation for their 'lack of rigour and clear thinking, the romantic pasticheries of the Festival of Britain and its offspring, the free empirical manner derived from Sweden, and the loose handling of prefabricated elements in works like the Hertfordshire schools'.[7]

Who were the signatories of the Brutalist declaration and their allies? Their challenge to mainstream modern architecture had close parallels in other fields and was to lead to a loose alliance of young painters, sculptors, critics and architects who gathered at the Institute of Contemporary Art (ICA).[8] The ICA was founded in 1946 by pre-war modernists: the British Surrealist Roland Penrose, the art critic Herbert Read and E.L.T. Mesens, a Belgian Surrealist who had settled in London before the war. The ICA was intended to champion the cause of modernism in London in the manner of the Museum of Modern Art in New York, especially to provide a counterpoint to the Neo-Romantic sympathies of the Arts Council. The terms in which modernism was first advanced by the ICA reflected the values of the generation whose interests had been shaped in the 1930s. There was an emphasis on the general, universal and international dimensions of modernism, but there was also an interest in modernism across the artistic spectrum, including architecture, film and music, and a commitment to foster the work of young artists. For a younger, post-war generation, the ICA was the door to International Modernism: the first exhibition, '40,000 Years of Modern Art', included key icons of modernism like Pablo Picasso's *Demoiselles d'Avignon* and juxtaposed exhibits to underline the parallels between primitivism and modernism. In contrast to the patriotic celebrations of the Festival of Britain, the ICA emphasised its international interests, with a programme of work by Picasso and Matta, and a series of Surrealist films, including *Un Chien Andalou* and *The Shell and the Clergyman*. Those with an interest in architecture could attend lectures and discussions chaired by J.M. Richards or, occasionally, Leslie Martin. Lectures in 1951, for example, featured current work like Powell and Moya's Pimlico flats, Drake and Lasdun's Hallfields housing estate and Fry and Drew's work at Chandigarh, presented and defended by the designers.[9] More important, at a time when foreign travel was far from easy, the ICA provided an opportunity to hear from and meet foreign architects. In 1951, Philip Johnson, admired as Mies van der Rohe's American collaborator, lectured on modern architecture, and Le Corbusier, in London for the Hoddesdon meeting of CIAM, was prevailed upon to open the ICA's exhibition 'Growth and Form'.

The ICA's presentation of modernism simultaneously attracted the younger generation and prompted the challenges to the institute's direction that were to define the position of the new avant-garde. During the early 1950s the formal business of the ICA was dominated by the older generation. But younger members, keen to become involved and already welcome to help with menial tasks like hanging exhibitions, started to seek a more active role.[10] The ICA's willingness in 1951 to allow Richard Hamilton to mount the exhibition 'Growth and Form' signalled the impact of the new generation. Equally important were the regular but informal meetings of a group of younger members that started in April 1952. By August this group, now convened by Reyner Banham, had acquired semi-official status as the 'Independent Group' in its dealings with the ICA management committee and was arranging a series of talks on a wide range of subjects, many of which touched on the links between the arts and a range of fields, from philosophy to technology: A.J. Ayer spoke on 'The Principle of Verification', Jasia S. Shapiro on 'Helicopter Design', Norman Pirie on 'Are Proteins Unique?', Banham on 'The Machine Aesthetic'.[11] By 1953, regular lecture series such as 'Aesthetic Problems of Contemporary Art' provided opportunities for artists and architects to discuss common issues and concerns. Topics like the 'Dadaists as Non-Aristotelians', or 'Probability and Information Theory and Their Application to the Visual Arts', encouraged speculation, perhaps some of it wild, but also a feeling of intellectual companionship with people in other disciplines who were breaking new boundaries.

Without a journal to serve as a platform from which to launch their views in the way that the *Review* had advanced the New Humanism or the New Monumentality in the late 1940s, this new avant-garde started meeting in a number of settings across London: in flats and pubs, at the Central School, in the Architect's Department at the LCC and, more regularly, at ICA lectures and the meetings organised by the Independent Group at the ICA galleries in Dover Street.[12] Publicity and a wider audience for these ideas were slow to come, although the *Architects' Yearbook*, long sympathetic to the continuity of modernist ideas from the pre-war to the post-war years, published occasional articles by members of the group.[13] From late 1952 things began to change. In October, Banham joined the editorial staff of the *Review* and started to write regular articles which reflected and publicised the interests of the group. Two years later, Theo Crosby, a sometime

participant in the Independent Group meetings and a friend of the Smithsons, took over the editorial direction of *Architectural Design*, changing the magazine from a journal with a technical bias and an interest in issues like housing and school building into the most effective vehicle for publicising and promoting the interests of this new outspoken group.[14]

What emerges from the various accounts of the Independent Group in the early 1950s is the sense of excitement and vitality that animates the activities of its membership as they sought to define their position as the new avant-garde. Naturally, this involved challenging the leaders of the ICA like Herbert Read along with other prominent members of the older generation modernists. Peter Smithson characterised the tension between the generations as a necessary spur to defining the position of the younger group: 'A part of the necessity for the Independent Group was taking position – literally in the "nest" of the previous generation – and that, I suspect, was always part of the excitement of the 1953–1954 meetings.'[15]

In architecture, it was the views of J.M. Richards and the circle around the *Review* that most attracted the fire of the group's architectural members, who were younger still than the young team assembled by Casson to design the Festival of Britain. Around 20 architects were loosely associated with the Independent Group, but the dozen or so core members had much in common. Most were of a generation born in the early 1920s, they had seen active service prior to finishing their architectural education, and they entered architecture by similar routes.[16] The largest contingent was trained at the Architectural Association, Sandy Wilson was from Cambridge and the Bartlett, James Stirling from Liverpool, and both Smithsons had studied at Newcastle. Banham, a key figure in the group, had gone from school to work at BAC (the Bristol Aeroplane Company) and had taught local history in Norwich before entering the Courtauld Institute as a mature student, where he wrote his PhD dissertation under Pevsner.

More important than their training was their agreement on the central importance of the pre- and post-war achievements of the leaders of the pre-war Continental avant-garde, particularly Le Corbusier and Mies van der Rohe. Those from the AA would have encountered the work of Le Corbusier and might have heard him lecture at the AA or the RIBA on one of his post-war visits to London.[17] At Liverpool, too, the ideas of Le Corbusier were enthusiastically interpreted by Colin Rowe.[18] But others, like Peter Smithson, found their way to the work of the pre-war masters by less direct means.[19] At Newcastle Smithson had been especially captivated by Swedish architecture, and his final-year project had been a cemetery in the manner of Asplund. In the summer of 1948, at a time when travel outside the sterling area was still difficult, Smithson visited Scandinavia to see Asplund's work at first hand and also met Markelius and the Danish architects S.E. Rasmussen and Arne Jacobsen. But within a year, and perhaps prompted by a first encounter with real classicism at the Royal Academy school under Albert Richardson, Smithson discovered the work of Mies van der Rohe. Inoculated, as it were, against the

New Humanism by his earlier Swedish interests, he prepared a design for a new Fitzwilliam Museum in Cambridge in the modern classical manner of Mies. Fired by the discovery of Mies's Minerals and Metals Research Building of 1942 at the Illinois Institute of Technology (IIT) – covered extensively by the *Architects' Journal*[20] – and armed with a copy of Philip Johnson's 1947 book *Mies van der Rohe*,[21] Smithson was able to follow the drawings and the details to see how Mies made architecture out of the constituent structural and constructional elements of the building (Figure 5.1). This approach to architecture seemed to him to be charged with the same kind of unadorned reality to be found in the weapons and equipment that the younger generation had encountered in wartime in the services: the jeep, the Sten gun or the Bailey bridge.

Revaluing Mies van der Rohe: Hunstanton School, 1950–54

The sense of excitement at the rediscovery of architectural principles, of making a 'real' modern architecture, of enclosing space with the naked ease of Mies van der Rohe, is reflected in the Smithsons' entry for the Hunstanton School competition of the spring of 1950. Even at the time of its completion in 1954, the building seemed strikingly new. But in 1950, when Mies's American work was so little known in Britain, the Smithsons' design must have seemed yet more original still (Figure 5.2).

The announcement of the results of the Hunstanton School competition sparked little interest in the architectural press.[22] That two young, recently qualified architects should win was due in large measure to the fact that the sole assessor was Denis Clarke Hall, an architect with considerable experience of school design, winner of the 1937 News Chronicle School Competition, and someone with an established sympathy for modern architecture.[23] Of the fifty-six schemes submitted, Clarke Hall chose to commend three: the Smithsons' winning submission and two schools planned on the 'finger

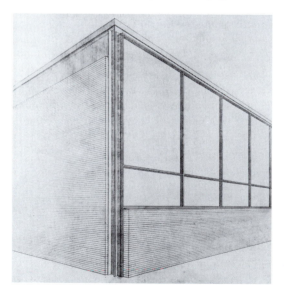

5.1 The first English publication of Mies van der Rohe's post-war work at the Illinois Institute of Technology: view of the corner of the administration building

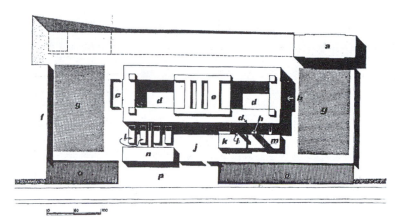

key
a, gymnasium and changing rooms.
b, caretaker's garden.
c, school garden.
d, green court.
e, main block.
f, 7 ft. high wall.
g, pitch.
h, water tower.
i, cycle sheds.
j, forecourt.
k, kitchen.
l, chimney.
m, adult housecraft.
n, workshops.
o, revetment.
p, car park.

i

ii

iii

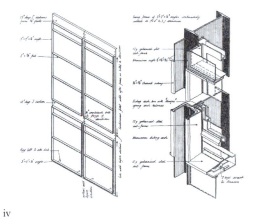

iv

5.2 Hunstanton School by Alison and Peter Smithson (1950–54): (i) site plan; (ii) exterior from the north-west; (iii) interior of the hall; (iv) construction details of the windows

plan' principle, which had become popular in the late 1940s.[24] The second placed entry, with its informal plan, long circulation routes and separation of the classrooms from the hall and dining rooms, was more typical of the approach to secondary school planning at the time than the compact formal plan of the Smithsons' entry. Planned around two open courts and the open volume of the hall and dining areas, the layout of the Smithsons' scheme was not a reversion to an older tradition of courtyard plans of the 1920s – which had given way to the open planning of the 1930s. Instead of grouping accommodation indiscriminately around a court, as in the 1920s, the Smithsons had succeeded by their systematic zoning of the principal teaching areas. Thus the classrooms were planned to face south with views across the site, while the craft rooms, which did not need a view, were placed on the northern, closed side of the site. The noisier workshops and the gymnasium were placed outside the main block altogether. Moreover, all the classrooms in the main block were placed at first-floor level, offering the advantage (at the cost of more, if shorter, staircases) of keeping all circulation, cloakroom, ancillary and administrative spaces on the ground floor.

The clarity of planning was matched by the directness of the architecture. The competition drawings, in the manner of Mies van der Rohe's drawings for IIT, were intended to show exactly what the building would look like, but architects in Britain still had too limited an understanding of Mies's work to appreciate how successfully the Smithsons had adapted his architectural vocabulary. The *Review* had almost ignored Mies's work in America,[25] and *Architectural Design* was hardly more generous in its coverage. Exceptionally, in July 1952, Mark Hartland Thomas reported from Chicago on Mies's current work and conveyed to British readers some of the qualities of his design approach, but this was the exception to the rule.[26] It would not be until the opening of the school in Hunstanton in September 1954, that the scale of the Smithsons' achievement was fully recognised.

The response was immediate. Philip Johnson, hailed by the *Review*'s editors as 'an American follower of Mies van der Rohe', introduced enthusiastically the *Review*'s coverage of the building. He judged it 'extraordinary' both as a school and as an interpretation of Mies:

> not only radical but good Mies van der Rohe. ... All the more credit to them for mastering and using the language so well –

in my opinion as well as anyone ever has on either side of the ocean, not excluding the midwesterners who have worked directly with Mies.[27]

A lengthy editorial, probably written by Banham, emphasised the 'ruthless' determination and the rigour with which the initial design had been translated into building. Mies, the 'master', had been known to 'cheat' to make his buildings look 'right', as in the corner detailing of the group of two-storey buildings at IIT in 1946 where an external metal cover section is placed over the fireproofing of the steel frame to suggest the true nature of the structure. By contrast, the Smithsons' building was praised for its absolute authenticity:

> At Hunstanton every element is truly what it appears to be, serving as necessary structure and necessary decoration. The brick panels in the end elevation are not only there to set off the glass visually, nor only to stiffen the frame – though that in Plastic Theory they must do. They were conceived from the very first, as were all the other elements, as performing structurally, functionally and decoratively as parts of an integrated architecture.[28]

The consequence of this direct form of building, as the *Review* acknowledged, was the need for a new level of control by the architect of every detail in order to anticipate the final appearance:

> This imposes an existential responsibility upon the architect for every brick laid, every joint welded, every panel offered up, for, apart from pipes laid in ducts (in the interests of maintenance and because a duct could serve to resist overturning moments), apart from these, literally every structural and functional element is visible, and, since there is nothing else to see, they are the totality of the architectural elements.[29]

With this new directness, the *Review* argued, it was inevitable that the nature of materials and the integrity of their surface would be revalued in a way that returned to the roots of the Modern Movement:

> There must be a new aesthetic of materials, which must be valued for the surfaces they have on delivery to the site – since paint is only used where structurally or functionally unavoidable – a valuation like that of the Dadaists, who accepted their materials 'as found', a valuation built into the Modern Movement by Moholy-Nagy at the Bauhaus.[30]

The local yellow gault brick, the standard steel sections, the bright handbasins, the elements of the Braithwaite water tower – familiar to anybody who travelled by rail[31] – the materials of Hunstanton were used 'as found' and, apart from the black painted steel frame, the colours of the building were those of the materials in their natural state.

The Smithsons claimed that the architecture of the Hunstanton School was shaped by a desire to build in the most direct and economical way possible.[32] At a conceptual level, this was reflected in the use of 'plastic theory', a new method of calculating the size of members, which made it possible to take account of form and configuration of a steel frame to give a leaner, more economical structure, a real consideration at a time of national steel shortage. At a more detailed level, this concern for directness and economy was evident in the way in which the windows were designed. Built on site to very fine tolerances, the details of the window construction were worked out by the Smithsons from a close reading of Mies's details. Such detailed design of a steel building in Britain was new, yet the Smithsons saw parallels with this approach and traditional ways of building. Like timber, they argued, steel was available in standard sections which could be bought 'off the peg' from any steel stock-holder, cut to length and welded into position:

> compare our system of building with medieval building; we are using steel in the same way as medieval builders used wood. They chamfered their wood and determined the positions of their pegs in order that their framing members should look well and contribute to the architecture of the building.[33]

This approach was the antithesis of the 'closed', prefabricated, industrialised system developed for the Hertfordshire schools and, the Smithsons claimed, more economical in its use of steel.

With such an ambitious first design, so different from the buttering and bodging of traditional wet construction still used by many mainstream modernists, it was inevitable that there would be occasional mistakes. The critics were quick to spot them. Johnson, for example, fastened on the difficulties caused by certain internal right-angled junctions between the main structural 'H' frames: 'In the main hall we have, for example, three different right-angle conditions in one room. Definitely not elegant!'[34] The editors of the *Architects' Journal* drew attention to the occasions where it was necessary to cut storey-high rebates in the brickwork with a carborundum wheel to ensure that the steel and the brickwork remained in the same plane, citing this as an example of formal considerations overriding the logic of transparency in construction.[35] Nor were the criticisms just about detail and construction. The Smithsons' formal design preoccupations were seen to take the upper hand, whatever Banham might later claim about the *je m'en foutiste* insouciance of Brutalists to mere formal issues. For architects who asserted that they saw 'architecture as the direct result of a way of life', it is ironic to see the footnote to the *Review*'s publication of Hunstanton: 'All the interiors were photographed without furniture, at the architect's request'.[36]

When it opened for the beginning of the new school year in autumn of 1954, Hunstanton School was billed in the *Architect and Building News* as the most remarkable school of the year, and the *Review* praised it as a building of radical novelty:

> The importance of the building is manifest at sight, and rests upon a radicalism, which becomes increasingly manifest upon inspection. This radicalism makes the building obtrusive, but it is a quality which has clear English precedent – as in the architects' namesake's work at Hardwick Hall, or in All Saints', Margaret Street. But it is here a radicalism which owes nothing to precedent, and everything to the inner mechanisms of the Modern Movement. It does not merely imply a special kind of plan or structure, but a peculiar ruthlessness – overriding gentlemen's agreements and routine solutions – which pervades the whole design from original conception to finished details.[37]

In its conception and execution the Hunstanton School was an impressive first reinterpretation by the new avant-garde of the ideas of the pre-war masters of the Modern Movement.

Homage to Le Corbusier: the Unité d'Habitation and the LCC slab blocks, 1950–57

Equally important to the exploration of the ideas of the pre-war masters was the widespread fascination with Le Corbusier's Unité d'Habitation at Marseilles and attempts to adapt his conception to English use. For Le Corbusier's admirers, to whom he was invariably 'Corbu',[38] the Unité represented more than just a contribution to the debate on housing. Towering above the sparsely developed suburbs to the south of Marseilles, with views of the mountains to one side and to the sea on the other, it had all the majesty of the great transatlantic ocean liners that Le Corbusier had used to suggest the massive scale of the utopian buildings in *La Ville Radieuse* (Figure 5.3). For the younger generation debating the direction of the 'New Architecture' it seemed not just a product of a modern mechanical age but

much more: a clear statement of the place of man in nature and a link back to the heroic traditions of a Mediterranean past.

Interest in the Unité was actively pursued by the newest recruits to the LCC's Housing Division. This interest ran counter to the prevailing enthusiasm for the New Humanism and contributed to the polarisation of attitudes between different generations of post-war modernists.[39] The different teams in the Housing Division working on different projects naturally developed different approaches: during 1951–55 the team working on the Ackroydon and Alton East estates were sympathetic to the New Humanism, while the group on the Bentham Road, Alton West and Loughborough Road estates were 'pro-Corbu'.[40] Personal reminiscences may emphasise the separate, almost tribal identity of these teams. But the differences between them reflected issues of principle, especially the strongly held views about the social role of architecture. Oliver Cox and A.R. Cleeve Barr and a number of the others working on the Ackroydon and Alton East estates had links to the Kenilworth Group, with whom they shared a commitment to the development of a modern architecture to serve society.[41] By contrast many of those working on the design of Bentham Road, Hackney, and the larger team working on Alton West at Roehampton were politically more pragmatic (though not necessarily right-wing), emphasising the need for an architecture independent of party political considerations and the importance of architectural and planning ideas for the transformation of society.

These divisions led easily to an identification, sometimes facile, of political attitudes with architectural values. The New Humanism and the enthusiasm for Swedish architecture was happily attacked as the 'People's Architecture', the architecture of social realism and hard-line communism, an equivalence famously celebrated in Stirling's vivid – if inaccurate – epithet 'William Morris was a Swede',[42] or in Banham's provocative account, 'Polemic before Khrushchev', of the impact of Khrushchev's redirection of the Communist Party's policy on those

i

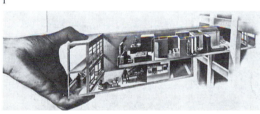

ii

5.3 Le Corbusier's Unité d'Habitation at Marseilles (1947–52): (i) general view; (ii) arrangement of the individual units

5.4 Maisonette block at the LCC's Bentham Road Estate (1951–56): the design prototype to demonstrate the use of the new deep-plan maisonettes to create a Unité-type 'slab block'

architects in the LCC who were card-carrying Party members.[43] Equally, this led to counter-charges that those opposed to the New Humanism were arrogant bourgeois revisionists or mere 'formalists', self-indulgently playing with architectural forms devoid of any social meaning.[44]

The value of the Unité d'Habitation as a paradigm for housing in London was caught up in these rivalries. Widely documented in Britain from the start of construction in 1947 in both the national architectural press and in student journals like *Plan*,[45] the Unité d'Habitation was presented simultaneously as the grand summation of thirty years of research on the form of collective housing and a universal solution to the problems of social housing. The building's progress was closely followed and keenly discussed. Despite the cost of travelling to Marseilles, the site was visited by students, who were thus familiar at first hand with the building and Corbu's innovative use of the Modulor and *béton brut*, the rough in-situ concrete used for the pilotis and the main structural frame.

The Unité also aroused fierce opposition. The vigour with which rival opinions were campaigned is suggested by an evening of discussion held by members of the LCC Housing Division in a pub in 1951.[46] The critics of Le Corbusier attacked the Unité for the primitive qualities of construction, others for its apparent lack of humanity. The most frequent accusation by those who believed that architecture should serve society was Le Corbusier's arrogance in seeking to impose such a complete but so arbitrarily derived a solution to the problems of mass housing: 'He is at fault when he suggests that it is the task of architecture to create a new way of life'.[47] Arguing that Le Corbusier proceeded on the basis of his own intuition alone, without the support of any social research, Cox and Barr reported darkly that 'in Moscow Le Corbusier is accused of Fascist tendencies'.[48]

A further sustained attack focused on the inappropriateness of a building like the Unité for London. The complications of combining Le Corbusier's ideas of a vertical garden city for a complete neighbourhood with the County of

London Plan's recommendations that housing be planned in 'mixed developments' was obvious. A conception as categorical as the Unité could only be adapted with difficulty to housing layouts that envisaged families living in houses on the ground and couples living in flats. To English eyes a combination of Unité flats and cottages ran the risk of creating resentments both for those in flats deprived of gardens and for those in houses overshadowed and overlooked by flats. Moreover even if the critics of the Unité allowed that these issues might be resolved by ingenious site planning, they still challenged the wisdom of such a deep plan and the prospect of a dark, damp *rue intérieure* in the cold and wet of northern Europe.

To the champions of Unité, the debate touched on fundamental questions of architecture and the city. It was not just about how to build housing in London but about the value of the work of the pre-war masters for the direction of the Modern Movement. The building was revered as the outcome of a triumphant struggle by Le Corbusier to sustain – and realise – a vision of the ideal form for living despite the seven changes of government, the three bankrupt main contractors and the myriad of other difficulties that had beset the project from the start. Drawing authority from the master's studies since the 1920s of housing and planning, Le Corbusier's defenders saw the Unité as promising to solve the central challenge of housing: to provide accommodation for individual families, large and small, and to bring these families together to form a community. This was to be achieved in a single building type, the basic building block for the new urbanism, that would meet all the immediate needs of the community for shops, nursery schooling, open space and other neighbourhood services. They argued that Le Corbusier, far from being arrogant, showed an extraordinary intuitive sensitivity to the needs of the typical family and the community of which it was a part. Here was a building that seemed to address at once both the pragmatic needs of everyday life and the larger issues at the heart of architecture.

For those familiar with the evolution of Le Corbusier's Citrohan house type, with its double-height living room and the sleeping/study balcony, the Unité was reassuringly familiar, an exemplary demonstration of the 'Engineers' Approach', the evolutionary refinement of a standard type celebrated in *Towards a New Architecture*.[49] Yet the different individual units assembled within the ordering frame of the Unité, like the bottles in a wine-rack, provided a wealth of dwelling type variations, from the single-person unit to flats capable of housing *familles nombreuses* with five children. The Unité offered a trenchantly simple solution to the problems of the neighbourhood, a real alternative to mixed-development projects with their separation of different kinds of families between different building types – houses for those with children and flats for those without. To those who criticised this form of housing as inhuman or unworkable for the British, with their inseparable attachment to the individual house and its garden, defenders of the Unité could point to advantages that everyone could appreciate. The Unité opened up the green space around the block, and it offered balconies, and with these the opportunity to throw open the individual dwelling to the outside world, to sun and view. Last but not least, it provided protected open areas for the neighbourhood on the roof. To English architects already wrestling to build even the most limited communal facilities with the straitened budgets of local authorities, the Unité appeared attractive because it offered so much more than mere housing. The provision of shops and services on the seventh floor and the protected play space, paddling pool, creche, running track and stage on the roof was firm evidence of Le Corbusier's claims to be addressing not just the questions of housing but the leisure and everyday pursuits of the community as well. Corbu's advocates were equally dismissive of charges that the deep section of the Unité would be unworkably dark in London's climate, pointing, by way of justification, to the success of the traditional London terrace house, with its narrow frontage and deep plan.

In town planning terms too, the Unité was an important counter-example to the form of development associated with the County of London Plan: the Picturesque suburban developments like the Ackroydon Estate or the New Humanism of the Lansbury Estate, Poplar. Corbu's admirers, like Sandy Wilson, writing in the *Observer*, denounced Lansbury as the architecture of 'cold feet' and of 'the fear of everything the architectural innovators of the last 25 years have offered us'.[50] By contrast, the Unité offered 'the grand scale of city life' necessary to the rebuilding of London and an escape from the cloyingly 'tasteful villages' like Lansbury with their 'pitched roofs, peephole windows and "folksy" details of the current Swedish revival'.

The LCC's younger architects promoted the Unité as a solution to London's housing and planning problems. But how to accomplish this within the limited provisions of the LCC's housing programme? It was clearly out of the question simply to build a Unité in London. The institutional and financial structure of local authority housing would not permit it. The most that could be done would be to build an interpretation of the Unité using the house types developed by a local housing authority such as the LCC. But how was this to be achieved? Even for Le Corbusier's most ardent admirers the task of adapting his vision for British use was daunting.

The starting point for a Unité-inspired block for the LCC had to be a new type plan for the individual dwelling.[51] Only by combining dwelling units with a narrower frontage and a deeper plan would it be possible to arrive at a 'slab block' bearing any resemblance to the Unité. For this there was no precedent in English housing practice at the time. The few modern blocks of flats, like Tecton's Spa Green or Powell and Moya's Churchill Gardens, were planned with staircase access, not the horizontal *rue intérieure* of the Unité. However, in 1950 the LCC's Housing Division was then engaged in the task of redesigning new type plans to replace those used during the 1940s by the Valuer,[52] though at this stage the new plan types were being developed in a form that could not be combined to create a block bearing any similarity to the Unité. Nevertheless, a small group sympathetic

to Le Corbusier's ideas – Peter Carter, Alan Colquhoun and Sandy Wilson – were assigned to develop a new maisonette plan. Offered the opportunity to use the new maisonette plan in the development of a site on Bentham Road, Hackney, the group reworked the earlier LCC maisonette plan type to suit a much deeper block (Figure 5.4). By using an internally ventilated bathroom, still something of an innovation, and by reducing the frontage to 12 ft, 3½ in. instead of the 15 feet for the standard maisonette plan, the group arrived at a new plan which could be used to create a deeper slab block with horizontal access.[53]

The results, tested in a prototype built at Purley in the summer of 1953, were very different from the basic dwelling unit of the Unité.[54] Within the LCC space standards it was impossible to provide the double-height living room of the original. Nor was it possible to plan a maisonette block with a *rue intérieure*. Instead access to the individual dwelling was to be provided from an up-to-date and much improved version of the old LCC access gallery, now serving the lower floor of each maisonette on every second floor. Fire escape was by means of a narrow balcony on the upper floor of each maisonette. Overall, the bulk of the building was much smaller than the Unité. Limited to two lifts and to a maximum of ten floors, the LCC blocks, with seventy-five units, were less than a quarter the size of the eighteen-floor Unité with 337 flats. Again, unlike the Unité, the LCC block could offer only a few different variants of the basic three bedroom unit. Following the principles of mixed development, the larger dwellings for families with children were planned in two-storey terrace houses on the same site, not as part of the slab block. Nor were there communal facilities of any kind within the LCC blocks. But for all these differences, the Bentham Road team were able to build a block of maisonettes which could legitimately claim direct decent from Le Corbusier's Unité.[55] For the first time, in place of the pre-war courts or the tower blocks of Swedish inspiration, here were two slab blocks raised above the ground on pilotis, offering views across London

of nature and sunshine. The site had been freed of building to provide a sculptural playground and enough open space for a typically English form of *loisir*, the game of neighbourhood football. The Unité d'Habitation had arrived in London, albeit in modified form. So too had some of the qualities of Le Corbusier's architecture. The new slabs had a formal clarity in the handling of the frame and massive pilotis of Doric proportions that echoed the structure of the Unité, unlike the smaller, spindly columns of Alton West. The distinction between the *béton brut* of the pilotis and the platform supporting the slab and the smooth pre-cast concrete of the slab's superstructure was an interpretation, wholly appropriate for English conditions, of the Unité's constructional logic. Bentham Road even managed to catch, as Banham wrote, some of the 'swagger' of the original Unité in Marseille.[56]

The blocks at Bentham Road established the viability of the Unité-inspired ten-storey slab block that was to be used by the LCC on a number of major developments during the

1950s and 1960s, notably at Alton West and Loughborough Road.[57] Perhaps the detailed design of the slabs on the later estates lack the raw strength of the prototype at Bentham Road, but the five slabs at Alton West, when viewed across the green sweep of rolling parkland, come closer to realising the vision of *La Ville Radieuse* – the belief that even in the city man should live with the benefits of nature – than any comparable development in Britain of the time (Figure 5.5).

The agenda of the new avant-garde: history and the Modern Movement

Both the Hunstanton school and the Bentham Road estate can be seen as part of a larger attempt to redraw the map of modernism, to rethink the direction of architecture at the time and to revalue the work of the pre-war masters. These buildings signal not just a simple rejection of the New Humanism but the engagement of the younger generation with the history of the Modern Movement and their attempts to define

5.5 Eleven-storey maisonette slab blocks at the Alton West Estate, Roehampton (1955–59). The layout of the six blocks across the mature parkland remains, despite the greatly reduced scale of the blocks, the most successful attempt in Britain to realise the ideal of Le Corbusier's *Ville Radieuse*

their position in relation to this. Banham's article in the *Review* introduced the New Brutalism in just these terms: 'The New Brutalism has to be seen against the background of the recent history of history, and, in particular, the growing sense of the inner history of the Modern Movement itself.'[58]

This history figured prominently in the discussions and publications. It is most obviously identified with the lectures by Banham at the ICA that would appear later as articles in the *Review* and were ultimately to form the chapters of *Theory and Design in the First Machine Age*.[59] But Banham's views were complemented by other interpretations of the development of the Modern Movement: at the ICA in 1954, for example, speakers as different as Lawrence Alloway and R. Furneaux Jordan contributed to a series of lectures on the 'Books of the Modern Movement' that examined key modernist texts, from Le Corbusier's *Towards a New Architecture* and Gertrude Stein's *Picasso*, to Roger Fry's *Vision and Design* and Herbert Read's *Art Now*.[60]

This interest in the history of the Modern Movement served not only to restate the continuum of interests of the new avant-garde with their precursors but also to establish a critical distance between the generations. In place of the older accounts offered by Pevsner in *Pioneers of the Modern Movement* and Giedion in *Space, Time and Architecture*, which had played a central role in legitimising the Modern Movement, now the discussion of the development of the Modern Movement no longer focused on legitimising the movement, but on its 'inner history'. The old and new histories shared much, but the new offered a more nuanced account of the development of the Modern Movement. The lecture series 'Books of the Modern Movement' and Banham's lectures, beginning with one on Futurism in early 1956, emphasised the diversity of avant-garde views, the different ways of understanding space and the changing interests in the machine and technology. The old unified view of modernism gave way to a frank recognition of the differences between De Stijl and Purism or the quarrels within the Bauhaus. The emphasis

was now on examining the credentials and achievements of those who had made modern architecture, on establishing the true succession of ideas and on weeding out those regarded as mere fellow travellers. Inevitably this was a process that tended to enhance the standing of old masters like Le Corbusier and Mies van der Rohe still further.

Equally important was the interest of the new avant-garde in the relationship between the Modern Movement and the great architectural traditions of the past. The pre-war masters had claimed continuity with an older architectural tradition as a measure of their own contemporary legitimacy. In *Towards a New Architecture* Le Corbusier had written passionately of his debt to Greece; Philip Johnson was emphatic about Mies van der Rohe's debt to Schinkel.[61] Following these examples and the lead given by contemporary essays, like Colin Rowe's 'The Mathematics of the Ideal Villa',[62] the younger generation discovered a new interest in architectural history. This was now to serve as a starting point for an approach to a modern architecture founded on principle, to provide a general guide to questions of design, composition and proportion free of the whimsy and arbitrariness of the New Empiricism. Banham's assessment of Rudolf Wittkower's *Architectural Principles in the Age of Humanism* (1949) illustrates the impact of new historical interpretations on 'a whole generation of post-war architects and students':

[Wittkower's book] is one of the phenomena of our time. Its exposition of a body of theory in which function and form were significantly linked by the objective laws governing the Cosmos (as Alberti and Palladio understood them) suddenly offered a way out of the doldrums of routine-functionalist abdications ... The effect of *Architectural Principles* has made it by far the most important contribution – for evil as well as good – by any historian to English Architecture since *Pioneers of the Modern Movement*.[63]

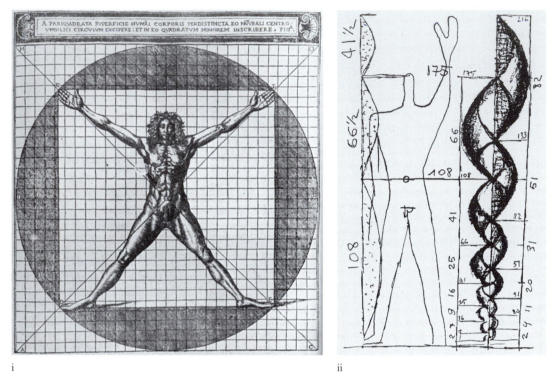

i   ii

5.6 Proportional systems and the human body: (i) Vitruvian Man from Cesarino's edition of Vitruvius, Como, 1521;
(ii) Le Corbusier's Modulor, 1948

History as principle rather than a quarry of possible forms might nevertheless be used pragmatically as a starting point for design. The Smithsons and others would eventually find the formality of classical planning to be inhibiting and formulaic, but in the early 1950s history seemed to offer a way of escaping from the confusion and lack of rigour so obviously visible at the Festival of Britain. In the planning of their Coventry Cathedral submission, the Smithsons explicitly claimed inspiration from the 'absolute, immutable, static and entirely lucid' geometry of the Renaissance. At Hunstanton, the formal, almost symmetrical planning might reflect both a view of classical composition inspired by Mies and an interest in Palladio; as Banham observed: 'neo-palladianism became the order of the day'.[64]

The interest in questions of dimension and proportion also underscored the continuity between the Modern Movement and the architectures of the past. For the new avant-garde the

study of proportional systems suggested a particularly fertile way of linking the principles thought to have been developed by Palladio with Le Corbusier's use of a system of proportions, the 'Modulor', in the design of the Unité (Figure 5.6). Conceived as a proportional and dimensional system related to the human body, the Modulor was first published in 1948.[65] Like the scale in music, Le Corbusier believed that the Modulor would provide a way of achieving a harmony through the use of a series of preferred dimensions derived from the mathematics of the golden section. The book had attracted universal interest when it was first published; even the *Review* was prompted to commission an article on the Modulor and the mathematics underpinning the concept of the golden mean from the mathematician Matila Ghyka.[66] The sustained fascination with the Modulor through the 1950s is evident from the articles on Le Corbusier's system and generally on proportional systems in modern architecture carried by journals as different as the *Architects' Yearbook* and *Plan*.[67] Some, like Peter Collins writing in the *Review*, remained sceptical of Le Corbusier's 'breathtaking ambitions'.[68] But more typical was the Independent Group's enthusiastic discussion of the topic at the ICA as part of the lecture series 'Aesthetic Problems of Contemporary Art'[69] and Wittkower's judgement of it as 'a fascinating attempt to co-ordinate tradition with our non-Euclidian world'.[70]

The use of the Modulor was also linked to the higher calling of the architect as one who could reveal in building the universal laws of nature. In an article in *Plan*, 'How to use the Modulor', which was prefaced by a photograph of the Unité under construction, Clive Entwhistle set out in ambitious terms his own view of the value of the Modulor:

> Measure–mensurate–'mens'–mentality–Menschen–mind–man. Mind is the symbol of man. Man is not merely the measure, but the measur*er*. Not in the linear sense only, but in the sense of constatation and comparison. In the sense of the appreciation of analogies: 'as above–so below'. It is this special ability that gives man, unlike his co-habitants of the planet, the possibility of self-development. It is thus his supreme function. By his appreciation of the relationship between the parts he can attain degrees of comprehension of the Whole.[71]

For the younger generation looking to the pre-war masters for direction, the discipline of the Modulor offered an approach of principle and a welcome release from the arbitrariness of the New Humanism. An article by Ruth Olitsky and John Voelcker, 'Form and Mathematics', conveys this excitement:

> It is seldom that chance timing in the publication of two books has been so fortunate as in the case of Dr Wittkower's *Architectural Principles in the Age of Humanism* and Le Corbusier's *Le Modulor*. Both books are concerned, broadly speaking, with interpretations of man's place in the physical universe. The first explicitly, through meticulous historical documentation; the second implicitly, through the development of a mind and an idea. Each book illuminates the significance of the other, and through them both it becomes possible to see the origins of many issues which are very much alive amongst architects at the present time.[72]

Olitsky and Voelcker's central conclusion is the continuity of a developing and active tradition which links Palladio to Le Corbusier and adapts to changes in cosmology. Like Wittkower, they saw Le Corbusier's Modulor as a recasting for a modern age of the understanding represented by the Renaissance's Vitruvian figure:

> A symbol reappears, transformed and enriched by 400 years of social revolution. L'Unité d'Habitation is without doubt the clearest expression to date of this symbol. In fact it would be true to say that the symbol would be meaningless without it and that is why it is cast into one of the building's walls.[73]

They applauded Le Corbusier's ability to adapt the Renaissance tradition to modern needs and to humanise a building as massive as the Unité and thus to make 'the physical universe … an intelligible place to live in'.[74] Like others of their generation their interest was fired by the links between Corbu's work and the classical tradition. For many contemporary architects the strength of this continuity gave legitimacy to modern architecture. Looking back on his days as a student in the late 1940s, James Gowan remembered sharing the same excitement: for students at that time a reading of *Towards a New Architecture* would have reinforced the conviction that the Modern Movement was attempting to recover the eternal values of architecture which had been obscured during the nineteenth century.[75]

The agenda of the new avant-garde: designing for a world of post-war plenty

To face the challenges of the post-war Britain, continuity with the past was not enough. A critical rereading of the past might help provide a sense of difference from the previous generation and suggest a starting point for something new, but the real concern of the new avant-garde was to confront the challenge of designing for the new post-war world. For some, like the Smithsons, this imperative might mean challenging the terms of continuity with the past and the traditional role of the architect.

By the early 1950s, the shortages and rationing of the 1940s had given way to economic expansion and a growing availability of consumer products, changes that were quickly recognised by designers and architects. These changes had commenced earlier in the prosperous United States than in war-torn Europe, but the effect was clearly felt in Britain. The war had ushered in dramatic changes in the way design was produced and consumed. Products were now designed, advertised, produced, distributed and sold in ways that were fundamentally different from the pre-war years and even the immediately post-war years. Gone were the days when someone like Ozenfant or Gropius was called on to design the bodywork for a Delage or an Adler. Ford's new Sedan and the new Plymouth Mercury were designed 'in house' by a team that linked the process of design through to production and sales (Figure 5.7). And what was true of the motor industry was true of other branches of manufacture.

The sense of living through a 'second machine age', which had superseded but not reversed the achievements of the first pre-war machine age, is enthusiastically spelt out in the introduction to Banham's *Theory and Design in the First Machine Age*, published in 1960, and very much a product of the debates that began in the Independent Group and around the ICA in the early 1950s:

5.7 Plymouth advertisement, 1955

This book was conceived and written in the late years of the Nineteen-fifties, an epoch that has variously been called the Jet Age, the Detergent Age, the Second Industrial Revolution. Almost any label that identifies anything worth identifying in this period will draw attention to some aspect of the transformation of science and technology, for these transformations have powerfully affected human life, and opened up new paths of choice in the ordering of our collective destiny ... Even a man who does not possess an electric razor is likely – in the Westernised world at least – to dispense some previously inconceivable product, such as an aerosol shaving cream, from an equally unprecedented pressurised container, and accept with equanimity the fact that he can afford to throw away, regularly, cutting edges that previous generations would have nursed for years ... we have already entered the Second Machine Age.[76]

How would the designer, the architect or the artist design for this second machine age? For Pevsner, writing before the war about the quality of design in England, it was the want of government action, of support for the Design in Industry Association or of some Werkbund-like organisation that had left English design so enfeebled when set beside what had been achieved in Germany.[77] Underpinning this judgement was the presumption that it was the duty of the educated designer to inculcate proper aesthetic and design standards, to wean the consumer from the adulterated taste of the market to which the manufacturer pandered. During the war, the opportunity for government action had been enormously increased, and taken. Government had sought out designers of ability to ensure that what was produced under its control was economical in conception, well designed and well made. The history of the government's utility furniture programme was one such example. Encouraged from the sidelines by journals like the *Review*, government had continued its sponsorship of good design after the war, and exhibitions of the best of British design like 'Britain Can Make It' and, of course, the Festival of Britain were the result.

But for a group with the iconoclastic preoccupations of the Independent Group, it was only natural to question this conception of design and the role of the designer. The intention of the Festival of Britain, with the exception of out-of-the-way exhibits as 'Black Eyes and Lemonade' at the Whitechapel Gallery, was seen as making available to 'the people' the 'good' design endorsed by an educated elite whose judgement of what was acceptable was the test for inclusion in the exhibition. To the younger avant-garde this stance was equally apparent in other pillars of British cultural life: in the role of the BBC, shaped by the Reithian ideal of public service; in the work of the newly formed Arts Council or the attempts by the Tate Gallery to champion the cause of modern art; in the claims by the *Review* to speak for the Modern Movement in Britain. The idea that popular culture and, by extension, the imagery of everyday life might constitute art or comprise direct inspiration for art was at odds with the didactic role of art and culture mapped out by these institutions.

To the younger generation the distinctions between high and low art were no longer clear cut. More familiar with different aspects of popular culture than their 'established' contemporaries, the members of the Independent Group took delight in the diversity and the strength of the images of popular culture, the magazines, science fiction, comics and those key symbols of consumer desirability, advertisements. To Lawrence Alloway the aesthetic standards set by the old elite, or by the American art critic Clement Greenberg, who dismissed popular art as kitsch, seemed hopelessly outdated:

> The elite, accustomed to set aesthetic standards, has found that it no longer possesses the power to dominate all aspects of art. It is in this situation that we need to consider the arts of the mass media. It is impossible to see them clearly within a code of aesthetics associated with minorities with pastoral and upper-class ideas because mass art is urban and democratic.[78]

Alloway called on artists and critics to expand contemporary understanding of the arts:

> Our definition of culture is being stretched beyond the fine-art limits imposed on it by Renaissance theory, and refers now increasingly to the whole complex of human activities. Within this definition a rejection of the mass produced art is not, as critics think, a defence of culture but an attack on it … The new role for the fine arts is to be one of the possible forms of communication in an expanding framework that also includes the mass arts.[79]

In architecture, too, old distinctions were challenged. By the mid 1950s the Smithsons were no longer concerned to find an alternative to the New Humanism but to create an architecture appropriate for this new world of post-war plenty, even if this meant breaking with the traditional definitions of the past:

> If Academicism can be defined as yesterday's answers to today's problems, then obviously the objectives and aesthetic techniques of a real architecture (or a real art) must be in constant change ... From individual buildings, disciplined on the whole by classical aesthetic techniques, we moved on to an examination of the *whole* problem of human associations and the relationship that building and community has to them. From this study has grown a completely new attitude and a non-classical aesthetic.
>
> Any discussion of Brutalism will miss the point if it does not take into account Brutalism's attempt to be objective about 'reality' – the cultural objectives of society, its urges, its techniques, and so on. Brutalism tries to face up to a mass-production society, and drag a rough poetry out of the confused and powerful forces which are at work. Up to now Brutalism has been discussed stylistically, whereas its essence is ethical.[80]

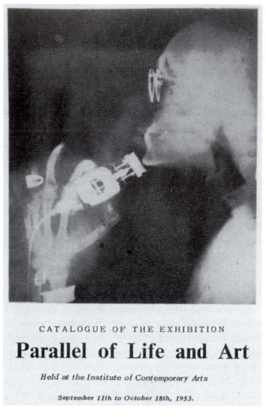

CATALOGUE OF THE EXHIBITION

Parallel of Life and Art

Held at the Institute of Contemporary Arts

September 11th to October 18th, 1953.

5.8 Cover of the catalogue to the 'Parallel of Life and Art' exhibition by Eduardo Paolozzi, Richard Hamilton and Alison and Peter Smithson at the ICA, 1953

One of the first manifestations of this determination to go beyond the traditional confines of art and the canon of modernism established by the founders of ICA was the exhibition 'Parallel of Life and Art', a collaboration between Eduardo Paolozzi Nigel Henderson, and Alison and Peter Smithson (Figure 5.8). Hung at the ICA in the late summer of 1953, the exhibition consisted of a hundred photographs of all kinds ranging from X-rays and microphotographs to landscapes and aerial photographs. Printed in such a way as to emphasise texture and grain, these photographs came to acquire a common identity and a strange and unpredictable emotional impact:

> 'Parallel' dealt almost exclusively in images drawn from anthropology and technology and, as objects to be exhibited in an art gallery ... they were a deliberate flouting, not only of conventional ideas of 'beauty', but also of the common concept of a 'good photograph'.[81]

Described as a 'locus classicus' of the new movement by Banham, the exhibition provoked an immediate and generally hostile reaction because of its denial of any conventional aesthetic of beauty.[82] But common to these photographs and to the architectural ideas of the Brutalists was the idea of abandoning established standards of beauty in pursuit of forms possessing the quality of 'image', a term interpreted by Banham as 'one of the most intractable and the most useful terms in contemporary aesthetics':

A great many things have been called 'an image' – S.M. della Consolazione at Todi, a painting by Jackson Pollack, the Lever Building, the 1954 Cadillac convertible, the roofscape of the Unité at Marseilles, any of the hundred photographs in *Parallel of Life and Art*. 'Image' seems to be a word that describes anything or nothing. Ultimately, however, it means something which is visually valuable, but not necessarily by the standards of classical aesthetics.[83]

The agenda of the new avant-garde: the machine aesthetic

One of the most potent sources of image in the new mass-production society was technology and the machine. Discussion of their importance for architecture and the arts figured prominently in the lectures and debates of the new avant-garde. For most the machine was no longer an abstract, remote or exceptional entity, as it might have been for the pre-war masters. Those who had served in the armed forces during the war would have been all too familiar with the up-to-date versions of the ships, planes and vehicles that had inspired the machine aesthetic of the 1920s. There was an awareness that access to machinery was far greater in the post-war years than ever before, even in Britain. On a day-to-day basis people relied more than ever on technology and machines, taking them for granted. The old fascination with the machine, the kind expressed by the Futurists, might live on, but in the Independent Group's debates there was also a recognition that the role of the machine in a mass-production society was different from that in the first machine age of the 1920s. The introduction to the catalogue of Richard Hamilton's 1955 exhibition 'Man, Machine and Motion' conveys something of this translation of feeling:

The relationship between man and machine is a kind of union. … This new affiliation, evoking much that is heroic and much that

is terrible, is with us, not only in the sky, but in every street where a boy joins magically with his motor-bicycle, his face whipped by the wind and stiffened by passion for which we have no name, like the machinery of motion, it is with us for all foreseeable time. It creates, as we watch, its own myth. The myth, the poetry, is needed: man has no other means of assimilating disruptive experience to the balanced fabric of thought and feeling.[84]

Photographs of Cooper Bristols and Mercedes racing cars with Carraciola or Stirling Moss 'up' expressed both the thrill and the danger of speed and something of the technical precision necessary to it.

But other photographs in the exhibition signalled a very different preoccupation. Far from remarking on technical issues, other photographs and captions commented on styling and the image of cars. The caption on the photograph of the Cadillac El Camino acknowledged that the consumer's response to the motor car had gone beyond a primitive Futurist excitement at the sheer pleasure of speed to an enjoyment of the car as status symbol and as a means of indulging fantasy:

The capsule chronicle of improving gear-change, from gloved grasp of massive lever to naked finger-touch on chrome plant-stem, is also a miniature history of the progress of automobile design from an approximate truce with mechanical forces to a pure creation of the human will – the driver no longer dresses for battle, but for the boudoir.[85]

Assisting Richard Hamilton with the exhibition was Reyner Banham, one of the leading voices in the discussion of the different ways in which machinery and technology might affect architecture and the arts. Hardly a driver himself, he nevertheless was no stranger to the Futurist thrill of movement and danger made available by the car,[86] but he recognised that in the post-war

i   ii

5.9 Cars of the first and second machine ages: (i) Delage 'Grand Sport'; (ii) Cadillac El Camino, 1954

world the role occupied by the machine was very different from that of the 1920s (Figure 5.9). In the article 'Machine Aesthetic', published in the *Review* in 1955, Banham argued that the most systematic statement of the old importance of the machine for architecture and the arts was to be found in *L'Esprit Nouveau* where Le Corbusier and Ozenfant advanced the proposition that 'objects of maximum utility and lowest price have simple geometrical shapes' and that these were entirely consonant with machine production and even with the forms of machines themselves.[87] Linking architecture with the machine at the time was, in Banham's view, plausible if not strictly logical:

> Nor – and this is the heart of the matter – was its falsity visible at the time, for automotive, aeronautical and naval design were currently going through a phase when their products did literally resemble those of Functionalist architecture. The Intelligent Observer, turning from one set of smooth simple shapes to the other, would see apparent and visible proof of the architect's claim to share the virtues of the engineer.[88]

This view of the machine aesthetic, however plausible in the early 1920s, could no longer be defended when the dictates of production engineering and sales began to determine form: 'The need to chase the customer led to the rapid evolution of an anti-purist but eye-catching vocabulary of design – which we now call Borax'.[89] After 1945 the old modernist view of the machine aesthetic ceased to be tenable:

After the second World War, in which a whole generation had been forced to familiarise themselves with machinery on its own terms, the disparity between the observable facts and the architects' Machine Aesthetic had become too obtrusive to be ignored. In the Jet Age these ideas of the 'twenties began to wear a very quaint and half-timbered look.[90]

The consequences of this new era of understanding were important. The task of the designer was no longer to translate the function of the car into form in the fashion of the supposedly innocent engineers of the 1920s, like the designers of the Lancia Lambda or the Bugatti Type 35. The designer was no longer answerable to simplifying assumptions about function but to the demands and tastes of the consumer. Now the designer was to appeal to popular taste, creating a car to enhance status, to suggest sex appeal or to create the illusion of boundless luxury or limitless power. The resulting forms, the splendidly sculptural chrome grille and fenders of the Buick Carlton de Luxe Convertible Sedan, or the dramatic tail fins of the Cadillac El Dorado, might be as fit a subject for iconographic analysis as the traditional high arts, like painting. But neither the modern car nor, to use Banham's term, 'Borax' provides the starting point for a new machine aesthetic applicable to architecture. With car designers changing designs season by season to play to the mood of the market, Banham argued that architecture could no longer afford to follow a visual code keyed to the automobile:

It is not merely that the car and the building are made of different materials, that one is mobile and the other static, but that the manner of consuming the two products is so different. Like the tree, the building is a long-standing investment. Compared with it the motor car is, like the fruit, a deciduous affair. Its season is the four or five year retooling cycle of the big manufacturers, and like the fruit it must have an appetizing exterior. In this situation Borax is entirely proper, though there are plenty of other design situations, notably architecture, in which it is grossly inappropriate.[91]

Banham concluded that the machine aesthetic was no longer sustainable in the terms in which Le Corbusier sought to embody it in the parallels between his buildings and the machinery and technology of the 1920s, like his Voisin car: 'The Machine Aesthetic is dead, and we salute its grave because of the magnificent architecture it produced, but we cannot afford to be sentimental over its passing.'[92]

But the passing of the old machine aesthetic of the first machine age of the pre-war years in no way lessened the importance of technology for a truly modern architecture. The machine played a central role in the new avant-garde. In addition to the Independent Group's own interest, sustained most obviously by Banham, the group invited speakers to talk on technological issues: in the first sessions in the summer of 1952 there were talks on the most recent jet aircraft by a designer from De Havilland and on the design of helicopters.[93] Nor were technical issues in architecture ignored. Theo Crosby at *Architectural Design* published articles by innovative engineers like Frank Newby, an occasional participant in Independent Group meetings, as well as surveys of current building technology based on US experience such as curtain walling, as a way of keeping the British avant-garde abreast of technical developments abroad.[94]

For Banham this interest in new technology was crucial if the Modern Movement was to retain its claim to modernity, although he recognised that architecture and technology might no longer be as compatible as they had been before. He wanted to alert architects not only to the technological differences between the 1920s and '30s and the 1950s, but to the need to keep up with engineers as the machine became an ever more pervasive force in society:

It may well be that what we have hitherto understood as architecture, and what we are beginning to understand of technology are incompatible disciplines. The architect who proposes to run with technology knows now that he will be in fast company, and that, in order to keep up, he may have to emulate the Futurists and discard his whole cultural load, including the professional garments by which he is recognised as an architect. If, on the other hand, he decides not to do this, he may find that a technological culture has decided to go on without him.[95]

Yet the architectural responses of the British avant-garde to the challenges of the second machine age remained uncertain. True, Bentham Road and Alton West had been built in pre-cast concrete with elements prefabricated on site, and Hunstanton had a steel frame designed using Plastic Theory. But the architecture of New Brutalism could not be presented as technologically sophisticated. More worrying was the response of the old masters themselves to technical progress. Despite the emphasis on making architecture out of structure and materials, Mies's use of structure remained conservative, searching for greater architectural refinement within a very narrow register of technical choice. Corbu's response was even more regressive. Working with the primitive qualities of reinforced concrete could be welcomed in Chandigarh as an appropriate response to conditions in the building industry in India. But could this same approach be defended in France, where the modernisation of the technology of building was proceeding apace?[96] Some might insist that Corbu's pursuit of architecture looked beyond the local accidents of technique to the loftier tasks of architecture. To address in a single building the problems of dwelling, community and the city as had Le Corbusier at Marseilles, was regarded by his supporters as already enough; to expect technical innovation as well was too much.

But some of Corbu's staunchest admirers remained troubled. They found that his mid-1950s buildings lacked the engagement with a mass-production society and the current technology that had been so exciting in his buildings of the 1920s and 1930s. Comparing the villa at Garches (1927) with the recently completed Maisons Jaoul, James Stirling voiced this regret:

> Garches is an excellent example of Le Corbusier's particular interpretation of the machine aesthetic … while Garches is not the product of any high-powered mechanisation, the whole spirit of the building expresses the essence of machine-power … There is no reference to any aspect of the machine at Jaoul either in construction or aesthetic. These houses … are being built by Algerian labourers equipped with ladders, hammers and nails, and with the exception of the glass no synthetic materials are being used; technologically, they make no advance on medieval building.[97]

The lack of engagement with modern technology robbed the Maisons Jaoul of the claim to be in the van of progress which had been one of the great qualities of Garches. While Garches promised liberation to a modern utopia, Stirling found the Maisons Jaoul 'almost cosy' and clearly intended for the status quo.

Who then could demonstrate how to marry architecture with the new technology? The work of architects in Britain involving new forms of construction was studiously ignored by the new avant-garde. For a group that talked with excitement both about the application of 'Borax' to American cars and kitchens and about the unadorned qualities of the high technology used in jet planes and racing cars, the prefabricated houses of the austerity years were irrelevant. The Hertfordshire schools, billed by some as harbingers of a new aesthetic, were passed by without reference.

The work of Charles and Ray Eames, little known in Britain in the mid-1950s, did attract the interest of the Independent Group. Banham recalled the excitement of encountering Charles's work, particularly the Eames chair and the Eames House, for the first time in 1949 in the Californian journal *Arts and Architecture*.[98] Geoffrey Holroyd, an occasional participant in the debates at the ICA, had visited the Eames House in the summer of 1953.[99] Frank Newby wrote an article about it in *Architectural Design* in 1954.[100] The Eames film *Communications Primer* was shown at the ICA in 1955.[101] Eames's use of the new means of bending plywood sheets to form three-dimensional curves, adapted from the technology of aircraft production, was known in Britain through the furniture he had designed with Eero Saarinen.[102] So too was the polemical force of the elegant assembly of material readily available from steel merchants to build his own house. But despite Eames's standing as an industrial designer this work failed to win him widespread recognition amongst the British avant-garde as an architect keeping up with the new technology.

More so than Eames, it was the eccentric figure of Richard Buckminster Fuller, the self-proclaimed 'comprehensive designer', who attracted the interest of the group.[103] Known as much for the streamlined Dymaxion Car – a telling point in a group interested in motor cars – as the Dymaxion House, his war-time minimal housing inspired by corrugated metal grain-bins and, above all, for his geodesic domes, Buckminster Fuller was forgiven his relentless self-promotion, his idiosyncratic English and what even his keenest supporters acknowledged as 'design myopia', because he could contrive the appearance of being at ease in the world of the engineer (Figure 5.10). Small matter that the architectural qualities of his work, particularly the cross collision of conservative furnishings and

5.10 A Marine Corps helicopter transporting one of Buckminster Fuller's geodesic domes

geodesic geometry in the interiors of his domestic domes, was a source of enduring embarrassment to his defenders. Photographed against images of a lightweight magnesium dome being airlifted into position by a Marine Corps helicopter, here was a man who could be presented as being at the cutting edge of the new technology, someone Banham could use to prod architects into thinking inventively about the possibilities of the second machine age.[104]

From theory to practice: competitions and projects of the mid-1950s

In 1955 the only indisputably Brutalist building was Hunstanton School and that had been designed in 1949, before the formation of the Independent Group, and long before the 'ethic or aesthetic' of the New Brutalism had been coined. But, although the editors of *Architectural Design* were still bemoaning as late as 1957 the absence of any further explicitly Brutalist buildings,[105] there were by the end of 1956 a number of buildings and projects that served to define the changing position of the new architectural avant-garde. Bentham Road had been followed by Loughborough Road (1954–57) and Alton West (1955–59) as demonstrations by the younger generation of the way to adapt the ideas of the pre-war masters. Various competition entries likewise provided an important means of exploring new ideas. Two of the most important competitions of the early 1950s were those for the rebuilding of Golden Lane on the edge of the City of London, announced in March 1952, and the expansion of Sheffield University, judged in November 1953. Both attracted an enthusiastic response from the new avant-garde.

The Smithsons' Golden Lane competition entry offers evidence not only of the way in which their work was evolving after Hunstanton, but also of the difference between their work and that of the older generation of modernists.[106] The competition attracted interest and a large number of entries because it focused on the problems of high-density housing. The brief called for housing for 400 inhabitants at 220 people per acre, the highest density recommended by the County of London Plan. The site was small, with no obviously interesting prospect. The winning scheme by Geoffrey Powell exemplifies the new orthodoxy: praised for its village-like character, the accommodation was to be divided into different types of dwellings, ranging from one-room to three-room flats in one twelve-storey block to three-room and four-room maisonettes in four-storey blocks (Figure 5.11). Powell used the different blocks of this mixed development to create an urban landscape centred on a piazza and in keeping with the grain of the surrounding city. But for all the skill brought to the layout of the scheme, the architecture of the winning entry remains diagrammatic. Looking at the bland elevations and uninformative perspective, it is easy to

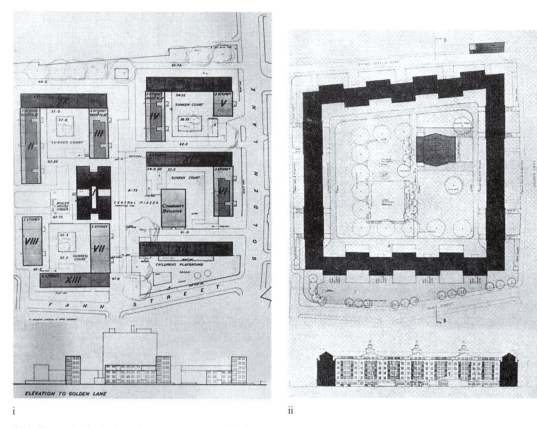

5.11 Entry for the Golden Lane competition: (i) the winning entry by Chamberlain, Powell and Bon; (ii) unplaced scheme by Gregory Jones

imagine the whole designed in the competent but unexceptionable manner of Churchill Gardens.

The schemes placed second and third displayed the same competence in organisation and layout and the same bland modern architecture. But the scheme placed fourth, designed by David Gregory Jones, a communist member of the LCC's Housing Division, was different both formally and in its approach to planning: the accommodation was placed in a single six-storey court running round the perimeter of the site to enclose the whole space. This relatively low building, which fitted well with the scale of the surrounding neighbourhood, was designed with pitched roofs and load-bearing masonry. The overall effect and the details, for example the spires over the access stairs, were reminiscent of some of the more

conservative Swedish architecture. Here was an example of the 'people's architecture' urged by the hard left and despised by Corbu's admirers as 'Commisars' Tudorbethan'.

The contrast between these schemes and the Smithsons' entry could not have been sharper (Figure 5.12). The *Architects' Journal* singled out the Smithsons' entry as designed by 'extremists – in the sense that Corbusier is an extremist in his design for the well-known flats at Marseilles'.[107] The Smithsons took as their starting point not the Unité but an earlier project by Le Corbusier for the rebuilding of Ilot Insalubre No. 6, an area of run-down, high-density housing in eastern Paris. In this project Le Corbusier assembled the individual dwellings in a wall of housing which was in places as high as sixteen storeys and in

 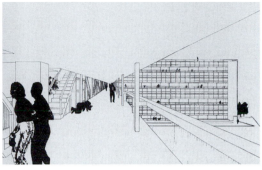

i   ii

5.12 Entry for the Golden Lane competition by Alison and Peter Smithson: (i) collage showing partial elevation; (ii) view along high-level street

which access to each dwelling was from a number of pedestrian routes that ran either down the centre or along the outside of the blocks they served. Developing this idea, the Smithsons proposed a layout based on a system of pedestrian decks at ground and upper levels crossing the site, linked at ground level to the surrounding streets. On this system of routes they planned a sixteen-storey wall of housing which, as in Le Corbusier's project, would follow the routes to enclose – in the manner later explored at Park Hill, Sheffield – large-scale spaces that might be put to grass, be planted with trees or house the playground and community building for the neighbourhood. The plans of the individual units were ingenious: designed to the space standards of the *Housing Manual 1949*, most were provided with a high-level 'yard' or private open space which owed its inspiration not only to Le Corbusier but to the Smithsons' encounters with the patterns of life in the East End. The brutal, no-nonsense aesthetic of the block, vividly conveyed in the combination of sketchy drawing and collage that illustrated the scheme, had something of the scale of the Unité and the same sculptural use of elements on the roof. It was also matched by a formal quality that the Smithsons claimed reflected the gritty reality of working-class life in London, as based on research with Nigel Henderson and his wife, Judith, a sociologist working in Bethnal Green.[108] The Smithsons envisaged for this project the same 'as found' use of materials – vitreous-enamel wall

panels and reinforced concrete frame – as at Hunstanton, but the composition was conceived in entirely different terms. Gone was the Palladian formality of Hunstanton. The Golden Lane project was instead a step towards the 'topological' freedom of Sheffield, a response to the characteristics and the context of the site, the pattern of the existing streets, the grain and scale of the surrounding city.

In the declamatory style of the avant-garde manifesto, almost an English parody of Le Corbusier's *La Ville Radieuse*, the Smithsons set out their claim to recover, in modern form, the structure of traditional working-class living. The tough exterior of the building, clad in stove-enamelled steel sheeting, 'like Mazawattee Tea and Stephens Ink advertisements', was to be the architectural parallel to the non-rhetorical form of architecture necessary for urban buildings. With people moving along the decks, following their hobbies and their interests in their garden yards, the Smithsons believed that the building would recover the liveliness of working-class areas where

> the vital relationship between the house and the street survives, children run about, (the street is comparatively quiet), people stop and talk, dismantled vehicles are parked: in the back gardens are pigeons and ferrets and the shops are round the corner: you know the milkman, *you* are outside *your* house in *your* street.[109]

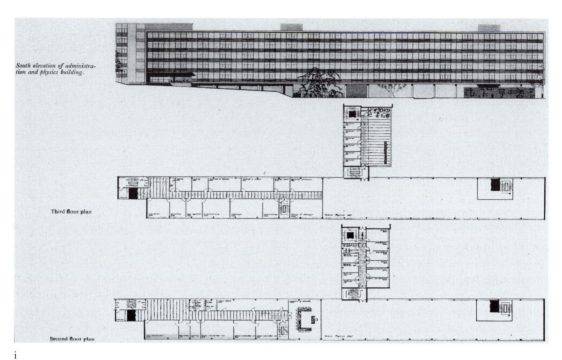

South elevation of administration and physics building.

Third floor plan

Second floor plan

i

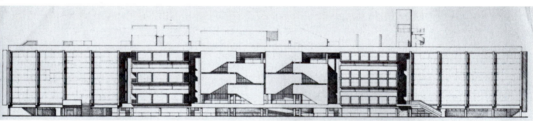

ii

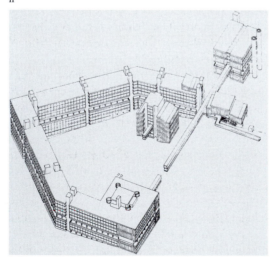

iii

5.13 Entries for the Sheffield University Extension Scheme competition, 1953: (i) the winning scheme by Gollins Melvin Ward; (ii) elevation of the entry by James Stirling; (iii) axonometric of the Smithsons' entry

The Smithsons had looked to the recent work of Le Corbusier, but their ideas for reshaping the fabric of the city already contained a critique of the ideas of the older generation whose values still dominated the CIAM debates. At Golden Lane the Smithsons were looking beyond the design of the individual building to the city as a whole. They were already drawing up the agenda that would form the basis for their contribution to Team X.

In the entries submitted for the Sheffield University competition the contrast between the work of the new avant-garde and the mainstream modernism of the older generation was quite as visible as it was at Golden Lane (Figure 5.13).[110] The jury had been chosen carefully, balancing the non-radical modernism of F.R.S. Yorke with the professional establishment values of Percy Thomas and the pragmatism of Gerard Young, Pro-Chancellor of the university. The winning project by Gollins Melvin Ward, a reinforced frame hidden behind bland glazed elevations, has much of the same accomplished planning and architectural neutrality of the winning scheme at Golden Lane and was damned with faint praise as 'routine functionalism' by critics as different as J.M. Richards and Banham.[111]

The submission by the Smithsons struck a very different note. It took even further the move from the classical conception of Hunstanton which had begun at Golden Lane. The entry, classed by Banham as the architectural project that best captured the 'threat' and the 'promise' of the exhibition 'Parallel of Life and Art', was conceived as a long block cranked to fit around and join the existing buildings of the university by means of a series of upper-level walkways linked to the 'street in the air' midway up the height of the new block. Designed as a continuous 'extrusion' interrupted at regular intervals by elements holding stairs, lifts and services, this linear building was to be built with a reinforced concrete frame and was to contrast with the specific geometry of the blocks housing the lecture rooms. The tough take-it-or-leave-it quality of the whole was likened by Banham to the no-frills industrial but sculptural qualities of Owen Williams' Dry Processing Plant for Boots at Nottingham (1931). Banham was later to judge this project, which owed little or nothing to precedent, as a potent example of an architectural order that was as 'other' as the paintings of Jackson Pollock.[112]

The Smithsons' Sheffield University project may be the closest architecture ever came to matching the ideals of the New Brutalism. However, the entry by James Stirling also deserves attention, not least for the way it illustrates the new avant-garde's explorations of the ideas and themes of Le Corbusier. Stirling's scheme was conceived as a number of separate blocks, each of which was handled differently, yet all in a manner derived from Le Corbusier. The administration, physics, art and architecture building, the largest building, was designed as a six-storey block raised above the ground on pilotis, crowned with a top floor conceived in the same sculptural terms as the Unité, and by virtue of its length having something of the same massive presence as the Unité. Planned as a heroic frame building, it had the added formal interest of needing to house not just one type of space but a variety of different types of accommodation, from staff rooms and offices to lecture rooms, which are clearly articulated each in their own terms within the discipline of the frame. This play with the character of the different spaces, particularly the sculptural qualities of the lecture rooms, goes back beyond Stirling's interest in Le Corbusier to an admiration for the work of Russian Constructivists and to Konstantin Melnikov's Workers' Clubhouse of 1926. But Stirling also explained these forms in terms of a fascination with the positive forms of space, an idea that he had come upon in the analyses of Renaissance buildings carried out by Luigi Moretti using plaster casts of their internal spaces and published in the Italian magazine *Spazio*.[113] For Stirling the task at Sheffield was to convey the overall hierarchical order of the volumes defined in this way within the discipline of a structural and constructional system appropriate to the particular building.

The order of the building established in this way created a rich contrast between the heavily sculptured forms of the auditoria and the blandness of the offices, while the rhythm of the structure and the explicit nature of the circulation routes provided an overall order that was immediately recognisable. This was, however, adapted, as with the staircase through to the circulation spine on the first floor, to the particular circumstances of the site. Designed in *béton brut*, apart from the white painted smooth-concrete beams at roof and first-floor level, the overall impression would have been of a building that

i

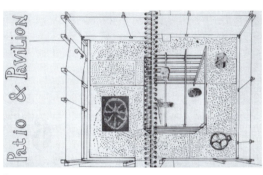

ii

5.14 The 'This is Tomorrow' exhibition at the ICA, 1956: (i) Group 1 assembling their exhibit, 'Robby the Robot'; (ii) the 'Patio and Pavilion' by Group 6

was more like a ship than the stripped classicism of the university's existing buildings, an impression heightened by Stirling's 'take it or leave it' comments on the way in which the 'aggressive' forms of the building might easily accommodate the consequences of weathering: 'like rust on a battleship'.[114]

Stirling's Sheffield scheme suggests more powerfully than the different variants of the LCC maisonette blocks the way in which the younger English avant-garde architects were prepared to incorporate the ideas of Le Corbusier. With themes drawn from the Unité, from the Villa at Carthage, perhaps from Le Corbusier's work at Chandigarh, Stirling showed how much invention and freedom this younger generation could draw from the pre-war masters. The outcome looked very different from the work of the preceding generation. Stirling's entry has no obvious similarities with the Smithsons' scheme. But set side by side with the winning entry, the schemes of the younger architects appear to share the same aggressive rejection of routine modernism and what were fast becoming the conventional compositional rules of the modern architecture: reinforced concrete, clearly expressed and clad with elevations which were

generally heavily glazed to emphasise the essential modernist distinction between enclosing walls and structure.

The new avant-garde by the mid-1950s

Projects by individual architects, the Smithsons' House of the Future and the Sugden House, continued into the late 1950s to reflect the issues discussed by the Independent Group. But the last collective expression of the range of interests and explorations driven by interests and explorations of the new avant-garde during the early 1950s was the exhibition 'This is Tomorrow', which opened in the summer of 1956.[115]

The idea of an exhibition that would show the work of painters, sculptors and architects originated with an invitation from the French group La Groupe Espace to the ICA in 1953. Asked to respond on behalf of the Institute, Leslie Martin contacted Sandy Wilson, who had raised the possibility of a project with other members of the Independent Group. Though the Groupe Espace proposal was turned down, it was the starting point for plans for an exhibition involving collaboration of the arts and architecture. By 1955 the idea had been taken over by Theo

Crosby, whose organising talents had secured the Whitechapel Gallery as a venue and the promise of collaboration of a number of artists and architects. They were to work together in small groups of painters, sculptors and architects, with each group producing independently an exhibit, like the stalls of market traders at an open-air market.

The exhibition opened in the August of 1956 and attracted public interest, not least because of Lawrence Alloway's promotion of the exhibition to the press, radio, television and newsreels, who gratefully recorded any interpretations of an exhibition that left most people bemused, if intrigued (Figure 5.14). Indeed, for all its impact and its later historical importance as one of the stepping stones to the world of Pop Art, most contemporaries found it difficult to establish the significance of the exhibition, particularly for the future of architecture. The catalogue, which opened with a demonstration of Ed Wright's new typography, did little to dispel the confusion, with its three introductions, written by Lawrence Alloway, Reyner Banham and David Lewis, that offered three different accounts of what the visitor was about to experience.

Banham's poem 'Marriage of Two Minds', written as a dialectic account of the development of the Modern Movement, presented cybernetics, Jackson Pollock and the acronyms 'RTP TNP IBM PMI PLM PSI ESP EEG ARB IOJ NPL ZDA' as the direct continuation of developments that had started with Pevsner's *Pioneers of Modern Design* at the turn of the century. Lewis returned to the certitudes of pre-war modernism, to the search for a constant and unchanging ideal to be discovered through the integration of architecture and the arts, as imagined by Mondrian, Malevich, Moholy-Nagy and other heroic figures of the 1920s:

Some of us, in our generation, recognise the need to move towards a wider and fundamentally different kind of inclusiveness – an integration of men closer in spirit to the aim of Mondrian and of the Bauhaus, but bearing the character of the present.[116]

Alloway struck a very different note, returning to themes familiar to the Independent Group and visible in the installations of groups 2, 6 and 12, and perhaps in those of groups 1, 8 and 10. He stressed the break with past views of modernism and affirmed the aims of the exhibition itself:

Early modern art is full of theories concerning the integration of the arts, with realisation of the ideals scheduled for another time. But yesterday's tomorrow is not today–and the ideal of symbiotic art architecture has not been achieved.[117]

Nor did he hold any hope of achieving the integration envisaged by Lewis. The collaboration between the artists and architects of the different groups was no more than 'antagonistic co-operation' remote from the ideals of the Bauhaus or the Arts and Crafts movement, which were falsely derived from 'a rosy fiction of the middle ages'. Far from seeing unity, Alloway insisted on the different character of the different groups in the exhibition: 'the independent competing groups do not agree on any universal design principles'. The exhibition was about opening up the field of art, recovering the sense of excitement of the 1930s and inviting the spectator, now the consumer, to play his part in making sense of a new array of products which might or might not be art:

An exhibition like this is, on the contrary, a lesson in spectatorship, which cuts across the learned responses of conventional perception. In This is Tomorrow the visitor is exposed to space effects, play with signs, a wide range of materials and structure, which, taken together, make of art and architecture a many-channelled activity, as factual and far from ideal standards as the street outside.[118]

Gone were the old roles of artist and spectator. Information theory and cybernetic learning processes provided the models for understanding the exhibits:

The freedom of the artist and architects concerned is communicated to the spectator who cannot rely on the learned responses called up by a picture in a frame, a house in a street, words on a page. As he circulates the visitor will have to adjust to the character of the exhibit (a walk through four cubes versus the sight of human symbols in a pavilion, and so on). This is a reminder of the responsibility of the spectator in the reception and interpretation of the many messages in the communication network of the whole exhibition.[119]

The differences in Lewis's and Alloway's introductions were as visible in the work of the different exhibition groups. Banham's review of the exhibition for the *Architects' Journal* captured the diversity:

What has come up is, roughly speaking, a range of graded possibilities between two seemingly irreconcilable extremes. Both extremes are to be seen in the big picture above … In the foreground … you see brickie A.J.A. Canning building a wall designed by architect John Weeks and painter Adrian Heath. The set up is as the Masters of the Modern Movement envisaged it. Architect and painter have settled for a simple rectangular aesthetic on a concrete-block module, and so completely sunk their personalities that execution can be left to a third party. Their contribution ended with the beautifully precise course-by-course drawings, showing variations in bond, the departures from the straight and narrow, which Canning had to follow. A tidy, unassuming, cerebral, minimal attempt to find a noblest common denominator for constructive art.[120]

This he contrasts with the exhibit constructed by Hamilton, John McHale and 'lady-brutalist' Magda Cordell:

If their [Weeks and Heath's] contribution is the leastest, what goes on in the background of the picture is the mostest … This section has optical illusions, ultra-violet light, Cinemascope, recorded sound, squashy floors, collage, science-fiction, van Gogh, topology, expanded metal, a juke box … and a general desire to smash down all barriers, prise open all watertight conventions, and get ideas and sensory responses on the move.[121]

The work of some individual groups was memorable: the exuberance of the Hamilton, McHale and Voelcker installation, with the outsize image of Robby the Robot carrying off the dumb blonde of American (and British) fantasy. The enigmatic assemblage of objects in the 'Patio and Pavilion' assembled by Paolozzi, Henderson and the Smithsons has prompted extended discussion both at the time and subsequently.[122] The former exhibit, identified in the catalogue with Hamilton's collage *What is it that makes Today's Homes so Different, so Appealing?*, with its representation of products, advertisements, mass production and throw-away consumer society, stands in obvious contrast to the latter, described in the catalogue as the symbolic representation of 'the fundamental necessities of the human habitat'. The objects and images in this exhibit may have been dismissed by Sandy Wilson as no more than a 'collection of ludicrously antediluvian objects',[123] but the exhibit, like the 'Parallel of Life and Art' exhibition before it, had disconcerting resonances both with the banal present, the garden sheds of early 1950s Britain, and the remote values of primitive societies. The objects representing the fundamental necessities – the head ('for man himself – his brain and his machines'), the wheel and aeroplane, the frog and the dog and the other 'antediluvian' objects – might appear to be associated with some unknowable rite, like the objects discovered at the excavation of a setting for some forgotten ritual. They fascinate but their meaning is obscure.

Whatever the significance of the individual exhibits, 'This is Tomorrow' held limited importance for the direction of architecture, even for the members of the new avant-garde. For those who had taken part in the debates and meetings of the Independent Group, the exhibition provided a final opportunity for a collaborative re-enactment of the group's interests, a valedictory celebration of the themes that had been discussed over the five years of fertile, if antagonistic, cooperation. The Independent Group had ceased to meet in the summer of 1955. 'This is Tomorrow' marked the end of the group's collective activity. But if the group no longer met, several of the more lasting ideas that it debated were now to be developed and applied in the work of individual members of the new avant-garde.

By the end of 1955, the clues to the future direction of modern architecture in Britain were already there for those who knew where to look. The work of Le Corbusier continued to fascinate: the buildings at Chandigarh were studied and admired, but however beautiful they were they seemed remote. More immediately relevant to English interests were the Maisons Jaoul, whose simple materials of brick, reinforced concrete, wood and glass seemed ideally suited to adaption for British use. Though it is easier to see it now, with hindsight, the work of the young avant-garde – whether for the practices in which they worked or (more rarely) on their own account – was establishing a new approach. At Lyons Israel and Ellis, James Stirling was launching a new practice with James Gowan, while Alan Colquhoun and John Miller were working on buildings like the Old Vic and the Regent Street Polytechnic. Bill Howell and the other members of the group who were soon to form Howell, Killick, Patridge and Amis were just starting construction at Alton West of the Le Corbusier-inspired slab blocks and were designing their own domesticated English Brutalist town houses in Hampstead. Sandy Wilson had just finished the design of a different version of the LCC's slab blocks. Voelcker was at work on designing a house for the jazz musician Humphrey Lyttleton. The Smithsons were soon to start on the design of the Economist Building. Taken together, these designs showed a sufficient

number of characteristics in common – a concern with the explicit logic of structure, the direct expression of materials and function – to make it possible to talk of a new emerging style.

This sense of a common approach was reinforced by the way the architectural press responded to their work, publishing photographs, drawings and column inches of critical comment. By 1955 *Architectural Design* was under the editorial control of Theo Crosby, and at the *Review* the influence of Richards was being balanced by the energies of Reyner Banham. In the *Review* Richards and Gordon Cullen still inveighed against public and official indifference to architecture and the design of towns and cities. 'Townscape' continued to rail against the failure of planning to maintain the best qualities of the British tradition of town building; Richards attacked the opportunities lost in rebuilding the City of London. The   *Review's* annual

5.15 The Department of Engineering, Leicester University, by James Stirling and James Gowan (1960–63)

'Preview' of work to be built, published from 1954, shows clearly that the older generation were building more than ever, though much of the new work failed to match the quality of their own earlier buildings. Their work might still be published, handsomely illustrated and judiciously reviewed, but cumulatively the older generation, those who had led the debate in the late 1940s, no longer had the weight or the critical edge to retain the leadership that was now passing to the younger avant-garde.

After 1955, promoted by a sympathetic press, the direction of the new architecture seemed set (Figure 5.15). For those familiar with the developments of the mid-1950s, the achievements of the late 1950s and the early 1960s, such as the flats at Ham Common, the Engineering Building at Leicester, the Gonville and Caius Hostel at Cambridge, even the little lecture room built at the Department of Architecture not far away, should have come as no great surprise. They can be readily seen as a realisation and exploration of ideas debated during the early 1950s in the loosely constituted circles around the Independent Group.

Notes

1 'The New Brutalism', *AD*, Jan. 1955, p. 1.

2 In the early 1950s the Smithsons' knowledge of Japan and Japanese architecture was still limited, they were first to visit Japan in 1960. See A. and P. Smithson, *Architecture without Rhetoric*, London, Latimer New Dimensions, 1973.

3 'New Brutalism', p. 1.

4 *Ibid.*

5 R. Banham, 'The New Brutalism', *AR*, Dec. 1955, pp. 355–61.

6 Banham has a natural claim to be the historian of the New Brutalism, not least because of his book *The New Brutalism: Ethic or Aesthetic?*, London, Architectural Press, 1966, but others have taken a different view of the balance of invention and influence in New Brutalist circles, see e.g. R. Middleton, 'The New Brutalism or a Clean Well-Lighted Place', *AD*, Jan. 1967, pp. 7–8.

7 'Thoughts in Progress: the New Brutalism', *AD*, Apr. 1957, p. 111.

8 For an account of the early years of the ICA and the Independent Group see A. Massey, *The Independent Group: Modernism and Mass Culture in Britain 1945–59,* Manchester, Manchester University Press, 1995, and D. Robbins, *The Independent Group: Postwar Britain and the Aesthetics of Plenty*, Cambridge, Mass., MIT Press, 1990.

9 The programmes of the ICA are recorded in the *ICA Bulletin* and summarised in Robbins, *Independent Group*. The list of architectural lectures makes interesting reading: (1952) Contemporary Italian Architecture by Richards, discussion of the Pimlico flats chaired by Richards; (1953) Chandigarh by Jane Drew, discussion of Tecton's Hallfields Housing Scheme chaired by Richards, discussion of the Time Life Building chaired by Richards.

10 The early years of the ICA were dominated by Read, and it is significant that on his departure to take up the Charles Elliot Norton Chair at Harvard in the summer of 1953, permission was granted for the first seminar series organised by the Independent Group, 'Aesthetic Problems of Contemporary Art'. The series began in Oct. 1953.

11 The list of lectures arranged by the group is given as part of the chronology of the group's activities in Robbins, *Independent Group*, pp. 12–48.

12 The activities of the group are vividly if partially remembered by its members; Robbins records the memories of a number of the key figures. Further evidence is provided in a film made by the Arts Council, *Fathers of British Pop*, and in more recent publications, e.g.: M. Girouard, *Big Jim: The Life and Work of James Stirling*, London, Chatto & Windus, 1998, especially chs 4 and 5.

13 For example the articles by Smithson on the Golden Lane competition and the ideas that were to form the basis for the Smithsons' Team X position: 'An Urban Project', *AYB*, 5, 1953, pp. 48–55; 'The Theme of Team X', *AYB*, 7, 1956, pp. 28–31.

14 See Theo Crosby's own account of his time with Fry and Drew and his move to join Monica Pidgeon at *Architectural Design* as executive editor: Robbins, *Independent Group*, pp. 197–9.

15 *Ibid.*, p. 194.

16 The core architectural members of the Independent Group were Peter Carter, Alan Colquhoun, Geoffrey Holroyd, Alison and Peter Smithson, James Stirling, John Voelcker, Sandy Wilson, the engineer Frank Newby and of course the critic Peter Reyner Banham. Others loosely associated with the group included Bill Howell.

17 Le Corbusier was a regular visitor to Britain during the late 1940s and early 1950s: he was in Britain for the CIAM meeting in Bridgwater in the summer of 1947 and later in the year for the celebration of the AA centenary, he was in Britain for the CIAM meeting at Hoddesdon in 1951, in 1953 he was in

London for the presentation of the RIBA Gold Medal and in 1959 he was in Cambridge to receive an honorary degree.

18 See e.g. Girouard, *Big Jim*, ch. 3. Le Corbusier's influence was strongly felt in Liverpool even before the war as a result of the presence of Gordon Stephenson, who had worked at rue de Sèvres on the Palace of the Soviets competition entry and returned to Liverpool to teach, see M. Crinson and J. Lubbock, *Architecture: Art or Profession?*, Manchester: Manchester University Press, 1994, ch. 3.

19 P. Smithson, 'Reflections on Hunstanton', *ARQ*, 2, pp. 32–43; Middleton, 'The New Brutalism or a Clean Well-Lighted Place', *AD*, p. 7.

20 *AJ*, 3.1.46, pp. 7–14.

21 P.C. Johnson, *Mies van der Rohe*, New York, Museum of Modern Art, 1947.

22 The competition was reported in the weekly journals: *AJ*, 11.5.1950, pp. 576–9; *A&BN*, 12.5.1950, pp. 486–8.

23 His best-known work was the Richmond High School for Girls, Richmond, Yorkshire, 1938–40. After the war he continued to work extensively on school design and had just designed the compact two-storey school arranged around a courtyard at Woodfield Road, Cranfield, Middlesex (*AJ*, 10.6.1954, pp. 709–14), before judging the Hunstanton competition.

24 The development of school planning principles is discussed below in ch. 10.

25 J.M. Richards, 'The Next Step?', *AR*, Mar. 1950, p. 173.

26 M. Hartland Thomas, 'The Mies Influence', *AD*, Jul. 1952, p. 183.

27 P. Johnson, 'School at Hunstanton', *AR*, Sep. 1954, p. 148.

28 'School at Hunstanton', *AR*, p. 153.

29 *Ibid.*

30 *Ibid.*

31 Braithwaite tanks, which held water for steam locomotives, were constructed out of modular cast-iron panels and were located throughout the railway network.

32 'Building the School at Hunstanton', *AJ*, 10.9.1953, p. 323. For a contemporary view of structural steelwork see K. Hajnal Konyi, 'Structural Steelwork', *AYB*, 1, 1945, pp. 164–81.

33 'Building the School at Hunstanton', p. 325.

34 'School at Hunstanton', *AR*, p. 148.

35 'Building the School at Hunstanton', p. 323.

36 'School at Hunstanton', *AR*, p. 152.

37 'The Story of Another Idea', *Forum*, August 1959, pp. 198–239.

38 Those in the know referred to Le Corbusier as 'Corbu', see e.g. Sandy Wilson's recollections in Robbins, *Independent Group*, p. 196.

39 See e.g. 'Le Corbusier's Unité d'Habitation', *AR*, May 1951, pp. 293–300; Banham, *New Brutalism*, p. 11.

40 The leaders of the New Humanists included Oliver Cox, A.W. Cleeve Barr and Philip Powell; the leading figures among the pro-Corbu group included Peter Carter, Alan Colquhoun, Bill Howell and Sandy Wilson.

41 Cox's and Barr's views on Roehampton are set out in 'Housing at Roehampton', *Keystone*, May-Jun. 1952, pp. 36–40; see also C. Barr, 'The People's Houses', *Keystone*, May-June 1952, pp. 44–5

42 Girouard, *Big Jim*, p. 72.

43 Banham, *New Brutalism*, p. 11.

44 It is, however, important to remember the extent of the common ground between the two sides. Oliver Cox professed a fierce admiration for Le Corbusier, as did members of the older generation like Maxwell Fry. A measure of the interest in Le Corbusier by members of the different architectural generations is to be found in J. Gowan, 'Le Corbusier – His Impact on Four Generations', *JRIBA*, Oct. 1965, pp. 497–500.

45 There was keen but not universal interest in the Unité: *Plan* ran regular reports on its progress, as did *AD*: Feb. 1948, pp. 29–31; Dec. 1949, pp. 295–6; Feb. 1950, p. 51; Jan. 1951, pp. 3–7. By contrast *OAP* made no mention of it. Nor was it mentioned regularly in the weekly journals: *AJ* mentioned it only twice between the start of construction in 1947 and completion in December 1951: 18.1.1951, pp. 92, 101; 13.12.1951, p. 698.

46 'Le Corbusier's Unité d'Habitation', *AR*, pp. 293–300. Sandy Wilson recalls in an unpublished account, 'Working in the LCC', that the debate, intended to settle 'once and for all' the disagreements between the two camps, proved less decisive than had been hoped and, though planned to run over two evenings in the pub on York Road opposite the LCC, lasted only one.

47 'Le Corbusier's Unité', p. 299.

48 *Ibid.*

49 Le Corbusier, *Towards a New Architecture*, London, John Rodker, 1927, pp. 81–138. An appreciation of the impact of Le Corbusier's ideas is given Gowan, 'Le Corbusier – His Impact', p. 499.

50 C.A. St John Wilson 'The Vertical City', *Observer*, 20.7.1952, p. 8. The article was seen by hard-left members of the LCC Housing Division as an attack on socially oriented architecture, and Wilson remembers being accused of 'throwing mud at Stalin'.

51 Since the 1920s the LCC Architect's Department had used a set of standard plans for dwellings of different types (*London Housing*, London, LCC, 1937, pp. 39–48). To develop a new type of block, a new set of type plans was therefore a necessity.

52 The LCC published new house plans in 1945 ('LCC Housing', *AJ*, 27.12.1945, pp. 465–72), and new plans were developed for new projects from the start of the reorganisation of the Housing Division under Whitfield Lewis. The next set of 39 type plans was published in summer 1953 as a loose-leaf folder, *Housing Type Plans*, London, LCC (n.d.).

53 The LCC's new maisonette plan was published in *AJ*, 13.8.1953, pp. 190–1.

54 'LCC Maisonette "Mock-Up" Erected at Purley', *AD*, Sep. 1953, pp. 258–9.

55 The designs for the Bentham Road Estate, Hackney, were published in *AR*, Jan. 1955, pp. 30–2, and more fully in *AJ*, 3.6.1954, pp. 676–81; the finished scheme was published in *Interbuild*, Feb. 1959, pp. 18–25.

56 Banham, *New Brutalism*, p. 90.

57 For a discussion of the use of the new slab-block type see M. Glendinning and S. Muthesius, *Tower Block: Modern Public Housing in England, Scotland, Wales and Northern Ireland*, London, Yale University Press, 1994, ch. 7.

58 Banham, 'New Brutalism', p. 356.

59 R. Banham, *Theory and Design in the First Machine Age*, London, Architectural Press, 1960; the book is dedicated to members of the Independent Group.

60 Robbins, *Independent Group*, pp. 26–7.

61 Johnson, *Mies van der Rohe*, pp. 12–16.

62 C. Rowe, 'The Mathematics of the Ideal Villa', *AR*, Mar. 1947, pp. 101–4.

63 Banham, 'New Brutalism', pp. 358–9.

64 *Ibid.*, p. 361.

65 The first English translation was published in 1951: Le Corbusier, *The Modulor: A Harmonious Measure of the Human Scale Universally Applicable to Architecture and Mechanics*, London, Faber & Faber, 1951.

66 M. Ghyka, 'Le Corbusier's Modulor and the Concept of the Golden Mean', *AR*, Feb. 1948, pp. 39–42. Ghyka, an internationally known mathematician, was also author of *The Geometry of Art and Life*, New York, Sheet & Ward, 1946.

67 R. Wittkower, 'Systems of Proportion', *AYB*, 5, 1953, pp. 9–18; C. Entwhistle, 'How to Use the Modulor', *Plan*, 9 (n.d.), pp. 3–6.

68 P. Collins, 'Modulor', *AR*, Jul. 1954, pp. 5–8.

69 Robbins, *Independent Group*, p. 23.

70 Wittkower, 'Systems of Proportion', p. 18.

71 Entwhistle, 'Modulor', p. 3.

72 R. Olitsky and J. Voelcker, 'Form and Mathematics', *AD*, Oct. 1954, p. 306.

73 *Ibid.*, p. 307.

74 *Ibid.*

75 Gowan, 'Le Corbusier – his impact, p. 499.

76 Banham, *Theory and Design*, p. 9.

77 N. Pevsner, *An Enquiry into Industrial Art in England*, Cambridge, Cambridge University Press, 1937.

78 L. Alloway, 'The Arts and the Mass Media', *AD*, Feb. 1958, p. 84.

79 *Ibid.*, p. 85.

80 'Thoughts in Progress', p. 113.

81 Banham, *New Brutalism*, p. 41.

82 Banham, 'New Brutalism', p. 356.

83 *Ibid.*, p. 358. It is interesting to note that an image of Santa Maria della Consolazione at Todi featured on the cover of the first edition of Wittkower's *Architectural Principles in the Age of Humanism* (London, Tiranti, 1949).

84 R. Hamilton, *Man, Machine and Motion*, London, ICA, exhib. cat., p. 2.

85 *Ibid.*, p. 14.

86 Girouard, *Big Jim*, p. 70.

87 R. Banham, 'Machine Aesthetic', *AR*, Apr. 1955, p. 227.

88 *Ibid.*

89 *Ibid.*, pp. 227–8.

90 *Ibid.*, p. 228.

91 *Ibid.*

92 *Ibid.*

93 Robbins, *Independent Group*, pp. 18–19.

94 F. Newby, 'Prestressed Concrete', *AD*, Jun. 1955, pp. 199–200. An example of the thorough discussion of technical issues is the article by D. Nield 'The Design of Large Metal Windows', *AD*, Oct. 1955, pp. 314–24.

95 Banham, *Theory and Design*, pp. 329–30.

96 In addition to the work of Jean Prouvé, the development of the large-panels system of building construction, actively encouraged by government, was an area of conspicuous technical advance; see e.g. 'Structures: La Préfabrication Lourde en France, les Procédés Camus', *Architecture d'Aujourd'hui*, 64, Mar. 1956, pp. 96–9.

97 J. Stirling, 'Garches to Jaoul', *AR*, Sep. 1955, p. 151.

98 R. Banham, 'Klarheit, Ehrlichkeit, Einfachkeit – and Wit Too!', The Case Study Houses in the World's Eyes', in E.A.T. Smith (ed.), *Blueprints for Modern Living: History and Legacy of the Case Study Houses*, Cambridge, Mass., MIT Press, 1989, pp. 183–97.

99 Robbins, *Independent Group*, p. 189.

100 F. Newby, 'The Work of Charles Eames', *AD*, Feb. 1954, pp. 31–5.

101 Robbins, *Independent Group*, p. 30.

102 In the photograph of the Smithsons, Eduardo Paolozzi and Nigel Henderson in the catalogue of the 'This is Tomorrow' exhibition, Peter Smithson is seated on an Eames chair. See also Banham 'Klarheit', p. 183.

103 E.g. John McHale's article 'Buckminster Fuller', *AR*, Jul. 1956, pp. 13–20.

104 See particularly the conclusion to Banham, *Theory and Design*.

105 'Thoughts in Progress', p. 111.

106 The results of the competition were extensively reported in the architectural press, e.g. 'Golden Lane Housing Competition', *AJ*, 6.3.1952, pp. 298–310; 358–62.

107 *Ibid.*, p. 358.

108 Judith Henderson was working with Peter Wilmot and Michael Young on the research project that would eventually be published as *Family and Kinship in East London*, London, Routledge & Kegan Paul, 1957.

109 A. and P. Smithson, 'An Urban Project', *AYB*, 5, 1953, pp. 48–55.

110 The Sheffield University competition, like the Golden Lane competition, attracted considerable interest: 'Sheffield Competition Winners', *AJ*, 26.11.1953, p. 652, 'Winning and Unplaced Designs in Competition for Sheffield University Buildings', *AJ*, 26.11.1953, pp. 718–32.

111 This term, which is used more frequently after 1952, is a measure of the difference between the avant-garde and less radical modernists; Richards uses the term in his article 'The Next Step?' in the *Review* in March 1950, and Banham is already using it by 1955 as a way of differentiating the Smithsons' Sheffield University entry from those of other less radical modernists: Banham, 'New Brutalism', p. 361.

112 *Ibid.*

113 James Stirling *Buildings and Projects 1950–1974*, London, Thames & Hudson, 1996, p. 29.

114 *Ibid.*, p. 28.

115 There is an extensive literature on 'This is Tomorrow'; for an introduction see the bibliography in Robbins, *Independent Group*, pp. 254–5.

116 'Introduction 3', *This is Tomorrow*, London, Whitechapel Gallery, exhib. cat., 1956 (no page numbers).

117 'Introduction 1', *This is Tomorrow*.

118 *Ibid.*

119 *Ibid.*

120 R. Banham, 'Not Quite Architecture, Not Quite Painting or Sculpture Either', *AJ*, 16.8.1956, pp. 218–19.

121 *Ibid.*, p. 219.

122 S.W. Goldhagen, 'Freedom's Domiciles: Three Projects by Alison and Peter Smithson', in S.W. Goldhagen and R. Legault (eds), *Anxious Modernisms: Experimentation in Postwar Architectural Culture*, Cambridge, Mass., MIT Press, 2000, pp. 75–96.

123 Quoted in Massey, *Independent Group*, p. 102.

6   Rethinking CIAM's ideal of the city

Standing in the shadow of the Lawn, the densest development in Mark Hall, Harlow New Town's first neighbourhood, the delegates for CIAM 8 would have seen for themselves an anglicised version of the planning that CIAM had been debating since the early 1930s (Figures 6.1 and 4.18). In July 1951 CIAM 8 convened at High Leigh near Hoddesdon in Hertfordshire for a meeting dedicated to questions of urbanism and planning, focused on 'The Heart of the City'. With Harlow and Stevenage, two New Towns under construction less than 30 minutes away by car, the theme must have seemed propitious to the MARS Group, which organised the conference.[1] Although Sigfried Giedion and the British hosts had agreed there would be a firmly imposed limit on the number of excursions, they readily acceded to the idea of a visit to Harlow to hear from the town's architect, Frederick Gibberd, about the most advanced of the British New Towns.

Harlow, more clearly than anywhere else in Britain, promised a first glimpse of a modern town, a first realisation of one of the great hopes of reconstruction. Like the other New Towns its conception owed much to Ebenezer Howard's vision of the Garden City and the campaigns of the Town and Country Planning Association from the 1930s and 1940s. But Gibberd's design of the town had a different parentage, combining the Picturesque approach to layout advocated since the war by the *Review* and the pre-war planning principles of CIAM, familiar to Gibberd as a member of the MARS Group. In 'Landscaping the New Town', written in the year after the first presentation of the plan for Harlow, he reiterated his belief in CIAM's approach:

> The technical solutions to the problems that a new town for 60,000 people raises are now generally agreed, at least in broad

6.1 The Mark Hall neighbourhood, Harlow, by Frederick Gibberd (1947–51). The Lawn is visible in the background in the centre of the picture

outline. They consist in making a distinct separation between areas for work, homes and play, in connecting those areas by a road pattern free of building in which traffic can flow easily, and in surrounding the whole by a well-defined agricultural belt. Industry is planned as a zone adjacent to the railway, with access to the regional road pattern: housing is arranged as a series of distinct neighbourhood units of from 6,000 to 15,000 people, each with its own schools, shops, and other services; and the town centre, with its business, shopping, and civic groups, is planned near to the railway station and industry.[2]

These ideas, combining as they did the thinking of CIAM with current interests in neighbourhood planning and new developments in road design, would have been familiar to most of the CIAM delegates. But the sources to which he turned for the design of Harlow, set out in his book *Town Design*, would have been less so.[3] The book is hardly radical but it is of interest because it shows how the values of the Picturesque and the New Empiricism could be linked to an older tradition of town design. It is in effect a restatement for the early 1950s of the approach to town design first set out in 1889 by Camillo Sitte in *Town Planning According to Artistic Principles*.[4]

The book shares from the start Sitte's concern for the shaping of space through buildings and owes much to the interpretation of these ideas offered by Raymond Unwin in *Town Planning in Practice*.[5] Thus in the discussion of 'civic areas', Gibberd illustrates the arrangement of buildings and spaces in towns and cities with examples as varied as Aylesbury and the Rockefeller Center, New York, in the same terms used by Unwin in his presentation of the spatial qualities of the little German town of Buttstedt. But Gibberd's intention was to demonstrate how this approach might be used for the design of the modern town, and the sections on industry and housing are illustrated with predominantly modern examples. The approach is similar to

Unwin's but the housing layouts and blocks of flats used to illustrate the text reflect the architectural values of the *Review* at the turn of the decade: Le Corbusier's work is mentioned, but projects from Sweden, Denmark and Switzerland provide the lion's share of examples.

Along with his analysis of the celebrated examples of central areas in Pisa, Venice and Florence, Gibberd included a number of recent developments to show how the same principles of spatial composition could be applied to the design of the modern town. Alongside Gibson's design for the rebuilding of the centre of Coventry and examples from the United States and Scandinavia, Gibberd saw nothing immodest in including his own design for the market square at Lansbury, Poplar, and his proposals for the civic centre at Harlow. The latter comprised three squares: one for entertainment and one for administration were both connected, in the manner of Sitte's linked squares, to the larger and centrally placed civic square. This was designed as an enclosed piazza, open along one side at ground level to give views down and across natural landscape into the valley along which the centre was to be built. Perhaps the centre as designed might have had some of the same qualities of Picturesque planning that critics admired in the layout of the Festival of Britain. But for the CIAM delegation there was not enough of the town centre to judge. The qualities of Harlow as a New Town had to be judged on the strength of the housing just completed as part of the Mark Hall neighbourhood.

Architecturally, the new neighbourhoods, set in the rolling Hertfordshire countryside, with mature trees interspersed by tracts of new planting, go some way to providing that very combination of Englishness and modernity that the *Review* was calling for. The different housing areas designed by Gibberd and his own team, by Richard Sheppard and Partners, and by other modernist practices like Yorke, Rosenberg, Mardall, or Fry Drew and Partners, sympathetically exploit the qualities of the site and the tradition of local materials. Brick, wood, white painted timber door and window frames, pitched tile and slate roofs are used to produce an architecture that is informal and pragmatically adapted to every demand of locality and landscape in order to create an identifiable sense of locality and place.

But what of the design of these neighbourhoods as urban fabric, as town? Here the most acute difficulty for Gibberd, as for the other New Town designers, was to marry his ideas on town design with the low densities imposed on the New Towns at their inception by the Reith Committee.[6] The committee's report had endorsed the low density of 30–50 people per acre recommended by the *Housing Manual* for suburban housing as the basis for house building in all the New Towns. At these densities the challenge was to create any feeling of urbanity at all. The designer might sidestep these constraints when considering the arrangement of the town centre, where might be found the opportunity for creating enclosure and urbanity. But in the residential areas, organised on neighbourhood principles, the task of creating some real distinction between town and country was more difficult. At Harlow, Gibberd wanted to avoid building what could appear simply as a series of hamlets set in the rural countryside:

If an urban character is to be achieved, housing groups must be to a comparatively high density – over 30 people per acre – and they must be compactly planned. Their separation must be either by broad strips of landscape or by a natural barrier – such as a wood. After the built-up area has been broken down to obtain a major contrast between building and landscape it has to be welded together again into an aesthetic whole. It is a town that has to be created, not a series of independent villages.[7]

The starting point for the planning of the Harlow neighbourhoods was the belief that they should be sufficiently compact to encourage residents to walk from one part of the neighbourhood to another. Any neighbourhood as large as 10,000 or 15,000 people, Gibberd argued, would be so large as to require its inhabitants to move around by bus, and would thus defeat any sense of identity. The neighbourhoods were therefore to be made smaller: with families housed within a 10 minute walk, or a quarter of a mile from the neighbourhood centre, the population was limited to 5,000 or less. At Harlow each neighbourhood was in turn made up of four or five residential areas housing around a thousand people, sufficient to sustain a primary school, corner shop and newsagent. These residential areas were then grouped around a neighbourhood shopping centre with more facilities, a church, a community hall and specialised shops like a butcher, a greengrocer and a local co-op.

In the design of Harlow's first neighbourhoods Gibberd sought to heighten the sense of urbanity by concentrating the housing as tightly as possible. Between the housing, areas of untouched landscape were to be preserved to demarcate the man-made and the natural:

A compact and urban type of building side by side with stretches of natural landscape will, by the contrast provided and the greater cohesion in the design, make an altogether finer environment than the more usual periphery of low-density development.[8]

Within the broad bands of natural landscape separating one neighbourhood from another, Gibberd was able to place schools and playing fields and thus to increase the area of green space buffering one neighbourhood from another. Within the neighbourhood, residential areas were designed by different architects so that variations in architectural approach might help to create a sense of place with its own character: the antithesis of the endless ribbon developments and suburban sameness of the inter-war years. In sections with headings like 'Street Pattern and Picture' Gibberd echoed Unwin's (and Sitte's) concerns with the visual qualities of planning. He urged architects to plan three-dimensionally: to compose spaces with the horizontal surfaces of roads, paving and planting and to contrast the verticals of walls and the facades of buildings. Drawing on a variety of examples, he pressed architects to strive for a sense of spatial containment untroubled by the effect of back gardens and access roads. Typical of what Gibberd wished to achieve was the feeling of urbanity and the succession of enclosed courts and unfolding prospects of his Somerford Grove estate, Hackney (Figure 4.14). There, at 140 people to the acre, he was able to use three-storey flats and two-storey terraces to make a number of linked 'out-door rooms' that have a more urban character than the surrounding areas of bye-law housing.

In Harlow, at 50–60 people to the acre, these effects were more difficult to achieve. Maxwell Fry and Jane Drew's design for Tanys Dell and the Chantry in Mark Hall North illustrates the problems (Figure 6.2).[9] The three- and four-storey blocks of flats are simply not tall enough to contain one side of an area which is defined by a succession of two-storey terraces that on the other side step uncomfortably down the slope of land falling away to the north. Even the views through the two-storey terrace to Old Harlow Church seem to dissipate into the openness of the surrounding area. The area adjacent to Mark Hall Moors, by Gibberd and his team, is hardly more successful, the containment and urbanity of the Somerford Grove estate are lacking. At Mark Hall Moors, the two-storey houses, some detached, some in echelon, others in terraces, achieve no greater sense of urbanity than do the conventional suburbs of the time. Only at the Lawn, the chosen starting point of the CIAM visit, does Gibberd come close to succeeding. Sheltered by nine mature oak trees, a ten-storey block of flats combines with a block of three-storey flats and terraces of two-storey housing to create a real sense of the town.

Nor were the urban qualities the architects were striving for in the residential areas any easier to create in the neighbourhood centre, the Stow, intended to serve the two Mark Hall neighbourhoods. In the centre's piazza between the shops

i

ii

iii

6.2 Views of the first housing areas 1949–52: (i) Tanys Dell by Fry, Drew and Partners; (ii) Mark Hall Moors by Frederick Gibberd; (iii) the Stow Neighbourhood Centre by Frederick Gibberd

and North Square a sense of enclosure and urbanity was achieved, at least before the street through the piazza became clogged with cars. But the piazza remained isolated from the rest of the built-up area of town, cut off from the surrounding housing by the uncertain relationship of both the back of the shops and of the exterior of the centre. This isolation undermined the success of the piazza at the heart of the Stow.

The Festival of Britain had demonstrated how Picturesque planning techniques might be used successfully. There, visitors walked from one highly controlled and contained urban 'room' to another, tempted from one space to the next by a shielded view or a vertical feature and the range of Picturesque devices detailed by the *Review*. But at Harlow the shortage of resources and the very limited size of centres like the Stow made such visual effects impossible. The linking of outdoor spaces of different sizes, the heart of the success at the South Bank, could not work at the Stow where there was only one space and nothing to link to except the surrounding low-density housing.

The *Review* and the failure of the New Towns

By the summer of 1953 enough of the first New Towns, Harlow and Stevenage, had been built to give an impression of how they would look when finished. Many were critical of what they saw. J.M. Richards was particularly outspoken. In an article, 'The Failure of the New Towns', he casti-gated the social and economic failings of the programme.[10] The shortcomings that he attacked were widely understood and acknowl-edged by government. The absence of social and commercial facilities to serve the new residential areas along with delays in constructing factories to provide employment were not only a stark measure of the shortage of capital for investment in the New Town programme but an indication of the general difficulties facing the New Town Development Corporations as they struggled to coordinate the different phases of each town's growth. Richards drew a close and unflattering comparison between the New Towns and the 'out-county' LCC estates, mere collections of houses that lacked social provision of any kind for their residents. What was the point of estab-lishing the elaborate machinery of a development corporation and spending government money so prodigally on the New Towns if the results were only little better than those estates, which served as an example of the failure of planning since the 1930s?

Richards' social and economic criticisms were not new, but his attack on the architectural quali-ties of the New Towns was. His central charge was the failure to create the urbanity necessary to the idea of a town:

> It should hardly be necessary to emphasise that a town is, by definition, a built up area, whose role is to provide for a partic-ular mode of living. It is a sociable place, for people want to live close together, and expresses itself as such through the compactness of its layout, through the sense of enclosure experienced within it and through being composed of *streets*. The new towns, by and large, have none of these attributes. They consist for the most part of scattered two-storey dwellings, separated by great spaces. Their inhabit-ants, instead of feeling themselves secure within an environment devoted to their convenience and pleasure, find themselves marooned in a desert of grass verges and concrete.[11]

The fact that under the guidance of the architects for the development corporations the standard of detailed design was higher than that of most suburban housing was scant consolation for the want of the traditional urban qualities, the streets and squares of most English market towns. Rich-ards laid the fault for this dismal state of affairs at the feet of the Garden City movement, and of Frederic Osborn and the Town and Country Planning Association in particular, who had insisted that Howard's ideas be interpreted as a prescription for low-density town building at no more than 12 houses to the acre. That Reith's New Towns Committee should have adopted this recommendation was due, in Richards' view, to the ineptitude of the Modern Movement. By advocating flats rather than houses, he argued, the modernists had lost public support. In doing so they had thrown away the opportunities offered by the New Town programme, the largest single programme of reconstruction to emerge from the war.[12]

6.3 'Prairie Planning in the New Towns': selected views of Harlow and Hemel Hempstead in Gordon Cullen's article in the *Architectural Review*

The force of Richards' attack was strengthened by an accompanying article by Gordon Cullen, 'Prairie Planning in the New Towns', which offered a visual indictment of the New Towns (Figure 6.3).[13] The photographs of Hemel Hempstead, Harlow and Stevenage, taken with a wide-angle lens, are damning. Pictures of vast expanses of rain-swept asphalt and grass, the absence of any vertical scale, either from trees or buildings, served to make Richards' points most effectively. What might have been achieved in the way of town design – but for the imposed constraints of low density and road layout – was illustrated by Cullen with the example of Blanchland, Yorkshire, a historic market town comparable in size to one of the New Towns at an early stage of development. No matter that Blanchland provided few of the community facilities offered already in Harlow, or that the houses lacked the gardens that people moving to the New Towns from London's East End found so welcome, the architectural

qualities of Blanchland were much closer to the values of the *Review*. Blanchland was the English equivalent of Sitte's examples of good design, the ancestors of the tradition of Picturesque town planning that had inspired the Festival of Britain. Gibberd and others might be adept in the use of established materials and traditional forms to create a sense of informality in the design of individual buildings or even groups of buildings, but architectural taste of this order could not make good the failure to recreate the Picturesque tradition in the New Towns. The *Review* saw the promise of reconstruction squandered. Hopes for a new tradition of town building had proved vain. The architectural qualities of the New Town programme as represented at Harlow were as anodyne as the very same suburban developments that had been attacked so roundly by the leading campaigners of the New Towns movement before the war.

CIAM: the rise of the younger generation

Richards' exasperation at missed opportunities was fully matched by the distaste shown by the new avant-garde. The younger generation was unimpressed by the urban forms of reconstruction: they were impatient with the new machinery of planning for its cumbrous processes and its built-in respect for the status quo; and they were dismissive of the results, whether at Lansbury or the New Towns. As the final year projects of students at the AA like Bill Howell, John Voelcker and others showed, many had been thinking adventurously, if not particularly realistically, about the future form of the city.[14] This frustration was trenchantly expressed by Alison and Peter Smithson. Writing in *Architectural Design*, they condemned both the Garden City movement and the founders of CIAM, the sources of inspiration for the form of the New Towns, for their failure to find a way of building towns suited to contemporary needs:

Each generation feels a new dissatisfaction, and conceives of a new idea of order. This is architecture. Young architects to-day feel a monumental dissatisfaction with the buildings they see going up around them. For them, the housing estates, the social centres and the blocks of flats are meaningless and irrelevant. They feel that the majority of architects have lost contact with reality and are building yesterday's dreams when the rest of us have woken up in today. They are dissatisfied with the ideas these buildings represent, the ideas of the Garden City Movement and the Rational Architecture Movement.[15]

These approaches were responsible for contemporary urban confusion. In Britain the Garden City had held sway for too long:

From the garden cities has come forty years of town planning legislation. They have fixed the density structure, the pattern of garden and house, and the aimless road system of our new council estates. They have perpetuated to this day the official opinion, in 1912, of what the deserving working man should have. The Garden City Movement has mothered the New Towns. In them the concept of 'balanced social structure', and the careful provision of survey assessed amenities, has reached its ultimate anti-climax.[16]

Elsewhere the ideas of CIAM had been more influential only to produce a form of town planning that was equally damaging:

Today in every city in Europe we can see Rational Architecture being built. Multistorey flats running north-south in parallel blocks just that distance apart that permits winter sun to enter bottom stories, and just that high to get fully economic density occupation of the ground area. Where the extent of development is sufficient we can see the working out of the theoretical isolates, dwelling, working, recreation of body and spirit, circulation, and we wonder how anyone could possibly believe that in this, lay the secret of town building.[17]

As the way forward, the article illustrated the Smithsons' Golden Lane competition entry, a housing scheme in Morocco by ATBAT, and examples of ideas on the design of towns that the British avant-garde were then exchanging with their Continental counterparts in the meetings of CIAM.

The 1953 CIAM 9 conference at Aix-en-Provence has long been celebrated as the point at which the younger generation of English and European architects, Alison and Peter Smithson, John and Anne Voelcker, Bill and Gill Howell, Jakob Bakema, Aldo van Eyck, Georges Candilis and Shad Woods, began to challenge the views and the authority of the generation that had founded CIAM.[18] But the issues that were to divide CIAM were already evident at the CIAM 8 meeting at Hoddesdon. It was at this meeting, the first attended by the Smithsons, the Howells and the Voelckers, the latter peripherally involved with organising the event, that the young English contingent had first encountered their young Dutch and French counterparts.

The Hoddesdon meeting was organised by the MARS Group, and Giedion and Richards had intended from the start to provide an opportunity to develop further the ideas first addressed at Bridgwater and aired at Bergamo. CIAM 8 was to move beyond the rigid analysis of the city that CIAM had adopted with the Athens Charter. The decision to focus on the 'Core of the City', both as a physical entity and as a key ingredient in the communal life of the city, introduced an order of complexity that burst the bounds of CIAM's rigid categorisation of the workings of the city in terms of the four functions: living, working, recreation and travel (Figure 6.4). The emphasis on the human and symbolic aspects of the core or the heart of the city was evident in the keynote addresses by both Sert and Giedion. In contrast to the language of CIAM in the 1930s, Sert now stressed the nature of the city as a social organism and the sense of community that was essential to its success, and

i   ii

6.4 The core of the city: (i) Piazza San Marco, Venice (ii) New Yorkers celebrating the liberation of Paris on the Plaza, the Rockefeller Center

quoted the MARS Group programme for the Congress:

> For a community of people is an organism, and a self-conscious organism. Not only are the members dependent on one another, but each of them knows he is so dependent. This awareness, or sense of community, is expressed with varying degrees of intensity at different levels. It is very strong, for example, at the lowest scale level – that of the family. It emerges again strongly at five different levels above this: in the village or primary housing group; in the small market centre or residential neighbourhood, in the town or city sector; in the city itself, and in the metropolis, the multiple city. At each level the creation of a special physical environment is called for, both as a setting for the expression of this sense of community and as an actual expression of it. This is the physical heart of the community, the nucleus, THE CORE.[19]

Giedion's historical review of the core of the city from antiquity onwards emphasised the same

humanistic concerns: 'Our present interest in the Core is a part of this humanising process or, if you prefer it, the return of the human scale and the assertion of the right of the individual over the tyranny of mechanical tools'.[20]

Nor was this emphasis limited to the pronouncements of the pre-war generation. The discussion of the panels presented by the different nation groups maintained the same emphasis on the city as a form of human association. Younger delegates, groups like De 8 from Amsterdam and Opbouw from Rotterdam, explained their work in terms of association and relationships using a language of abstraction and complexity that contrasted strongly with the reductive terms of the Charter of Athens.[21]

The change in direction already detectable at Hoddesdon in the summer of 1951 was to be clearly seen at the next meeting two years later at Aix. Hoddesdon had ended on a positive note and apparent agreement at Le Corbusier's suggestion that the next congress seek to formulate a 'Charte de l'Habitat', a declaration for housing parallel to the United Nations declaration of human rights. Planning for the Aix conference proceeded through 1952, first at a council meeting in Paris in May and later at an 'Interim

Congress' held in June at Sigtuna near Stock-holm. In London in May 1953, Bill Howell, already a member of the CIAM council as representative of 'junior members', convened a meeting of the British delegation to prepare material for the next congress. He undertook to present the work of the LCC Housing Division's architects who were working on the slabs proposed for Alton West, his 'Marseilles pups'. John Voelcker was to submit panels describing the 'Zone Scheme', AA student work for housing for Stevenage. The Smithsons undertook to present a number of panels describing their competition entry for the Golden Lane competition.[22]

Whatever the terms in which their entry for the Golden Lane competition had first been conceived, the Smithsons now saw this as a vehicle for exploring a number of the themes of direct relevance to the coming CIAM conference. An article in the *Architects' Yearbook* of 1953 suggests the parallels between their views and the issues briefly voiced at Hoddesdon. Titled 'An Urban Project', with the subtitle 'Pilot Project, an Application of the Principles of Urban Re-Identification', the article explicitly offered the Golden Lane project as a paradigm for an approach to the design of community which went beyond both the English neighbourhood unit and Le Corbusier's Unité:

> The assumption that a community can be created by geographic isolation is invalid.
>
> Real social groups cut across geographical barriers and *the principal aid to cohesion is looseness of grouping and ease of communications* rather than the rigid isolation of arbitrary sections of the total community with impossibly difficult communications, which characterise both English neighbourhood planning and the Unité concept of Le Corbusier.[23]

For the Smithsons, talk of association and community in the city were not mere abstractions. Through living in Bethnal Green they were conscious of the web of associations to be found in an established urban community, and

6.5 Street party, Bethnal Green by Nigel Henderson

through Nigel Henderson's wife, Judith Stephen, they were familiar with the investigation of the social structure of the area that was being undertaken by Peter Wilmott and Michael Young (Figure 6.5).[24] The Smithsons' project for Golden Lane was intended as an attempt to retain the advantages of the traditional city street but in a different form, maintaining the elements, the house and the street, and the relationship between them, to promote the established qualities of community. Hence their emphasis on the house as the first 'finite city element' and the street as the second. Central to reconstructing the relationship between house, street and city, they argued, was the need for a huge increase in density and the provision of upper-level streets to ensure that higher densities did not result in the loss of the street and other forms of public space, as inevitably occurred in the conventional high-rise city: 'It is the idea of the street that is important – the creation of effective group-spaces fulfilling the vital function of identification and enclosure making the socially vital life-of-the-street possible' (Figure 5.12).[25] In their project the form of these upper-level streets was to meet the needs of a traditional community but in novel form. Thus, the Smithsons demanded, 'streets would be *places* and not corridors or balconies. Thoroughfares where there are shops, postboxes and telephone kiosks.'[26] Anticipating a number of issues that were to come to the fore at Aix, the Smithsons presented their project as a demonstration of the new pattern of urban association:

> The time has come for a reorientation of urban thinking, a turning away from the hitherto functional theory of CIAM, towards a human theory based on the associations of people with each other and their work. These associations are the primary concern of the planner; precisely defined they can become finite plastic realities re-establishing man's stature – his identity – the task of these decades.
>
> The reidentification should start with a renewal of the house-street relationship.[27]

Though the British contingent was happy to make common cause against CIAM's pre-war view of the city, the work they assembled reflected the different interpretations of the word 'habitat' which clouded the discussions at Paris and Sigtuna. The Smithsons' project, with its concern to knit the new building into the tissue of the surrounding city, was closer to a view of habitat defined in ecological terms that emphasised less an analysis of separate organisms, more their interaction with each other and their environment. By contrast, Howell's LCC housing, inspired by the Unité, was closer to the narrower understanding of habitat favoured by Le Corbusier that focused on the dwelling and the facilities immediately associated with it. Shorn of the range of facilities provided in the Unité, the blocks at Alton West represented a more restricted view still of the meaning of the term.

CIAM 9: an international role for the British avant-garde

The meeting at Aix failed to live up to expectations. Hopes that the congress would formulate a 'Charte de l'Habitat' proved vain. The material presented at the six different commissions proved difficult to compare, the *grille* format proposed at Bergamo and tried at Hoddesdon

proved incapable of providing a common basis for discussion of the existing city, let alone of securing agreement on an issue as contentious as the Charte de l'Habitat. But Aix saw for the first time the impact on CIAM's debates of the younger generation. More than the debate on architecture and the ideas that were to emerge as the New Brutalism, it was the series of exchanges and discussions at a succession of CIAM events and meetings, beginning with CIAM 9 at Aix that did most to establish the international credentials of the new British avant-garde.

Aix marked the explicit recognition of the tensions between the two generations: hopes of a gradual transfer of responsibility for the direction of CIAM to the younger generation, voiced at Hoddesdon two years before, foundered on the disagreement between the old guard and the 'youngsters' (also referred to as the 'youngers'). Van Eyck's attack on Gropius, prompted more by Gropius' 'Ticky Tacky with TAC' than any determination to challenge the power of the founding generation, conveys an impression of rancorous disagreement.[28] Some of the younger delegates like Bakema and van Eyck urged collaboration with the CIAM establishment, even if the Smithsons seem to have remained aloof – cut off perhaps by their inability to speak French – presenting Golden Lane in a format which denied even the limited utility of the *grille*. But alongside these tensions, the Aix meeting must also be remembered for collective enjoyment of events like the party on the roof of the Unité and the exciting sense of affinity and common interests shared by the younger generation.[29] Perhaps in these terms the friction between generations was no more than a product of a sense of shared identity amongst '*les jeunes*', a necessary way of defining a common position.

In many ways the formal business of the congress conducted during the meetings of the six commissions proved less important than the informal contacts that rapidly developed among the younger generation.[30] It was the sense of contact with others thinking along the same lines, the sense of 'affinity of aims and methods',[31] that was so vital: 'policy arguments were like the wind in the tree tops; under which the younger generation's discovery of each other went on feverishly'.[32] This sense of affinity, of replacing the old analytical methods of CIAM with a new interest in the associations and interactions that were essential to understanding the nature of the modern city, developed during the presentation and discussion of the *grilles* of the youngsters. Projects like De 8's Nagele scheme or Opbouw's Alexanderpolder village by Bakema explored questions of association in a more flexible way than was compatible with the old neighbourhood unit way of thinking. These explorations were matched by the youngsters' other key projects: the Smithsons' Golden Lane scheme, Voelcker's presentation of the Zone project by students from the Architectural Association, and Candilis and Woods' presentation of their work for ATBAT in Morocco.[33]

This sense of common identity also grew out of the shared difficulties of finding somewhere affordable to stay and to eat, and out of the meal-time conversations and exchanges that were an essential part of CIAM meetings for the younger generation. Alison Smithson's memories of the sense of difference between generations in social terms say a lot about the context in which the alliance of the younger generation was formed:

The older generation were elsewhere, in one or more hotels; quite aloof, for they were the 'old family' ... we never thought to enquire where they were. The aloofness engulfed certain middle generation also: BBPR (Begioso, Banfi, Peresutti, Rogers) for example; although the Voelckers had worked in their Milan office during 1950 and had, with the Howells, been taught at the Architectural Association by Ernesto Rogers: BBPR were only persuaded to eat one evening meal with the young English ... more alongside us, not very communicative and offering less comradery than complete strangers ... this lack of connective will was to prove the rotten core of CIAM.[34]

Above all, the youngsters left Aix with a sense of shared purpose and excitement at the possibility of international collaboration.

But when put to the test, hopes of establishing a common position even within the younger generation proved elusive. In the aftermath of Aix a number of English and Dutch youngsters agreed to meet at Doorn, near Utrecht, to prepare a common statement in preparation for the next meeting of CIAM and to ensure that the Aix meeting's failure to formulate a Charte de l'Habitat should not be repeated.[35] The shared impatience with the rigidity of the Athens Charter was real enough, but what was to be put in its place?

For both the English and the Dutch the quality essential to the functioning of community, be it village, town or city, that was so comprehensively absent from CIAM's earlier analysis of the city was the quality of association. From the Bantu village to the western European metropolis, this was the central ingredient of the city as an organism, visible in the irreducible elements of any settlement. It was this that linked the house to the street and, beyond, the streets to the district and the city.

The Dutch – van Eyck, Bakema and Hans Hovens Greve – had started to investigate these questions in their studies of neighbourhood centres for existing cities and of new villages for recently reclaimed polderland, in the studies of the Opbouw group and De 8. At Hoddesdon, Bakema and Greve, both of Opbouw, had spoken of their belief that 'the relationship between things and within things are of greater importance than things themselves'.[36] It was these relationships that they believed were the key to successful design of a community and which they sought to demonstrate in the design for Alexanderpolder. Van Eyck, more poetically and more philosophically inclined than Bakema, had become fascinated by a range of interpretations of relationships and relativities and was working to develop an 'aesthetic of number' in architecture which would be of value in the layout of communities like Nagele. Van Eyck too had signalled his rejection of the rigid formulae

6.6 Opening page to 'The Story of an Other Idea' by Aldo van Eyck, 1959

The city is the ultimate community, 'the tangible expression of an economic region'.

$$
\left.
\begin{array}{llll}
\text{Hearth + Doorstep} & = \text{House} & 1 \\
\text{House} \times k + x & = \text{Street} & 2 \\
\text{Street} \times k^1 + y & = \text{District} & 3 \\
\text{District} \times n + z & = \text{City} & 4
\end{array}
\right\}
\begin{array}{l}
\text{Elements} \\
\text{of City}
\end{array}
$$

where

k = 40–50 families

k^1 = 2,500 people

n = apparently infinity as world cities, London, New York, etc supported by infinite regions.

x = craft tradesmen, (workshop-shop in house) doctors, newspaper vendors, tobacconists, public houses, private car parking, telephone kiosks, postbox, nursery schools, private open space.

y = workshops, allotments, shopping centre, small hotels, public car parking, churches, primary schools, public open space.

z = administration, factories, market gardens, hospitals, main shopping, hotels, public car parking, secondary schools, universities, museums, art galleries, concert halls, cathedrals, theatres, cinemas, major open space, protected areas.[38]

of CIAM and the four-functions analysis of the city and had emphasised the need to provide for the whole variety of needs of the community, not just in static terms but as they might evolve through time, ideas most fully conveyed in his essay of quotations and images, 'The Story of an Other Idea', published in the Dutch journal *Forum* nearly six years after the Aix conference (Figure 6.6).[37]

For the British, the term 'association' had comparable if not directly similar resonances. To the Smithsons, the idea of association set out in 'An Urban Project' was linked to the world they saw in the East End of London and their attempts to grasp the order of the city around them. In terms comparable to van Eyck's 'aesthetic of number' they sought a formal identity for the associations they were studying:

The Smithsons were already familiar with the work of Wilmott and Young, whose research for the book *Family and Kinship in East London* was being conducted around Bethnal Green during 1953–54 and which mapped kinship networks and key relationships of mother and daughter, husband and mother not just in social terms but spatial terms as well. Wilmott and Young's work and the visual evocation of the world of the urban working class in the photographs of Nigel Henderson[39] and Richard Mayne,[40] which were to figure prominently in the Smithsons' discussions on urban living in the late 50s, would have provided a visual and social anthropological parallel to the architectural and planning ideas that they were developing at the time.

Despite the wrangling over the exact form of words, the 'Doorn Manifesto' is a statement of a common position and stands as the single most coherent and succinct summary of the young-sters' position. It was also a clear statement of the hopes for the next CIAM meeting. It starts by identifying the different positions within CIAM:

We of the youngers received a shock at Aix, in seeing how far the wonder of the 'Ville Radieuse' had faded from CIAM ... **Today we each recognise the existence of a new spirit. It is manifest in our revolt from mechanical concepts of order and in our passionate interest in the complex rela-tionships in life and the realities of our world** ... We must find the means of real-ising in architecture the idea of a cosmos continuously in change, **inconceivably complex, yet at each moment exqui-sitely finite.**[41]

Following a summary of the Athens Charter, the manifesto set out the youngsters' central hopes for a new direction:

As a direct result of the 9th Congress at Aix, we have come to the conclusion that if we are to create a new Charte de l'Habitat, we must redefine the aims of urbanism, and at the same time create a new tool to make this aim possible.

Urbanism considered and developed in the terms of the Charte d'Athènes tends to produce 'towns' in which vital human associations are inadequately expressed.

To comprehend these human associa-tions we must consider every community as a particular total complex.

In order to make this comprehension possible, we propose to study urbanism as communities of varying degrees of complexity.

These can be shown on a Scale of Asso-ciation as shown below [Figure 6.7]

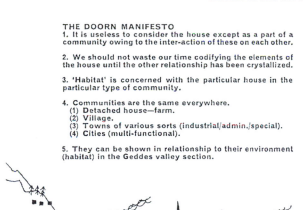

THE DOORN MANIFESTO
1. It is useless to consider the house except as a part of a community owing to the inter-action of these on each other.

2. We should not waste our time codifying the elements of the house until the other relationship has been crystallized.

3. 'Habitat' is concerned with the particular house in the particular type of community.

4. Communities are the same everywhere.
   (1) Detached house—farm.
   (2) Village.
   (3) Towns of various sorts (industrial/admin./special).
   (4) Cities (multi-functional).

5. They can be shown in relationship to their environment (habitat) in the Geddes valley section.

6. Any community must be internally convenient—have ease of circulation; in consequence, whatever type of transport is available, density must increase as population increases, i.e. (1) is least dense, (4) is most dense.

7. We must therefore study the dwelling and the groupings that are necessary to produce convenient communities at various points on the valley section.

8. The appropriateness of any solution may lie in the field of architectural invention rather than social anthropology.
Holland, 1954

6.7 Alison and Peter Smithson's diagrammatic representation of the 'Scale of Association'

We suggest that the commissions operate each in a field not on a point on the Scale of Association, for example

isolated buildings
villages
towns
cities.

This will enable us to study particular functions in their appropriate ecological field. Thus a housing sector or satellite of a city will be considered at the top of the scale … and can in this way be compared with developments in other cities, or contrasted with numerically similar developments in different fields of the Scale of Association. **This method of work will induce a study of human association as a first principle, and of the four functions as aspects of each total problem.**[42]

The language of Team X would be later enriched by terms like 'clusters', projects like the Smithsons' Hauptstadt Berlin would lead in new directions, but the ideas set out in the Doorn Manifesto remained through the 1950s a starting point for the younger generation's explorations of a new approach to architecture and planning based on the changing patterns of living. In 1956, looking back on the Doorn meeting, the Smithsons summarised what they felt had been achieved:

It became clear that what goes to the making of life falls through the mesh of the four functions – lies, in fact, beyond the scope of analytic thinking. The meeting therefore, attempted to formulate a new way of thinking about urbanism that would consider each problem as an entity, as a unique example of human association at a particular time and in a particular place.[43]

CIAM 10 at Dubrovnik and the demise of CIAM

At a general meeting of CIAM in Paris in July 1954 the signatories of the Doorn Manifesto were invited to draft guidelines for CIAM 10; the CIAM 10 Committee, or Team X as it now came to be known, now acquired official status. But the preparations for CIAM 10 were to cause even more difficulties than those for the meeting at Aix. Disagreement within Team X and between Team X and the old guard, particularly those based in America, were to lead to the postponement of the meeting by a year, a change of location and a succession of disputes about the form of the guidelines for CIAM 10. It was not until six weeks before the congress that the agenda was finally settled at a hastily convened meeting at Padua between Team X and the leaders of the old guard. Here it was agreed that the Dubrovnik meeting would have as its sole purpose the preparation of the Charte de l'Habitat and that, at Giedion's suggestion, this was to be accomplished by two committees working in parallel. The first, composed of representatives of the older generation, was to summarise the work of CIAM since its foundation in the form of a charter similar to the Athens Charter; the second, principally the members of Team X, was to study the material prepared for CIAM X in order to extend the work of CIAM to include the latest thinking.[44]

The format adopted for the Dubrovnik meeting exacerbated the divisions between the two generations. Though the different commissions combined younger and older generations, CIAM X seemed to be divided into two parallel congresses. Untroubled by the old guard, Team X was able to continue the investigations it had started at Doorn. The thirty-nine grids presented at the meeting were hung to correspond to the different scales of settlement identified at Doorn, and these were considered by four commissions, established at Padua, which reflected key interests of Team X: organic unity; mobility; growth and change; and the relationship between urbanism and habitat.[45] The Smithsons submitted four housing projects, each exemplifying a different scale of association which ranged from Burrows Lee Farm, an isolated farm in Surrey, to a project for twelve-storey terraces for an industrial suburb in a large city. Howell presented a design for a town house type for infilling in existing residential areas, Voelcker a design for a house type for established villages. Bakema showed the latest version of the Alexanderpolder and Van Eyck the Nagele project and a number of the playgrounds he had built in Amsterdam. Despite the differences in the approach between the Dutch and the English there was a willingness to recognise the value of the others' contribution. The Smithsons and Voelcker were particularly intrigued and excited by van Eyck's playgrounds; van Eyck was especially interested in the Smithsons' close housing and the terraced housing projects. But despite these shared interests, agreeing a summary of the proceedings of the four commissions was inevitably problematic: Peter Smithson's summing up of the discussions of the first commission was challenged by the Dutch for failing to acknowledge their contributions or the full range of issues that had been covered and for unilaterally describing the work of the commission as being the study of 'clusters'. But at least by the end of the congress the younger generation retained a sense of common purpose, a commitment to the principles of the Doorn Manifesto.

This sense of common purpose amongst Team X was in contrast to the acrimonious discussions of the future of CIAM that surfaced in the plenary sessions. Leading figures of the older generation questioned publicly the effectiveness of CIAM in its current form. Before the meeting Le Corbusier had urged the transfer of power and responsibility to the younger generation, and during the congress Cor van Eesteren raised publicly the possibility of disbanding CIAM altogether. Encumbered by an increasingly unworkable constitution and a dramatic increase in the number of members, the majority of whom neither submitted work nor played an active part in the discussions of the working commissions, CIAM had become unwieldy and institutionalised. To those who remembered its original purpose, CIAM in its current form was collapsing. To survive, it would have to be dissolved in order to be reborn. As the delegates voted in favour of reforming CIAM, few foresaw that they had already started the process of dissolution.[46] It can now be seen that the Dubrovnik meeting marked the point at which the demise of CIAM began and the new international avant-garde emerged from the shadow of the old. As part of Team X, the British, the Smithsons, the Voelckers and the Howells, along with the other youngsters, had emerged as leading voices of a new European avant-garde.

From Aix to practice

The Smithsons' urban proposals of the mid 50s – of all the British contingent, they remained the most actively involved in debating urban issues – have a quality of abstraction about them and a remoteness from the pragmatics of reconstruction and planning. At a time when the centre of cities like Berlin and Bristol were actually being rebuilt, the Smithsons schemes have a speculative quality that enabled them to rise above the emerging orthodoxy of planning to address questions to which architects did not yet have answers. These very qualities precluded any immediate application of their ideas.

But the new concerns with association and community voiced at Hoddesdon and at Aix did find a resonance in practice. The reaction to the low densities and the strict separation of functions of the first generation of new towns like Harlow can be seen in the density of development of projects like the LCC's design for a new town at Hook, Hampshire,[47] or in the design of the centre for the new town at Cumbernauld, near Stirling.[48] In both, the designers hoped that a multi-level central area with a variety of different uses would create that richness of association that was believed lie at the heart of 'community'. In housing, too, there was reaction against the simplicities of early CIAM formulations. The new approach is exemplified by projects which sought not just to provide dwellings but to address the larger issues of community. At the Park Hill estate, Sheffield, designed and built between 1953 and 1959 by Jack Lynch and Ivor Smith, both Peter Smithsons' students at the Architectural Association, the debt to Team X is clear.[49]

i

ii

6.8 The Park Hill Estate, Sheffield (1953–59), by Sheffield City Architect's Department (Jack Lynn, Ivor Smith and Frederick Nicklin, designers) (i) view of the open spaces contained by the cranked wall of the block; (ii) an upper-level pedestrian street

With its streets in the air, its multiplicity of uses and its provisions for the needs – shopping, recreation, leisure, as well as living – of a whole community close to the very centre of the city, Park Hill is a translation into practice of Team X's new approach to urbanism and the value of human association in the making of community (Figure 6.8).

Nor was the new approach limited to the youngsters of Team X. Denys Lasdun, who had

worked before and after the war with Lubetkin, designed two 'Cluster Blocks' in Bethnal Green which suggested common goals to those of Team X but drew inspiration from different sources.[50] With the 'Cluster' at Usk Street, for which design work started as early as 1952, and then Claredale Street from 1954, Lasdun put forward a radical alternative to the slab blocks of the Hallfields Estate, Paddington, on which he had worked with Tecton. These 'Housing

i

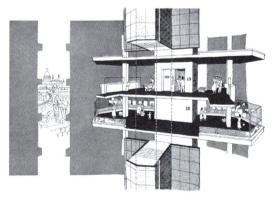

ii

6.9 'Cluster block' at Bethnal Green by Denys Lasdun (1954–59): (i) view from a typical street in Bethnal Green; (ii) arrangement of the entrance to the maisonettes and the communal drying and play areas

Clusters' offered light, view and all the benefits of the housing of *La Ville Radieuse*, but did so in a way that took account of the surroundings in Bethnal Green. The access bridges to the double-storey maisonettes and the communal drying yards on every other floor may be viewed as a reformulation of the qualities of the back-yards and alleys that Bill Brandt had captured in his photographs of the East End; they serve to encourage the chance neighbourly contacts provided by the traditional streets of the East End. The design of these blocks acknowledges both the nature of the local context and the needs of community in a way that the early tradition of CIAM housing simply did not (Figure 6.9).

Projects such as these signalled the rise of the new approach to urban issues. By the mid 1950s across much of Europe CIAM's pre-war formulation of the ideal of the city was under attack in both debate and in practice. Projects like Hook New Town or the new housing at Park Hill or Bethnal Green were illustrated and discussed in journals like *L'Architecture d'Aujourd'hui*, *Casabella*, the Dutch magazine *Forum*, and Swiss *Werk*, underlining the way in which British architects were now addressing themes of general interest. From 1955 onwards the British contingent were to play an active part in a European-wide debate on the nature of architecture and the city.

Notes

1   The official account of CIAM 8 at Hoddesdon is J. Tyrwhitt, J.L. Sert and E.N. Rogers (eds), *The Heart of the City: Towards the Humanisation of Urban Life*, London, Lund Humphries, 1952. In addition there were extended reports of the proceedings in the architectural press, e.g. 'CIAM 8', *AD*, Aug. 1951, pp. 227, 256; 'CIAM 8', *AJ*, 19.7.1951, pp. 66–9.

2   F. Gibberd, 'Landscaping the New Town', *AR*, Mar. 1948, p. 85.

3   F. Gibberd, *Town Design*, London, Architectural Press, 1953.

4   C. Sitte, *Der Städtebau nach seinen künstlerischen Grundsätzen*, Vienna, C. Gaeser, 1889. A complete and thus influential translation into English by G.R. Collins and Christiane Craseman Collins was published by the Phaidon Press, London, in 1965.

5   R. Unwin, *Town Planning in Practice: An Introduction to the Art of Designing Cities and Suburbs*, London, Fisher & Unwin, 1909.

6   For a discussion of the founding of the New Towns see J.B. Cullingworth, *Environment and Planning 1939–1969. Vol. 3: New Towns Policy*, London, HMSO, 1979, ch. 1; D. Hardy, *From Garden Cities to New Towns: Campaigning for Town and Country Planning 1899–1946*, London, E. & F.N. Spon, 1991, ch. 5.

7   Gibberd, 'Landscaping the New Town', p. 85.

8   F. Gibberd, 'The Design of Residential Areas', *Design in Town and Village*, London, HMSO, 1953, p. 27.

9   The different residential areas in the two Mark Hall neighbourhoods and the Stow shopping centre are described in detail in 'Harlow New Town', *AR*, May 1955, pp. 311–29.

10 J.M. Richards, 'The Failure of the New Towns', *AR*, Jul. 1953, pp. 29–32; see also J.M. Richards, 'Failure of the New Densities', *AR*, Dec. 1953, pp. 355–61.

11 Richards, 'Failure of the New Towns', p. 31.

12 *Ibid.*, p. 32.

13 G. Cullen, 'Prairie Planning in the New Towns', *AR*, Jul. 1953, pp. 33–6.

14 Representative of these students' schemes were the Zone Project by Pat Crooke, Andrew Derbyshire and John Voelcker (fifth year students in 1952), exhibited at Aix, and the project for Stevenage by Bill Howell and others illustrated in *Plan*, 8, 1950, pp. 24–31.

15 A. and P. Smithson, 'The Built World: Urban Reidentification', *AD*, Jun. 1955, p. 185.

16 *Ibid.*

17 *Ibid.*, p. 186.

18 On the emergence of the younger generation and the formation of Team X, see E. Mumford, *The CIAM Discourse on Urbanism 1928–1960*, Cambridge, Mass., MIT Press, 2000, chs 3 and 4; the special number of *Rassegna* devoted to the post-war CIAM meetings, D. Matteoni (ed.), 'The Last CIAMs', *Rassegna*, 14, Dec. 1992; and F. Strauven, *Aldo van Eyck: The Shape of Relativity*, Amsterdam, Architectura and Natura, 1998, especially ch. 6. The recollections of the Smithsons provide a complementary view of the same events, A. Smithson (ed.), *Team 10 Meetings 1953–1984*, New York, Rizzoli, 1991.

19 J.L. Sert, 'Centres of Community Life', in Tyrwhitt *et al.*, *Heart of the City*, p. 6.

20 S. Giedion, 'Historical Background to the Core', in Tyrwhitt *et al.*, *Heart of the City*, p. 17.

21 See e.g. Bakema's description of the Opbouw group's proposals for a community core in Rotterdam: J. Bakema, 'Relations between Men and Things', in Tyrwhitt *et al.*, *Heart of the City*, p. 67.

22 Alison Smithson remembers the meeting convened by Bill Howell in *Team 10 Meetings*, p. 17.

23 A. and P. Smithson, 'An Urban Project', *AYB*, 5, 1953, p. 49.

24 This work was eventually to be published as P. Wilmott and M. Young, *Family and Kinship in East London*, London, Routledge & Kegan Paul, 1957; Judith Stephen is not acknowledged in the credits.

25 A. and P. Smithson, 'An Urban Project', p. 50.

26 *Ibid.*

27 *Ibid.*, p. 54.

28 Strauven, *Aldo van Eyck*, p. 256.

29 Something of the mood of the Aix meeting is conveyed in Smithson, *Team 10 Meetings*, pp. 17–20.

30 The six commissions were: (1) Urbanism, (2) Synthesis of the Arts, (3) Formation of the Architect, (4) Construction Techniques, (5) Legislation and (6) Charte de l'Habitat. The youngsters were spread across different commissions, though membership seems to have been fluid and some people moved from one session to another: the Smithsons and the Howells joined Commission 6, along with Woods, van Ginkel and van Eyck of the youngsters, Lasdun joined Commission 3, Voelcker Commission 2, while Candilis and Bakema were part of Commission 1.

31 J. Voelcker, 'CIAM 10, Dubrovnik 1956', *AYB*, 8, 1957, p. 44; see also *Arena*, Jun. 1965, p. 12.

32 Smithson, *Team 10 Meetings*, p. 20.

33 The Smithsons presented a *grille* titled 'Urban Reidentification' showing their Golden Lane project, including Henderson's photographs of Bethnal Green. The Voelcker's *grille* showed the Zone project by students of the Architectural Association. Other members of the MARS Group showed *grilles* showing the Golden Lane project by Chamberlain Powell and Bon, the Hallfield Estate, Paddington, by Drake and Lasdun, Churchill Gardens by Powell and Moya and the Alton Estate West at Roehampton. *Grilles* presented by other members of what was to become Team X included the latest version of van Eyck's Nagele project, Bakema and Opbouw's Alexanderpolder project, and Candilis and Woods' work for ATBAT. For a fuller description of the *grilles* presented at Aix see Mumford, *CIAM Discourse on Urbanism*, pp. 227–38.

34 Smithson, *Team 10 Meetings*, p. 18.

35 The Smithsons described the mood after Aix in A. and P. Smithson, 'The Theme of CIAM 10', *AYB*, 7, 1956, p. 28.

36 Bakema, 'Relationship between Men and Things', p. 67.

37 A. van Eyck, 'The Story of an Other Idea', *Forum*, 7, 1959, pp. 198–239.

38 A. and P. Smithson, 'An Urban Project', p. 49.

39 Nigel Henderson's photographic essay on Bethnal Green was published in *Uppercase 3* (n.d., no page nos.). His photographs also appeared on the *grilles* presented by the Smithsons at Aix.

40 R. Mayne, 'Portrait of Southam Street', *Uppercase 4*, London, Whitefriar Press (n.d.), pp. 63–119.

41 The Doorn Manifesto is reproduced in van Eyck 'Story of an Other Idea', p. 231.

42 *Ibid.*

43 A. and P. Smithson, 'Theme of CIAM 10', pp. 28–9.

44 The most succinct summary of CIAM 10 is provided by J. Voelcker, 'CIAM 10, Dubrovnik', *AYB*, 8, 1957, pp. 43–52.

45 For a summary of the projects presented at CIAM 10 see T. Crosby, 'Contributions to CIAM 10', *AYB*, 7, 1956, pp. 32–9, and Mumford, *CIAM Discourse on Urbanism*, pp. 249–58. The *grilles* presented by the Smithsons are reproduced in R. Landau, 'The End of CIAM and the Role of the British', *Casabella*, 14, Dec. 1992, pp. 44–5.

46 W. Howell, 'CIAM is dead ... Long Live CIAM', *AJ*, 6.9.1956, p. 332.

47 LCC, *The Planning of a New Town*, London, LCC, 1961.

48 'Cumbernauld New Town', *AD*, January 1962, p.15.

49 'Park Hill 1 + 2', *AD*, September 1961, pp. 393–404.

50 'Housing Cluster: Bethnal Green, London', *AD*, April 1956, pp.125–28; see also W. Curtis, *Denys Lasdun, Architecture, City, Landscape*, London, Phaidon, 1994, pp. 46–52.

PART II

Rebuilding Britain

7 Preparing for reconstruction
Plans for housing, 1942–45

Early in the summer of 1942 the outcome of the war was still undecided, the U-boat attacks in the Atlantic were at their highest level yet, the Allied victories of El Alamein and Stalingrad still lay in the future. However, it was already clear that Britain no longer faced the immediate threat of defeat. At home the bombing had eased and the pressures created by the war had begun to wane. At last government found itself in a position to prepare more purposefully and actively for the eventual transition from war to peace and reconstruction.[1] The change in the tempo of government action is reflected in the reconfiguration of the committees and the committee structure for reconstruction. In March 1942 Minister Without Portfolio Greenwood resigned his post and the responsibility for reconstruction passed to Sir William Jowitt, Paymaster General and chairman of a newly constituted Committee on Reconstruction Problems. Complementary to this was the formation of a new Official Committee on Post-War Internal Economic Problems (the IEP Committee), which started to meet from February 1942 under Sir George Chrystal, secretary to the War Cabinet on reconstruction. Staffed with senior civil servants from different departments, it was capable of the detailed 'nuts and bolts' planning of reconstruction in a way that previously had not been possible.[2]

Strengthened by these changes, though with Jowitt still lacking a seat in Cabinet, the reconstruction committees set to work. The job at hand was no longer to initiate post-war planning but to consolidate and coordinate the number of proposals made by departments as a result of the initiatives taken by Greenwood and his Reconstruction Committee the year before. Just securing coordination between departments was to prove exceptionally difficult – something like housing might involve as many as six departments, each with its own priorities.[3] The scale of these tasks can be judged by the workload of the IEP Committee, which received over forty papers on reconstruction in its first month.[4] Some papers might treat relatively straightforward issues like the post-war postal union, others covered weightier questions about post-war aviation or post-war food production. Beveridge's first proposals for the reform of social insurance, one of the key areas of policy for the future welfare state, were just one of the many papers submitted to this committee. Issues like the control of post-war inflation, which had proved so damaging to government plans for reconstruction in 1918–20, were of central strategic concern to the IEP Committee.[5]

Complementary to this central task of coordination performed by the IEP Committee was the growing activity within departments. The early summer of 1942 saw a further change in the tempo of reconstruction as ministries first started to prepare proposals for reconstruction in their own areas of responsibility. It is against the background of this huge expansion of planning for peace that the discussion of physical rebuilding must be set. However urgent the calls by campaigning organisations for actions on a particular front, for the establishment of a central planning authority, or for a pledge on post-war house construction, government saw no alternative but to consider all contending demands as part of the overall task of preparing the country for the return of peace.

Progress by separate departments, although uneven, was undeniable. The cause for planning advanced rapidly during Lord Reith's last months in office as Minister of Works and Planning in the spring of 1942, even if it then stagnated under Lord Portal. The creation in February 1942 of a single Ministry of Town and Country Planning[6] was followed in August by the publication of the reports of two committees established to consider the most difficult technical questions: the Scott Committee to report on land use, and the Uthwatt Committee to recommend a solution to the problems of betterment and compensation.[7] On housing, progress was brisker, eased by the existence of a long-established departmental responsibility for housing under the Ministry of Health and well-defined mechanisms for consultation with local authorities. Preparation for the post-war housing drive illustrates how effectively and quickly the reconstruction committees and the different departments could work together. Planning for reconstruction had changed gear, and in the spring of 1942, less than a year after the IEP Committee's establishment, the outlines of a post-war housing programme had already been drafted.[8]

Plans for the post-war housing drive

Planning the work of the building industry in the period immediately after the war was a central issue for the IEP Committee both because physical rebuilding would be central to every aspect of reconstruction and because of the massive impact that the resources in labour and materials needed by the building industry would have on the rest of the economy. Housing, the largest component of any plan for a post-war building programme, first appeared on the agenda of the committee in April 1942.[9] By November, with submissions from the two key departments, Health and Works, already to hand, the IEP Committee started to press for progress on key policies: the standardisation of designs and components; increased production in the building materials industry; and the introduction of a system of licensing or rationing for house building in order to reduce the impact of the housing programme on the building industry as a whole.[10]

In March 1943 the Ministry of Health submitted calculations on the likely scale of demand for housing.[11] In May the IEP Committee considered four key issues: the scale and timing of the programme, the relationship between housing and town planning, the agencies responsible for constructing housing, and finally, the capacity of the building industry.[12] Through the summer of 1943 the departments worked to answer these issues and complete the draft programme. In November 1943, Lord Woolton, the new Minister for Reconstruction, was given a seat in the Cabinet, a reflection of the growing importance accorded by the government to post-war housing as a whole, and was calling for a resolution of the programme.[13]

In January 1944 the main Reconstruction Committee presented to the Cabinet its *Memorandum on Post-War Housing* setting out the key elements of the government's programme for housing.[14] The memorandum envisaged a three-stage timetable for the programme: an emergency period lasting for the first two years after the war, during which some form of accommodation would be provided for all those without a home of their own; a second longer period of five years when new housing construction was meant to overtake the demand for housing; and finally a third period running on for ten years after the war in which government aimed to replace substandard housing and make good the pre-war hopes of clearing the slums. The most fully detailed plans were for the emergency period. These provided for the construction of 100,000–200,000 permanent houses in the first year after the war and for a further 180,000–200,000 houses in the year after that. Significantly, the Reconstruction Committee reversed decisions taken earlier and now agreed that, given the demands on the building industry during the emergency period, some form of temporary accommodation would be necessary to meet the most urgent, short-term need for housing.[15] This temporary programme would provide housing of strictly limited life for an additional 200,000 families until such a time as the permanent programme was well under way.

Meanwhile, progress was made on two other issues. First, time was devoted by both ministries of Works and Health to encouraging the local authorities to secure sites for permanent housing, a necessary first step for the programme, whose start date was fixed as January 1945.[16] Second, there was further discussion of the need for temporary housing, which led in February to the announcement by Portal in a major speech on post-war housing that active planning of the temporary programme should begin forthwith.[17] In May 1944 further publicity for temporary housing was generated by the erection of a prototype house, hand-built, outside the Tate Gallery, which both the public and the press were encouraged to visit and comment on.[18]

In June 1944 the key housing issues under consideration by the Reconstruction Committee and its housing subcommittee appeared to approach resolution. A technical committee of the ministries of Health, Works and Town and Country Planning was studying the relationship between housing and town planning.[19] The Ministry of Labour was making plans to expand the supply of building labour through a massive expansion of the training programme for the industry.[20] The committee under the Minister of Health had agreed a clear recommendation on who should be responsible for building housing in the first, emergency phase of the reconstruction programme. Because of the economic uncertainty of this period and the need for the strictest control of resources, the local authorities rather than private enterprise were to be responsible for implementing the programme.[21]

Investigations by the specialist committees working on the technical issues crucial to the success of the programmes were also ready. It was these committees, established by the different departments, that provide the most obvious bridge between the campaigning organisations of the early years of the war and the plans that government was making for reconstruction. Their activities see the real clashes between the aspirations for a better post-war world and the pragmatic need to face the availability of resources in post-war Britain. Their membership and the evidence they assembled ensured recognition and representation of the ideals of reconstruction, even if these ideals were adapted during the work of these committees to face the necessary test of implementation. Membership of these specialist committees enabled architects to make direct contributions to plans for reconstruction.

The activities of the two most important bodies, the Burt Committee and the Dudley Committee, touched directly on the issues being decided by the IEP Committee for the economy as a whole. The Burt Committee was established in 1942 jointly by the ministries of Works and Health to consider alternative, non-traditional forms of construction for the permanent housing programme in the hope of by-passing the shortage of traditional materials and labour that had so restricted the housing programme after World War I.[22] The Dudley Committee was set up in the spring of 1942 by the Ministry of Health to advise on space and equipment standards for post-war housing. By the time its recommendations were published in 1944, the Dudley Committee had gone further. Not only had it presented suggestions for the way in which post-war dwellings were to be planned internally to meet the changing patterns of family life, it had collaborated with a team from the Ministry of Town and Country Planning to set standards for the layout of housing. The Dudley Committee made no recommendations on the appearance of housing but its findings were to have a direct impact on the design of the housing built by local authorities at every level, from the arrangement of kitchen and living room, to questions about density and the proportion of flats to houses.

The report of the Dudley Committee

Convened under the aegis of the Central Housing Advisory Council, the committee chaired by Lord Dudley included representatives of the women's movement, the medical and sanitary professions, local government and the construction industry.[23] Four of its members were architects. The two senior architects covered a range of interests. Louis de Soissons was best known as the architect of Welwyn Garden City; and as the architect to the Duchy of Lancaster estates he also had experience of urban housing. Lancelot Keay, City Architect to Liverpool, was an established expert on local authority housing, city-centre flats and large-scale suburban developments like Speke. Of the two other architects, Jocelyn Adburgham, whose designs had appeared occasionally in *Ideal Home*, was experienced in domestic architecture. Judith Ledeboer, the secretary to the Dudley Committee, was a recent graduate of the Architectural Association and winner of the RIBA-sponsored Industrial Housing Competition.[24]

There were obvious parallels between the task before the Dudley Committee and that which had faced the Tudor Walters Committee in 1917.[25] The Dudley Committee saw their enquiry as an attempt to update the Tudor Walters Report by examining and interpreting the successes and failures of housing between the wars. They turned to the same kind of organisations and sources in assembling evidence, and the structure of their report is broadly comparable to that of its predecessor. But there the parallel ends. Printed on twenty-three quarto pages and backed by eleven pages of technical notes, the report of the Dudley Committee looks decidedly thin by comparison with the ninety-seven foolscap pages of the Tudor Walters Report. But despite its brevity the Dudley Report did represent a way of addressing the problems of inter-war housing and set a new point of departure for post-war housing.[26] As the committee assessed the qualities of the housing built after World War I and debated the kind of housing to be built after the war, their discussions focused on two issues of overriding importance: the arrangement of the family's activities within the home, and the choice of the type of dwelling – flat, semi-detached house or terrace house – an issue with important consequences for town planning.

The question of how best to arrange the different household activities inside a dwelling had been examined at length by the Tudor Walters Committee. Their report reflected, for example, working-class life at a time when even in urban areas the majority of families cooked on an open range. But since then there had been widespread change. Now, with the general availability of gas and electricity, and the experience of the war itself, people's expectations of household amenity had changed. The Dudley Committee felt that the standards for post-war housing should be higher than those of 1918:

> The experience gained by the vast number of women now in industry and in the services will influence their attitudes to housing: for war-time factories and hostels often provide high standards of services and equipment, which will make women intolerant of inferior conditions in their own homes.[27]

Women might be intolerant of the old, but what did they expect of the new? The Dudley Committee collected evidence to answer this question, and by the end of the summer of 1942 a large number of groups and organisations were invited to present their views. These included professions, the women's movement, the building industry and representatives of large local authorities like the LCC, Liverpool and Leeds. The list of invited speakers reads like a roll call of

THE UNPLANNED KITCHEN
She must wash in the kitchen. She has hardly room to move. The baby lies on the floor before the fire.

i

ii

7.1 The depressed condition of pre-war housing for working families: (i) 'The unplanned kitchen', from the article 'Plan the Home' by Elizabeth Denby published in *Picture Post*; (ii) poor-quality working-class housing in Somers Town, St Pancras

the pre-war campaigns for slum clearance and better housing during the 1930s.[28] Some, like the Society of Women Housing Managers, were professional groups. Others were confessional bodies like the Union of Catholic Mothers. Others represented political interests, for example the Woman's Co-operative Guild held strong links with the Labour Party. More important in shaping the views of the Dudley Committee were broad-based national organisations like the National Union of Townswomen's Guilds and the National Federation of Women's Institutes. Influential too were the Fabian reform organisations like the Women's Group on Public Welfare, the Kensington Trust and the National Council for Social Service. Evidence from these groups was very different again from the views of

architectural writers on the home like Anthony Betram, author of *The House, a Machine for Living In* (1935), or the contributors to *The Book of the Modern House* (1937), edited by Patrick Abercrombie, for whom the task of rethinking the home was essentially a question of design.[29]

The central issue for the women's groups, across the spectrum, was the guarantee of a minimum standard of housing, a decent and healthy setting for the housewife and her family (Figure 7.1). These points had been made in radical terms in 1939 by Margery Spring-Rice, a doctor and director of the Kensington Trust, in a Penguin Special, *Working Class Wives*.[30] Spring-Rice's book was not only an indictment of poor housing, poor diet and poverty, but a catalogue of pre-war housing conditions seen through the eyes and experience of working-class housewives.

What had seemed radical in 1939 appeared less so in 1942. With further deterioration of housing conditions during the war, there was growing support for the conviction that improving housing conditions was one of the most effective ways of defending the interests of children, women and the family generally. War-time studies of the family under the strain of evacuation such as *Our Towns* (1944), by the Women's Group on Public Welfare,[31] were confirmed by Spring-Rice and her collaborators. Convinced of the need to improve conditions for the working-class housewife, the women's organisations greeted the investigation of the Dudley Committee as a heaven-sent opportunity to secure better housing for those in greatest need.

By the summer of 1942 at least eight surveys were being carried out by different organisations in response to the committee's enquiries.[32] The Women's Advisory Housing Council was responsible for the largest enquiry, with over 40,000 questionnaires sent out. A second major survey, organised by the National Federation of Women's Institutes, was administered nationwide through local institutes. Though the results were open to challenge, the surveys were greeted with enthusiasm by the membership of these bodies, and both the Women's Advisory Housing Council and the National Federation of Women's Institutes felt they had sufficient clarity to press these views on the committee.

Both surveys offered clear guidance on the Dudley Committee's chief concerns on the internal arrangement of the home and the type of dwelling that people wanted. The response to the latter issue was unequivocal: surveys showed an overwhelming desire to live in houses rather than flats. Preferences for the planning of the layout of the kitchen, dining area and living space were more varied. The Women's Advisory Housing Council survey canvassed opinion on both the working kitchen plus living/dining room and the dining/kitchen/utility room plus living room arrangements under discussion by the Dudley Committee. The surveys concluded that most respondents favoured a layout with a small working kitchen, though large enough to do the family washing, and a dining/living room, ideally with a parlour or sitting room as well. However, the Women's Advisory Housing Council cautioned against taking the results of the surveys too literally, saying that they felt many respondents had been overly influenced by existing forms of housing and that good design might possibly reverse these stated preferences.

The results of these surveys gained added weight when taken together with the results of the widespread survey on housing carried out by Mass-Observation for the Advertising Guild. Launched in August 1941, and available to the Dudley Committee in outline form before being published in 1943 as *People's Homes*, this survey corroborated earlier findings and provided the most comprehensive assessment of current preferences.[33] Based on 1,200 household interviews with families ranging from the tenants of city-centre slum tenements to the owner-occupiers of detached houses in seaside towns, the survey provided a wealth of information on different aspects of family life, both within and outside the home. Under the heading 'Inside Homes', the survey addressed issues from 'Feelings about the Home: Satisfactions and Frustrations' to the provision for specific activities in 'The Kitchen-Living Room; the Parlour' or 'Washing Bodies' and 'Anti-Dirt'. Of direct interest to the Dudley Committee was the survey's exploration of preferences for houses over flats, and a series of related questions on the neighbourhood and the world outside the home. The tone of *People's Homes*, with its anecdotal evidence and 'anthropological' asides, is very different from the tabular information and the earnest recommendations of the Women's Advisory Housing Council and National Federation of Women's Institutes surveys. Nevertheless, the results of the three surveys were broadly similar. And on the key issues, the arrangements for cooking and eating and the form of the dwelling, the measure of agreement was remarkable.

People's Homes identified broad changes in the way people ate and cooked which supported the other two surveys. Typical of these changes was the view of respondents on the parlour. Like the Women's Advisory Housing Council survey, the Mass-Observation enquiry showed 'fairly strong demand' for a parlour or second living room, a 'best' room away from the pressures of family life:[34]

> If people's wishes are listened to, it will in effect mean a minor revolution in working-class housing. People are no longer content to eat and live in the same room: what they want today is two living rooms, one for every day in which to eat and relax, another where visitors may be entertained and which they like to keep for best.[35]

What emerged most strongly from all three surveys was the strength of the desire to live in a house, not in a flat. Dismissing the possibility of a more positive image for the flat, and discounting the location problems of the semi-detached house, Mass-Observation's findings showed that for 79 per cent of respondents a small house or bungalow was their ideal form of house.[36] The continuing attraction of the small house surrounded by its own garden, equipped with labour-saving devices, easy to keep clean and warm, emerges from all three surveys as clearly as it shone out of the prospectuses of speculative builders in the years before the war. The evidence before the Dudley Committee left no doubt that the detached house was regarded as the most popular form of post-war home.

The arrangement of the post-war dwelling

With this conclusive evidence the task of making recommendations on the internal layout of the dwelling was comparatively straightforward. On space standards, the Dudley Committee proposed an increase of between 9 per cent and 16 per cent over pre-war local authority norms.[37] More important was the discussion of three alternative arrangements for the layout of the ground floor of a typical two-storey house, with a bathroom and three bedrooms on the upper floor

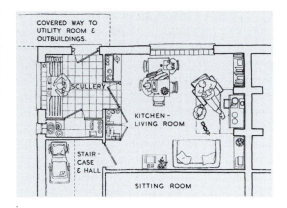

i

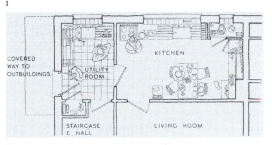

ii

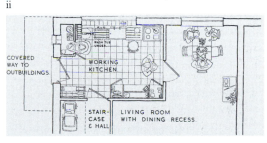

iii

7.2 The three alternative layouts for key activities within the home proposed by the Dudley Committee: (i) the kitchen/living room layout with a separate scullery, the alternative best suited to rural housing; (ii) the dining/kitchen arrangement with separate utility room and living room; (iii) the working kitchen with dining arranged in a recess off the living room

(Figure 7.2). In the first alternative, intended for use in rural and mining areas, the coal range would be retained and located in the kitchen/living room where it would continue as the principal source of heat for both cooking and heating the home. A scullery was to accommodate the washing of dishes and clothes. The second and third alternatives were for urban houses serviced by gas and electricity, and were regarded by the committee as equally applicable to either house or flat. The first of these two alternatives provided a kitchen/dining room of 110 square feet in which the family might eat occasionally, with an adjacent 35 square foot utility room for laundry. The main living room of 160 square feet, freed from cooking and other household tasks, would offer some of the benefits of the inter-war parlour, though the committee set its face against the genteel association of the parlour: 'We think the expression "Parlour" carries an implication which is old fashioned and obsolete. Therefore we do not employ it.'[38]

The final alternative provided – to judge from the surveys – a less popular arrangement of cooking, eating and living. It included a working kitchen of 100 square feet with sufficient space to allow for laundry work. It was, in effect, an up-to-date scullery equipped with a cooker and enlarged to meet the criticisms levelled at the shortage of space of inter-war kitchens. The family would dine in a 'dining niche' in the 210 square foot dining/living room, which was planned in such a way that, cleared of its table, it would provide a space sufficiently large to hold a party or similar event.

More difficult to interpret than the evidence on the internal layout of the dwelling was the type of housing that people said they wanted. The evidence from the surveys seemed incontrovertible. When questioned about housing preferences, people said that they wanted to live in houses. But how did these views square with the growing concern for the impact of the semi-detached house on the form of the city, urban sprawl and increasing commuting times?

The starting point for the Dudley Committee's discussion of the rival advantages of houses and flats was the experience of pre-war housing. One consistent criticism of pre-war estates, from bodies like the National Council for Social Service, concerned with the social impact of local authority housing, had been the lack of variety of types of accommodation on both cottage and tenement estates.[39] Both Thomas Young's study of life at Becontree[40] and Ruth Durant's study of

the LCC's Watling Estate[41] decried the lack of provision for social and communal activities, the absence of shops and schools, but above all they criticised the standardisation of household types and sizes which contributed an overwhelming sense of monotony to many of the LCC's suburban estates. These views were shared by housing reformers like Elizabeth Denby. Before the war she compared the low level of British housing achievement with what she had seen on the Continent and asked, '[Why] indulge in the extremes of *beehive* building in the centre and *chicken-coop* building on the outskirts of the town?'[42] Why isolate different types of families, the old from the young, denying the variety and diversity of a well-established community?

To avoid such monotony the Dudley Committee emphasised the need for a wider range of accommodation to be provided in the same development than had been common before the war. Municipal agencies such as the Association of Municipal Corporations, the National Council for Social Service, the Association of Urban District Councils and major local authorities like the LCC, Manchester and Liverpool all stressed the need to provide for the full range of households, from single people and newlyweds, to large families and old people in the same development.[43] The provision of diverse dwelling types was one way of meeting one of the most damaging criticisms of the social failings of the inter-war estates.

This had important consequences for the debate on the forms of housing. Given the distribution of the size of families, local authorities as different as Liverpool and Welwyn Garden City thought it advantageous, notwithstanding the general antipathy to the flat, to include a proportion of small dwellings to accommodate smaller households and single people.[44] But the case for increasing the proportion of flats beyond a minimum of 5 per cent to answer this need was vigorously opposed, at least in the narrow context of a simple comparison of the attractions of the flat and the house.[45] Evidence from the surveys and the experience of the local authorities confirmed that objections to the flat were firmly rooted in the problems caused by the failings of existing designs like the LCC's gallery-access flats, where noise, lack of privacy, worries about children's safety, 'gangsterism' and the difficulties of refuse disposal and coal delivery caused continual aggravation.[46]

Framed simply in terms of the choice between one type of dwelling or another there was general agreement that houses were simply preferable to flats for the great majority. But how did the committee judge the matter when it was set in the wider context of the planning issues with which housing was inevitably bound up? When considered in conjunction with the need to limit urban sprawl, with the need to balance densities and land costs, or with the necessary connection between home and work, how appropriate was a simple choice between flat and house?

Housing and planning

To avoid rethinking the form of housing without due consideration of the necessary relationship with planning, a joint study group was set up involving members of the Dudley Committee and the ministries of Health and Town and Country Planning. In addition to Lancelot Keay and Louis de Soissons, the senior architectural members of the Dudley Committee, this group included two leading planners, Thomas Sharp and William Holford.[47] Patrick Abercrombie, closely involved with the County of London Plan, did not take part in the joint study group, but the team working on the plan was represented by Gordon Stephenson and Terry Kennedy.[48] By June 1943 the study group was meeting regularly and had considerably expanded the agenda for discussion. Questions about density and residential location had already been touched on in the discussion of housing form, but only in very limited terms. Now the study group set about examining housing issues in the wider context of planning.[49]

Again the discussion of large-scale planning started from the preoccupations of the pre-war years, focusing on the containment of uncontrolled urban growth, one of the central themes in the British debate on planning in the late

1920s and 1930s. The study group's principles for directing the pattern of reconstruction at a regional level were clearly in line with the aims of the campaign to contain urban growth. It argued for:

> the restriction of future housing on the periphery of the larger towns, on the grounds that it increases the burden of workers' travel, isolates the townsman still more from the country and makes it difficult to provide a full social life in a physically distinct community.[50]

But rejection of sprawling 'chicken-coop' building on the outskirts of existing towns now raised the question of how to distribute the new housing to be built after the war.

Some of those consulted by the study group, like Frederic Osborn and the Town and Country Planning Association, favoured radical policies of decentralisation, arguing that reconstruction provided a unique opportunity to redirect the population away from existing cities towards low-density New Towns: 'Though infinitely preferable to the tenement flat solution, the suburban extension of a city already creates its own set of problems … Long process though this may be, decentralisation is in our opinion the only fundamental solution.'[51] However, the study group and the Dudley Committee favoured a more pragmatic and less costly approach, with the creation of some New Towns, some expansion of smaller towns, and the rebuilding of the housing destroyed in the centres of existing cities. Clearly this policy was not only much more in keeping with Forshaw and Abercrombie's proposals for London, but also more acceptable to the large local authorities, who had a major stake in continuity with the status quo as the basis for post-war housing.

The implications of this approach for housing densities were far-reaching. While it might be possible to build in New Towns and even on the outskirts of small towns at the 40–50 people per acre densities of the inter-war cottage estates or the Garden Cities, it would be unreasonable to expect such low densities in cities like London, Liverpool or Manchester. On the strength of their pre-war experience, most large local authorities favoured higher densities for all but suburban developments, as their submissions to the study group clearly showed.[52] Manchester, which had generally opposed the building of high flats, hoped to achieve an aggregate density for mixed layouts of houses and flats of twenty-five dwellings, or about eighty people per acre, and a density of up to forty-five flats per acre in layouts for flats alone. London, Liverpool and the Association of Metropolitan Councils argued for higher densities, particularly where developments could be placed next to playgrounds, parks or other open spaces, and cited the cost of land as a prime consideration. Other factors, too, weighed in favour of higher densities. The need to place housing near work in the centre of the city, albeit at higher densities, and thereby reduce the journey to work for working-class households was an important consideration for many authorities like Birmingham and Manchester.[53]

The balance of evidence submitted on density was against the low densities of the suburban developments of the pre-war years, even though the Dudley Committee recognised that in the long term densities would probably fall: 'In general, the tendency towards a lower overall density for towns as a whole will no doubt continue.'[54] To accommodate a range of different types of development the committee recommended a range of densities from thirty people per acre for open developments outside towns to 100 people per acre for town centres. Provision was even made for a maximum density of 120 people per acre for 'large concentrated urban areas', although this was still well below the maximum of 200 persons per acre suggested by Forshaw and Abercrombie for the central areas of London.[55] Yet even these proposed densities were of considerable importance for the debate on housing form: how else but by building flats could higher densities be achieved?

To judge from pre-war experience high densities invariably meant building blocks of flats: certainly the predominant form of local authority housing in city centres had been flats and tenements.[56] Even the committee's own calculations suggested that at 120 people per acre between 25 per cent and 30 per cent of the population would have to be accommodated in flats.[57] But of more general relevance in establishing the case for the flat as the necessary response to higher densities were the recently published studies by Forshaw and Abercrombie which accompanied the discussion of density in their plan for London (Figure 7.3).[58] They proposed a combination of housing and flats in 'mixed layouts' to suit different densities. As might be expected, in their Zone 3, the outer zone for London, where densities were to be set at 100 people per acre, the majority of dwellings would be in the two- or three-storey houses and only 13.5 per cent of all dwellings would be in blocks of eight or ten storeys. Nor was it surprising that in Zone 1 at 200 people per acre virtually all dwellings were to be in high blocks. But significantly, even at 136 people per acre, the density for the intermediate zone, over 60 per cent of all dwellings would have to be in tall blocks to achieve the generous provision of open space and communal facilities that the planners considered necessary. To achieve densities of 100 people per acre or more the flat was essential.

Mixed development and the neighbourhood

Instructive though these studies of density might be they were diagrammatic in the extreme. They gave little indication of how this kind of housing would appear in practice. To judge from the architectural shortcomings of many of the slum-clearance schemes of the mid-1930s, higher densities did appear to create just the kind of environment which Osborn and the Town and Country Planning Association had denounced as so damaging to family life. To most architects the inter-war experience of flat building was exemplified by the drab Neo-Georgian gallery-access housing built by the LCC. Judged on this basis higher densities might well appear to involve a reduction in housing quality. There were of course more positive examples. Elizabeth

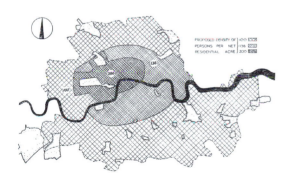

i

7.3 Forshaw and Abercrombie's studies of density: (i) estimates of the result of different densities on the mix of houses and flats for a notional site of 93 acres; (ii) the three density zones proposed for post-war London

Denby had championed Continental housing, particularly the programme of municipal flat building in Vienna.[59] Yorke and Gibberd's *The Modern Flat* showed what could be done in other countries,[60] and even during the war new and influential ideas on flats were to find their way from Sweden to England.[61] In England, too, there were successful pre-war examples of modern flat building like Kensal House in West London or Quarry Hill in Leeds, well known to the committee (Figure 7.4).[62]

But too often these outstanding English examples were no more than single buildings, individual architectural successes rather than prototypes for a new approach to housing layout. What was needed was not new styling but a new organising principle to guarantee an escape from the drabness and the monotony of the typical pre-war tenement estate.

The approach to this problem endorsed by the joint study group was the planning of new developments in 'neighbourhoods', the aim of which would establish well-defined and easily identifiable communities charged with the vitality and variety of existing areas of the city. Mixed layouts of flats and houses were seen as the natural form of housing for neighbourhood planning to ensure the necessary variety of different types of households for a balanced community. In addition to this variety of housing the neighbourhood was to offer facilities for use by the local community: a school, shops, open space and, ideally, a community centre or local hall.

In 1943 the concept of neighbourhood planning was new to England. Forshaw and Abercrombie's use of the idea in the County of London Plan was one of its first English applications (Figure 7.5). Its advocates could point to a number of positive approaches to the creation of the neighbourhood community. From Continental examples English housing reformers had learned to build common facilities for a community living in large developments. Denby had praised the Viennese custom of providing facilities like creches, kindergartens, laundries and drying rooms for large housing blocks like the

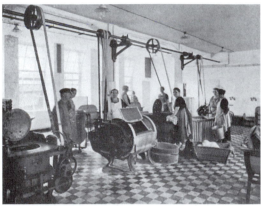

i

ii

iii

iv

7.4 Examples of modern flats with communal facilities: (i) the Karl-Marx-Hof, Vienna (1926–30), a development with a population of 5,000 in 1,400 apartments; (ii) Karl-Marx-Hof, the communal washing and drying rooms; (iii) Kensal House, Ladbroke Grove (1934–36), a view showing the nursery school and the 68 flats beyond; (iv) a model of the Quarry Hill development of 500 flats showing the central boiler house, shops, swimming and paddling pool and other communal facilities

Washingtonhof and the Karl-Marx-hof. Delegations from big cities such as Manchester, Leeds and London had studied Continental estates at first hand; a delegation from the LCC visited estates in Copenhagen, Paris, Vienna and Berlin and returned impressed by the scale of provision of communal facilities and the sense of community that this appeared to foster.[63]

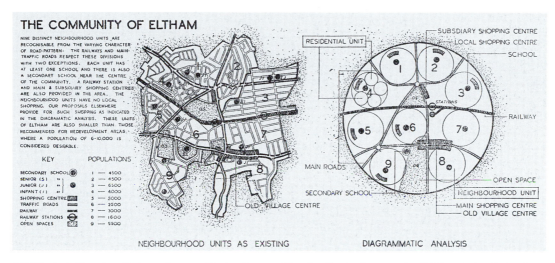

7.5 The 'neighbourhood' idea as illustrated in the County of London Plan by the example of Eltham in South London

An alternative view of neighbourhood planning, unrelated to the practice of public housing, had also developed in the United States. Here the emphasis was not on the single large development or complex but on dividing the rapidly growing suburbs into a number of readily identifiable neighbourhoods. These ideas, set out as early as the 1920s by Clarence Perry, were already established practice in the work of architect planners like Henry Wright and Clarence Stein.[64] Neighbourhoods were to be defined by major traffic arteries or natural boundaries such as rivers or other changes in topography and were to accommodate 5,000–10,000 people and have the full range of communal facilities such as schools and shops necessary to the day-to-day life of its residents.

While English planners were already familiar with the US discussion on the neighbourhood, the most immediate source of English information on the topic was the work of the National Council for Social Service (NCSS). Through its role in coordinating various forms of charitable and voluntary social work the NCSS had built up a considerable understanding of the social problems of pre-war housing, especially the sense of isolation and the lack of community felt by so many tenants on new suburban estates. In 1937 the NCSS had arranged its annual conference

around this theme and had maintained an interest in the subject during the debate on reconstruction.[65] In 1942 the NCSS focused attention on the problems of community in the city and initiated an enquiry, the results of which were later published as *The Size and Social Structure of a Town*.[66] In this the NCSS had supported the concept of the neighbourhood in the planning of new developments, urged an ideal size for the neighbourhood unit, recognised the need for a variety of different types of housing to ensure a mix of different households, and argued for the provision of local communal facilities such as elementary schools, shops and a village hall in terms very similar to contemporary US proposals.[67]

Forshaw and Abercrombie's use of the neighbourhood in the County of London Plan developed both from American ideas and from the recommendations of the NCSS; indeed, Wesley Dougill, one of Abercrombie's chief assistants at the LCC, had been a member of the NCSS enquiry team in 1942. Basing their plan on an analysis of London as a conglomeration of different communities, rather than one massive city, Forshaw and Abercrombie argued that each of London's separate communities could be subdivided quite naturally into a number of neighbourhood units of between 6,000 and 10,000 people, centred on a school and a group of local shops. With a balanced community of different types of households, these new neighbourhoods would continue the long established pattern of London's growth, avoiding the faults of inter-war sprawl and the social problems that went with it.

The idea of the neighbourhood as recommended by the NCSS and developed in the Country of London Plan was immediately attractive to the joint study group. It appeared to provide a form of social structure for the housing to be built after the war:

> For the proper social functioning of the large town … it is necessary to work out some organisation of its physical form which will aid in every way the full development of community life and enable a proper measure of social amenities to be provided and arranged to advantage in each residential neighbourhood. The conception of the 'neighbourhood unit' arises out of an acknowledgment of the necessity of doing this and offers the means of doing it.[68]

Planned as mixed developments, the neighbourhood would provide a way of avoiding both the harshness of the tenement block and the anomie of the cottage estates, and would answer the Dudley Committee's demands for socially balanced communities. At all but the very lowest densities the flat would be a natural part of this new residential landscape, providing social diversity and an element of architectural variety.

The 1944 *Housing Manual* and the forms of post-war housing

With pressure from the IEP Committee to agree plans for post-war housing, the translation of the Dudley Committee's recommendations into ministerial policy was swift. The publication of the Dudley Report in May 1944 was followed shortly by the Ministry of Health's publication of a new version of its *Housing Manual*, the prin-ciple means by which the ministry circulated advice on housing to the local authorities.[69] Just as the Tudor Walters Report had determined the form and the content of the *Housing Manual 1919*, so the Dudley Report now determined the recommendations of the new manual.[70] While the main body of the Dudley Report and the new manual might be seen as an appropriate and largely uncontentious updating of earlier *Housing Manuals*, the recommendations on housing layout, on the value of the neighbourhood unit to planning and on the need for mixed development were entirely new. The Dudley Committee's arguments for the implementation of higher densities in housing and the need for flats at densities over 100 people per acre represented a significant break with the conventional wisdom of the pre-war years. Coming so soon after the presentation of Forshaw and Abercrombie's County of London Plan, the Dudley Report and the *Housing Manual 1944* established a new orthodoxy. In 1944, as local authorities responded to the urgings the of Ministry of Town and Country Planning to draw up plans for post-war housing, this new orthodoxy provided the most comprehensive vision for rebuilding the housing areas of Britain's cities. During the first five years of reconstruction there were minor changes to the provisions of the *Housing Manual 1944*. Space standards were trimmed to meet government's determination to reduce public spending. But the central recommendations on the design of the individual dwelling and on housing layout were repeated unaltered in the enlarged *Housing Manual 1949* (Figure 10.7).[71] In these terms the work of the Dudley Committee and the joint study group would shape the form of residential development across Britain into the 1950s (Figure 7.6).[72]

Above all, the work of the Dudley Committee demonstrated how the general aspirations for a better world could be harnessed to the government's plans for reconstruction. In its membership and in the evidence drawn from different sources – from the women's movement and those campaigning for better housing or demanding an improvement in the living

7.6 The use of mixed development of houses and flats to provide housing at 90 people per acre, a study illustrated in the Ministry of Housing and Local Government's *The Density of Residential Areas*, 1952

conditions of working-class wives – the Dudley Committee showed how ideas on improvement could be translated into officially sponsored recommendations and then through into a blueprint for government action. Here was a visible connection between the idealism of the reforming campaigners and the necessary pragmatism of government plans for reconstruction.

The work of the Dudley Committee was crucial to the post-war housing programme. But it was only one area of war-time planning for housing. Government had learned from painful lessons after World War I that the building industry would be unable to meet the demands for building immediately after the war. It would therefore have to consider how the houses it proposed to build were actually going to be constructed. As in other fields, the answer to this question was to be explored by another specialist committee, the Burt Committee, whose work would come to be as important as that of Lord Dudley and his team.

Notes

1 For an overview of the preparations for reconstruction see P. Addison, *The Road to 1945: British Politics and the Second World War*, London, Jonathan Cape, 1975, ch. IX. For a discussion of plans for physical reconstruction see J.B. Cullingworth, *Environmental Planning. Vol. I: Reconstruction and Land Use Planning 1939–47*, London, HMSO, 1975.

2 The role of this crucial committee is discussed in Cullingworth, *Reconstruction*, pp. 19–52. The papers for the various Cabinet reconstruction committees are to be found at PRO/CAB/87; those dealing primarily with physical reconstruction are to be found at CAB/87/1–12; 35–7. The papers for the IEP Committee are at PRO/CAB/87/54–7.

3 Cullingworth, *Reconstruction*, pp. 21–3.

4 PRO/CAB/87/55.

5 The need to learn from the lessons of 1918–20 was a continual refrain; Cullingworth, *Reconstruction*, p. 25. See also PRO/CAB/87/55/IEP(42)17.

6 A detailed account of the establishment of the Ministry of Town and Country Planning is provided by Cullingworth, *Reconstruction*, chs II and III.

7 *Ibid.*, pp. 71–3.

8 The first draft of the post-war housing programme, 'Preliminary Discussion of the Building Programme and Housing Policy' (PRO/CAB/87/55/IEP(42) 17, 43, 65) was assembled for the IEP's 23rd meeting on 27.11.1942. By May 1943 the Cabinet's Committee on Reconstruction Problems was presented with a more developed version of this earlier paper: 'Post-War Housing Policy' (RP/ IEP(43)24).

9 PRO/CAB/87/55, at the meeting of 23.4.1942.

10 PRO/CAB/87/55/IEP(42)65.

11 PRO/CAB/87/55/IEP(42)23.

12 PRO/CAB/87/55/RP/IEP(43)24.

13 Addison, *Road to 1945*, pp. 236–58.

14 PRO/CAB/87/7/R(44)18.

15 The Central Housing Advisory Committee's Sub-Committee for Temporary and Permanent Housing Construction under Lewis Silkin had reported their opposition to the construction of temporary housing in December 1943, see below ch. 8, especially note 21. Official support for a programme of temporary housing, opposed hitherto, surfaced for the first time in the Memorandum on post-war housing, especially paragraphs 3 and 14.

16 PRO/CAB/87/7/R(44)19.

17 Lord Portal's speech in the House of Lords on post-war housing was summarised in *AJ*, 17.2.1944, p. 142–4.

18 'Emergency Factory Made House', *AJ*, 11.5.1944, pp. 344, 349–57. The full range of prototypes sponsored by government were on display outside the Tate Gallery by November, *AD*, Nov. 1944, pp. 251–5.

19 The work of this committee, first mooted in January 1943, was to be published as the second part of the Dudley Report (see below).

20 This was later to appear as a White Paper: Ministry of Labour, *Training in the Building Industry*, Cmnd 6428, London, HMSO, 1943.

21 For files on the Committee on Housing by Private Enterprise *see* The Poole Committee, PRO.

22 For an account of the work of the Burt Committee see below, ch. 8.

23 The papers of the Dudley Committee are at PRO/HLG/37/62,63,64,65; the papers circulated to the committee, identified by the prefix PD, are to be found in file 63. The members of the committee are listed in the report. The chairman, Lord Dudley, was an industrialist with iron and steel interests and had served as chairman of the Council for Research on Housing Construction, whose report had been published in 1934.

24 'Industrial Housing Competition', *AJ*, 12.9.1940, pp. 201–8.

25 *Report of the Committee Appointed by the President of the LGB and the Secretary for State for Scotland to consider Questions of Building Construction in Connection with the Provision of Dwellings for the Working Classes in England, Wales, and Scotland* (the Tudor Walters Report), Local Government Board, London, HMSO, 1918. For a discussion of the work of the Tudor Walters Committee see M. Swennarton, *Homes for Heroes: The Politics and Architecture of Early State Housing in Britain*, London, Heinemann Educational Books, 1981, ch. 5.

26 *The Design of Dwellings* (the Dudley Report), London, Ministry of Health, 1943.

27 *Ibid.*, p. 10.

28 See the papers of the Dudley Committee, PRO/HLG/37/63, papers 1, 5, 9.

29 A. Betram, *The House, a Machine for Living In: A Summary of the Art and Science of Home-Making Considered Functionally*, Harmondsworth, Penguin, 1935; P. Abercrombie (ed.), *The Book of the Modern House*, London, Hodder & Stoughton, 1937.

30 M. Spring-Rice, *Working-Class Wives*, Harmondsworth, Penguin, 1939.

31 The Women's Group on Public Welfare, *Our Towns: A Close-Up*, Oxford, Oxford University Press, 1944, p. 103.

32 These organisations were the Women's Advisory Housing Council, the National Union of Townswomen's Guilds, the Women's Group on Public Welfare, the Women's Gas Council, the National Council of Women, the National Federation of Women's Institutes and the Standing Joint Committee of Working Women's Organisations.

33 *People's Homes*, London, John Murray, 1943.

34 *Ibid.*, pp. 104–8.

35 *Ibid.*, p. xii–xiii.

36 *Ibid.*, pp. 218–22.

37 *Design of Dwellings*, pp. 33–50, especially Appendix II.

38 *Ibid.*, p. 14.

39 As an organisation that coordinated the activities of a number of voluntary and charitable groups involved in social work, the National Council of Social Service had engaged with the social problems of housing during the 1930s. The Eighth Annual Conference, held in 1937, was devoted to the theme of the social problems of the new estates, and the proceedings were published as *New Housing Estates and their Problems*, London, NCSS, 1937.

40 T. Young, *Becontree and Dagenham*, London, Pilgrim Trust and Becontree Social Survey Committee, 1934.

41 R. Durant, *Watling: A Survey of Social Life on a New Estate*, London, S. King & Son, 1939.

42 E. Denby, *Europe Rehoused*, London, George Allen & Unwin, 1938, p. 262.

43 See the evidence under 'Variety of Type of Accommodation', *House Plans, Urban*, PRO/HLG 37/63,PD11, p. 1.

44 *Ibid.*, pp. 2–3.

45 *Flat Plans*, PRO/HLG37/63,PD16, p. 2.

46 *Ibid.*, p. 3.

47 The need to set up a joint study group between the two ministries was first raised in January 1943. When finally established it consisted of: Sharp as chairman, de Soissons and Keay from the Dudley Committee; Holford; Gordon Stephenson and R.T. Kennedy, both of whom had worked on the County of London Plan at the Ministry of Town and Country Planning; Ellicott, from the Ministry of Town and Country Planning; Pointon Taylor, from the Ministry of Health; and Miss Crowther Smith from the Ministry of Information. The secretary was Judith Ledeboer, who was also secretary to the main Dudley Committee. The study group was assisted by W. Allen from the Building Research Station, who advised on lighting and the space around buildings. The draft report was subject to scrutiny (and amendment) by George Pepler.

48 Stephenson and Kennedy's role on the County of London Plan team is mentioned in G. Cherry (ed.) *Pioneers in British Planning*, London, Architectural Press, 1981, p. 16.

49 'The Relationship of Housing to Town Planning', PRO/HLG37/65; the joint study group's papers are unnumbered.

50 *Ibid.*, p. 1.

51 See the evidence submitted to the Dudley Committee: 'Layout', PRO/HLG37/63,PD29, p. 8.

52 *Ibid.*, pp. 15–18; *House Plans, Urban*, pp. 3–4.

53 *Flat Plans*, p. 2.

54 *Design of Dwellings*, p. 56.

55 *Ibid.*, pp. 59–61.

56 It is difficult to form a comprehensive picture of the volume of flat building before 1939, though A. Ravetz, 'From Working Class Tenement to Modern

Flat: Local Authorities and Multi-storey Housing between the Wars', in A. Sutcliffe (ed.), *Multi-Storey Living: The British Working Class Experience*, London, Croon Helm, 1974, does provide a useful summary of achievements in Leeds, Liverpool and Manchester. Certainly the LCC restricted cottage developments to suburban estates: LCC, *London Housing*, London, LCC, 1937.

57 *Design of Dwellings*, p. 60.

58 J. Forshaw and P. Abercrombie, *The County of London Plan 1943*, London, Macmillan, 1943, pp. 79–83.

59 Denby, *Europe Rehoused*, pp. 148–83. See also the report by the International Housing Association, *Housing in Vienna*, Frankfurt and Stuttgart, Julius Hoffmann, 1933.

60 F.R.S. Yorke and F. Gibberd, *The Modern Flat*, London, Architectural Press, 1937, was probably the best-known book on flats, but other books such as H.I. Ashworth's *Flats: Design and Equipment*, London, Pitman & Sons, 1936, provided information more relevant to working-class flats.

61 Journals such as *Architectural Design* gave considerable prominence to Swedish ideas on housing, e.g. 'Housing Forum: Sweden', *AD*, March 1944, pp. 52–7.

62 The Dudley Committee visited a number of blocks of flats in London, Birmingham and Leeds, including Kensal House and Quarry Hill. At Quarry Hill they were particularly impressed by the communal facilities, the Garchey waste disposal system and the lift installation, which convinced them of the possibility of using lifts more widely. Overall, however, they found the estate very drab.

63 See e.g. *Working Class Housing on the Continent and the Application of Continental Ideas to the Housing Problems of the County of London*, London, LCC, 1936; and *Report of the Birmingham Deputation Visiting Germany, Czechoslovakia and Austria*, Birmingham, City of Birmingham, 1930.

64 C. Perry, 'The Neighbourhood Unit, a Scheme for the Arrangement of the Family Life Community', *Regional Survey of New York and its Environs,* Vol. VII, 1929. The most widely known example of this neighbourhood idea was Radburn, New Jersey, designed by Wright and Stein and widely publicised. For a discussion of the evolution of the neighbourhood idea in US planning see L. Mumford, 'The Neighbourhood and the Neighbourhood Unit', *Town Planning Review*, 1953, pp. 256–70.

65 See e.g. NCSS, *New Housing Estates*, and the frequent articles on housing problems in the *Social Service Review* between 1937 and 1942.

66 The NCSS produced two pamphlets on this theme: *Social Factors Influencing the Composition and Size of an Urban Unit*, London, NCSS, 1942, and the report of an NCSS survey unit, *The Size and Social Structure of a Town*, London, George Allen & Unwin, 1943.

67 Other developments by Wright and Stein laid out on the neighbourhood principle include Chatham Village, Pittsburgh.

68 'Neighbourhood Planning', PRO/HLG37/65, p. 2.

69 Ministry of Health, *Housing Manual 1944*, London, HMSO, 1944.

70 Local Government Board, *Housing Manual 1919*, London, HMSO, 1919.

71 Ministry of Health, *Housing Manual 1949*, London, HMSO, 1949.

72 See e.g. Ministry of Housing and Local Government, *The Density of Residential Areas*, London, HMSO, 1952.

8 New ways of building for houses and schools

The discussion of plans for the post-war building programme surfaced first during the summer of 1941 at the meetings of the Reconstruction Committee under Arthur Greenwood. The scale of destruction already caused by the Blitz gave weight to concerns that the capabilities of the building industry, reduced by the war, would be unable to meet the demands.[1] It was not until after the reconfiguration of the reconstruction committees in 1942 and the establishment of the Committee on Post-War Internal Economic Problems (IEP Committee) that government was in a position to address reconstruction in concerted fashion.[2] But with estimates of future demand for building from different departments, development of a national building programme gathered pace. By the end of the year the Committee on Reconstruction Problems and the Lord President's Committee were in a position to discuss the well-developed drafts of the national programme that the War Cabinet had requested in early November, and to consider how plans for the housing drive would mesh with those for schools, factories and all other forms of construction.[3]

Pivotal to government's discussion of post-war rebuilding was the central difficulty of balancing the country's expectations with the resources that it believed would be available when the war ended. The boom after World War I and the accompanying inflation was still a vivid memory and a clear warning of what would inevitably happen again if demand and supply were not carefully controlled. In the spring of 1942 the IEP Committee had reviewed the painful experience of boom and slump between 1918 and 1921, when purchasing power that had built up during the war, combined with the need to replace material and stocks run down during the years of hostilities, had fuelled a surge in demand.[4] The sudden removal of war-time controls and subsidies and a return to an open economy had only aggravated the boom, which had then been followed in the summer of 1920 by a slump of corresponding ferocity. Given the damage sustained across the economy since 1939, there was every reason to believe that the same pattern would be repeated on an even grander scale unless the government could act to prevent it.

The challenge of reconciling plans for the post-war housing programme with the demands for other forms of building illustrate the scale and complexity of the task facing the government. Having identified the housing programme as the largest and most urgent priority for the construction industry, the government had to find a way of accommodating the programme's needs to the capacity of the building industry and the demands for construction in other fields, all of which had to take account of the demands for labour and resources from other sectors of the economy.

To meet this challenge the government needed to plan on a number of fronts, coordinating the work of different departments through the central reconstruction committees. Drawing on the lessons of the period after World War I, the IEP Committee argued that it would be necessary to continue in some form or other the system of determining priorities for building work and the rationing of labour and materials already established during the war.[5] A second priority for the success of plans for post-war building was to get the building industry back into action as soon as possible after the war by securing an adequate workforce for both the building and the building materials industries. To achieve this officials from a number of ministries, Works, Labour, Health and the Board of Trade, explored both how skilled labour might best be released from the services as part of the general process of demobilisation after the war and how to increase recruitment into the industry. This required delicate negotiations with the building unions and a long-term commitment to training in the building industry, set out in the White Paper *Training for the Building Industry*, published in 1943.[6] Finally, a third area of planning arose from the concern to encourage the building industry to explore ways of saving labour, particularly skilled labour, and economising on the use of materials that would be in short supply after the war. This was to be achieved most effectively not by the lowering of standards, which government hoped to raise by the various reconstruction programmes, but by developing new forms of construction for a variety of different building types.

The programme of investigating these new forms of construction to ensure the saving of traditional skills and materials was the responsibility of the Ministry of Works. To oversee the preparation of the building industry for post-war reconstruction it had established the Directorate of Post-War Building in 1941 under the general charge of Sir James West, Chief Architect to the Ministry of Works, working with Hugh Beaver as Director.[7] Faced with this massive undertaking, the directorate, working in concert with its sister organisation, the Directorate of Building Materials, established a series of committees to coordinate the study of the different tasks ahead. Three groups of committees were set up, each concerned with different areas of policy. One was concerned with design and design policy for different building types, housing, schools, factories and agricultural buildings, with the architectural use of building materials, and with certain kinds of architectural problems particular to certain building types, such as architectural acoustics; each of these separate subject areas was then investigated by a separate study committee, which would frequently overlap in membership with other study committees and with the main Design Policy Committee. The second broad area of study was policy for structures, with a set of five study committees to explore different forms of construction. The third major area of study was the examination of future policy on installations and services. To complement this already awesome array of committees, there were four further committees: the Standards Committee, the Code of Practice Committee, the Building Standards Committee and a Publications Board, responsible for informing the industry of the findings and recommendations of all these different committees. In all, the expertise assembled by the directorate provided the skills and resources for the most thoroughgoing investigation of building in Britain. The flow of publications, particularly the Post-War Building Studies series, provide impressive evidence of the scale and the quality of this investigation.[8]

The work of the Burt Committee

The search for viable alternatives to traditional forms of construction was central to the planning of the post-war building programme. Housing, the largest single element in the programme, was naturally given the highest priority. In September 1942 an interdepartmental committee on house construction was appointed by the Minister of Health, the Secretary of State for Scotland and the Minister of Works

to consider materials and methods of construction suitable for the building of

houses and flats, having regard to efficiency, economy and speed of erection,
and to make recommendations for post-
war practice in the light of all relevant findings of the Study Committees coordinated
by the Directorate of Post-War Building of
the Ministry of Works.[9]

The committee assembled by Sir George Burt
was knowledgeable, bringing together people
with experience in the building industry, architecture, government service and the Building
Research Station (BRS). A number of members,
Lancelot Keay, Louis de Soissons and Judith
Ledeboer, were also serving on the Dudley and
other committees, easing considerably the difficulties of coordination.

The first stage of the Burt Committee's work,
completed within a month of its establishment,
consisted of three separate pieces of work. The
committee established for the first time performance standards for housing in terms of strength
and stability, moisture penetration and sound
insulation to simplify the process of comparison
of traditional forms of construction with any new
alternatives. Second, the committee prepared a
report summarising the work being carried out
by other study committees on the value of non-
traditional materials as substitutes in traditional
forms of construction. Finally, the committee
assembled information on past forms of non-traditional house building. One of the most valuable sources of this information was the
assessment of the different alternative forms of
housing construction that had been investigated
by the BRS during the early 1920s. Drawing on
the information obtained by the BRS from
houses built on its experimental site at Ealing,
and by collecting evidence from the variety of
local authorities and private sponsors who had
been engaged in developing these systems, the
committee was able to assemble quickly a comprehensive survey of 19 different systems of non-
traditional construction. These ranged from the
'no-fines' mass concrete system used to build less
than a thousand houses in the early 1920s to the
10,000 steel 'Weir houses' which had been built

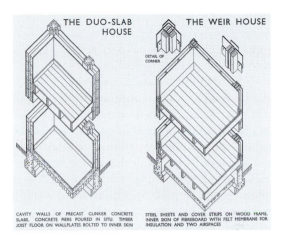

THE DUO-SLAB HOUSE   THE WEIR HOUSE

DETAIL OF CORNER

CAVITY WALLS OF PRECAST CLINKER CONCRETE SLABS. CONCRETE PIERS POURED IN SITU. TIMBER JOIST FLOOR ON WALLPLATES BOLTED TO INNER SKIN

STEEL SHEETS AND COVER STRIPS ON WOOD FRAME. INNER SKIN OF FIBREBOARD WITH FELT MEMBRANE FOR INSULATION AND TWO AIRSPACES

8.1 Forms of non-traditional house construction developed between the wars: the Duo-Slab house, built with
precast concrete slabs and concrete piers, and the Weir
house, constructed with sheet-steel external panels
mounted on a timber frame

by unemployed shipbuilders in defiance of the
local building unions (Figure 8.1). The assessment of these non-traditional systems on the basis
of the committee's standards and on evidence,
such as it might be, of their performance in practice was published in 1944 as Part II of *House
Construction*, the committee's first report.[10]

It was natural that the Burt Committee
should have started its investigations by assessing
pre-war experience in this field, but its members
held out little hope of using the majority of these
systems for post-war housing. The committee
was able to recommend the development of the
'no-fines' concrete system, but refused to
endorse the various timber, steel-frame and
metal-panel systems without radical reappraisal.
Not surprisingly, the report reads more like a
cautious case for further research than a basis for
immediate action. If non-traditional construction was to make a real contribution to the post-
war building programme, the committee recognised that it needed to encourage the submission
of more proposals and to speed up its ability to
assess them.

By the middle of 1943 the committee had
addressed these two issues. Its ability to assess
the growing number of proposals was greatly

strengthened in July with the setting up of a technical subcommittee to advise the main committee.[11] This smaller group, working directly under Burt himself, consisted largely of architects from the BRS and a small number from private practice, including Anthony Chitty from Tecton who acted from August 1943 as the committee's technical officer in charge of a newly formed technical section. The technical subcommittee vetted all proposals and reported on those regarded as promising. If a proposal was approved for further development, the main committee would request the Directorate of Post-War Building to issue a licence for the construction of a demonstration house, perhaps by the sponsor or by the Ministry of Works at its test site at Northolt. This would then be assessed by a team from the BRS under Frederic Towndrow, the Controller of Experimental Building Development at the Ministry of Works.[12]

In February the position of the Burt Committee was further strengthened by its reconstitution with wider terms of reference as a full standing committee of the Directorate of Post-War Building.[13] Here was confirmation of the critical importance of non-traditional forms of construction for government's plans for post-war building. Equally important was the committee's success in increasing the number of proposals. By the end of 1943 the technical subcommittee had already received over 500 submissions, of which it considered 234 'had reached a stage of development worth the Committee's notice'.[14] During 1944 proposals continued to flood in and were forwarded to the committee for consideration.[15] Of these only a small number were granted a licence to build a demonstration house. The committee's second report, published in November 1946, describes only nine systems in detail.[16] But by the final meeting of the committee in May 1947, 101 systems had been investigated in detail and recommended by the committee for a licence. Of these, nineteen were based on pre-war experience, while the remaining eighty-two were a product of wartime experiments, a measure of the interest in the field throughout the later years of the war.[17]

The Burt Committee's engagement with the temporary housing programme began later than its work on non-traditional forms of permanent construction, and then only after overcoming initial hostility to the idea.[18] The question of a temporary housing programme had been addressed first by a committee under Lewis Silkin, established by the Central Housing Advisory Committee in the summer of 1942 to report on the case for temporary housing alongside the permanent housing programme.[19] Again the membership of the Silkin Committee overlapped with that of the Dudley and the Burt Committees, with the ubiquitous Keay serving on all three, and Towndrow, appointed coordinator of the government's experimental housing programme in March 1943, on both the Silkin and the Burt Committees.

The Silkin Committee's first report shows that two approaches to emergency housing were being considered for the first phase of the housing drive. The first, much influenced by US experience, reflected very closely the form of 'demountable trailer homes' of about 600 square feet and of strictly limited life developed by the Tennessee Valley Authority to provide temporary housing for workers on sites where there was no existing housing.[20] This was opposed by Keay, who argued that temporary housing would inevitably be inferior to permanent housing and would consume resources that could be used more profitably for the permanent programme. The second approach took the form of a 'divided minimum house' of around 850–900 square feet of the kind built by Keay in Liverpool in 1940, which might be temporarily divided into two independent dwellings but could be converted back to a single dwelling when circumstances allowed. Pushed by Keay and backed by the majority of the Silkin Committee, this form of housing was considered by the Burt Committee and in the summer of 1943 plans were in hand to build a demonstration block of this type on the Ministry of Works' testing ground at Northolt.[21]

But the Silkin Committee's urging of Keay's divided minimum house was overtaken by the growing interest in the design of a temporary house. Already in late 1943, C.J. Mole, the senior architect at the Ministry of Works, and his deputy Arthur Kenyon were working with the assistance of Dr Stradling at the BRS on a design for a mass-produced temporary house to be produced by the motor industry.[22] In the Ministry of Aircraft Production, broadly similar ideas were being explored as early as 1942 with the formation of a group of engineers and designers called the Aircraft Industries Research Organisation on Housing (AIROH) and with the preparation of a case for maximum factory production of housing and for the full use of the technical and scientific advances made in the aircraft industry during the war.[23]

Crucial to the development of the temporary rather than the divided minimum house was the recognition by the end of 1943 in the central reconstruction committees responsible for the post-war housing programme that the acute demand for housing in the 'emergency period' immediately after the war could only be met by some form of temporary housing. The need for a temporary housing programme was presented in the IEP Committee's *Memorandum on Post-War Housing* of January 1944, and in February Lord Portal committed government to the launch of a temporary housing programme and the promise of a prototype for public inspection by the spring.[24] What had been a side interest of a small team at the Ministry of Works and the BRS, and backed by the Burt Committee, suddenly became a central element in the government's housing programme, backed by the authority of Churchill himself, who commanded in early April that 'the erection of these emergency houses will be carried out by exceptional methods, on the lines of a military operation … The success of this undertaking is not to be impeded by reliance at any point on traditional methods.'[25]

Proposals for non-traditional house building

By its last meeting, Burt's technical subcommittee had considered over 500 submissions.[26] Many were trivial or simply irrelevant. Typical were Mr J. Faulkner's modest and unworkable 'Inexpensive Victory House' or the torrent of correspondence from Mr Cameron Jeffs, working under the motto 'Troutstream and Thatch', who urged the advantages of Goodyear tyre canvas and thatch sprayed with cement as a form of cheap housing. Occasionally the proposals were more extravagantly silly: Mr Fryer, self-styled director of British Builders (Mobile) Ltd, pressed the committee to accept his offer of the design secrets of the 'Car-a-Car' car, the 'Car-a-Car' train and the 'Car-a-Car' houseboat as the basis for the design of emergency housing. Small wonder that the technical section should have been described by one correspondent as 'inverted Micawbers always looking for something to turn down'.[27]

Fortunately there was no shortage of serious proposals. While the building unions and small contractors may have been anxious at the prospect of the widespread use of alternative forms of house building, a number of building firms welcomed the opportunity. Of the sixty-one firms listed in the Burt Committee's final report, twenty were builders and contractors, five were engineering firms with links to the building industry, and fourteen were firms with a major interest in materials, components or fittings.[28]

Firms with capital available for developing new forms of construction, or those like Wates which had developed new ways of using materials like precast concrete for government contracts such as the development and construction of the Mulberry harbours, might be encouraged to sponsor a system by the prospect of securing a contract, 'a slice of the action', in the post-war building programme. A number of firms were able to secure advance guarantees from government for the production of substantial numbers of houses: the British Iron and Steel Federation was able to secure an order for 30,000 steel houses as early as 1941. William Airey and Son Ltd was encouraged by the success of its inter-war system of small-panel construction to develop a modified version for post-war use which won approval from the Burt Committee and was guaranteed in 1946 a production run of up to 20,000 houses.[29] Other firms were attracted by the opportunity to secure the continuation of production during the difficult period of the transition from war to peace. Proposals by the British Power Boat Company for the Jicwood plywood house were submitted as a way of using manufacturing capacity which would otherwise be underused with the decline in orders for motor-torpedo boats and other light craft after the war.[30] The AIROH temporary aluminium bungalow developed for the temporary housing programme by sections of the aircraft industry and the Ministry of Aircraft Production was conceived in similar terms.[31]

In architectural circles there was an active interest in non-traditional construction, and many of the systems that were being developed were designed in conjunction with architects. Early in the war a number of younger architects made the case for the application of prefabrication and, by extension, of non-traditional methods of building to the urgent problems of housing. In November 1941 R. Penny and Henry Watson, a Coventry production engineer and a member of the Coventry Housing Committee, founded the Committee for the Industrial and Scientific Provision of Housing (CISPH) to look at ways of speeding up the production of housing. In January 1942 Denis Clarke Hall, best known as the winner of the *Daily Chronicle* Schools Competition of 1937, was persuaded to join CISPH, bringing a keen interest in prefabrication and a mass of research on different applications in building.[32]

Meeting irregularly in London over the next 18 months, CISPH eventually grew to 30 members, most of them architects. It investigated ways of extending the mechanised production of building components and materials and of accelerating and systematising the process of their assembly. Drawing on Clarke Hall's researches and the experience of other members, the committee sought to identify the reasons for the failure of these ideas in the past and looked to the examples of motor-car and caravan production to find a way of applying them to the production of housing. Though it published two

reports, CISPH established formal links neither with the Burt Committee nor with any other bodies responsible for the government's post-war building programme.[33] Like the short-lived but more visible campaign by the Association of Architects, Surveyors and Technical Assistants (AASTA) for the use of prefabrication and non-traditional forms of construction for air-raid shelters and emergency accommodation,[34] the work of CISPH is more important as an illustration of architectural interest in the subject than a substantive contribution to its application in practice. Both AASTA and CISPH exemplify the interest by young and often politically radical architects in applying non-traditional forms of construction to the solution of social problems like housing shortages and their willingness to accept the architectural forms that would result.

More important as a source of ideas for new forms of construction for both the permanent and the temporary programmes was the extraordinary achievement in the United States of building mass-produced, prefabricated developments at great speed to house the workforce for the rapidly expanding munitions industry.[35] This housing was known to those working at the BRS, and in 1943 members of the Burt Committee visited the United States to see this achievement at first hand.[36] What they saw impressed them. From 1934 US industry, with the backing of New Deal federal agencies, had been experimenting with ways of speeding up the production of low-cost housing, generally by building on the American tradition of lightweight timber construction. A number of New Deal public works programmes called for the creation of new communities, often in rural areas where it was difficult to build conventional housing, and where prefabricated units were the simplest and quickest way to house a new workforce. The lightweight demountable units designed and built for the Tennessee Valley Authority whose work was widely illustrated in war-time Britain, were typical of this kind of housing, designed for delivery by road with three sections to a house.[37] Other US federal agencies had an equally distinguished record of achievement in this field. The

Farm Security Administration employed Californian architects like Vernon de Mars and Burton Cairns to design low-cost housing for migrant workers in the western United States. The results at Yuba City, California, attracted international attention as a successful marriage of modern design with constructional innovation.[38]

With the beginning of the war in Europe and the need for a rapid expansion of the defence industries, ideas in the United States about low-cost housing and community site planning were developed still further. When the federal government set about increasing the volume of war-time house building for the defence industry, it turned to modern architects such as de Mars, William Wurster, Walter Gropius, Marcel Breuer, George Howe, Louis Kahn, Hugh Stubbins, Antonin Raymond and even Frank Lloyd Wright to encourage the construction industry to experiment with new ways of building and frankly to encourage the employment of architects. In 1941 at Carquinez Heights, in Vallejo, California, 1,700 units of housing and community buildings were constructed for defence workers in the Vallejo shipyards. The houses were factory built on an assembly line from stressed skin and glued plywood panels. The entire complex was built in seventy-three days. Such achievements – from Wurster's housing in Vallejo to the housing built in Pennsylvania by Gropius and Breuer and by Howe, Stonorov and Kahn – were widely illustrated in the United States and impressed the team from the Burt Committee as an inspiration for British practice.[39]

Just as impressive as the quality and the novelty of the design and construction of the individual house was the speed with which the Americans were developing whole settlements, many of them the size of small towns. Vanport, Oregon, an early development on this scale, was built to house the 45,000 workers in the Kaiser shipbuilding plants engaged in the mass production of Liberty ships, and this was soon followed by others. At McLoughlin Heights, near Vancouver, Washington, 4,452 hectares of dairy and garlic farms were transformed with a mix of temporary and permanent housing to provide a new

town with city-wide water, sewage and electricity systems, four schools, recreation and daycare centres, a branch library, a medical clinic and two shopping centres – the larger of which boasted thirty-three shops covering 4,645 square metres and the largest food store in the region. Nor was McLoughlin Heights exceptional: new communities of similar size were being developed to accommodate the furious growth of the defence industries in California, Michigan, Oklahoma and along the East Coast.[40]

The US war-time effort was soon broadcast to a wider public, through publications, films and the Museum of Modern Art's exhibition 'American Housing in War and Peace' (Figure 8.2).[41] This exhibition opened in London in July 1944, attracting widespread interest and an enthusiastic response from the British architectural press. The *RIBA Journal*, for example, declared much of the work to be of 'quite superlative excellence' and urged British architects to learn from the US example.[42]

The majority of British architects were keen to accept the challenge, though some of the established members of the profession had reservations. The year before, a memorandum on 'House Construction of a Definite Limited Life' prepared by senior figures in the RIBA in response to an enquiry from the CHAC Committee chaired by Lewis Silkin had equated non-traditional construction with low standards and rejected out of hand any thought that houses might be manufactured in a factory by a workforce 'unskilled in any craft but the assembly of ready-made houses by means of a spanner'.[43] The memorandum may have made a number of sensible points but its tone, with the call for a return to traditional skills and the expansion of the system of apprenticeship, was rejected by many architects as reactionary. A debate convened by the RIBA six months later, in April 1944, to determine the profession's stance on prefabrication indicated instead the strength of desire of most architects to be closely involved in any new developments in construction methods. Architectural opinion seemed wholeheartedly behind the need for a more inventive approach

8.2 Non-traditional forms of housing developed in the United States were widely covered in the British journals and exhibited at the Royal Institute of British Architects

to housing. At the well-attended RIBA debate, chaired by the vice-president, it was agreed to recommend full professional involvement in the development of non-traditional construction.[44]

The RIBA debate had rallied the forces of those in favour of non-traditional forms of building. The press had warmly encouraged this approach through its widespread and enthusiastic coverage of experiments in countries like the United States and Sweden. Editorial reaction in the *Architects' Journal* and *Architectural Design* was highly critical of the RIBA memorandum. By the summer of 1944, the problem facing many architects was not whether to become involved in these developments, but to decide what non-traditional buildings would look like. Establishment figures like Grey Wornum and young Turks like Anthony Chitty were already engaged in the design of both temporary houses and non-traditional permanent houses.[45] Generously covered in the professional press, this kind of design came to acquire a certain gritty glamour, an exciting sense of making real plans for the post-war world.

Non-traditional forms of construction for permanent housing

By the end of 1944 government plans were beginning to bear fruit. During the summer of 1944 the ministries of Works and Health published jointly a memorandum for local authorities on government plans for temporary housing, the BRS published a report on the demonstration houses it had built at Northolt, and the Burt Committee published its first report on new ways of building permanent housing.[46] The result of these endeavours was a wide variety of different approaches to house building using steel, concrete and timber, though because of the post-war rise in the cost of timber, until 1950 steel and concrete systems of construction were to prove more popular than any form of timber construction.

The most widely used type of steel-framed house was the British Iron and Steel Federation (BISF) house designed by Frederick Gibberd and developed as a number of variants (Figure 8.3).[47] The structure was a metal frame of cold-rolled sections assembled in units which were

i

8.3 The British Iron and Steel Federation house type 'A', designed by Frederick Gibberd: (i) general view; (ii) details of the construction

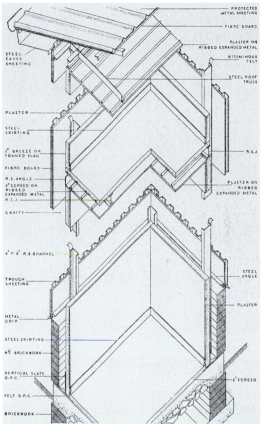

ii

light enough to be handled by two men. The uprights of these units were placed 3 ft 6 in. apart and spot and ridge welded to a transverse beam at ground-floor, first-floor and eaves levels. The roof structure was formed of a light-weight steel truss, the floors of cold-rolled steel joists. External walls were of concrete render on steel sheet to first-floor level, with horizontally ribbed steel sheeting galvanised and painted above. Party walls were of two independent 3 in. skins of foamed slag, and internal walls were of plasterboard panels bonded to fibreboard and skimmed in situ. Heating was by open fire in a masonry hearth with an encased flue above.

The different forms of concrete construction recommended by the Burt Committee can be divided into three basic types: systems using small- or large-scale precast units and in situ no-fines construction. Typical of the first were the Orlit, BCCF, Permabuilt and Airey houses, the most popular of this type.[48] The Airey house, developed by William Airey and Son Ltd from their Airey Duo Slab house and built in large numbers in Leeds before the war, used a system of single-storey precast concrete posts and small concrete panels, which were small enough to be easily handled by one or two men (Figure 8.4). The concrete posts were cast around a steel tube and connected by a steel lattice joist at first-floor

level, and the resulting goalpost frames were then erected at 1 ft 6 in. centres with the upper floor frames located by dowels onto the frames beneath. The cladding panels, 3 ft long and 9¾ in. high, were attached like concrete weatherboarding to the posts with copper wire twisted around a softwood fillet cast into the back of each post. The panels were laid without mortar and placed to give a staggered vertical joint. The roof was of traditional timber construction finished with tiles or slate. Internally the walls were lined with sheets of plasterboard or cellular plywood backed with additional thermal insulation and fixed to the softwood fillet on the posts. Easily erected by unskilled labour and requiring no special equipment, the Airey 'rural type' houses were well suited to rural or scattered sites. Today, they are still a common

i

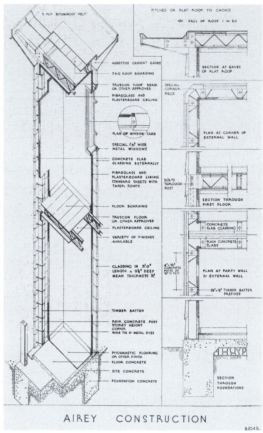

AIREY   CONSTRUCTION

ii

8.4 The Airey house: (i) a pair of Airey 'rural type' houses (ii) details of the construction

sight on the edge of villages as far apart as the Fens and the Scottish Borders.

The most popular large-panel system, in terms of the volume of post-war production, was that developed by Wates Ltd (Figure 8.5).[49] During the war the firm had helped to develop precast concrete techniques for a variety of harbour works, floating docks and other civil engineering projects, and the experience acquired in this way formed the basis for its large-panel approach to house building. Based on a 12 in. module, the structure consisted of tray-shaped panels 7 ft 6 in. high and 2, 3 or 4 ft wide, cast in metal moulds and with provision for window openings where necessary. Panels were lifted into position by a mobile crane and positioned with a special jig which enabled the contractor to dispense with normal scaffolding and ensured that the structure was plumb straight and that the overall dimensions were accurate. At first-floor and roof levels, horizontal panels were shaped to receive the precast concrete floor panels or the lightweight trussed timber roof. Horizontally the panel joints were interlocked in a bed of mortar while the vertical joints were filled with grout after erection. There was no reinforcement between the large panels, but the horizontal panels at first-floor and roof levels were provided with reinforcement to ensure continuity and to resist lateral loads from the floor or

roof. Internally the houses were fitted out with prefabricated panels to reduce working time on site to a minimum.

The most common form of in situ concrete construction, the no-fines system, was developed by a number of sponsors (Figure 8.6).[50] The common characteristic of this approach was the construction of the walls of the house from cement and large aggregate only, omitting the fine aggregate of normal concrete – hence 'no fines' – to leave small voids uniformly distributed throughout the structure. The rough concrete finish that resulted was rendered to improve the appearance and to reduce water penetration. This form of construction offered excellent thermal properties: an 8 in. thick wall of no-fines concrete rendered externally offered the same standard of insulation as an 11 in. brick cavity

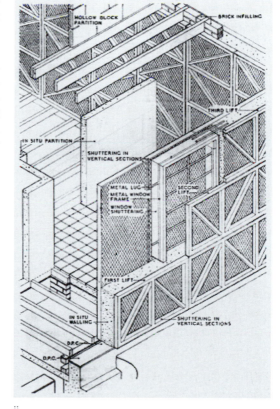

8.5 The Wates large-panel system of construction: (i) a Wates house under construction; (ii) details of the constructional system

wall. Unlike the large-panel systems, which made use of expensive reusable shuttering, no-fines concrete used much cheaper, reusable shuttering and the principal differences between one proprietary system and another are to be found in the design of the shuttering system. The system developed before the war by the Scottish Special Housing Association was based on the use of steel channels and angle sections faced with 14 swg perforated steel plates. Simpler was the system devised by Wimpey. Shuttering frames, one or two storeys high, were lined on the inner face

8.6 The 'no-fines' system of construction: (i) a Wimpey 'no-fines' house in the process of erection; (ii) details of the 'no-fines' construction system showing the steel-mesh shuttering

with plywood, while the outer face was made of some open mesh material, such as small patterned expanded metal or heavy gauge woven wire cloth, to assist in checking the progress of pouring and to ease the placing of the concrete around the window openings. Simpler still was the system investigated at Northolt by the Ministry of Works. Smaller frames covered in wire mesh were used to give three 'lifts' to a storey height, making it easier to accommodate window and door openings than the full or double-storey height lifts of the Wimpey system. Taken over by Laing's and developed further as the 'Easiform' house, houses of this form of construction were built in large numbers during the late 1940s and early 1950s.[51]

Bungalows for the temporary housing programme

As with the permanent non-traditional housing programme, government was keen to encourage a variety of approaches to the design of the temporary bungalow that Lord Portal had announced in February 1944. The first visible result of his announcement was the erection on the terrace of the Tate Gallery three months later of four different prototype temporary bungalows developed by ARCON, Tarran Industries, Uniseco Structures and the Ministry of Works (Figure 8.7).[52] All were built differently. The Ministry of Works' Portal house, named after Lord Portal, the Minister of Works, was designed in steel and intended for factory production by the motor industry, though the prototype was hand built by tool-setters from Briggs Motor Bodies of Dagenham and Pressed Steel in Cowley in four days. Only one was ever built. Both the Tarran and the Uniseco houses used timber as a framing material for panels made of cement and treated sawdust, or of asbestos cement sheeting on woodwool slabs. The ARCON bungalow used a lightweight metal frame.

Before the end of the programme in 1948 other forms of construction had been tried which not only used different materials but also varied

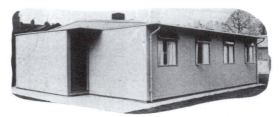

8.7 The four 'officially approved' temporary bungalows exhibited at the Tate Gallery in 1944. Top to bottom: the Ministry of Works' Portal house; the ARCON house; the Uniseco house; the Tarran house

markedly in the proportion of labour spent in factory production as opposed to on-site erection.[53] The AIROH aluminium bungalow, for instance, prefabricated in sections like the

Tennessee Valley Authority's demountable houses, is an example of factory-based manufacture, while the ARCON house demonstrates the advantages of an 'open' approach based on the on-site assembly of standardised but widely available building components.

The AIROH house consisted of four sections each 7 ft 6 in. wide, the maximum size transportable by road (Figure 8.8).[54] These sections were structurally discrete and joined on site in the manner of the wings to the fuselage of an aircraft. Each section was built up on a chassis like that of a motor car, to which were attached the wall panels of 20 gauge aluminium sheet finished internally with bitumen-bonded insulation. The roof consisted of a trussed assembly attached to both external and internal walls so that the whole section would act like a deep trussed beam when lifted by crane for transport or assembly. Internal wall linings and partitions were of plasterboard, the ceilings of fibreboard, the floors were made of tongue and groove boarding on joists fixed to the section's chassis. All the services, including a slow combustion stove for central heating, were provided by the Ministry of Works' standard kitchen/bathroom unit, which was built into one of the house's four sections. All glazing, wiring and finishing work, including painting, was completed in the factory.

Finished sections were delivered to the site by low loader ready for erection on a pre-prepared site slab, similar to those used by other temporary bungalows, which contained all mains services. The four sections were levelled by means of the jacking points positioned at three of the section's four corners, the sections joined together and the joints sealed. With site labour kept to a minimum, it was claimed that the house could be erected on site, after some experience, by an unskilled labour in 30–40 man-hours, depending on the experience of the gang.

The factory-based construction of the AIROH house stands in sharp contrast to that of the ARCON house.[55] For this, components were supplied by a variety of manufacturers to an 'agent', typically a large contractor who would act as coordinator of supplies and deliveries for

i

ii

iii

8.8 The AIROH bungalow: (i) the production flow line; (ii) a 'slice of house' being delivered to a demonstration site off Oxford Street; (iii) the finished house

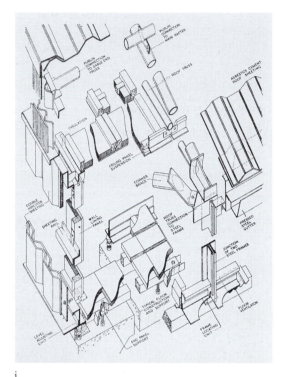

i

ii

8.9 The Mark V ARCON bungalow (i) details of the construction; (ii) the finished dwelling

sites in the locality. These components would be delivered as required and assembled on site by a general builder. The number of hours needed for erection might be greater than with the AIROH house, but factory production would be reduced and the level of skills required on site would be minimal.

The basic structure of the final version of the ARCON house, the Mark V, was a light steel frame of cold-rolled sections mounted on a foundation frame and roofed with a tubular steel truss (Figure 8.9). The external walls and roof were of moulded asbestos cement sheeting used in double thickness for the walls and single thickness for the roof. Interior walls were lined with storey-height plasterboard panels backed with insulation and bonded onto light timber frames. This form of external wall construction gave thermal insulation comparable to that of an 11 in. brick cavity wall. Internal partitions were also of plasterboard, the ceiling of fibre-board on light wooden frames, and the floor of tongue and groove boarding nailed to battens set in a cement screed laid on a pitch and tar damp-proof membrane over the site slab. The ARCON house used the standard Ministry of Works service core but located it on the entrance side of the house to produce a more elegant plan than those of the other temporary bungalows, with a kitchen overlooking the road and a marginally larger hall.

Assembly of the house started with the levelling of the foundation frame. With this in position, the main steel frame was welded together, along with the surrounds for windows and doors. Next came the cladding and the bolting into position of the windows and doors. Levelling and alignment during erection could be adjusted in a number of ways built into the design to master the tolerances that naturally arose. Finally, with electrical circuits connected to the service core, the house was lined and partitioned internally. Assembly could be completed by a team of thirty-five labourers, with between six and nineteen men on site at any one time, in eight hours, longer than the time taken to erect an AIROH house, but balanced by savings in factory production time.

Non-traditional building for schools

Early on in its consideration of the national building plan, the IEP Committee had granted priority to the housing drive in the allocation of labour and resources. But other forms of building were no less urgent. The plans being prepared for post-war school building illustrate the difficulties faced by other, less favoured sectors.[56] With 60 per cent of resources already guaranteed for housing, and thus only 40 per cent left for all other forms of building, how were old schools to be modernised and new schools built?

Those starting to plan the post-war school building programme in 1942 faced the same double challenge as those planning the housing programme: to make good the destruction caused by the war and to plan for the rising expectations generated by the debate on reconstruction.[57] The first issue, rebuilding the schools destroyed or damaged by enemy action, was a large enough task in itself, though the more easily quantifiable of the two. Schools had been hit as badly as the housing they served during the Blitz and during the flying bomb attacks of 1944. As the Blitz was drawing to a close in May 1941, school inspectors reported to the Board of Education that nationally over 10 per cent of elementary schools had been damaged by bombing. But this national picture took no account of the sharp variation between one area and another: blitzed cities like Plymouth, Liverpool and Coventry had suffered much more heavily than most. London had suffered most of all.[58] In the first night of heavy raiding in September nineteen schools in the LCC area were damaged, mostly in Bow and Poplar. A fortnight later twenty-seven elementary schools had been destroyed, 120 had been badly damaged, and forty-nine schools were closed because of unexploded bombs and mines. By mid-October this scale of destruction showed no signs of abating: the LCC reported eighty-six schools destroyed, 137 damaged beyond the possibility of immediate repair, and 309 'slightly' damaged schools. This damage, together with schools closed through unexploded bombs, meant that over half the LCC schools were unavailable for schooling or other uses. At the end of the Blitz over 10 per cent of the county's elementary schools were destroyed or seriously damaged. As attacks eased and shifted to other cities, many of the lightly damaged schools were repaired and put back into commission, or places made available in standard Ministry of Works' huts which provided for two classrooms and a space for cloaks. But the schools in London and the South East were again to suffer disproportionately during the flying bomb and rocket attacks of 1944 and 1945. By the end of the war 218 of the LCC's schools had been rendered unusable and a further 1,094 had been less extensively damaged.[59]

Destruction on this scale already represented a major claim on the resources to be made available for the national building programme. But more important still for the demand for school building was the effect of rising expectations encouraged by the debate on post-war educational policy. Like so much of the agenda for reconstruction these developments were a product of the pre-war campaigns for reform.[60] A succession of reports on education had examined the deficiencies of the current system and made a number of recommendations for radical change: the Hadow Reports of 1926 and 1931 and the Spens Report of 1938 had set the terms of the educational debate and brought forward demands for the reorganisation of elementary schools and the establishment of some form of universal secondary education. Proposals to raise the school leaving age and the aim of replacing the schools identified on the 'blacklist' drawn up by the local education authorities as long ago as 1925 only added to the demand for school building.

With the debate on reconstruction just beginning in 1940, plans for continuing and expanding these educational reforms gathered pace. Senior figures at the Board of Education began to draw up the set of proposals, published in 1942 as the 'Green Book', *Education after the War*, that were eventually to form the basis for the Education Act 1944.[61] Early on, it was clear that these proposals would have a direct effect on the scale of school building after the war. If educational reform was not to be held back by the shortage of school accommodation, plans for a post-war school building programme would have to be drawn up alongside those for housing.

By early October 1941, Robert Wood, Deputy Secretary of the Board of Education and a key figure in the official discussion group, was pressing for formal recognition of the resources that would be needed for post-war school building as part of the work of the Directorate of Post-War Building. At the first meeting of the Post-War Projects Committee in December, the question of resources for the post-war schools programme was included on the agenda. Shortly thereafter Reith urged the Board of Education to establish a committee similar to the Burt Committee already set up by the Directorate of Post-War Building for other types of building. The result of these initiatives was the formation in January 1942 of a committee under the chairmanship of Robert Wood to examine the problems of post-war school building in the emergency period after the war when shortages of labour and materials would be most acute.[62]

The war-time debate on school building: the Wood Committee, January 1942 to December 1943

Wood and his committee produced two reports. The first was ready in draft form for consultation in May 1942, barely three months after starting work.[63] The second, prepared by an enlarged committee and after a period of consultation with the local education authorities and other interested parties, was published as *Standard Construction for Schools*, the second of the Post-War Building Studies.[64] By comparison with the wealth of information produced by the Burt Committee, neither of the two Wood reports gave specific advice on how schools should be built. In the first report the committee had shown in very general terms how typical primary and secondary schools might be built after the war, using either a system of standardised 'bays' or a system of dimensional coordination based on a two-way grid. The committee had favoured the latter because it believed that it offered a more suitable basis for the prefabrication and standardisation of classroom units and the different types of accommodation required in even the simplest school but said nothing about the form of construction. Despite the enlargement of the committee to meet the criticisms of the first report, especially those voiced by the Ministry of Works,[65] the second report again concluded in favour of the grid system because of the advantages it offered for standardisation of construction throughout the school. And again it said little about the way in which schools should be built beyond urging 'the prefabrication of structural elements and the wider use of prefabricated materials' to meet the shortages that would certainly confront the post-war school building programme. The most specific guidance offered by the committee was that a system of construction based on a lightweight steel frame of cold-rolled sections would not only best suit the kind of designs they envisaged but would be capable of being produced 'in large quantities by mass-production to standard sizes'.[66] While government had already encouraged the development of a range of alternative forms of construction for housing, there were no equivalent prototypes for schools.

Faced with the prospect of accepting mass-produced huts as the only way to meet the huge demand for school places immediately after the war, or of devising some system of construction which could provide school places as cheaply and as quickly as huts, senior officials at both the Board of Education and the Ministry of Works were keen to build a school to demonstrate the ideas put forward by the committee. In early 1944 Wood started discussing with the education authorities in Kent the adoption of a school from the county's programme for this purpose, but this plan was overtaken by the absolute ban on building imposed in the summer of 1944 after the beginning of the flying bomb campaign.

Over the next two years a number of authorities were approached on the same basis, but to no avail.[67]

More important as a demonstration of the way in which the principles set out in the Wood Report might be translated into practice were the proposals submitted by a number of manufacturers and development teams for the construction of a Wood Report school.[68] From mid-1944 the Burt Committee was involved in evaluating systems put forward by Tarran, Uniseco, ARCON and a number of other sponsors who were keen to extend the work that they had done on non-traditional forms of house building to other fields like schools. But despite the experience these sponsors could already draw upon, their proposals for schools were far behind the progress made in the field of housing. As the war drew to a close, local authorities found themselves in the difficult position of having either to accept the 'HORSA' huts being urged by the Ministry of Education as the only certain way of meeting the immediate demand for school places and keeping to the timetable of raising the school leaving age, or face the risk and expense of developing a system of non-traditional school building for themselves.[69]

Non-traditional building in practice: school construction, 1945–50

How were local education authorities to meet this challenge? Short of qualified design staff, denied workers and materials, many authorities simply found it easier to take up the offer of HORSA huts, particularly to provide places in secondary schools. Cambridgeshire, a pioneering county before the war under its Chief Education Officer Henry Morris, known for its 'village colleges' and its willingness to employ a leading modernist like Gropius, faced a double challenge. In many rural areas where population was falling schools were being closed but in urban areas where the need for places to meet the raising of the school leaving age was acute, huts were widely used. The first new schools, which were largely of traditional construction, were

only included in the building programme of 1951 and not opened until 1953.[70]

A small number of authorities were prepared to take the initiative and set about the task of developing a non-traditional system of building schools. One of the first in the field was Middlesex, where C.G. Stillman was appointed County Architect in late 1945.[71] A member of the Ministry of Education's technical working party appointed to reconsider the findings of the Wood Committee, he immediately set about the task of adapting the approach that he had developed before the war as County Architect to West Sussex to post-war conditions. The schools that he designed for Middlesex during the late 1940s share the 'finger' plan type that he had first developed at schools like Littlehampton: a series of standardised classrooms, each 24 ft by 24 ft, with corridor access – the 'finger' – planned at right angles to a main corridor leading to an entrance block containing the school hall, staff rooms and all non-standard accommodation (Figure 8.10). The key to the Middlesex system was the continued use of a lightweight steel frame placed at 8 ft 3 in. centres to create the repeated standard bay for the classrooms. These were entered from the corridor, whose roof, supported on the light steel frame, was lower than the classroom roof to give clerestory lighting to one side.

These late 1940s Middlesex schools have a pinched 'utility' look about them which even today serves as a reminder of the shortages and the difficulties of the time (Figure 8.11). With the bland repetition of the bays on the glazed elevation and the unrelieved run of the corridor on the other, they are very similar to the classroom blocks Stillman was building in the 1930s but built in less durable fashion and fitted out with cheaper components and finishes. The standardisation of the bay and the limited degree of prefabrication that this made possible represented little advance over the ideas already in use before the war, but Stillman's hopes of large-scale experimentation were frustrated by the particular nature of the Middlesex programme. The restricted site of many of the county's schools

i

ii

8.10 C.G. Stillman's proposals for school design: (i) pre-war school at Selsey, West Sussex, showing the repeated classroom units; (ii) post-war proposals showing the repeated classroom elements and separate non-standard accommodation

favoured 'one-off' designs which precluded the use of mass production on the same scale as in neighbouring Hertfordshire. By the beginning of the 1950s Stillman's designs were beginning to look dated. As cost control of the school building programme became tighter from 1950 onwards, the inefficiencies of the 'finger' plan, with its high proportion of circulation space, seemed less and less defensible, and Middlesex moved like other authorities to a more compact

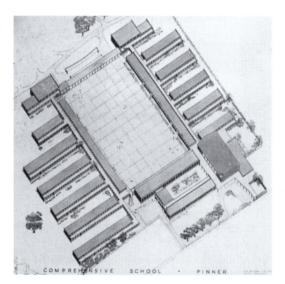

8.11 Proposed layout of Headstone Lane Comprehensive School, Pinner, Middlesex, 1947, one of Stillman's early Middlesex plans

system of planning which militated against the use of the repeated bay system that was the key to Stillman's designs.[72]

The other county that was involved from the first in trying to develop a system of non-traditional school building was Hertfordshire. Under the leadership of John Newsom, appointed Chief Education Officer in 1940, the county had set about planning for education after the war in 1943. In answer to government pressure to draw up a programme of post-war school construction which would show how the county would respond to the opportunities created by the 1944 Education Act, and taking account of the growth of population in the area, Newsom and his planning team had recognised early on that the county would need to provide for a massive increase in the number of school places. Rather than rely on Ministry of Works huts, Newsom was convinced from the start of the advantages of building cheap lightweight schools, along the lines suggested by the experiments in school design by Stillman and others just before the war.

Without an Architect's Department, Hertfordshire was persuaded to establish a department large enough to take on the design of the 176 schools that it calculated in 1946 would be necessary to meet the county's needs. Having failed to attract their first choice, Stillman, the county appointed Herbert Aslin, formerly

Borough Architect at Derby. By the end of 1945, Stirrat Johnson-Marshall had been appointed as his deputy, and with his help a young hand-picked staff was attracted to Hertfordshire, many coming direct from the services or from schools like the Architectural Association.

The story of the Hertfordshire team and its achievements has been told many times,[73] but the outline of the development of the county's school system bears repetition in order to emphasise the team's achievements when set beside the work on non-traditional forms of building being carried out not just on schools but on housing as well. The speed of development of the Hertfordshire system was astonishing. From late 1945, when Johnson-Marshall was appointed it took barely twelve months before work started on the site of the first school, Burleigh Infants School in Cheshunt, and only two years before this school and the school at Essendon were ready for occupation. By comparison Stillman, with a system developed before the war and tested in prototype form at West Sussex in 1945 immediately before his Middlesex appointment, had not done nearly as well. How was the Hertfordshire achievement possible?

Determined not to put their faith into a proprietary system, Aslin and his team chose to design their own system for the county's use. As Andrew Saint put it, 'they wanted to compose not an essay or a book but a language and vocabulary, and to write the first literature in it all at the same time'.[74] The key was the successful collaboration between the county team and Earnest Hinchliffe of Hills and Company in West Bromwich, who was already interested in the opportunities for postwar reconstruction. In 1943 Hinchliffe had designed and developed the Hills Pressweld House, built around a lightweight steel frame, and had approached the Ministry of Education to see if a comparable system of construction would be of interest to those responsible for post-war school building.[75] By the time that the Hertfordshire team had made contact with him through the Ministry of Education, Hinchliffe had already

8.12 A trial section of the Hills Pressweld frame in its mature form around 1953, showing the essential components of the frame, the columns and various forms of beams, and a number of different windows and cladding types

erected an experimental classroom unit, based on an 8 ft 3 in. bay, at his works at West Bromwich and was preparing to manufacture a series of standardised components, cladding slabs and roof and floor units, for this and his Hills Pressweld houses (Figure 8.12).

The team was thus able to start with a system on which considerable development had already taken place. But it was the foresight of the team to see the potential of this system and, as the programme developed, to rewrite the grammar of the original Hills design to produce a flexible yet coherent system that led to the success of the Hertfordshire schools. In many respects the original Hills design met the recommendations of the Wood Committee: it started with the officially commended 8 ft 3 in. module and used a lightweight steel frame. But from the start the Hertfordshire team was certain that it could be improved. The first major improvement was to change from the 'bay' system used by Hinchliffe to the greater flexibility of a full modular grid system (Figure 8.13). It was the modular grid that made it possible to standardise and prefabricate not just the classrooms but all the accommodation required for a whole school. It was this, despite the cumbrous nature of the 8 ft 3 in. module, that provided the key to the informality

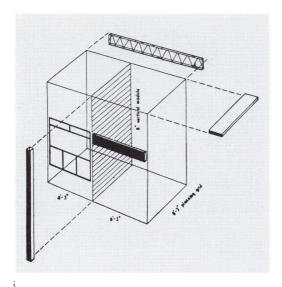

i

8.13 The modular coordinating grid used in all the Hertfordshire schools: (i) the basic three-dimensional grid; (ii) the relationship in section between the grid and different components

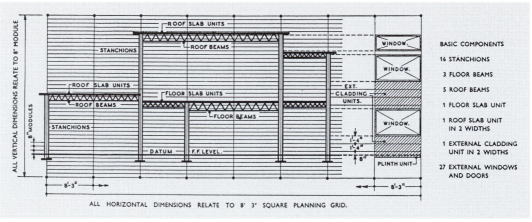

ii

in planning that so appealed to the educationalists under Newsom. With this grid system it became possible in a way that simply was not possible with the rigidity of the bay approach to abandon the insistent regularity of the finger layout for a freedom of planning on different levels, with classrooms in echelon, or with classrooms and other spaces opening into one another. Here was the practical evidence of the superiority of the grid over the bay for school planning and a demonstration of how prefabricated schools like those in Hertfordshire could meet the changing needs of educationalists in a way that traditionally constructed schools could not.

The first two schools built with the Hertfordshire system, Burleigh Infants School at Cheshunt and the village school at Essendon, show the characteristic qualities of the system and the variety that could be achieved with it (Figure 8.14).[76] The starting point for the planning of the two schools is the same, but their appearance is very different. In both schools the junior classrooms open off a corridor which houses coats and lavatories; in both the infants classrooms are treated as virtually self-contained pavilions, complete with their own entrances, outdoor space and cloakrooms. As a result the different proportion of infants to juniors in the two schools is

8.14 The first two first schools built under the new system in Hertfordshire, Burleigh Infants School, Cheshunt (1946–48) and Essendon Village School (1947–48): (i) view of the Cheshunt model; (ii) plan of the Cheshunt school; (iii) the early Hills structural frame at Cheshunt; (iv) general view of Essendon; (v) plan of Essendon; (vi) the entrance area at Essendon

reflected directly in their layout. At Cheshunt the staggered infants classrooms on the flat site give the impression of loose informality, of a blend of the open-air classrooms of the pre-war years with a Scandinavian holiday camp.[77] At Essendon the school stands on a ridge overlooking a valley. It commands the site, and its clearly visible form conveys the order of its organisation.

However much the two schools differ in their appearance, they are made with the same kit of parts. The same Meccano-like constructional system with its square fabricated columns and light steel trusses is used to make the classrooms and the hall, the corridors and the staff rooms. The system easily accommodates all the major elements of school plans as varied as Cheshunt and Essendon. Contemporaries admired the potential of the system but were critical of certain details. The horizontal precast concrete cladding units, for example, attracted particular criticism for the way they seemed to deny the lightness of the structure. At Essendon the cladding gives the distinctly odd impression of a monolithic hall supported on spindly lightweight columns. And one of the Hertfordshire team noted of the early cladding system: 'there are, however, inconsistencies resulting from present-day conditions such as the necessity of cladding a very light frame with a clumsy intractable material which is neither a panel nor a wall permitting a clear expression of the structure'.[78] But the strength of the Hertfordshire approach was that the design team could learn from its mistakes, and the system did then improve. Thus later schools were designed with different cladding: at Croxley Green, the next school in the programme, the team tried vertical concrete cladding panels; and at Aboyne Lodge (1949–50), with more success, they tried stove-enamelled metal panels.[79]

Whatever their views on the details of the system, contemporary critics were agreed that schools like Cheshunt and Essendon embodied a completely new way of approaching the design of schools. The results might have little to do with the traditional language of architecture; Cheshunt was regarded as formally confused by a number of critics. To Richard Llewelyn Davies

and John Weeks, the first view of a Hertfordshire school suggested an unresolved conflict between a 'resolution to avoid monumentality' on the one hand and the desire to make the buildings legible in conventional architectural terms on the other. But they went on to argue that this first impression was misleading, and that the schools had a positive architectural aesthetic all their own:

The schools really come to life, however, as one walks round them. Then the isolated blocks which seem a little dull in themselves, and a jumble when all seen together, begin to show a logic in their placing with relation to each other ... The architect, trying to analyse the impression he has received, feels baffled. Most of the normal elements of architecture are missing. There is no recognisable formal element whatever, proportions seem almost accidental, spaces and places are divided in the most elementary manner ... There is an utter and refreshing absence of conscious detailing. There are no materials except glass, steel and plaster.[80]

To anyone familiar with the subsequent development of prefabrication and its application in schools, or to any visitor to one of the schools today conscious of the way these buildings have weathered (with precious little maintenance) over the last 50 years, it is difficult to recover the sense of novelty that impressed contemporaries. But their impact was undeniable. Robert Townsend, responsible for experimental building at the BRS during the war, recognised the 'crude and tentative' quality of some of the detailing but thought the Hertfordshire system full of 'all sorts of interesting possibilities'.[81] By comparison with the other schools illustrated in his review of post-war schools, he put Hertfordshire ahead of all other authorities in creating a new architectural aesthetic for prefabrication, in allowing a spatial freedom unmatched elsewhere and in their bold use of colour.[82] In the late 1940s a younger generation of architects and architectural students looking for evidence of the new architecture eagerly seized on the qualities of Cheshunt and Essendon. Henry Swain, then a student at the Architectural Association, recalls:

> I can't impress on you too much how different these buildings looked. Seen in the context of the Modern Movement, everything monstrous big and reinforced, here was something light and delicate and hammered out of the process of studying the problem. It was totally new, it didn't seem to have roots in anything.[83]

Non-traditional building in practice: new forms of house building, 1945–48

What had government programmes achieved as the first, most intense, phase of reconstruction was coming to an end in 1948? With the economy struggling to recover from the war and with labour and most building materials in short supply, it was soon clear that war-time hopes for a massive housing drive and the speedy reconstruction of war-damaged cities were impossible to achieve. In quantitative terms, far fewer houses had been built than the government had planned. The temporary housing programme had provided 156,667 houses, against a target of 158,100, but had taken far longer than originally planned to produce this number.[84] One year after VE Day, fewer than 30,000 dwellings had been completed. Two years after the end of the war – the target date for the completion of the programme – the number had increased but still stood at only 97,000.[85] Less successful still was the permanent, non-traditional housing programme. The 1945 White Paper on housing held out the hope that 200,000 dwellings would be completed in the first two years after the war. By the end of 1946 only 2,769 houses had been built; two years after VE Day only 7,850 had been completed, and a year later the number was still only 36,000.[86] By September 1950 only 117,359 permanent non-traditional houses had been built, a much smaller contribution to the post-war housing drive than had been envisaged

at the time of the White Paper's publication in March 1945.[87]

These difficulties in the production of housing were due in large measure to rising costs and, after 1948, to an increasingly unfavourable comparison in terms of value for money with conventional housing. Both reflect the problem of addressing key issues, particularly costs, during the planning of both the permanent and the temporary programmes. The context in which the exploration of non-traditional construction began had emphasised the paramount need to save the resources of the traditional building industry and increase the use of non-building labour. With both houses and schools the emphasis was more on saving traditional building resources and less on saving money, although from the start there was an implicit assumption that the increased use of prefabrication and off-site factory production would reduce costs.

The Burt Committee did not look at costs; its brief was to encourage and evaluate alternative forms of construction in terms of performance. Questions of cost were considered separately by BRS using information from its demonstration site at Northolt and from prototypes built by sponsors of the systems under investigation.[88] Equally, although the costs of the temporary housing programme were included in the discussion of the programme from the start, they were treated as subservient to the overall priority of meeting the acute demand for housing during the emergency period. As costs rose, the relative costs of one type of house against another became an important factor in deciding which types of permanent housing to continue building, though it was the social priorities of housing that demanded the continuation of the temporary housing programme through to 1948.

In practice the cost of both temporary and permanent housing programmes was much higher than expected. As labour and materials became more freely available, temporary and permanent non-traditional construction programmes became uncompetitive with the standard and cost of traditionally built housing. There were exceptions: Wates built more no-fines houses after 1950 than before, and the Cornish Unit system of building (closely akin to the Airey system) continued to be used after 1950 in remote rural areas. But these were exceptions to the general rule. The results of an investigation into the cost of the permanent non-traditional programme carried out by the BRS showed that of the fourteen systems examined in detail, all except two in situ concrete systems (whose shuttering costs were excluded) were more expensive than traditional brick construction, and this by a considerable margin: six of the fourteen were 10 per cent more expensive, and one was over 20 per cent more. After examining the way in which the non-traditional programme had balanced savings in conventional materials and labour against off-site labour and equipment costs, the study concluded damagingly that 'the investigations provide a striking illustration of the relative ease of economising in particular scarce resources compared to the difficulty of providing cost reductions, and the absence of any *a priori* reason for the former to coincide with the latter'.[90]

But if non-traditional housing was not cheaper, what were its advantages when traditional materials and skills ceased to be in short supply? Conceived at a time of shortages, the general thrust of design and innovation in non-traditional forms of building had been to find substitutes for traditional ways of building the shell of the house – to match the qualities of the conventional house, not to offer fundamental innovation.[91] A form of construction designed to use materials such as sheet timber or aluminium as a substitute for traditional materials was found to have peace-time costs (because of the changing value of the pound relative to the dollar) that simply could not have been anticipated in wartime. A non-traditional house that could offer the standards of space and comfort of a conventional house might be viable at a slightly higher cost during the period of greatest austerity, but as costs rose for authorities such as the LCC that were grudgingly willing to try the new systems of building, many of the new systems became too

expensive to offset the advantages of the ready availability of non-traditional materials and speed of construction.

Moreover, non-traditional housing had other disadvantages. To the local authorities who were expected to take the financial risk of building this kind of housing, its durability was suspect.[92] Members of the Glasgow Housing Committee, invited to inspect and comment on the systems being reviewed by the Burt Committee, were sceptical that non-traditionally built houses would last long, let alone the full sixty years of their financial life, if occupied by traditional Glasgow tenants.[93] The LCC Housing Committee shared these doubts, despite the urging of the county's architect, Forshaw.[94] Pressured by the Ministry of Health and the Ministry of Works to use new ways of building housing, the LCC reluctantly agreed to try a number of Braithwaite and Hills houses on their out-county estates, principally as a way of legitimately skirting the control of skilled labour and traditional materials in the region. Of all the different forms of non-traditional houses, the Housing Committee favoured the Orlit and Airey houses, both of precast concrete construction, because they were closest to traditional construction.

Nor did the appearance of non-traditional housing have much to offer. Most sponsors chose not to exploit the architectural potential of new forms of construction and disguised their designs to look as much like conventional houses as possible. A few were frank, some brutally so, in expressing the form of their construction. Very few had the straightforward simplicity of the BISF houses designed by Frederick Gibberd. Contemporary comments in *Architectural Design* and the *Architectural Review* record a muted enthusiasm for what were generally regarded as a series of worthy rather than exciting designs.[95]

If non-traditional construction offered a poor substitute for traditional methods of building, housing built in this way was of little value to those trying to replan war-damaged cities. The huge programme of housing and communities being built for the US defence industry had excited those preparing plans for reconstruction in Britain, but these lessons were difficult to apply to the most urgent of British problems, rehousing in the London area. Here the issue was not just to build housing but to do so in ways that were compatible with the existing fabric of the city and with the new plans being made for post-war development. Abercrombie's plans for the county of London and for Greater London envisaged an increase in the population density in the existing built-up area to 100 people per acre in the areas of lowest density and to 200 people per acre in the central residential areas. Temporary bungalows, which could at most be laid out at a density of forty people per acre, were thus of little use in the East End, or indeed almost anywhere within the county, and threatened to pre-empt the use of sites for the permanent housing programme.[96] In London and other big cities the use of temporary bungalows was limited to small groups on playing fields, in parks or on housing sites too small for multi-storey housing. Even permanent non-traditional housing was restricted to suburban sites like the LCC's Oxhey or Debden estates.[97] Designed with a maximum of two storeys, this form of housing was inadequate where the demand for housing was most acute, and none of the systems of non-traditional construction had yet been adapted to multi-storey use. Often built on sites on the fringe of the city or on the unpopular out-country estates developed by the LCC as far as 20 miles from Charing Cross, large estates of temporary and non-traditionally built housing came to acquire a negative image, looking at best like an ingenious, if utilitarian, response to the problems of austerity and the housing shortage.

The contrasting fortunes of the non-traditional housing and schools programmes

Looking back at the period of reconstruction, it may seem that government plans started from the essentially optimistic and simplifying assumption that technical ingenuity could provide a way of meeting the demands that would be made of the building industry. To those who had just come through a war in which government had been expected to find solutions to war-time challenges such as maintaining supplies of food and munitions across the Atlantic and launching an invasion of Europe across the Channel, war-time plans the for a non-traditional building programme must have seemed more plausible than they do to us. That the housing programmes fell short of producing the number of dwellings expected is readily understood, taking into account the shortage of labour and materials that the country then faced. But that so many of these designs should have been found to compare so unfavourably with conventional housing suggests that the plans to meet housing demand in this way were flawed. In the world of post-war shortages any dwellings were welcome, even ones that looked so different. But most non-traditional permanent houses and temporary bungalows were not regarded as anything more than mere substitutes for conventional housing. They never came to be valued in their own right.

Gibberd's BISF houses, for example, were not so different in their appearance from traditionally built houses, and some non-traditional houses were disguised to look like their conventionally built neighbours. But those that looked as inescapably unconventional as their construction or could not be disguised were generally viewed askance. Those who lived in them might welcome the benefits of their comfort and their equipment and even come to view them with affection, but they never came to be valued for their newness and their otherness. Unlike the Airstream caravan or the Citroen 2cv they never established a new canon, an acceptable image of a 'machine for living in'.

With non-traditional schools the position was different. As with housing, non-traditional schools had first been seen as a substitute for traditional construction. And as with housing the first priority was to provide accommodation rather than to save costs. Indeed the control of costs imposed on housing from the outset by the Ministry of Health was not imposed on school building by the Ministry of Education until 1949. But when cost controls on schools were established, and subsequently tightened, the costs of non-traditional schools were generally higher than those of schools built in the traditional way. However, by ingenious planning and paring away circulation areas, Hertfordshire was able to contain costs, so that a Hertfordshire system school in the early 1950s was broadly comparable in cost to a first-class traditionally built school.[98] Backed by the cost analysis techniques developed later by James Nisbet and others at the Ministry's Architects and Buildings Branch, the cost control of school building, both traditional and non-traditional, became possible and yielded an ability to plan and control value for money in a way that had no parallel, at this point, in housing.[99]

Most importantly, however, non-traditional schools offered more than just a substitute for traditional construction for the same money. Contemporaries recognised that the better non-traditional systems, like Hertfordshire's, offered innovation in design that was valuable in itself:

> Unlike the non-traditional houses the non-traditional schools are not merely a forcing of new methods into old forms. A new product has been created with the new methods and materials. This makes non-traditional schools something more than a *pis aller* dependent entirely on the lack of availability of traditional resources for their usefulness.[100]

To teachers and educationalists trying to recast the educational system at both primary and secondary level, struggling to bring it into line with the ideas that had been first raised by Hadow in 1931 and then reinforced by the 1944 Education Act, the openness of the Hertfordshire schools and those like them was much more attractive than the rigidity of schools planned and built in traditional fashion. Developed by the county's own architects in conjunction with the educationalists, the Hertfordshire schools were conceived from the start in terms of the user. Planning and architectural ideas, the linking of

spaces, the separation of uses, the use of colour, could all be tried in advance on the educationalists and the teachers who would use the schools. This was in sharp contrast to the development of non-traditional housing, where the systems were developed by their sponsors with no possibility of discussion with the ultimate clients, the local authorities and their tenants.

It was the ability of groups like the Hertfordshire team and their educational advisers to develop a new approach to the design of schools out of the need to use non-traditional forms of building that caught the imagination of designers and users alike:

> The architects have justified their existence as distinct from that of engineers in selecting and adapting the machine so that it provides pleasure and a sense of well-being as well as efficiency. It is for this reason that the non-traditional schools have been regarded as a contribution to architecture.[101]

The architectural qualities of schools like the Hertfordshire schools were recognised by contemporary critics. Llewelyn Davies and Weeks, writing in the *Review*, presented the schools not just as a contribution to the debate on school building or as a display of technical ingenuity in system design, but as an important statement about the nature of a modern architecture, a first demonstration of the architecture of industrialisation. The results, they argued, were strange, 'other', creating a spatial order unlike the conventional formal language of architecture.

Schools like Burleigh and Essendon were a demonstration of the way in which new materials and methods of construction, intelligently used, could produce an architecture which might still occasionally be crude and tentative, but which was 'forceful and genial' in its novelty. Non-traditional houses and the prefabs of the temporary housing programme might be ingenious in technical terms and might be viewed with affection by their tenants in spite of their design. But to teachers, to children and their parents, schools like Essendon were an early and refreshing indication of the way that new materials and means of construction might lead to an architecture which was genuinely of the modern age.

Notes

1 For a discussion of the reduced capacity of the wartime building industry, see C.M. Kohan, *Works and Buildings*, London, HMSO, 1952, chs XVIII and XIX.

2 This committee was served by an 'official' counterpart that brought together senior civil servants from each of the key departments and was thus capable of addressing the detail so necessary to the preparation of the different programmes for post-war reconstruction; J.B. Cullingworth, *Environmental Planning. Vol 1: Reconstruction and Land Use Planning*, London, HMSO, 1965, pp. 19–32.

3 P. Addison, *The Road to 1945: British Politics and the Second World War*, London, Jonathan Cape, 1975, pp. 236–58.

4 PRO/CAB/87/55 see also M. Bowley, *Housing and the State 1919–44*, London, George Allen and Unwin, 1945, ch. 2.

5 PRO/CAB/87/3, the Memorandum by the Official Committee on Post-War Internal Economic Problems, *Post-War Housing Policy*, RP/IEP(43)24, 25 May 1943, brings together the proposals made for determining priorities and methods of rationing for post-war building work, including IEP(43)2, 'The Economic Background of the Post-War Building and Constructional Programme', 14 January 1943.

6 Ministry of Works, *Training for the Building Industry*, Cmnd 6428, London, HMSO, 1943.

7 The background to the formation of the Directorate of Post-War Building is to be found in R.B. White, *Prefabrication: A History of its Development in Great Britain*, London, HMSO, 1965, pp. 123–4; see also 'Directorate of Post-War Building', *AJ*, 12.3.1942, p. 206.

8 Published by the Ministry of Works from 1944, the Post-War Building Studies kept the professions abreast of the recommendations of the different committees working under the umbrella of the Directorate of Post-War Building. By the end of the first series in 1946, 33 titles had been published.

9 Minister of Health, Secretary of State for Scotland and Minister of Works (the Burt Committee), *House Construction, Interdepartmental Committee on House Construction, First Report*, Post-War Building Studies 1, London, HMSO, 1944, p. 1. The second report was published in 1946 as Post-War Building Studies 23 and the third in 1948 as Post-War Building Studies 25. The papers of the Burt Committee are to be found at PRO/HLG/94/1–16. The work of the Burt Committee is discussed in White, *Prefabrication*, pp. 152–60.

10 Burt Committee, *House Construction, First Report*, Part II, pp. 42–92.

11 The reorganisation of the Burt Committee in February 1944 is reported in the committee's second report and summarised in White, *Prefabrication*, p. 155.

12 Government was engaged, sometimes in conjunction with private sponsors, in a limited programme of experimental building on its own demonstration site at Northolt. Here, during 1943, thirteen demonstration blocks of different forms of construction were erected under the direction of the Ministry of Works' Chief Architect, C.J. Mole, and his deputy, A.W. Kenyon, advised by an independent architectural panel consisting of Lancelot Keay, C.H. James and Cecil Howlitt. A comprehensive report on the work carried out at Northolt is provided in Ministry of Works, *Demonstration Houses: A Short Account of the Demonstration Houses and Flats erected at Northolt by the Ministry of Works*, London, HMSO, 1944. The contribution of the BRS is described in *The History of the Building Research Station*, London, HMSO, 1948.

13 White, *Prefabrication*, p. 155.

14 PRO/HLG/94/13.

15 PRO/HLG/94/13.

16 Minister of Health, Secretary of State for Scotland and Minister of Works (the Burt Committee), *House Construction, Second Report*, Post-War Building Study 23, London, HMSO, 1946.

17 Minister of Health, Secretary of State for Scotland and Minister of Works (the Burt Committee), *House Construction, Third Report*, London, HMSO, 1948.

18 For a general discussion of the temporary housing programme see B. Vale, *Prefabs: A History of the UK Temporary Housing Programme*, London, E. & F.N. Spon, 1995; B. Finnimore, *Houses from the Factory: System Building and the Welfare State*, London, Rivers Oran Press, 1989.

19 The papers for the CHAC Sub-Committee for the Temporary and Permanent Construction of Housing (the Silkin Committee) are to be found at PRO/HLG/37/66.

20 The committee heard at its second and third meetings of US experience of temporary housing. It also took evidence from a wide variety of different sources in Britain. They were well aware of the work being undertaken by the Ministry of Planning and Works on the development of the BCF system of construction for huts and hostels and by groups such as the Committee for the Industrial and Scientific Provision of Housing (CISPH) and the Committee on Post-

War Building set up by the National Federation of Building Trade Employers in April 1942. They would also have been familiar with the pressure from architects and journals like the *Architects' Journal* to start working on the design of genuinely temporary housing: *AJ*, 9.4.1942, pp. 260–8.

21 At its meeting on 17 December 1943 the committee considered a draft report strongly influenced by Keay which pronounced against any form of temporary housing and recommended that a prototype 'divided minimum house' should be built at Northolt. Keay had already built housing of this type in Liverpool; 'Convertible Part Houses at Liverpool', *AJ*, 11.9.1941, pp. 184–5.

22 Mole and Kenyon appear to have started work in the late summer of 1943 on translating into practice the CHAC recommendation for a 600 square foot house for factory production; White, *Prefabrication*, p. 139.

23 White, *Prefabrication*, pp. 141–8. White refers to the ideas of CISPH as a possible source of inspiration for the AIROH house, *ibid.*, p. 131.

24 *AJ*, 17.2.1944, p. 129.

25 PRO/CAB/124/465 (the directive from Churchill 5.4.1944). Churchill may still have been largely indifferent to questions of reconstruction, but he seems to have been an enthusiastic supporter of emergency factory made temporary houses (EFMs); see e.g. his directive of 3.9.1944 in even stronger vein to Woolton and the Reconstruction Committee, PRO/CAB/124/465.

26 PRO/HLG/94/13.

27 White, *Prefabrication*, p. 154.

28 M. Bowley, *The British Building Industry: Four Studies in Response and Resistance to Change*, Cambridge, Cambridge University Press, 1966, pp. 207–22.

29 *Ibid.*, pp. 212–13.

30 *Ibid.*, p. 209.

31 Vale, *Prefabs*, p. 15–20; White, *Prefabrication*, pp. 141–4.

32 CISPH produced two reports: *Housing Production I*, London, 1943, and *Housing Production II or the Application of Quantity Production Technique to Building*, London 1943. The full committee was chaired by Harry Weston, Chairman of the Coventry City Housing Committee, and included Ove Arup, Donald Gibson, Denis Clarke Hall, Max Lock, C.A. Monoprio, Edric Neel, Howard Robertson, Felix Samuely and Lewis Silkin; the technical subcommittee consisted of H.J. Spiwak, Arup, Clarke Hall, Gibson, Neel and Samuely. It activities are discussed in White, *Prefabrication*, pp. 124–31.

33 White, *Prefabrication*, p. 131. CISPH did present evidence to the Burt Committee shortly after the Burt Committee's establishment. More important

were the informal contacts it enjoyed through those like Lewis Silkin who were actively shaping the fortunes of the temporary housing programme: Lord Portal, soon to be Minister of Works and Buildings, was a regular visitor to CISPH meetings, while Edric Neel was to play an important role as one of the founders of ARCON; Finnimore, *Houses from the Factory*, pp. 21–35.

34 See ch. 1.

35 See D. Albrecht (ed.), *World War II and the American Dream*, Cambridge, Mass., MIT Press, 1995. A popular contemporary account was provided by H. Casson, *Homes by the Million*, Harmondsworth, Penguin Books, 1946. See also the view of the Burt Committee team that visited the US: Ministry of Works, *Methods of Building in the USA*, London, HMSO, 1944.

36 PRO/HLG/94/7 & 9; the visit was also reported widely in the architectural press: 'MOW's Mission to the USA', *AJ*, 10.2.1944, pp. 121–3.

37 See e.g. the Penguin Special by D. Lilienthal, *The Tennessee Valley Authority: Democracy on the March*, Harmondsworth, Penguin Books, 1944, and J. Huxley, 'TVA, an Achievement of Democratic Planning', *AR*, Jun. 1943, pp. 138–66.

38 P.S. Read, 'Enlisting Modernism', in Albrecht, *World War II*, pp. 8–11.

39 *Ibid.*, pp. 12–15, and G. Hise, 'The Public Architecture of William Wurster 1935–50', in M. Treib (ed.), *An Everyday Modernism: The Houses of William Wurster*, Berkeley, University of California Press, 1995, pp. 138–63.

40 These developments were covered in the contmeporary journals, for example 'Cities while you wait', *Pencil Points*, April 1943, pp. 48–55, and in British reporting of American achievements, for example Casson, *Homes by the Million*. For a more recent assessment see G. Hise, *Magenetic Los Angeles, Planning the Twentieth-Century Metropolis*, Baltimore, The John Hopkins University Press, 1997, chs 4 and 5.

41 The exhibition was widely reported in the British press; see e.g. 'US Wartime Housing', *AR*, Aug. 1944, pp. 30–60; 'Housing in War and Peace', *AJ*, 27.4.1944, pp. 65–8.

42 'American Housing in War and Peace', *JRIBA*, Jul. 1944, pp. 227–30.

43 'House Construction of a Definite Limited Life', *JRIBA*, Nov. 1943, pp. 282–3. Keay, President of the RIBA 1946–7, appears to have influenced the drafting of the memorandum.

44 'Prefabrication', *JRIBA*, May 1944 pp. 163–9.

45 Grey Wornum, for example, was involved in the design of the Unibuilt house with R.H. Sheppard; see G. Wornum and J. Gloag, *Houses Out of Factory*, London, Allen & Unwin, 1946. Anthony Chitty was

engaged, also with Richard Sheppard, in the design of the all-plywood Jicwood house; C. Mardall and J. Vulliamy, 'Towards an Architecture: Post-War Housing in Britain', *AR*, Oct. 1948, p. 179.

46 Ministry of Health and Ministry of Works, *Temporary Accommodation: Memorandum for the Guidance of Local Authorities*, London, HMSO, 1944. For the report on the Northolt demonstration houses see White, *Prefabrication*, p. 155.

47 All the different forms of construction recommended by the Burt Committee were described in the committee's reports. The three variants of the BISF house designed by Gibberd are described in Burt Committee, *House Construction, Second Report*. In addition they were widely published in the architectural press; for the BISF 'B' type see also *AJ*, 20.9.1945, pp. 205–13; *AD*, Oct. 1945, pp. 235–6.

48 The Airey system is described in 'Official Permanent Prefabricated Houses', *AD*, Dec. 1945, p. 300. Descriptions of the Orlit, BCCF and Permabuilt systems are to be found in the 'Housing Notes' feature published on a frequent basis in *AD*.

49 The Wates system is described in 'The Wates System of House Construction', *AJ*, 16.8.1945, pp. 119–23.

50 The no-fines system of construction had been developed between the wars and is described in Burt Committee, *House Construction, Third Report*, pp. 34–37.

51 Coventry, where Donald Gibson, who had a long-standing interest in non-traditional forms of construction, was City Architect, was one of the cities to build large number of no-fines dwellings in the late 1940s; see below, ch. 10, notes 81 and 82.

52 The first prototype of the Ministry of Works' Churchill house (also referred to as the Portal house) was published in *AD*, May 1944, pp. 101–4; Jun. 1944, pp. 125–32. The other prototypes were published during the course of the summer: the Tarran house in *AD*, Jul. 1944, pp. 150–6; the Uniseco house in *AD*, Nov. 1944, p. 270; the ARCON house in *AD*, Nov. 1944, pp. 252–5.

53 Ministry of Works, *Temporary Housing Programme*, Cmnd 7304, London, HMSO, 1948, pp. 3–8.

54 White, *Prefabrication*, pp. 141–8, provides a helpful account of the AIROH bungalow; see also *AD*, May 1945, pp. 115–16.

55 ARCON stands for 'architectural consultants', and was a practice consisting of the architects Edric Neal, Rodney Thomas and Raglan Squire, who worked closely with a number of companies including ICI, Stewart and Lloyds and Turners Asbestos Cement Co Ltd. The construction of the ARCON bungalow is described in *AJ*, 30.11.1944, pp. 404–7.

56 The national building plan and the problems of balance between the demands of the different sectors is discussed in N. Rosenberg, *Economic Planning and the British Building Industry*, Philadelphia, University of Pennsylvania, 1961, chs II and IV.

57 For a discussion of the relationship between the educational developments of this period and school building see: P.H.J.H. Gosden, *Education in the Second World War*, London, Methuen, 1976; G.A.N. Lowndes, *The Silent Social Revolution*, Oxford, Oxford University Press, 1969; S. Maclure, *Educational Development and School Building: Aspects of Public Policy 1945–73*, Harlow, Longman, 1984; and A. Saint, *Towards a Social Architecture: The Role of School Building in Post-War England*, London, Yale University Press, 1987, especially ch. 3.

58 Gosden, *Education in the Second World War*, ch. 2, especially pp. 38–42.

59 *Ibid.*, pp. 61–7.

60 Pre-war developments are summarised in Lowndes, *Silent Social Revolution*, ch. XIII, and Maclure, *Educational Development*, ch. 1.

61 Gosden, *Education in the Second World War*, ch. 11.

62 The immediate background to the formation of the Wood Committee is discussed in Maclure, *Educational Development*, pp. 11–17.

63 Board of Education (the Wood Committee), *The First Report of the Committee on School Planning*, London, HMSO, 1942; the papers of the Wood Committee are to be found at PRO/ED/136/680.

64 Board of Education (the Wood Committee), *Standard Construction for Schools*, Post-War Building Studies 2, London, HMSO, 1944.

65 The first report of the Wood Committee was not well received. The Ministry of Works argued that it would not carry conviction because it failed to acknowledge fully the debate on school building that had developed in the late 1930s and because the committee failed to include key figures like C.G. Stillman, County Architect for West Sussex, whose ideas on prefabrication for schools seemed particularly relevant for the time. He and Denis Clarke Hall, another leading innovator in school design, were nominated to the Wood Committee by the RIBA. For a discussion of Stillman's influence on the Wood Committee see White, *Prefabrication*, pp. 103–7.

66 Wood Committee, *Standard Construction for Schools*, paragraph 23a.

67 Maclure, *Educational Development*, p. 15.

68 Ministry of Education, *The Story of Post-War School Building*, Pamphlet 33, London, HMSO, 1957.

69 The HORSA hut was developed from the standard 72 ft by 24 ft MOW hut and was universally acknowledged as no better than a stop-gap measure; Maclure, *Educational Development*, pp. 26–8; Kohan, *Works and Buildings*, pp. 379–82.

70 Cambridge County Council, *Minutes of the Education Committee*, 1949, p. 177; 1950, p. 70; 1951, p. 149, 272.

71 The ideas first tried by Stillman in West Sussex were eventually to be recommended by the technical working party appointed by the Board of Education in 1946 to reconsider the findings of the Wood Committee; see Ministry of Education (Cleary Committee), *Report of the Technical Working Party on School Construction*, London, HMSO, 1948; see also Maclure, *Educational Development*, p. 30. These ideas were also presented for post-war consumption in a number of articles, e.g. 'School in Standard Bay Units' *AJ*, 7.6.1945, pp. 421–7, and in Stillman's book (with R. Castle Cleary), *The Modern School*, London, Architectural Press, 1949.

72 'Post-War Schools in Middlesex', *OAP*, Apr. 1955, pp. 178–86, Jun 1955, pp. 319–25. For a general discussion of the impact of the cost controls on school building introduced in the early 1950s see below, ch. 10.

73 See especially Saint, *Towards a Social Architecture*, ch. 4.

74 *Ibid.*, p. 65.

75 Coventry was a centre of experimentation with non-traditional construction, due in part to encouragement by Gibson and other members of CISPH; see 'Experimental Housing, Coventry', *AJ*, 7.10.1943, pp. 255–8; Saint, *Towards a Social Architecture*, pp. 65–6.

76 The two schools were described extensively in the architectural press: 'Four Schools in Hertfordshire', *AR*, Sep. 1949, pp. 161–8; 'Standardisation in the School Programme of the Hertfordshire County Council', *AD*, Sep. 1949, pp. 210–5; 'Planning the New Schools', *ABN*, 16.1.1948, pp. 47–53.

77 Saint, *Towards a Social Architecture*, p. 72.

78 'On the Design of Primary Schools by the Herts County Council Architects' Department', *AJ*, 16.10.1947, p. 346.

79 'Schools in Herts, Building Programme', *AJ*, 20.10.1949, pp. 431–40.

80 R. Llewelyn Davies and J.R. Weeks, 'The Hertfordshire Achievement' *AR*, Jun. 1952, p. 371.

81 R. Townsend, 'Towards an Architecture: Post-War School in Britain' *AR*, Sep. 1949, p. 157.

82 *Ibid.*, p. 155.

85 Ministry of Health, *Housing Return for England and Wales, 30th April 1948*, Cmnd 7417, London, HMSO, 1948, p. 31 (table 10).

86 *Ibid.*, p. 20 (table 2b).

87 Bowley, *Building Industry*, p. 223.

88 The results of the BRS enquiry were published in two reports: *New Methods of House Construction*, New Building Studies, Special Reports 4 and 10. For a discussion of these results see Bowley, *Building Industry*, ch. IX, pp. 236–50.

89 *Ibid.*, p. 247.

90 It is important to remember that the shell of a conventionally built house amounted to no more than 40 per cent of the total, so that the remaining costs remained quite unaffected by experiments with non-traditional construction. The range of possible savings was therefore strictly limited from the outset; White, *Prefabrication*, p. 167.

91 *Ibid.*, pp. 222–8.

92 Papers of the Burt Committee, PRO/HLG94/13.

93 Forshaw's enthusiasm for non-traditionally built housing was checked by the opposition of the Valuer and the general scepticism of the Housing Committee. Forshaw's case for non-traditional construction was made in a variety of papers, e.g. GLRO/LCC/Min/7618, HP453, 'Post-War Housing Application of Proprietary Systems of Prefabrication and LCC Type Plans', and the ensuing discussion.

94 See e.g. Mardall and Vulliamy, 'Towards an Architecture', pp. 179–88. The same issues were a constant refrain in the 'Housing Forum' articles in *AD* during the mid-1940s.

95 'Siting the Temporary House', *AJ*, 30.11.1944, pp. 399–403.

96 LCC, *Housing: A Survey of the Post-War Housing Work of the London County Council 1945–49*, London, LCC, 1949, and GLRO/LCC/Min/7301, meeting of 7.11.1945, items 17 and 18.

97 Bowley, *Building Industry*, p. 278.

98 *Ibid.*, pp. 276–83.

99 *Ibid.*, p. 263.

100 *Ibid.*, p. 277.

9 Housing versus architecture
London 1940–49

In March 1945 the government published its White Paper on housing, setting out for the first time the plans it had been preparing for the post-war housing drive since 1942.[1] The White Paper came out at a difficult time. With the Allied armies already across the Rhine and the end of the war in Europe in sight, there was widespread feeling, sharply expressed in the press and by members of Parliament, that government should keep the public informed of what was described as the centrepiece of plans for rebuilding.[2] As the Reconstruction Committee assembled what seemed like the definitive plans for both the permanent and temporary programmes, housing problems were hugely worse than they had been the summer before.

The flying bomb campaign which began in June 1944 had thrown the committee's calculations into disarray. Worse still, to this daily round of destruction was added, after September, the more destructive power of the V2 rockets. Although the intensity of the flying bomb attacks was significantly reduced as the Allied forces advanced across northern Europe, denying the Germans launch sites for the V1s, V2 rocket attacks continued into 1945. Concentrated on London and Kent, the impact of the attacks was ferocious. At the end of the first month over 21,000 dwellings were still being damaged every day. In only three months, from June to September 1944, the renewed bombing campaign had destroyed or seriously damaged 150,000 houses, as much as 66 per cent of the total number of houses damaged during the first five years of the war.[3]

The government's overriding priority was to bring the deterioration of housing conditions in London under control. In September Lord Wolton, Minister of Reconstruction, launched a campaign led by Sir Malcolm Tristram Eve, chairman of the War Damage Commission, to bring the housing situation in the capital back to where it had been at the start of the flying bomb campaign.[4] Under Sir Malcolm Tristram Eve the Emergency Repair Service dramatically increased the resources for short-term emergency housing: in June 28,000 men were working on housing repairs; at the start of August – with workers poached from other essential services and with the Emergency Repair Service seeking the release of skilled men from the forces – the housing workforce had been more than doubled to 60,000, and the number continued to rise to a maximum of 143,000 in mid-March 1945.[5]

Despite these short-term measures the new wave of attacks was to have far-reaching effects on plans for new housing. Priority given to housing in the general discussion of reconstruction intensified. More than ever people needed reassurance that government was responding effectively to this level of destruction and that plans for the post-war programme would be rethought.

With the immediate housing crisis under control, the Cabinet set about considering the long-term consequences of the attacks. It created a powerful housing subcommittee that included the Cabinet ministers Ernest Bevin, Henry Willink, Sir John Anderson and Lord Portal to address the new problems of housing.[6] This committee started to reconsider the government's plans for housing. Assumptions about manpower that had underpinned the planning of the whole of the national building programme had now to be rethought. The two White Papers on manpower published in the summer and autumn of 1944 anticipated the shortages in the workforce after the war and the difficulties that would be faced in determining priorities not only between civilian and military needs before victory in Japan but, most critically, between competing sectors of the economy as reconstruction got under way.[7] As a result of the destruction of housing by flying bomb and rocket attacks and the resulting massive jump in demand for labour and materials, the overall manpower budget for the post-war building industry was now revised downward and the problems of launching the permanent housing programme during the two-year emergency phase of the housing programme acknowledged. The manpower and timetabling calculations that underpinned the first crucial phase of the housing programme – the emergency phase immediately after the end of the war – were simply out of date.

The outcome of rethinking the housing programme was to focus attention solely on the two-year emergency period. An immediate consequence of this was the expanded importance of the temporary programme. In November, Lord Woolton, Minister of Reconstruction, announced to the Cabinet that orders for over 180,000 temporary houses had been placed, with hopes of production starting in January.[8] A second, far-reaching consequence was the scaling back of the first phase of the permanent housing programme. In place of the previous plans for 300,000 permanent dwellings, the subcommittee was no longer prepared to commit to a target for fear that any realistic assessment of output would prove unacceptable to public opinion. The figure of 20,000 dwellings finished by the end of the first year was 'floated', not as a target but as 'an indication to Departments of the extent to which preliminary work [was] to be put in hand for building work in the second half of the year, if labour [was] available'.[9] Significantly, the terms of the plans had shifted: they were no longer discussed in terms of houses completed but in terms of the number under construction.

With pressure mounting in the Houses of Commons and the Lords for a comprehensive government statement on housing, the White Paper was finally rushed out at short notice for a debate scheduled for the end of March. The prospects offered were not promising. It set out in general terms three principal objectives for the housing campaign: the provision of a separate dwelling for every family for which it was thought 750,000 houses would be needed; the completion of the slum clearance programme under way when the war broke out, for which a further 500,000 houses might be needed; and 'a progressive improvement in the conditions of housing in respect both of standards of accommodation and of equipment', in a continuous programme of new building over an unspecified number of years.[10] The most explicit commitment on the permanent housing programme was the undertaking to build, or to be building, 300,000 houses by the close of the second year after the end of the war in Europe. Very little was said about the complex task of translating these objectives into a programme of action with specific targets and a timetable for their achievement, or of reconciling the comprehensive housing programme with the demands of repairing war-damaged housing.

The first priority was the commitment to the completion of the repair of war-damaged housing. This, the White Paper explained, would ensure the largest number of houses available for use in the shortest time. In 1945 this task was still enormous. While most of the damage inflicted before June 1944 had been made good, the houses damaged by the flying bomb and rocket campaigns were far from repaired. According to the White Paper, the 'winter target', the first-aid repairs to 719,000 houses, was to be completed by the end of March. But even if this optimistic target were to be achieved, over 290,000 houses would remain below the standard of 'tolerable comfort'.[11] Not until these repairs had been completed would the labour and materials necessary for the permanent programme become available.

The housing needs of London

The translation of the national housing programme announced in the White Paper into a plan of action was set by the needs and resources in different parts of the country. Housing was a local not a national issue. Aggregate national figures on the urgency of the need for housing concealed dramatic variations between different areas. In areas which had survived unscathed by damage, the immediate need for housing was small, more a reflection of hopes for better housing encouraged by discussion of reconstruction or a product of changes in the distribution of population. In cities that had suffered during the early years of the war, such as Bristol, Coventry and Liverpool, most housing had been repaired, if only temporarily, by 1944. Their first priority was now to rehouse people still in billeted, shared or temporary accommodation. It was in London, where the full weight of the flying bomb and rocket attacks had fallen, that housing conditions were worst, and the housing shortage was most acute.

Within London, the aggregate figures of housing need convey little. There were sharp variations in the level of destruction from one borough to another.[12] In the north and west damage was limited. In Hammersmith, for example, only 4 per cent of the total area of the borough was damaged; in Hampstead the equivalent figure was only 5 per cent. Even central West End boroughs like Westminster and Kensington recorded similar levels of damage. But in the East End, particularly in the areas near the docks, damage was widespread. In Poplar 18 per cent of the area of the borough was classed as damaged.

In Stepney damage was worse still, with 22 per cent of the borough classed in these terms.

Just north of the City of London, Finsbury had suffered badly both during the Blitz and the flying bomb campaign, with 18 per cent of the area of the borough war-damaged.[13] By 1945, of the borough's 9,899 dwellings, 9,015, or 91 per cent of the total residential stock, had been damaged in some way or another. Many were only 'slightly damaged'. But this official designation concealed the difficulties of living in slightly damaged houses without glass, with missing roof tiles or slates and falling ceilings (Figure 1.2). Blast damage aggravated the defects of houses shoddily built in the boom years of the nineteenth century; buildings built on inadequate foundations settled unevenly, and the inadequate bonding of brickwork caused walls to bulge and chimney flues to leak. In addition to the outright hardship caused by slight damage, there was the homelessness caused by more serious destruction. A substantial number of Finsbury's dwellings, 642 of them, were uninhabitable; 1,006 were either totally destroyed or needed to be torn down. The Borough Surveyor estimated that by the end of the war Finsbury had lost 11 per cent of its housing stock.

The shortage of housing in the borough, severe before the war, increased during the war despite the overall fall in population. In 1944, partly due to evacuation, the population was down to 26,700 from a pre-war high of 68,000. By mid-1945 the number of residents in the borough was estimated at only 30,000, barely half the 1939 total; even by 1947 it had only reached 35,347. But despite these changes in population the housing shortage grew more acute: the net effect of the war-time bombardment was to make housing more overcrowded than it had been when Finsbury was the third most overcrowded borough in London. From late 1944, temporary relief from overcrowding was available in the form of Uniseco huts. Finsbury was allocated seventy-five of the 3,000 available for the London area as a whole, but in Finsbury, as in many other central boroughs, the ability to take more huts was strictly limited by the shortage of sites unencumbered by debris.

The challenge for those responsible for building new housing was great. There was now a clear expectation that the hopes encouraged by the war-time debate on reconstruction should be translated into action, and that those living in temporary accommodation or pre-war slums should be offered new housing built to the new standards that had been established during the war by the Dudley Committee. How were these aims to be realised, given the shortage of resources the country now suffered? While ministers struggled at the national level to allocate scarce resources to the different parts of the housing programme in different regions, housing committees, local authority officers and the professionals brought in to help them struggled to decide at the local level what kind of housing to build. Faced regularly with the difficulties of confronting face-to-face the anger and despair of people desperate for housing, of wives and husbands battling for their children or fighting to save a failing marriage, what were those responsible for these decisions, like the chairman of a housing committee, to do? Should the immediate problems of the shortage be palliated by securing more temporary housing at the expense of longer-term plans for permanent housing? Or was it better to build new housing as quickly as possible, even if it meant reverting to old-fashioned pre-war designs, or reletting contracts that had been interrupted when war broke out? Or again, would it be better still to look to the long term, holding out against those clamouring for housing now, to build designs that would answer the aspirations that had developed during the war? These important questions were an early and direct test of the way in which the long-awaited task of reconstruction was to be carried out in practice. Would the idealism of war-time debate survive the pragmatic challenges of immediate social need?

The work of the London boroughs

Different authorities responded to these challenges in different ways. London, with the most pressing shortage of housing in the country and the widest variation in the size of housing authorities and resources available to them, provides a comprehensive illustration of the ways in which local authorities set about the task of designing and building housing. East End boroughs like Poplar and West Ham could afford much less than rich West End boroughs like Westminster and Kensington. Small boroughs like Finsbury faced a scale of problem quite different from that of the LCC, with its responsibility for building housing across the whole of the greater London area. In the London area the opportunities confronting the designer were more complicated than elsewhere. The call to build at the higher densities recommended in the County of London Plan inhibited designers from falling back on the standard cottage or terrace house type of the pre-war years. Instead they had the altogether more novel task of designing flats that were an improvement on the widely criticised pre-war tenements.

For local authorities the discussion of plans for post-war housing was first prompted by the Ministry of Health's Circular 2778 of October 1943 which required local authorities to prepare an estimate of post-war housing needs and assemble land for housing.[14] London authorities set about plans for house building in a number of different ways. Some authorities, like many others across the country, had no separate Architect's Department and sought to embark on the construction of houses with only minimal architectural advice, leaving the task of design to draftsmen or architectural technicians working in the Surveyor's or Engineer's Department.[15] This was the case in Poplar, one of the poorest boroughs, where there was no Architect's Department.[16]

Other authorities might choose to place a greater emphasis on good design and turn to the services of private architectural practice. This might provide a way of getting architects with a national reputation to work on housing, generally regarded in the pre-war years as a mundane form of employment. It had the added advantage of reducing the need to establish a separate Architect's Department, with all the overhead costs, just to cater for what many hoped would be a short-term emergency. This was the case in Westminster. Here the Conservative-controlled City Council was planning the development of 33.3 acres between Lupus Street and Grosvenor Road as a self-contained neighbourhood unit along the lines suggested in the County of London Plan.[17] The design of the housing for this area, the 'flagship of the City's plans for reconstruction', was to be decided by open competition. This attracted widespread interest and over 200 entrants. That Philip Powell and Hidalgo Moya, fresh out of the Architectural Association, won the competition in June 1946 amongst other entrants with far greater experience of housing added a buzz of excitement to the project (Figure 4.16).[18]

In other boroughs private architects were simply engaged by the local authority without competition, often on the strength of pre-war ties. Islington opted for an approach to housing that it knew would produce housing cheaply and quickly: H.C.H. Monson carried on his established relationship with the borough as he had before the war, building housing that was dispiritingly similar to his drab 1930s tenements blocks.[19] Other boroughs were more adventurous. Paddington employed architects working in the office of the borough's Director of Housing for small-scale developments like the flats at St Mary's Square but engaged Tecton to design larger projects like the Hadfields Estate (1948–54).[20] In Hackney, Frederick Gibberd, known for his pre-war modernist developments such as Pulman Court and his co-authorship of *The Modern Flat*, built a number of housing developments, of which Somerford Grove is the best known (Figure 4.14).[21] Hackney also hired other modernists: Edward Mills designed the small block of flats at Kenmure Road and Norman and Dawbarn designed the Sandringham Road Estate, one of the first small-scale examples of mixed development.[22]

In Finsbury, one of the poorer boroughs and amongst those with the worst housing conditions before the war, housing was a key issue in local politics.[23] The leaders of Finsbury Council saw modern architecture and the continuation of the borough's pre-war collaboration with Tecton as a way of giving their vision of reconstruction a recognisable identity: modern architecture was to advertise the council's determination to improve housing conditions. The Labour-dominated council's hopes of building ultramodern housing as the showpiece of plans to transform the borough had been overtaken in 1938 by the threat of war. Now in 1945, with a Labour national government, Labour in control at the LCC and still in command in Finsbury, all looked set to put in hand plans that had been cut short by the war. For Lubetkin and Tecton, with their long-standing commitment to linking architecture with social issues like housing, it was as important as it was to Finsbury councillors like Dr Chuni Lal Katial or Harold Riley to demonstrate how modern architecture could be used to improve housing conditions. Tecton's designs for Finsbury were intended to go beyond the mere provision of accommodation to address the expectations of higher standards that had been awakened during the war (Figure 4.17).

The LCC's plans for post-war housing

Finsbury's programmes were small, they could do no more than build in penny packets. The central duty of building new housing for London lay with the LCC.[24] Only the LCC had the power and the administrative resources necessary to meet the targets set by the government's housing campaign. As the major housing authority in the country faced with the largest single programme of housing, the LCC had to be seen to respond to the political pressure for decisive action on housing, and its example would do much to shape the way housing was built during the period of reconstruction. The evolution of the LCC's post-war housing policy is worth following in some detail because it illustrates vividly the way in which the immediate need for housing was reconciled with the longer-term hopes of improving housing standards and design.

Unlike many of the boroughs, which had only started systematic consideration of post-war house building in response to the Ministry of Health's circular 2778, the LCC began planning its post-war housing programme as early as October 1940.[25] Ten weeks after the beginning of the Blitz in early September, Thomas Dawson, chairman of the Housing and Public Health Committee, instructed his officers to start planning a response to the acute problems of housing that he recognised the LCC would have to confront after the war. Discussions during these first months between Forshaw, the County Architect, and Westwood, the Valuer, were critical in determining the way in which the LCC eventually started building housing immediately after the war.

With the immediate problems created by the Blitz under control, progress on plans for post-war housing gathered pace through the summer of 1941. At a succession of meetings with key officers, and occasionally in more formal meetings with the elected members, London's post-war housing needs were mapped out. By September 1941 the scale of the problem had been agreed. It was estimated that 100,000 families had been 'displaced by enemy action'; of these about 50,000 might return to homes that could be repaired. For the remaining 50,000 new accommodation would have to be built.[26] This new housing was to be built in the first two years after the ending of the war. By November, the informal committee of officers, the Valuer, the Architect, and the Chief Engineer, prepared a report, 'Post War Housing: The Achievement of Rapid Results', which was to have a decisive influence on the LCC's post-war housing programme.[27] The document reflected the general line of argument the Valuer had been putting forward since the summer. It identified two key issues that needed to be resolved in order to achieve 'rapid results': first, the need to meet the shortage of land and to reduce the time spent in acquiring new sites, and second, the necessity of cutting the length of time needed to prepare detailed layouts and designs for each development.

The latter was the easier of the two problems to solve. Given the limited resources of the Architect's Department, the officers agreed that there should be a greater measure of standardisation of design. Despite criticisms of the monotony of the pre-war estates, the number of house types was to be reduced to an absolute minimum, a decision justified by the Architect's Department on the grounds that 'the Council may have either variety or speed but not both'.[28] These plan types were to be combined in the small number of standard block types based on those developed in 1934 and 1936. To facilitate rapid construction still further, the same internal arrangements were to be repeated on each floor (Figure 7.2). For those sites where plans already existed or where the war had interrupted development, the committee of officers hoped that the development would be pushed ahead as rapidly as possible on the terms already agreed. For sites already in the LCC's possession, plans were to be prepared promptly in order to cut the delay in the letting of contracts. Finally, to ensure that the limited resources of the Architect's Department did not hold back the layout and design of schemes, a panel of selected architects of proven experience was proposed to work up standard designs for sites that were yet to become available. Forshaw, the County Architect, agreed to support this programme as a whole, notwithstanding his reservations about putting his name to the pre-war designs of his predecessors. But he did so in return for the chance to redesign the development planned for Woodberry Down, Hackney, the largest single site in the LCC area.

As ever the other central problem for the post-war programme, the shortage of land for housing, was less tractable. But here again a return to pre-war practice was agreed as the simplest way forward, despite the potentially high political costs. The development of London sites already in the LCC's possession was to be given the highest priority. But officers recognised that the amount of land required to house so many was so great that it would be necessary to purchase additional land outside the LCC area wherever large parcels became available, a return to the policies pursued after World War I.[29] Naturally, this twin-pronged policy raised the possibility of conflict between the LCC and other local authorities. Within the LCC area it might affect the division of responsibility for housing between the metropolitan boroughs and the LCC, though officials hoped that conflict here might be countered by limiting the role of the boroughs to war-damage repairs only, leaving the LCC responsible for new housing.[30] Outside the LCC area, the proposed land policies would aggravate the long-sensitive relationship between the LCC and adjoining authorities. In the 1920s the development of LCC out-county estates like Becontree had caused friction in the surrounding area. Local residents had resisted plans to house what they called London slum dwellers in their neighbourhoods and Essex County Council had been slow to provide services, such as schools, for LCC families. However, LCC officials believed that conflict might be delayed, if not avoided, by concealing the plans for the purchase of land until the sale was complete, as they had in the 1920s.[31] Finally, any differences between the dictates, still shadowy at this stage, of the County of London Plan and the LCC's housing strategy were to be resolved by the County Architect, who was centrally involved in the development of both.

The paper submitted by the officers the year before was endorsed by the council in July 1943 as the general basis for post-war policy.[32] Under the general compulsion to provide housing as soon as possible after the war, the LCC was now committed to a programme which was in most respects indistinguishable from what it had been doing before the war. To officers schooled in the established departmental attitudes of the council, this had obvious virtues. In place of some vision of reconstruction, this was a realistic programme, based on tried and tested methods. The officers were ready to deal with London as they knew it. They were unlikely to be moved by the way these housing proposals would influence the interests of other authorities: the cut and thrust of dealing with the boroughs or the

officials of adjacent authorities were skills that they had mastered long before the war. The criticisms made of the LCC's pre-war estates like Becontree or Watling could be discounted in the face of the need to provide housing as fast as possible, or could be addressed, as the officers' report suggested, by a number of straightforward measures like the inclusion of community centres or the provision of a site for a health centre. The idealism of reconstruction was overtaken by the demands of routine practicality, all in the name of 'rapid results'.

From policy to programme

During 1943 the different departments were busily engaged in translating this broad strategy into a programme of action. By December the LCC was able to answer to the Ministry of Health's circular 2778.[33] Even at this stage the programme of around 10,000 dwellings was very much smaller than had been envisaged two years before. Overall only 5,427 flats and 4,635 cottages were to be started in the first year after the war, and much of this reduced programme was to be a continuation of the work the LCC had already begun before the outbreak of war in 1939. Excluding the rebuilding of 1,281 war-damaged flats, nearly a third of the total remaining programme, 1,319, were flats on which the contracts had been suspended or terminated at the outbreak of war. Well over half of the remaining two-thirds, 1,683 out of 2,747 flats, had been designed to working drawing stage when the war broke out. Of the 5,017 additional flats to be built after the first year's programme just over half, 2,505, were on sites where development was well in hand before the war. On the cottage estates, too, the position was similar: two-thirds of the 4,653 cottages in the programme were on sites where house building had been proceeding rapidly before the war; only one-third of cottages were to be built on new sites.[34]

Limited though these plans were they had to be reduced still further to take account of the effects of the flying bomb and rocket attacks.

Repairing damage done by these attacks or finding sites for emergency housing swallowed up the scarce resources, labour, materials and land so necessary to the permanent programme for new housing. By the June 1945 meeting of the Housing Committee, the Architect and the Valuer set out what they thought could be realistically achieved in the first year of the council's programme.[35] The outlook was bleak. Within the county only 1,934 dwellings had been ready for tendering in May 1945. A further 210 were to be ready for tender in June. More comfortably, 2,831 dwellings, including the reinstatement of war-damaged flats, were to be ready by July. And by October a further 1,771 would be ready to go to tender. The position on the cottage estates was only slightly better with the promise of 341 dwellings ready for tender in September. The Architect and the Valuer could give no indication of the time that letting the contracts might take, nor the expected completion dates for each project. More troubling still, even these figures turned on the optimistic assumption that the preparation of layouts and designs could proceed without delay. In retrospect the timetable presented by the Architect and the Valuer seems unrealistic, as it took no account of delays, despite the growing evidence of the difficulties of keeping to schedule. In July, for example, there was an acrimonious discussion of the failure to keep to the production timetable for the Debden estate. Work on site was to have started in August but the Valuer's and Engineer's Departments were accusing the Architect's Department of holding up progress by the failure to produce key layout drawings on time.[36]

Coming as it did at a time when the political pressure for rapid progress on housing was mounting both nationally and in London, news of the drastically reduced targets prompted the LCC's Housing Committee to declare housing 'an utmost emergency'.[37] By October, confronted with mounting concern that coordination between the different departments within the LCC was not as effective as it should be, the LCC's senior officers resolved to streamline the output of housing by consolidating all aspects of production in a single department. Given that the Architect's Department was already overstretched, it was inevitable that the overall responsibility for housing, including the design of housing and housing layouts, should pass to the Valuer, who already bore the responsibility for initiating all housing developments.[38] This amounted to the surrender of the Architect's central task to the Valuer and sparked private but vigorous protest from senior members of the architectural profession, like Lancelot Keay, to the LCC leaders. They remained unmoved.[39] For Forshaw this was an unacceptable affront, and within six months he had resigned to join the Ministry of Health as Chief Architect and Housing Consultant.

Reshaping the administrative structure responsible for the London housing programme, the LCC had done more than merely streamline its internal administration. It had signalled the priorities that it wished to uphold: rapid results were to be more important than the new housing standards set by the Dudley Committee or the quality of design. Set beside the urgent need for housing at the end of 1945, war-time aspirations for reconstruction seemed even more remote and utopian than they had before the war ended. But as the continuing debate on reconstruction indicated, people were not prepared to abandon all hope of improving standards. Without thinking too hard about how it was to be done, the public expected those in charge of the country's housing programmes to square the circle: to achieve both quantity and quality. The challenge to architects was to show how this could be achieved.

Housing built by the LCC Valuer, 1945–49

The most immediate problem in designing new housing for London was the flat. The task of designing housing to normal densities seemed by comparison straightforward. Here the principal issue was construction, and the way that non-traditional construction in particular might shape architectural form (Figure 9.1). New types of developments combining flats and

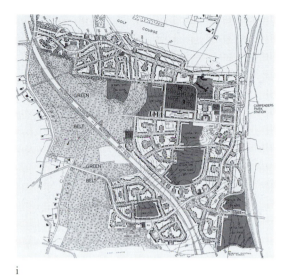

i

ii

9.1 The Oxhey Estate, 15 miles from Charing Cross and without shops or services when the estate was first occupied: (i) site plan; (ii) general view showing permanent, non-traditional BISF houses

houses , the mixed-development layouts recommended in the County of London Plan for use in the suburbs and districts where the density might be between seventy and 100 people per acre, seemed to present architects with less difficulty than the arrangement of large groups of flats. Mixed-development estates like Norman and Dawbarn's Sandringham Road Estate in Hackney or Gibberd's Somerford Grove, also in Hackney, were widely praised for combining terraces and squares, traditional elements of London housing, with an appreciation of the non-doctrinaire modernism of Scandinavia. However, their approach could not achieve the higher densities of 136 people per acre and more recommended in the County of London Plan for the central boroughs. Here multistorey flats had been shown by Forshaw and Abercrombie to be necessary, and architects needed to find a way of designing housing of this kind.

To the Valuer and his team at the LCC the solution existed in the form of tenement block that the council had used before the war. Defending LCC policy, Isaac Hayward, leader of the LCC from 1947 to 1965, made it clear that accelerating housing production was more important than the design of a new form of block of flats; politically the number of new houses

counted for more than architectural quality.[40] The Valuer and his team did not deny the advantages of gradual improvement to the house types they were using, but the LCC was simply not prepared to hold up the production of new housing to give architects time to get their designs right.

Many of the in-county 'flatted estates' that were started in the first two years after the war were built just as a continuation or renegotiation of contracts let before 1939. The Tufnell Park Estate is typical of such estates, one of those chosen specially to illustrate the council's housing achievements under the Valuer (Figure 9.2).[41] Work on 272 flats in the Tufnell Park Estate had already started shortly before the war and was resumed under the renegotiated terms of the same contract in 1946. Any latitude for redesign was thus strictly limited. Designed on the basis of the type plans approved by the LCC in 1934 the individual blocks were provided with gallery access to dwellings which had a separate bathroom and a kitchen with a gas cooker and a gas-heated copper boiler for hot water. The system of gallery access, much criticised before the war, remained unaltered. The gallery still eroded privacy in the kitchens, bathrooms, and bedrooms which looked on to it and overshadowed the same rooms in the flats beneath.

9.2 A general view of the Tufnell Park Estate (1946), an example of the post-war completion of estates started before the war

It was not just the layouts and the planning of these blocks that continued pre-war practice; their architectural treatment remained essentially unchanged as well. Based on the Neo-Georgian tradition started under Topham Forrest in the 1920s, the LCC blocks were treated as singular houses on a grossly inflated scale.[42] On the elevations there might be some indication of a classical base, perhaps a suggestion of vestigial pilasters and an attic storey to crown the symmetrical whole. On the gallery access side, such architectural control as existed focused on composing the verticals of the stair towers and the horizontals of the galleries. No formal means of reading the individual dwelling was apparent; this was invariably concealed behind a pattern of fenestration conceived in terms of the facade of the block as a whole. The results were dull, though occasionally, as at the China Walk Estate, the design might achieve a careful dignity helped

by a keen attention to the detailing of traditional construction. After the war in estates like Tufnell Park the compositional scheme remained while construction and detailing were sacrificed in the interests of economy. Even in the eyes of relatively conservative commentators like the editor of the *Architect and Building News*, the outcome was a 'housing architecture [which] is unimaginative, and detailing that is coarse'.[43]

That the Tufnell Park Estate should be finished in a continuation of pre-war practice might be accepted by the LCC Housing Committee as the price for rapid results, but there were widespread expectations that the new housing started from scratch after the war should be built to higher standards. In December 1945 the LCC announced the new type plans which were to be used in future developments.[44] To replace the limited range of pre-war plans, four new type plans were introduced, offering designers the opportunity to develop layouts with staircase-access flats, four-storey maisonettes, three-storey blocks combining maisonettes and flats, and an improved version of the gallery-access flats. Drawn up with the recommendations of the 1944 *Housing Manual* in mind, the new plans were slightly larger – with higher rents – and offered other benefits: lifts in blocks of five storeys, coal hoists in four-storey blocks, improvements in the design of the kitchen and in hot water supply and storage and, on some large estates, full central heating.

Typical of the in-county block dwellings designed to these new standards was the Minerva Estate in Bethnal Green (Figure 9.3).[45] Despite the availability of new plan types, 253 flats were planned in eight parallel blocks in the old gallery-access manner so that all the living rooms face each other across a strip of grass only 60 ft wide, while all the kitchens look over asphalt parking areas. In questions of detail, these plans showed some of the improvements intended to meet the most damaging criticism of the pre-war estates. In all but two of the blocks there is a playground and sun playroom on the top floor, and just over one acre of the 7¼ acre site was reserved for a community centre and a public house which was

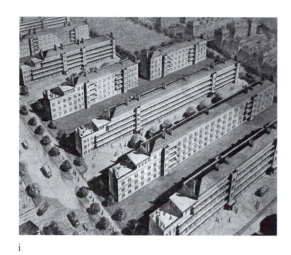

i

9.3 The Minerva Estate (1948–51), an example of post-war housing built by the Valuer unconstrained by pre-war work: (i) axonometric view of the site; (ii) plan of one of the blocks

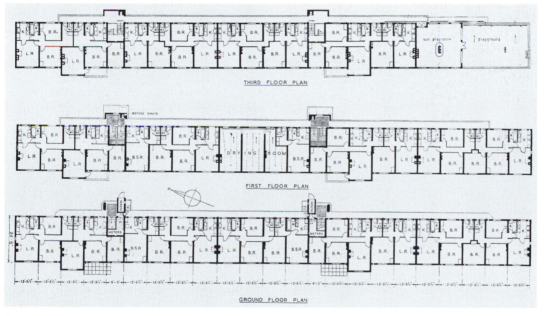

ii

to be built later. The individual block and flat plans represented some improvement over the pre-war norm: there were two dust chutes on the long access gallery and drying rooms on the first floor. Water heating by electricity in most blocks was viewed as an advance on the pre-war gas coppers, and the standard of the kitchen fittings and finishes was improved. Minerva Street was also one of the first estates on which the LCC experimented with a new form of monolithic reinforced concrete construction, which the Valuer claimed would lead to lower costs and faster construction.

But for most contemporaries the Minerva Estate was really no different from pre-war practice. Its publication in the *Architects' Journal* was met with letters protesting at the low quality of LCC housing design.[46] What is particular to the LCC housing of the late 1940s is the relentless aridity of the site planning, with the placing of the parallel blocks determined by the accidents of site geometry, unrelated to orientation or the needs of the individual dwellings. In its appearance Minerva Street is typical of the developments of this period with its elevations of unrelieved monotony and thin and skimpy detailing; these schemes lack either the authority of the Neo-Georgian details or the interest of the moderne that enlivens many of the pre-war schemes. At Minerva Street, as commentators were quick to point out, the only virtues that could be claimed for the design were its cheapness and the speed with which the blocks could be erected.

Two major developments, the Woodberry Down estate in Hackney and the Ocean Estate in Stepney, stand out as being different from the LCC's continuation of pre-war practice. As the largest single development within the LCC area in the late 1940s and as an exception to LCC policy of allocating all design to the Valuer, Woodberry Down provides an interesting indication of the approach to housing that Forshaw might have taken had he been allowed the freedom to practise as he wished (Figure 9.4).[47] Forshaw seems to have envisaged Woodberry Down as a positive response to pre-war criticism of LCC estates. Unlike the typical block estates of the 1930s – for example the King's Mead Estate, Hackney, planned with uniform five-storey blocks without lifts – the Woodberry Down site was planned as a mixed development with a number of different house types. These were to range from two-storey cottages and cottages with maisonettes above to five-storey blocks and to a new type of eight-storey block with lifts. The last in particular seem to have attracted the Valuer's criticisms as a wasteful and expensive way of providing housing that could have been accommodated equally well, and at a similar net density, in the standard pre-war 1936 or 1934 gallery-access blocks. For Forshaw, however, the new blocks were an attempt to establish a new approach for LCC 'flatted blocks' that would meet the standards recommended by the Dudley Committee. Designed with staircase rather than with gallery

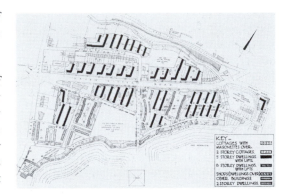

i

ii

iii

9.4 The Woodberry Down estate (1946–48), the principal estate designed by the LCC Architect's Department during the late 1940s: (i) site plan showing the mix of houses, maisonettes and flats; (ii) a view of the development across the West Reservoir; (iii) the new eight-storey blocks

access, the blocks were higher than previous LCC blocks, to make economical use of the single passenger lift per block that Forshaw proposed. Arguing his case against the Valuer in front of the Housing Committee, and drawing on the experience of Quarry Hill in Leeds, Forshaw successfully defended the use of lifts and staircase access as a way of overcoming the long-standing and deep-seated antipathy of the English working classes to living in flats.[48] In spite of the Valuer's objections that the cost per flat would be around 4 per cent higher than that of the council's 1936-type flats, and that the staircase system would mean the loss of seventy-six of the total of 384 flats, Forshaw was able to win the Housing Committee's support, though the Comptroller's backing was only offered on the strict understanding that the Woodberry Down approach would not be used as a general precedent for housing elsewhere in London.

The architectural treatment of Woodberry Down was diverse. The five-storey blocks, like Lonsdale or Leighfield House, planned with gallery access and now with lifts, were treated in a simplified Neo-Georgian style with an elaborate cornice combined with round-cornered balconies in a streamlined fashion. The eight-storey blocks were handled differently. They were designed in a simplified classical manner with heavy cornices and a rusticated base marking a certain emphasis to the entrance of each staircase. The form of the whole block was articulated by the emphasis placed on the final staircase unit at each end and by the rhythm of the balconies on the two principal facades. Elsewhere on the estate were a number of five-storey gallery-access blocks designed in a style that drew inspiration from Sweden and were viewed more sympathetically. With their straightforward elevations, simple pitched roofs and the direct treatment of brick elevations, these blocks were praised for showing how to raise the quality of design without compromising the production of housing.[49]

Most critics did not favour the architecture of the estate. R. Furneaux Jordan, president of the Architectural Association, was scathing:

The Valuer – for all one can see to the contrary – tosses a coin to decide between 'Georgian' roofs and flat roofs; if it comes down tails the details are streamlined a little more, and that's 'modern'. As simple as that! Except … when middle period Dudok towers break the Georgian skyline, and heads and tails get a little mixed … At Woodberry Down the flats in the lower half of the building have balconies on one elevation, the flats in the upper half have them on the other; the roof is flat, but the cornice is a pretty full-blooded affair – architrave, frieze and cornice to be correct – with the windows of the top floor punctuating like metopes. The Valuer should leave such *tours de force* to Sansovino, who did them better.[50]

But Woodberry Down still remains the most interesting development built by the LCC between 1945 and 1950. Cyril Walker, publicly defending the housing work of the LCC in February 1949 when his direction of the LCC's housing programme was under attack, chose the eight-storey blocks as the best illustration of the high quality of the council's flats.[51] In the gale of criticism of the standard of design of the LCC's housing unleashed in the architectural press by the 1949 exhibition of the LCC's housing work, the new five-storey blocks and the eight-storey blocks at Woodberry Down were spared, where the older type of tenement housing was not.[52] But as isolated examples they could do little to offset the overall impression of the poor standard of LCC housing under the Valuer.

The approach taken by the LCC had other opponents. When consulted on the form of housing it favoured – rather than on the difficult choice between more or higher-quality flats – the public had been unusually outspoken in its condemnation of the old-style gallery-access tenements which were the pre-war norm in most cities. The 'experts', housing reformers, planners and architects, agreed. The search for a new approach to the design of the flat was important and not necessarily at odds with giving the production of housing the high priority it deserved. The access gallery more than any other feature seemed to exemplify the failure of the pre-war tenement type.[53]

These criticisms, made by experts and public alike, were made sharper still by the comparison, upsetting to the LCC, with the housing work of a number of boroughs. Presented with the opportunity to explore and experiment, the architects working for the boroughs showed what could be achieved with similar resources. Set against the achievement of Tecton in Finsbury, of Powell and Moya in Westminster, or Norman and Dawbarn in St Pancras, the work of the Valuer's office looked regressive and unimaginative.

Quantity versus quality: the London housing programme, 1945–50

In 1945, the numerous London authorities made different decisions about the balance between quantity and quality. A number of the boroughs had refused to surrender hope that reconstruction could provide the opportunity for radical improvements in housing. The LCC had taken a different view. As the authority with prime responsibility for London's post-war housing programme, it had taken the decision early on to give priority to building as many dwellings as fast as possible and had reaffirmed this commitment with the transfer of all responsibility for housing to the Valuer. This was justified on the grounds that coordination of housing production within a single department would make it possible to achieve the LCC's housing targets. How far had the Valuer, by 1949, been able to secure in practice the rapid results, the 50,000 houses in two years, that he had first promised in 1942 and then again in 1945?

By 1947, the seemingly attainable targets of two years before were well beyond reach.[54] Already in the summer of 1946, a year after the war had ended, progress seemed pitiably slow: although sites for nearly 12,000 houses were being prepared, and tenders for over 7,500 houses had been approved, only 90 houses had

actually been finished. By the end of the year, the position had not radically improved: a year and a half of 'housing drive' had produced only 466 completed dwellings. By the end of the second year, the number of completions was still only 759, hardly the rapid results that had been expected. Even in September 1949, as the responsibility for housing design finally slipped from his control, the Valuer had only completed 16,542 dwellings, less than half the planned total for the first two years after the war.

The Valuer might reasonably cite the difficulties that beset the national housing programme as grounds for delays to the LCC's programme.[55] Shortages of labour and materials affected all authorities: demobilisation was slower than had been forecast and competition for skilled labour within the national building programme was fiercer than expected, despite the priority given to housing. Materials like bricks, plasterboard, timber and steel were all, at various times and for different reasons, the cause of delays to the programme. Difficulties in the management of the programme created acute problems across the country, particularly in the early years as different central government departments tried to coordinate the availability of labour and materials in different regions with the programmes of the different local authorities. The aim of most local authorities to build as rapidly as possible only compounded the difficulty of matching the number of permitted housing starts to the resources available, with the result that completion rates lagged far behind the number of starts.[56]

In mitigation the Valuer might have argued that in London the situation was yet more difficult still. Not only was competition for labour and materials between housing and other forms of building intense, but the competition for resources between new housing and war-damage repairs was sharper than anywhere else.[57] The sheer scale of destruction during the flying bomb attacks had generated a backlog of repairs which still had not been cleared by April 1945, notwithstanding the heroic efforts of the specially created London Housing Executive.[58] The effect of this substantial repair campaign was to consume materials and labour intended for the start of the permanent housing programme and to disrupt completely the plans that had been drawn up for its launch. Regardless of pledges to complete the bulk of the London war-damage repairs by the beginning of March 1945, the task that faced the London Housing Executive and the boroughs when the war ended was formidable. In March 1946, 350,000 houses in London were below the standard of 'reasonable comfort' and in need of 'second stage' repairs.[59] In September 1946 nearly three times as many men were working on war-damage repairs – 65,000 on authorised and 22,000 on licensed work – as on permanent new housing, where there were 21,000 on authorised and 8,200 on licensed work.[60]

Given labour and materials the problem of war-damage repairs was tractable, allowing resources to be switched to new housing. By March 1947, the numbers of men working on war-damage repairs and on permanent new housing were almost level.[61] Only 83,000 houses needed two-stage repairs, barely a quarter of the total of the year before.[62] Thereafter the build-up of men on new work proceeded rapidly, while the volume of repair work slowed to a trickle. By the end of 1947, repairs had been almost beaten. The consequences of this huge programme of repairs was, however, most damaging to the LCC's permanent programme. In the spring of 1945, the Valuer fought to have layouts and contract drawings ready for the earliest moment when the Ministry of Health would allow local authorities to go out to tender. But with only 15,000 men for new housing for the whole of the London region, there simply was not the labour force to take on the programme that the LCC had drawn up.[63] Nor could priorities be rearranged to make extra men available. The London Housing Executive had given the highest priority to war-damage repairs precisely because this form of work was the most effective way of rehabilitating and bringing into use as many houses as quickly and as cheaply as possible.[64] Given the case that the Valuer and the

LCC had made for deciding the arrangements for the LCC's housing programme on the basis of these same priorities, how could the Valuer challenge the view of the London Housing Executive? Priority to war-damage repairs during the immediate post-war years had denied the Valuer any possibility of achieving 'rapid results'.

At the time when the new organisation for housing was agreed in December 1945, it was intended that these arrangements would be reviewed in at least three years' time. But in 1948, with the London programme delayed by the same difficulties that beset the national programme, the LCC postponed the thorough-going review that had been promised. Then in February 1949, following an attack on the quality of the design of LCC housing by J.M. Richards on the BBC's Third Programme in December, the whole issue was thrown wide open to public discussion.[65]

The timing of Richards' attack was prompted partly by the LCC's proposed review of the administrative arrangements for housing and partly by the progress of the Valuer's plans for the Putney-Roehampton estates for 21,000 people, the largest of the council's post-war housing schemes. In December this had been roundly criticised by Richards in *The Times* and in the *Architects' Journal*.[66] Following a call in the *Architects' Journal* in March for a critical debate of the LCC's housing work, the LCC leader, Isaac Hayward, proposed to arrange

> a comprehensive exhibition, specially for qualified architects, at which will be displayed photographs, plans and working drawings of the Council's estates, including *any* which have been the subject of adverse comment, and invite the *Architects' Journal* to publish the opinions of the visitors.[67]

The offer, welcomed by the *Architects' Journal*, had been preceded by a certain amount of defensive bluster by Hayward and Gibson, the Chairman of the Housing Committee, reflecting a recognition by the LCC leaders of the need for change. In 1949, with the housing shortage less urgent than it was five years before, and an approach to housing by the LCC that was widely regarded as, at best, dull and reactionary, was it surprising that Hayward should have chosen to surrender the Valuer to his architectural critics? For an LCC leader keen to exploit the publicity value of the image of the LCC as a force for modernisation, what better way of securing a change of direction?

The LCC exhibition opened in April 1949. If the correspondence columns of the architectural press provide a measure of contemporary professional reaction, critical judgement swung against the Valuer.[68] While the scale of the difficulties ranged against him was readily acknowledged, there was strong and widespread feeling in the profession that this could not offset the mediocrity and the monotony of the schemes on display. Most damaging to any defence of the LCC was the contrast of its housing work with that of the metropolitan boroughs. If London boroughs rich and poor, St Pancras, Westminster, Finsbury and Hackney, could produce housing that answered to the ideal of a New Britain – at a cost which was claimed to be comparable to the work of the LCC – why could the LCC not do the same?

Neither officers nor the leaders of the LCC chose to mount a sustained defence of the quality of the LCC's housing work, and in October it was confirmed that responsibility for the layout and design of housing should be transferred back to the Architect's Department, a decision that was interpreted as a triumph for the architectural profession.[69] By early 1950 Robert Matthew and Leslie Martin – with H.J. Whitfield Lewis fresh from Norman and Dawbarn in charge of the housing section – were designing new prototypes for LCC housing which broke away completely from the types used under the Valuer. Looking to Sweden for inspiration and to the tenets of the New Humanism, the designers of the LCC's new Ackroydon Estate and the first phase of the Roehampton Estate produced designs that seemed to answer the ideals of reconstruction so much better than the 'stale

chocolate' of estates like Tufnell Park or Minerva Street.[70]

In retrospect, the triumph of architectural values over the priority given to production has a ring of inevitability about it. It all seems a part of the gradual adoption of the Modern Movement as the chosen style for New Britain that seemed to have been achieved by the mid-1950s. But was this inevitability so obviously true to contemporaries? To LCC politicians it was less the quality of the Architect's layouts and designs than the failure to achieve rapid results that left the Valuer without a defender. Far more damaging to the LCC than an attack on the appearance of the LCC's new housing was the mounting chorus of frustration shouted by those who were still waiting for their new homes. To get 'rapid results' Londoners might be prepared to forgo the ideals of reconstruction, but if the Valuer failed to deliver the number of houses that he had promised, then, whatever the reasons, he was not fit to retain total control of the LCC programme.

In the competition for resources, for labour and materials, war-damage repairs had been given priority because it was the quickest and cheapest means to increase the number of available dwellings. The LCC might do all it could to muscle its way to the head of the queue of authorities waiting for resources, but it could not reverse this priority. The Valuer's approach thus fell victim to the very social priorities that he had advanced in justification for his own approach in the mid-1940s (Figure 9.5). Unable to achieve rapid results, what could he answer to charges that he was building to lower standards than the London boroughs or local authorities elsewhere?

Hayward, his predecessor Lord Latham and officials like the Valuer seemed to identify their own preferences with those they ascribed to Londoners. In criticising mixed-development estates or the housing designed by the younger generation of architects, the Valuer claimed to be speaking for the 'ordinary' people. But what did Londoners really want? Popular attitudes to housing in the late 1940s suggest that Londoners were keen to have higher standards than the

i   ii

9.5 The face of housing needs in London: (i) ex-servicemen and their families squatting in Abbey Lodge, Hanover Terrace, London, in September 1946; (ii) the key to a newly completed flat at Woodberry Down being handed to the first tenants in 1948

debate on reconstruction suggested would become available. Who would willingly turn their back on central heating, or refuse the advantages of lifts in blocks of flats? Tenants in the new 1950s estates like Roehampton showed considerable enthusiasm for their new homes.[71] But this was less an enthusiasm for modern architecture and more a sense of liberation from the oppressive world of sharing with the in-laws or the trials of heating water in a pan on a gas stove for the children's baths. There is nothing to suggest that these Londoners would not have been equally enthusiastic at the prospect of moving into the kind of housing being built by the Valuer, as long as it was not too remote from work. As contemporary surveys of housing emphasised, what people wanted was a home of their own. Whether it was 'modern' or not remained a matter of indifference beside the supreme importance of 'homeness' and 'ownness'.

The post-war housing programme might not have provided opportunities for modern architecture on the ambitious scale that its advocates had hoped for as the war ended. But sufficient housing was built by a number of London boroughs, Finsbury, Hackney, Westminster and others, to show that it was not necessary to choose between the ideals of reconstruction and the social priorities of housing. Tecton, Powell

and Moya, and Norman and Dawbarn had shown how to develop a new approach to the flat and how to build modern housing at costs, and to a timetable, that were comparable with housing built elsewhere.

The LCC's post-war programme had been less successful. The return to pre-war practice had not brought the expected benefits. Public distaste for the LCC's pre-war housing, clearly expressed in war-time surveys of opinion, had been muted during the post-war housing shortage: there had been general acceptance of the housing policy pursued by the LCC in the first few years after the war. But the Valuer had been unable to deliver the 'rapid results' that he had promised in 1945, because he could not overcome the problems that beset the housing programme nationally; if anything, the difficulties that he faced in London were more acute than elsewhere. Unable to offer quantity or quality, he had to surrender the design of housing back to the architect.

The success of modern architecture at the LCC in the early 1950s was established by the successful combination of an in-house architectural team of proven ability – Matthews, Martin and the housing section under Whitfield Lewis – with politicians like Hayward who recognised the value of architecture as a way of giving formal identity to the modernising and reforming

9.6 The old and the new housing team at the LCC in November 1950: Cyril Walker (Director of Housing and Valuer), Reginald Stamp (Chairman of the Housing Committee) and H.J. Whitfield Lewis (Principal Housing Architect) inspect a model of the LCC's Princes' Way (Ackroydon) Estate at Wimbledon

policies of local government (Figure 9.6). Finsbury, St Pancras, Westminster and other progressive boroughs of the late 1940s were examples to be followed at a much larger scale by the LCC in the major developments of the 1950s at Roehampton and Loughborough Road (Figures 4.20 and 5.5). After 1950 the potent combination of progressive local government and modern architecture was to establish well-designed housing estates like Roehampton as one of the most enduring images of the New Britain.

Notes

1 Ministry of Health, *Housing*, Cmnd 6609, London, HMSO, March 1945.
2 MPs of all parties had become critical of the government's handling of both the war-time problems of housing and the failure to keep them informed of the plans for the housing campaign. This frustration was vented in the debates in the Commons on housing; see e.g. *Hansard* 16.3.1945.
3 C.M. Kohan, *Works and Buildings*, London, HMSO, 1952, ch. 10, pp. 222–38. For a fuller account of the rocket attacks see two books by N. Longmate: *The Doodlebugs: The Story of the Flying Bombs*, London, Hutchinson, 1981, and *Hitler's Rockets: The Story of the V2s*, London, Hutchinson, 1985.
4 Kohan, *Works and Buildings*, ch. 10.
5 *Ibid.*; I. Bowen, 'The Control of Building', in D.N. Chester (ed.), *Lessons of the British War Economy*, Cambridge, Cambridge University Press, 1951, pp. 139–43.
6 The subcommittee was proposed by Herbert Morrison and established in September 1944. The membership changed over time but included the following members of Cabinet: Sir John Anderson (Chancellor of the Exchequer), Ernest Bevin (Minister of Labour), Henry Willink (Minister of Health), Lord Portal (Minister of Works), W.S. Morrison (Minister of Town and Country Planning); it was chaired by Lord Woolton and served by a team of high-level civil servants. Its meetings are covered in PRO/CAB/87/34 and 36 and the papers in PRO/CAB/87/35 and 37.
7 Minister of Labour, *Manpower: Re-Allocation of Manpower between the Armed Forces and Civilian Employment*, Cmnd 6548, 1944; Ministry of Labour, *Manpower: Re-Allocation of Manpower between Civilian Employments*, Cmnd 6568, 1944.
8 PRO/CAB/87/35, the memorandum of 3.11.1944.
9 PRO/CAB/87/37, the memorandum of 28.2.1945.
10 Minister of Health, *Housing*, Cmnd No.6609, London, HMSO, March 1945, p. 2.
11 *Ibid.*, p. 5.
12 A summary of comparative statistics on war damage is to be found in *Administrative County of London Development Plan*, London, LCC, 1957, p. 28. The index of destruction used in these statistics is based on the area of continuous, serious damage, it therefore understates the extent of the damage to the housing stock, as is evident from the example of the Finsbury statistics. For details of damage in the LCC area see GLRO/CL/HSG/1/15.
13 See the report by G. Hebson, *Report on Housing in Finsbury*, London, Metropolitan Borough of Finsbury, August 1945, section III; N. Bullock, 'Fragments of Utopia: Housing in Finsbury 1945–51', in *Urban Studies*, 26, 1989, pp. 46–58.
14 Ministry of Health, *Post-War Housing*, Circular 2778, 1943.
15 It is easy to forget how few local authorities employed an independent Architect's Department; see below, ch. 10, especially notes 10 and 11.
16 See e.g. the flats presented in the exhibition 'Poplar Builds', *AJ*, 2.12.1948, p. 501; 'Poplar Builds',

Keystone, Jan. 1949, pp. 9–11; see also 'Public Housing in Poplar', in *Survey of London: Poplar, Blackwall and the Isle of Dogs*, Vol. XLIII, London, Royal Commission on the Historical Monuments of England (Athlone Press), 1994, pp. 37–45.

17　Plans for the replanning of Pimlico were first discussed in 1943; plans were agreed in outline form in April 1944: J. Rawlinson and W.R. Davidge, *Report on the Replanning of Pimlico*, London, City of Westminster, 27.4.1944. For a more resolved version of the plan for Pimlico see *A New Plan for Pimlico*, London, Town Planning and Improvements Committee, Westminster, 9.1.1946.

18　See e.g. the comments in the architectural press when the results of the competition were announced: *AJ*, 30.5.1946, pp. 411–16 ; *ABN*, 24.5.1946, pp. 122–7; 31.5.1946, pp. 138–9; *Builder*, 25.5.1946, pp. 500–9.

19　'Canonbury Court Estate', *Builder* 3.9.1948, pp. 270–1; 'Bentham Court, Essex Road', *Builder* 23.9.1949, p. 387.

20　The flats at St Mary's Square designed under the direction of the Borough Engineer are described in *AJ*, 7.10.1948, pp. 331–4. The flats being designed by Tecton soon after were first published in *AJ*, 11.11.1948, pp. 441–4.

21　Somerford Grove attracted considerable attention at the time, e.g. *AR*, Sep. 1949, pp. 146–9. Gibberd also designed the Beechholme Estate, *AR*, Oct. 1953, pp. 239–41; the Beckers, Rectory Rd, *Builder* 14.7.1961, pp. 62–4; Kingsgate Estate, Tottenham Road, *AR*, Apr. 1961, pp. 272–5.

22　The flats by Edward Mills at Kenmure Road were published in *AJ*, 5.5.49, pp. 413–15, the Sandringham Road Estate by Norman and Dawbarn in *AJ*, 30.9.1948, pp. 309–15.

23　Bullock, 'Fragments of Utopia'; J. Allen, *Berthold Lubetkin: Architecture and the Tradition of Progress*, London, RIBA Publications, 1992, chs 8 and 9.

24　There were extended discussions between the LCC and the boroughs on responsibility for new housing from at least as early as March 1942. The boroughs pressed hard for the right to build at least some new housing and fiercely resisted the LCC's attempts to restrict them to the repair of war-damaged housing alone; GLRO/CL/HSG/1/12.

25　GLRO/CL/HSG/1/12. For a general account see N. Bullock, 'Ideals, priorities and harsh realities: reconstruction and the LCC, 1945–51', *Planning Perspectives*, vol. 9, 1994, pp. 87–101.

26　GLRO/LCC/CL/HSG/1/12, the meeting of 7.8.1941.

27　GLRO/LCC/CL/HSG/1/12, the meeting of 17.11.1941.

28　*Ibid.*, item 4c. Before the war the LCC had used type plans as a way of reducing the time involved in designing individual blocks; see e.g. London County Council, *Housing*, London, LCC, 1937, pp. 39–44.

29　The Valuer's pre-war policy is set out in GLRO/LCC/CL/HSG/1/31.

30　GLRO/LCC/CL/HSG/1/12: the conference of 3.7.1942, especially Paper B.

31　For a discussion of the Valuer's views on how to provide for the 50,000 new homes see GLRO/LCC/CL/HSG/1/12, the conference of 3.7.1942, especially Paper C.

32　GLRO/LCC/MIN/7310: 21.7.1943.

33　GLRO/LCC/MIN/7616.

34　GLRO/LCC/MIN/7616: 'Post-War Housing Programme' (HP 300).

35　GLRO/LCC/MIN/7618: 'Post-War Housing, The First Year's Programme' (HP453).

36　GLRO/LCC/CL/HSG/2/14: 30.7.1945. Relations between the Architect's and the Valuer's departments had not improved with the appointment of Cyril Walker as Valuer on Westwood's death in 1944.

37　GLRO/LCC/MIN/7301: 18.7.1945.

38　For the discussion surrounding this decision see GLRO/LCC/MIN/7301: 7.11.1945, item 19 (HP251); 14.11.1945; and the papers of the Civil Defence and General Purposes Committee: GLRO/LCC/MIN/2796, GLRO/CDGP 928 and 928a.

39　The protests made by Keay and others, along with an account of a meeting with the senior figures at the RIBA, are contained in GLRO/LCC/MIN/2796; GLRO/CDPG 928a.

40　For Hayward's defence of LCC policy see *AJ*, 31.3.1949, pp. 293–4.

41　LCC, *Survey of Post-War Housing of the LCC 1945–49*, London, LCC, 1949, pp. 44–5, 52; *Builder* 12.12.1947, pp. 675–7.

42　Typical of these tenement estates was the China Walk Estate (1928–34), LCC, *London Housing*, London, LCC, 1937, pp. 56–61.

43　From a letter by the editor of *Architect and Building News*, cited in *AJ*, 26.5.1949, p. 475.

44　'LCC Type Plans', *ABN*, 15.2.1946, pp. 103–8; 23.8.1946, pp. 117–20.

45　'LCC Housing, Minerva Estate, Bethnal Green', *AJ*, 27.3.1947, pp. 253–6, and 'LCC Flats in Monolithic Reinforced Concrete at Bethnal Green', *ABN*, 14.3.1947, pp. 169–73.

46　E.g. 'LCC Housing, Need for a Critical Reassessment' *AJ*, 17.3.1949, pp. 251–3.

47　For the Woodberry Down estate see LCC, *Survey of Post-War Housing*, pp. 47–50; the estate as a whole, but the eight-storey flats in particular, received more coverage in the architectural press than any of the housing developments designed by the Valuer: *AD*, Jun. 1946, p. 151; *AJ*, 3.3.1949, p. 209; *ABN*, 18.2.1949, pp. 143, 145–9.

48 GLRO/LCC Min/7617, meeting of 261.1944; GLRO/LCC Min 7300, HP 323, Woodberry Down.

49 E.g. the letters from Lionel Brett, *AJ*, 19.5.1949, p. 451; from Edward Mills, *ibid.*, p. 452; from Colin Penn, *ibid.*, p. 452; and from E.B. Musman, *AJ*, 2.6.1949, p. 498.

50 R. Furneaux Jordan, *AJ*, 26.5.1949, p. 474.

51 C. Walker, 'The Housing Programme of the LCC', *ABN*, 18.2.1949, pp. 143–6.

52 The 1949 exhibition of the LCC's housing work was reported extensively in the press, particularly the *AJ*. *Architectural Design*, for example, was also critical of the LCC, though in more muted terms: 'The LCC v the Rest', *AD*, Jan. 1949, p. 2. *AJ* published accounts not only of the exhibition but of the profession's response to it. Most of the 30 or so letters received were hostile to the LCC and only a very few, notably letters from Albert Richardson, Clough Williams-Ellis and E.B. Musman, were in favour: *AJ*, 26.5.1949, pp. 476–83.

53 'Abolish the Balcony Access', *AJ*, 24.4.1947, p. 336.

54 These figures are taken from the monthly statistics in the Ministry of Health's *Housing Returns for England and Wales*, London, HMSO.

55 For a discussion of the difficulties affecting the national programme see N. Rosenberg, *Economic Difficulties in the British Building Industry 1945–49*, Philadelphia, University of Pennsylvania Press, 1960.

56 The difficulties caused by the failure to coordinate local authority programmes with the resources available is examined by J.A. Chenier, *The Development and Implementation of Post-War Housing Policy under the Labour Government*, Oxford, DPhil dissertation, 1984.

57 The important issue of war-damage repairs has not received sufficient attention, but see Kohan, *Works and Buildings*, especially ch. 10, and GLRO/LCC/Cl/HSG/1/15, 'Post-War Housing – Repair of War-Damaged Houses 1941–46'.

58 The London Housing Executive was created by Woolton, the Minister of Reconstruction, to coordinate the work of the different departments and local authorities who were dealing with the acute housing shortage in London at the time; see Kohan, *Work and Buildings*, pp. 222–5.

59 Ministry of Health, *Summary Report for the Year 1946–47*, Cmnd 7441; London, HMSO, 1948, p. 173.

60 These figures are taken from the regional breakdown of figures for the national building programme for the September quarter 1946; PRO/HLG/68/116.

61 *Ibid.* (figures for the March quarter 1947).

62 Ministry of Health, *Report of the Ministry of Health for the Year 1947/48*, Cmnd 7734, London, HMSO, 1948, p. 246

63 *Ibid.*, p. 246; and GLRO/Cl/HSG/1/15.

64 Contemporary figures show that with a completion rate of 2.25 houses repaired per man year of employment (for 1946), war-damage repairs were a markedly more productive way of securing more houses than the permanent programme, traditional or otherwise: I. Bowen, 'Housing Statistics', *AJ*, 104, 1946, p. 206.

65 The scheme was announced in the press: 'London Housing Project, Homes for 21,000', *The Times*, 27.11.1948, p. 4. Richard launched his attack the following week.

66 See e.g. the short notice, *AJ*, 2.12.1948, pp. 502, 505, on the quality of LCC architecture for the Roehampton development. This anticipates Richards' attack on LCC housing design in spring 1949. See also P.L. Garside, *Town Planning in London 1930–61: A Study of Pressures, Interests and Influences Affecting the Formation of Policy*, London School of Economics, PhD dissertation, 1979, part V: 'The LCC and Planning 1945–55.

67 'Housing: A Special Announcement', *AJ*, 5.5.1949, p. 401.

68 'The LCC Housing Exhibition', *AJ*, 12.5.1949, p. 426; 26.5.1949, pp. 474–95. The extended correspondence on the exhibition filled the columns of *AJ* until June: 'LCC Housing, A Final Word', *AJ*, 16.6.1949, pp. 537–8. Other journals took a softer line but did not support the Valuer. *Architect and Building News* allowed the Valuer space to defend the design of LCC housing (see note 51 above), but no journal offered wholehearted support.

69 The terms of the decision were spelt out neutrally by most of the architectural press, e.g. 'The Future Organisation of Housing Work for the LCC', *ABN*, 23.12.1949, p. 653, but the *Architects' Journal* took a more triumphalist line: 'LCC New Housing Architects', *AJ*, 16.3.1950, p. 329.

70 President of the RIBA Goodheart-Rendell disparaged the standards of official architecture by likening it to chocolate made by machine: 'repetitive and slightly stale' (quoted in A. Powers, 'Goodheart-Rendell: the Appropriateness of Style', *Britain in the Thirties*, Architectural Design Profiles 24, p. 51).

71 By the early 1950s, the LCC had appointed a sociologist, Margaret Willis, to assess attitudes to different forms of housing: M. Willis, 'Living in High Flats', *JRIBA*, Mar. 1955, pp. 203–4. For a less partisan point of view see the material assembled by the staff of the Geffrye Museum from interviews with the Whitley Point Tenants' Association and the Shepherd's Bush Local History Society; both are referred to in S. MacDoul and J. Potter, *Putting on the Style: Setting up Home in the 1950s*, London, Geffrye Museum, 1990.

10 Building by the local authorities
Schools and housing

The idea that the state should play the central role in reconstruction of post-war Britain had been widely accepted since the early years of the war. In the first post-war decade, the state had played the dominant role in both housing and school building, the two largest components of the national building programme: in housing, for example, by 1955 74 per cent of all new dwellings had been built by the state. Progress had not been as fast as hoped, but in the difficult circumstances of the post-war years the scale of the achievement in numerical terms alone was undeniable. But what of the architectural quality of this output? The difficulties faced by the LCC during the late 1940s illustrate the problems that resulted from pitting social – and thus political – priorities against arguments about the quality of housing. Was the approach adopted by the LCC typical? How had the public sector, the vast mass of local authorities, responded to the unprecedented demand for housing and schools? Was it simply a question of production, of building as many houses or school places as possible, or did building by the public sector answer more ambitious aspirations for a better future?

These questions are complicated by the fragmented nature of the state. The state in the form of central government built very little. Instead, building for the public sector was the responsibility of a large number of different authorities which, though not completely autonomous,

were not agents of central government but popularly elected, legally independent bodies with independent powers of taxation. On inspection, what is most apparent about these authorities is both their number and their variety. In the mid-1950s, housing alone was being built by 1,529 different authorities, which varied dramatically in size: some such as the rural district councils were small and might build no more than a dozen houses in any one year; others at the opposite end of the scale, like the LCC, held the primary responsibility for the housing needs of a population of around 10 million. In addition to size, there were important differences between local authorities of different types and central government. Given the number, variety and the differences between types of authorities, an account of the building work of the public sector is best approached in terms of the different kinds of authorities and the programmes of buildings for which they were responsible.

The local authorities and their architects

By 1957, nearly half (48 per cent) of all architects were working for government, the majority (28 per cent) for local authorities.[1] The employment offered by the local authorities was diverse. The LCC ran an Architect's Department with more than 750 architects and over 2,000 technical and administrative staff. The department was arranged into major divisions for housing, schools, planning and general needs, each of which was headed by a deputy responsible for all the work of that division; the Housing Division alone employed over 300 architects.[2] At the other end of the spectrum were small rural district councils where a few architectural assistants, not necessarily fully qualified, worked under the direction of the district council's engineer or surveyor.

Different kinds of authorities ran different building programmes. School building was principally the responsibility of the county councils. By the late 1940s, all but two of the sixty-two county councils employed a chief architect and had an independent Architect's Department whose main architectural concern, along with building fire stations and other occasional buildings, was building schools for areas with a population of anything between 250,000 and 750,000.[3] The next tier of local authorities, the cities or county boroughs, were responsible for building both housing and schools. These authorities ranged from industrial and commercial centres like Birmingham, with a population of millions to county towns like Gloucester, with around 30,000 inhabitants. The range of building undertaken by cities, generally more complex than that of the county councils, included special projects ranging from the monumental to the utilitarian, from law courts to fire stations. Prior to the war the responsibility for all the building work of these authorities – architecture as well as bridges and other public works – was generally in the hands of the Borough Engineer or Surveyor, with some of the architectural work farmed out to private practice. By 1957 this was changing: forty-seven of the eighty-three county boroughs had appointed chief architects with their own independent departments. Significantly, however, Birmingham, the country's second-largest city, appointed a City Architect, A.G. Sheppard Fidler, only in 1952, and even then he was but one of a number of deputies to the City Engineer, Herbert Manzoni, himself qualified as architect and engineer. Not until January 1954 was the Architect's Department granted full

independence.[4] Cambridge had to wait almost another decade, until 1963, before a City Architect was appointed.[5]

The responsibility of the remaining local authorities, the 318 non-county and twenty eight metropolitan boroughs, and the 564 urban and 474 rural district councils, was confined almost entirely to housing. Few employed chief architects or maintained a separate Architect's Department: only fourteen non-county and five metropolitan boroughs and only six of the 1,038 district councils did so. Thus in the great majority of these authorities housing would have been designed in-house by architects or architectural assistants working under the council's engineer.[6] But although few of these lower-tier authorities had an independent Architect's Department, they did employ large numbers of architects. By 1957, 71 per cent of the architects working in the public sector – or 35 per cent of the entire architectural profession – were working for a borough or council engineer.[7]

What kinds of departments were responsible for what kind of work? A basic distinction can be drawn between those designing schools and those working on housing, which together represented the greater part of all building by the state.[8] For school design, of the 145 local education authorities the majority, 107, or 74 per cent, could call on the resources of their own Architect's Department. For housing, only a few, at most seventy-two, of the 1,529 housing authorities could call on comparable resources. Inevitably most housing schemes were designed by architects or architectural assistants working – and very occasionally acknowledged – under the direction of the Engineer. Some smaller local authorities found they could not justify the cost of an Architect's Department and made use of private architectural firms to design schools and housing. Equally a small number of the largest authorities commissioned private architects, chosen from a panel of approved architects, as a way of promoting new ideas and of meeting the peaks of demand for schools and housing. In school building certain practices, Sheppard, Robson and Partners, the Architects' Co-Partnership, Yorke Rosenberg and Mardall, and Denis Clarke Hall, came to acquire an established expertise that education authorities large and small were keen to buy in.[9] In housing a number of the London boroughs fostered close and fruitful relationships with certain practices: Finsbury with Tecton (and Emberton), Hackney and Gibberd; Monson with Islington; Macmorran and Poplar; Chelsea with McManus and Armstrong, and Westminster with Powell and Moya. However, most local authorities, especially the smaller ones, preferred to keep design work in-house, both to save the cost of fees and to ease the burden of coordination between departments.[10]

School building: links between central and local government

Besides the differences in the internal organisation of local authorities for the building of schools and housing, there were important differences in the relationship between central and local government in the fields of housing and education. The transfer in 1951 of the responsibility for housing from the Ministry of Health to the newly created Ministry of Housing and Local Government (MOHLG) combined housing and planning in a single department and was meant to strengthen the hand of central government. But even this new, larger ministry was never to exert the same influence on either housing policy or the form of housing that the Ministry of Education exercised on teaching and the design of schools. By contrast, the relationship between the local authorities and the Ministry of Education was frequently held up as a paradigm for general emulation by other government departments.[11]

Through its Architects and Buildings (A&B) Branch, the Ministry of Education was in the position not only to advise local authorities on school design and to comment on their proposals for new building, but crucially, with the establishment of the Development Group in 1949, to build new projects.[12] By building a series of experimental schools in conjunction with different local education authorities, A&B

Branch was able to influence the form of the modern school, to show by example the way forward to new developments. Local authorities were not coerced into adopting the views or the advice of the Ministry of Education, they retained their individual identities and approaches and many went their own way. But at least those who wished to do so could call on the assistance of central government.

The way in which A&B Branch and the Development Group worked in the early 1950s owed much to the Hertfordshire schools programme. Though nationally known, the Hertfordshire programme was only one of a number of approaches to the prefabrication of schools that had been developed during the late 1940s. Nevertheless, the Hertfordshire experience did much to shape the way the Ministry of Education came to manage the whole business of school building. This was in large measure due to Stirrat Johnson-Marshall, who as deputy to Herbert Aslin, the Hertfordshire County Architect, played a key role during the three critical years after the war. In August 1948 Johnson-Marshall left Hertfordshire to join the Ministry of Education as head of A&B Branch, where he worked alongside Anthony Part, a progressive civil servant of outstanding ability, under the informed guidance of John Maud, the Permanent Secretary at Education. One of the conditions of Johnson-Marshall's acceptance of his new post was that A&B Branch should not merely advise local authorities but should actually build a number of experimental schools. To undertake this, the Branch was split into two. Research, experimentation and development work was to be the task for a new Development Group, to which Johnson-Marshall was able to attract former Hertfordshire colleagues and others from organisations like the Building Research Station and the LMS Development Group who had an interest in research and development. The second group, the territorials, were to continue the established task of vetting the annual programmes and plans for individual schools submitted by education authorities. Working in this way the territorials were to play an important role in winning the support of individual authorities for the Development Group's new ideas.

By the time Johnson-Marshall left the Ministry of Education in 1956, A&B Branch had already begun to affect the form of school building in three important ways. First, it was responsible for circulating information on the most successful new developments and their costs among different education authorities and their architects everywhere in England and Wales. Following the success of the Post-War Building Studies series, the Ministry of Education in 1949 began to publish a series of Building Bulletins in which current thinking was set out by those directly involved in the work.[13] *New Primary Schools* (Building Bulletin 1), by David Medd, one of the first to join from Hertfordshire, provided a summary of the Hertfordshire experience; Building Bulletin 2 set out the thinking on secondary schools. Later bulletins addressed questions of cost and primary school layout, as well as describing some of the branch's development projects.

Second, the way in which the A&B Branch affected the form of school building was through the politically delicate but critical task of securing better value for money in school building. The arrival in 1951 of the new Conservative government was met by loud calls for cuts in government expenditure, and the Ministry of Education was faced with the imperative need to reduce costs without compromising the school building programme.[14] A&B Branch was called upon to give advice on how to limit building costs. This was a new departure. In the first years after the war, when the immediate priority was to increase the number of school places, costs had been less pressing than solving the shortages of labour and materials. In place of the ad hoc methods of controlling cost used before the war, the A&B Branch had instituted in 1950 a means of control based on the cost per place. But to meet the call for cost savings involved calculating how much a school actually cost to build and whether the newly established cost per place was reasonable. Answering these questions involved A&B Branch in new and fundamental research into the cost of buildings.

Central to this inquiry was the attempt to examine the wide variation in the cost of schools built in different ways in different parts of the country. For the first time the separate elements of a building, the foundations, steelwork, cladding and roofing, were costed independently. This form of comparative costing was of no great value where a building was designed and built as a singular, one-off assignment. But given the system of organising the school-building programmes and the increased use of prefabricated or rationalised building methods, the value of this approach to cost analysis was greatly enhanced. An elemental analysis of cost made it possible for the first time for the architect, and the client, to understand how the overall cost of the school was allocated across the different elements of a school and thus to determine at the design stage priorities for expenditure. This pioneering system of cost control, which was developed by the A&B Branch's senior quantity surveyor, James Nisbet, was described with exemplary clarity in *Cost Study* (Building Bulletin 4)[15] and taken up by a number of other ministries in their own efforts to control expenditure. In school building this method of cost control had the very real benefit of enabling the annual programme to survive more easily the cuts in expenditure imposed by the Conservative government between 1951 and 1954.

The effects of this system of cost analysis went further than simply limiting expenditure. As local authorities struggled to keep their school-building programme within the costs imposed by central government, their architects found it increasingly important to confer with A&B Branch architects to see how to meet the new cost targets. Local education authorities (LEAs), architects and teachers were forced to reconsider school design, abandon wasteful plan types, and avoid expensive forms of construction. Inevitably the new system of cost control led to a greater uniformity in every aspect of school building, from basic configuration and planning to the use of materials and details of construction.

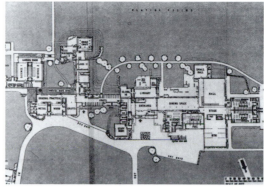

i   ii

10.1 St Crispin's Secondary Modern School, Wokingham (1951–53), the first of the Development Group's live projects: (i) general view showing the four-storey classroom block and the elements of the school; (ii) plan

The third way in which A&B Branch was to influence school building came as a complement to its increasingly sophisticated control of costs. To demonstrate that the cost targets being recommended could be met in practice, the Development Group built a number of prototype schools to show local authorities – who were generally too short of design staff to experiment on their own account – how they might set about the design of the new secondary and comprehensive schools called for by the 1944 Education Act. From 1949 to 1957, the Development Group was to develop five different school building systems. All were of lightweight rather than traditional construction: two of the systems were in steelwork, one was in aluminium, and two were in precast concrete. All were based on the 3 ft 4 in. horizontal module adopted by the Ministry of Education in 1948.

St Crispin's School, Wokingham, designed in 1949–50 by David Medd (and others) and built in 1951–53, was the first development of the Hertfordshire system based on the Hills light steel frame (Figure 10.1).[16] At Wokingham the Ministry of Education's newly agreed 3 ft 4 in. module replaced the less flexible 8 ft 3 in. module used at Hertfordshire. Just as important as the development of the Hertfordshire system was its adaptation to meet the demands of building a new secondary school. In place of the single-storey primary schools for which the Hertfordshire system was originally conceived, Wokingham was designed with a four-storey classroom block with additional single-storey rooms, with long enough clear spans to accommodate a hall, a gym and specialised teaching spaces for arts and crafts. Designed to a brief that was being prepared while the text of Building Bulletin 2, *New Secondary Schools*, was being written, the thinking behind Wokingham immediately influenced the layout and construction of new secondary schools across the country. In contrast to the formality and monumentality of most pre-war grammar schools, and even some secondary schools built after the war, Wokingham was informal in layout and architecturally unassuming. The plan, according to the bulletin, was not derived from a 'preconceived plan pattern', but was allowed to grow out of the problem itself – the educational needs and activities of each of its parts'.[17] These were readily identifiable. The classrooms were housed in a four storey block, the other facilities were at ground-floor level in separate one-storey blocks. All were linked under cover. The overall effect was picturesque rather than formal and owed much to the Hertfordshire schools: the same aesthetic of assembly, the same low-key qualities that Llewelyn Davies and Weeks had described as the 'otherness' of the Hertfordshire schools.[18]

The other four systems designed by the Development Group had much in common with Wokingham. All shared a number of common components, like windows, doors and cladding, but were built around quite different structural systems. After the hot-rolled steel frame used at Wokingham, the Branch designed a system based on the cold-rolled steel frame developed by John Brockhouse and Company which was first used at The Parks Secondary School in Belper (1953–55).[19] Later this was developed further to form the basis of the system used by the Consortium of Local Authority Schools' Programmes (CLASP) established by Nottinghamshire County Council in 1956.

There was also an aluminium system developed from the Mark I Bristol Aircraft Company (BAC), tried first at Limbrick Wood School, Coventry, in 1951–52,[20] and later as a Mark II BAC system at Lyng Hall Comprehensive School, Coventry, in 1953–55.[21] Finally, there were two methods of construction based on prestressed and prefabricated concrete, the Intergrid and the Laingspan systems. The latter was developed in the late 1950s and tested at the Arnold Grammar School in Nottingham in 1957–59, but was little used.[22] The Intergrid system was more successful. It was designed by the Development Group in conjunction with the contractor Gilbert-Ash and an engineer, Alan Harris, with experience of prestressed, prefabricated concrete in France.[23] By late 1952 the team had designed a method of concrete construction capable of meeting the challenges that the Hills system had answered at Wokingham. The Intergrid system could provide up to four storeys of classroom accommodation and the long spans needed for halls and gyms. It could also accept without leaking the cladding systems, tiling and concrete panels that had already been developed for lightweight construction. The technical secondary school built at Worthing in 1953–55 was the prototype for this form of construction and was viewed by A&B Branch as the most successful of its five experimental systems (Figure 10.2).[24] Later Intergrid was to be successfully exploited by Bovis, who had taken over

Gilbert-Ash, the owners of the rights to the system, and during the 1960s several hundred schools were built using this system and its derivatives, many of them in Scotland.

i

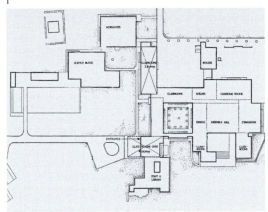

ii

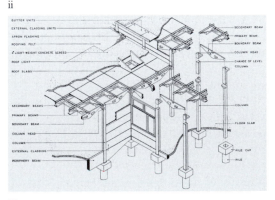

iii

10.2 Worthing Technical Secondary High School, Worthing (1953–55), built with the Intergrid precast concrete structural system: (i) general view; (ii) plan; (iii) the Intergrid system

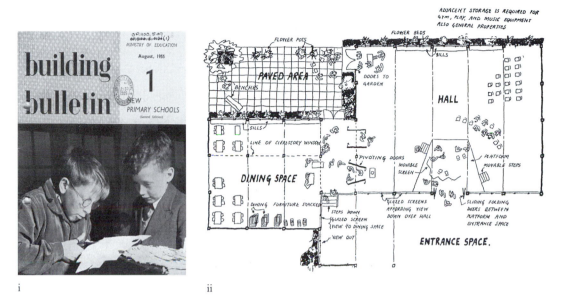

i   ii

10.3 Planning principles for the new primary school: (i) the new child-centred approach as illustrated on the cover of Building Bulletin 1, New Primary Schools; (ii) diagrammatic representation of new layout

School building by local authorities

Schools built by the LEAs with the advice and encouragement of central government are still seen, as they were at the time, to have been a success.[25] True, the principal proponents of this view have been the educationalists and the architects closely engaged in their creation. But notwithstanding the changes in educational ideology since their construction, the reputation of the school building programmes of the 1950s remains largely untarnished. In *Education*, the national weekly journal of record in education in the 1940s and 1950s, teachers and educationalists praised the new primary schools, and the smaller number of secondary schools, for the sympathetic environment they provided for new developments in teaching.[26] The architectural press, too, feted the new schools as the most successful and the most familiar face of modern architecture. The award of the *Gran Premio con Menzione Speciale* to the small CLASP primary school at the Milan Triennale in 1960 is a reminder of how English school building was viewed in Europe, a token of the international recognition of its qualities.[27]

This success was due in part to the way the new schools answered the needs of teachers and pupils. The approach to the planning of the primary school in Building Bulletin 1, *New Primary Schools*, drew together the ideas of child-centred teaching practice that had already gained momentum in the 1930s and emerged as the dominant educational ideology by the early 1950s (Figure 10.3). To Christian Schiller, chief inspector of primary schools at the Ministry of Education and a champion of these views, it was important that school buildings should serve the child. The child and its education was central, and any investment in building should serve this focus.[28] In architectural terms liberation was as necessary from the inhibiting effect of the inflexible buildings and rigid class layouts of the pre-war years, as was a shift away from formality and architectural display (Figure 10.4).[29]

These views were shared by A&B Branch and were directly to affect post-war school building. At A&B Branch architects and educationalists worked together in a way that promoted the exchange of ideas on the relationship between the form of buildings and the nature of education. In the Development Group too architects

i

ii

10.4 In Neo-Georgian or modernist styling, the symmetrical quadrangle plan remained in widespread use during the 1920s and '30s: (i) Fairlop School, Ilford (1933), designed by L. Reynolds and J.F. Cavanagh; (ii) Junior and Mixed Infants School at Southall (1937), designed by W.T. Curtis, County Architect, Middlesex

and educationalists worked together so that the form of the new secondary schools under development reflected the Ministry of Education's latest thinking on education and its determination to transform the educational system. The overlap of educational and architectural ideas is evident from the start of the series of Building Bulletins. *New Primary Schools* opens with a discussion of the new approach, 'How can the architect make his best contribution to the creation of this [school] environment? The basis of the school design is not only a schedule of areas and building regulations but the needs and activities of growing children and their teachers.'[30] In place of the conventional illustrations of school architecture, it offers a series of hand-drawn diagrams of site layout, classroom layout, equipment for playing, and different ways of using the building and using its spaces. For many of the architects in A&B Branch, like David Medd and Mary Crowley (later Mary Medd), school building was more about providing for children and their education and less about architecture.

How successfully were the ideas of A&B Branch translated into practice? The overall impression given by the eighty schools built by different authorities and shown in March 1953 at the 'Britain Builds for Education' exhibition, arranged by the Building Centre, is of the extent to which these values had penetrated the designs of private practice and the county architects

who might, for other types of buildings, still be producing designs of pre-war monumentality.[31] In place of the axial symmetries and the self-conscious display of architectural features, whether classical, arts and crafts or 1930s moderne, the schools exhibited at the Building Centre and those frequently illustrated in *Official Architecture and Planning*, the *Architects' Journal* and the *Builder* share an informality of layout and simplicity of purpose that established, despite varieties in the configuration of plans and different approaches to construction and detailed design, an overall impression of a common approach.

Of course there were education authorities with special needs: the LCC faced the task of building new comprehensive schools, many for well over a thousand children, on small and expensive urban sites. Schools like the new comprehensive at Tulse Hill, with its nine-storey classroom block, looked very different from the schools being built by most education authorities.[32] These, however, did resemble each other. They shared common characteristics shaped by the same considerations: the new approach to education, the need to control costs and a shared motivation to exploit non-traditional construction. To a critic like J.M. Richards, the new school building programme was important for modern architecture generally and for the emergence of a modern vernacular: 'In the development of modern school architecture and

i

10.5 Local authority use of non-traditional school construction: (i) the BAC system of lightweight construction as used at Cornwall Technical College, Trevanson, Cornwall; (ii) the Vic Hallam's Derwent system of timber construction used at Hackenthorpe Primary School, Derbyshire (1953)

ii

the consolidation of the efforts of the pioneers, we can see at work the process whereby architectural style is created.'[33]

This resemblance was in part a reflection of common educational priorities and partly a result of the way in which designers of schools, the LEAs and central government adopted common responses to the need to reduce the cost of school building. The reduction in funding began in 1949 with the introduction of a cost limit per place.[34] This was followed by a succession of annual reductions that led to a halving of the real cost per place between late 1949 and 1953. More effectively than was the case with housing, the damaging effect of these cuts was countered by the changes made in the design of schools, not in the standards of construction or in the overall quality of school buildings.

To meet these targets school architects and the architects of A&B Branch explored a number of ways of reducing costs. The two major savings were to be found in reducing the size of the building

and in cutting the costs of construction.[35] Prompted by government's general encouragement of non-traditional construction, many education authorities had high hopes that lightweight construction and the extensive use of prefabrication would lower costs. But in practice major savings were difficult to achieve. In 1955, despite the work of the Development Group, the Ministry of Education estimated that only 25 per cent of schools were built using a complete system of prefabrication.[36] The authorities who favoured this approach were widely scattered. They ranged from the Home Counties, where Hertfordshire, with a rapidly rising school population, regarded prefabrication as the only means of meeting its targets for new school places, to rural counties like Cornwall, where the lightweight aluminium BAC system offered advantages of speed and cost over traditional construction in a region short of materials and labour. For most authorities complete prefabrication was not cheaper than traditional building. The Hills and Intergrid systems, for example, cost about the same as first-class traditional building and offered the same degree of performance, if not durability.[37] Their principle advantage was that both were faster to erect and needed less site labour than traditional building.

However, these complete systems did not represent the sum of all non-traditional school building. The publicity that the Hertfordshire achievements attracted has overshadowed the history of widespread experimental work carried out by other authorities. Even at a time of steel shortage, as at the start of the 1950s, local authorities across the country continued to engage in an impressive range of experiments with different approaches to non-traditional construction (Figure 10.5).[38] Lancashire, a large authority, had the advantage of a big programme with which to develop alternatives to traditional building.[39] Smaller counties like Northamptonshire were also keen to experiment. Here, the County Architect opposed the use of a proprietary system and his department was encouraged instead to use readily available prefabricated components, rolled-steel joists and metal windows, alongside traditional materials like brick.[40] In general, however, by 1955 most education authorities were making extensive use of prefabricated components, if not of whole proprietary systems, as a means of meeting the reduced allowance per place or speeding of construction.

Even more successful as a way to cut costs was to reduce the size of school buildings; and architects, encouraged by A&B Branch, looked intensively at ways of doing so. To reduce the cube of the building, for example, ceiling heights were trimmed, a limited though relatively pain-free way of reducing cost. By far the most effective way to cut costs was to reduce floor area, and to do so by reducing the amount of space used solely for circulation.[41] In secondary schools the use of double- rather than single-banked corridors offered immediate savings. In primary schools real savings were made by the shift from the 'finger plans' of the late 1930s and 1940s to the more compact layouts of the 1950s, a shift made possible by the double use of the hall as dining room and circulation space (Figure 10.6). The Development Group estimated that this reduced the proportion of the area given over to circulation from 23 per cent to 7 per cent and the area for non-teaching accommodation from 38 per cent to 25 per cent. Overall, these new compact plans made it possible to reduce the area per place by nearly 40 per cent in under five years without cutting the areas available for teaching, thus enabling architects to meet the demands for economy without compromising quality.[42]

One result of this pressure to reduce costs was to encourage a convergence on successful solutions to the layout of schools. With a large

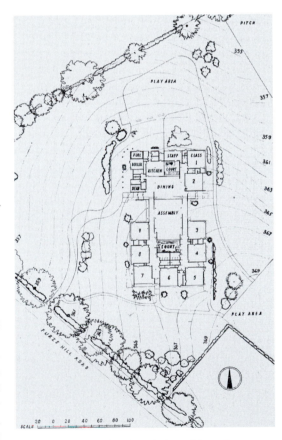

10.6 In contrast to the 'finger' plans of the early post-war Middlesex and Hertfordshire schools, the schools of the early 1950s were generally more compact, a trend illustrated by the Summerswood Primary School, Borehamwood (1950–52), one of the early Hertfordshire compact plans

number of architects working on the design of schools and with information on new buildings and new design ideas rapidly circulated by the Ministry of Education and through the architectural press, a common approach, a familial resemblance – though not necessarily a common 'style' – for the design of the modern school, soon evolved, winning approval from professionals and public alike. Differences between the approaches of individual authorities remained: in Hertfordshire, schools built under Aslin looked very different from the schools built in the two neighbouring counties of Middlesex and Essex. Schools built in Middlesex under Stillman and in Essex under H. Connolly differed from those in Hertfordshire – and each other – in construction and in appearance. But schools in all three counties reflected the same pressures to cut circulation and to replace the loose layouts of the late 1940s with the more compact plans of the early 1950s. With flat or gently sloping roofs, their modest 'domestic' scale, large windows, the frequent use of lightweight and prefabricated construction, bright colours, and with their generally light and spacious appearance, the architecture of the new schools had much in common. It was this generic quality that was recognised in the editorials and reviews of school building in the pages of *Official Architecture and Planning*, the *Builder* and the *Architects' Journal*.

The role of central government in housing design

Compared with school building, the administrative arrangements for house building were both looser and more varied. For a start, the task for central government of communicating with 1,500 housing authorities was a less personal activity than that facing the Ministry of Education in its discussions with far fewer education authorities.[43] Moreover, to add further complexity, the division of responsibility for housing between central government departments was less straightforward than that for school building.[44] Until 1951, housing was the respon-

sibility of the Department of Health, but the size of the housing programme and its economic consequences was of direct concern to other departments like Labour, Works and, less immediately, the Board of Trade. The housing programme also influenced the overall economic assumptions made by the Treasury. Finally, as the largest single land use in any city, housing was of immediate importance for planning decisions, and the work of the Ministry of Town and Country Planning, an overlap of responsibilities so critical that in 1951 responsibility for housing was transferred from the Department of Health to the newly formed Ministry of Housing and Local Government (MOHLG). Here, under Evelyn Sharp, housing was to play a subordinate role to planning.

Formally the MOHLG had powers to compel local authorities to comply with government policy; more immediately it could also coerce authorities through the economic powers that came with subsidies, it could even threaten to refuse to sanction a loan, but in practice such sanctions were never used. Indeed the ministry was put in a 'remarkably weak' position in its dealings with the local authorities.[45] Much of its advice and guidance was in the form of informal contacts through local 'territorial' staff working with individual authorities. Given that no more than 250 of the 1,500 housing authorities built over 100 dwellings a year, and most built far fewer, this system of informal contacts was appropriate for most schemes.[46] But the larger authorities with major building programmes tended to exercise a considerable measure of freedom in the way they worked within the parameters of government policy, for example in the choice of the proportion of flats they built. Nor was it unknown for large authorities to use their political muscle to demand, and receive, special treatment or particularly favourable interpretations of key aspects of policy such as subsidies.[47]

The system of subsidies was an obvious mechanism by which central government could influence the activities of the local authorities. Before the mid-1950s subsidies had little direct effect on the form of housing. During the whole of the first post-war decade subsidies were paid at a flat rate per dwelling of whatever form or type of £16.50, increased in 1952 to £26.70. In addition there was an expensive site subsidy payable for each dwelling for blocks of flats over four storeys to assist authorities building housing in central areas. It was not until after 1956 that government, as a way of further encouraging slum clearance, introduced a new system of subsidies that encouraged high-rise housing by progressively increasing the level of subsidy per dwelling for higher blocks.

More important for the form of housing in a number of large cities were the decentralist policies promoted by central government planners at the MOHLG. From the start of the 1950s central government planners had encouraged a twin policy of containing urban growth through the extension of greenbelts around cities and by relocating those wishing to move or those not rehoused in clearance schemes to New Towns. With the curtailment of the New Town programme this was to continue – under the provisions of the Town Development Act 1952 – by a policy of overspill which enabled overcrowded older cities to export population to smaller, less crowded towns, often some distance away. As slum clearance programmes got under way again after 1954, estimates were made of the proportion of the existing population that might need to be relocated in this way. These varied from 5 per cent for Greater London to 18 per cent for Birmingham and Liverpool and to 23 per cent for Manchester and Salford.

The 1952 Act was viewed with a mixture of hostility and misgiving by central and by local authorities for a variety of reasons, not least because of the complexity of the administrative arrangements it proposed. The response of many of the authorities designated as 'exporters' was more hostile than most. They saw a twin threat. First, the proposed reduction in population, with its implications for rates, threatened the financial well-being of many authorities; second, the loss of housing land challenged the autonomy of their housing programmes. To preserve these –

and they were an important part of the local political process – housing authorities like Liverpool or Birmingham realised that they would have to abandon completely the low-density housing schemes that they had been building since the war for developments that required less land. Higher densities were necessary and, according to the conventional wisdom of the time set out in the MOHLG pamphlet *The Density of Residential Areas*, this inevitably meant building more flats.[48]

In addition to strategic policies like these, central government continued to offer guidance and advice to local authorities on questions of design, as it had since 1919. Here, the principle instrument of policy was the *Housing Manual*. The latest edition, published in 1949, continued the guidelines set by the 1944 manual, which in turn formalised as advice to the local authorities the recommendations of the Dudley Committee.[49] The 1949 manual starts by clarifying the relationship between housing and planning, density and the neighbourhood unit, the problems of redevelopment areas and the special nature of rural housing, and then focuses on themes identified by the Dudley Committee: housing layout, standards of accommodation, and heating and equipment. Better illustrated and offering more adventurous advice on the appearance of new housing than previous editions, the 1949 manual grouped its photographs of successful post-war housing to illustrate a number of key architectural concerns (Figure 10.7). For rural housing the photographs showed ways of siting new housing in the landscape, the role of colour and texture of materials in combining old and new work on the same street, the importance of planting, the recognition of regional distinctions and local materials, and the sensitive task of incorporating non-traditional housing types into traditional rural and village settings. The examples of urban housing covered a comparable variety of issues: the handling of front gardens, the treatment of the street and of landscape as an element in housing layout. Stylistically, the 1949 manual encouraged diversity, illustrating buildings that ranged from the

i   ii

10.7 *The Housing Manual 1949* went further than previous manuals in illustrating what the Ministry of Health architects considered to be good design: (i) landscaping and low-density layouts; (ii) higher-density, mixed-development layouts

restrained classicism of Louis de Soissons's semi-detached houses at Welwyn Garden City to the radical modernity of Tecton's flats on Rosebery Avenue for the Borough of Finsbury.

Advice in the manual was complemented in a number of ways. The recommendations on density provided in the Dudley Report were supplemented by the publication in 1952 of *The Density of Residential Areas*, which spelt out in systematic terms the limits of density for different housing types and linked the use of the flat to densities over 100 people per acre. Other publications such as *The Appearance of Housing Estates* and *Design in Town and Country* reflected the concern of central government to raise the quality of neighbourhood and housing design, which Macmillan, Minister for Housing, acknowledged to be too often 'dull and

depressing'.[50] The latter publication, published in 1953 with essays by Sharp, Gibberd and Holford, was part of a concerted attempt to raise standards of design for both rural and urban housing.

Taken together, these publications made up a considerable body of information and advice on which local authorities could draw for guidance on planning, layout and the design of housing, from the individual dwelling to the neighbourhood. Coupled with the advice that authorities might expect from the ministry inspectors on any individual project, this was the sum of guidance that central government provided to local authorities during the late 1940s and early 1950s.[51]

With the easing of the shortage of resources and the passing of the need for central monitoring of the use of building materials, the vetting of each local authority scheme for loan sanction changed from close scrutiny to merely confirming conformity with the standards set by the MOHLG. Generally, as production increased, control by the MOHLG became looser on all but the most controversial schemes. Thus from the mid-1950s a certificate from the local authority's architects stating that the project complied with the ministry's requirements was sufficient to secure loan sanction.[52] The relationship between central and local government in all but the most important or most controversial schemes was thus very much more remote than it had been and than it then was in the case of school building. For most authorities this was of little consequence. Many of the smaller authorities faced with the need to build more houses would have fallen back on their pre-war experience, updated only to take account of the new standards and changes in the regulations.

But what of the novel challenges faced by authorities where densities were high and where even the ministry's density calculations showed that a combination of housing and flats, a mixed development, was necessary to meet the target densities? Who could offer advice on the design of housing that fell outside the run of familiar examples? Until 1957 there was no equivalent for housing of the Development Group at the Ministry of Education's A&B Branch to explore new ideas or circulate information on experimental projects.[53] The Post-War Building Studies might deal with some technical issues, for example with new forms of construction, but there was no equivalent of the Building Bulletins published by the Ministry of Education. With so many challenges, and only limited guidance from central government, the form and the quality of the design of housing depended on the approach adopted by each authority. Indeed, a nationwide picture of what was built can only be formulated by reviewing the work of a number of individual authorities.

The housing work of individual authorities

The LCC

The London County Council, the country's largest housing authority, was unlike all others both in the size of its housing programme and in the professional and other resources it could command. It was also exceptional in that it enjoyed a number of advantages as housing authority to the capital. In its dealings with central government it benefited from formal advantages such as a housing programme agreed directly by Parliament and was thus exempted from the need to seek loan sanction approval from the MOHLG. Equally important, given the informal nature of dealings on housing with the MOHLG, it was able to use its location so close to the heart of government to catch the ear of officials and politicians alike. In its dealing with its voters, the LCC enjoyed advantages over other authorities because it was the London boroughs who had first responsibility for housing. Because of its regional role the LCC Housing Committee was shielded from the relentless local pressure to build that was felt so strongly by the boroughs and by other large cities. It was also fortunate in being one of the few authorities for which the overspill arrangements envisaged in the Town Development Act 1952 appeared to work well. In its regional role the LCC at first sent Londoners, many from the East End, to the New Towns and after 1952 to expanding market towns like Huntingdon and Haverhill. As a result the LCC was also partially shielded from the growing shortage of housing land experienced by many other authorities from the early 1950s onwards.

Perhaps it was this very exemption from the immediate and unrelenting pressures for production that enabled the LCC and its architects to play a national role in housing design.[54] With the transfer of responsibility for design back to the Architect's Department in 1950, the LCC established itself nationwide as the leading authority for housing design, backed by a Housing Committee with members like Evelyn Dennington who believed in design – modern design – of high quality. Teams working under Whitfield Lewis in the Housing Division responsible for the designs first at Ackroydon and Alton East, then at Bentham Road and Alton West, were to dominate much of the debate on the form of housing and were, as we have already seen, to play a critical role in developing the form of the tower block and the slab block for use by local authorities. Ideas tested on these sites were pressed into service by other authorities.

These well-documented achievements should not obscure the account of what the LCC was building elsewhere (Figure 10.8). The ideas tested on the pioneering estates like Alton East and Alton West were repeated and adapted elsewhere, on the Fitzhugh Estate at Trinity Road, Wandsworth, the Loughborough Road Estate, Lambeth, and the Picton Street Estate, Camberwell.[55] But other teams in the Housing Division were building in more traditional ways.[56] Through into the 1960s, the LCC was putting up large mixed-development estates built

traditionally in brick with pitched roofs and gentle picturesque site layouts at the Fayland Estate, Wandsworth, and the Forest Estate, Lewisham. These estates represent a modernisation and a softening, but still a continuation, of the housing which the Valuer had been designing in the 1940s.[57] Architects working in the Valuers Department continued during the 1950s with the approach that they had used in the late 1940s on out-county estates like Sheerwater near Woking, or the Debden Estate in Essex.[58]

The LCC was exceptional in the quality of its staff, the diversity of the different approaches it pursued and the resources it could command. It could support its own development group to work on new type plans; it even built prototype dwellings on an occasional, experimental basis. By the mid-1950s the balance between production and design was the reverse of what it had been in the 1940s, when every aspect of housing production was controlled by the Valuer. Freedom given to architects to develop Alton East or West seemed unconstrained by the

i

ii

10.8 Work by different sections in the Housing Division of the LCC Architect's Department: (i) the Lough- borough Road Estate, Lambeth (1954–57); (ii) the Forest Estate, Lewisham (1955–58)

demands of production, except in the most general sense. Type plans and standardisation were set aside in the interest of design freedom: it became a matter of pride to Colin Lucas, leader of the group that designed Alton West, that no design was repeated.[59] The number of dwellings built was not a pressing matter, even cost targets were treated with a certain disdain.[60]

The LCC's approach to housing in the 1950s contrasts starkly with the emphasis on production that dominated the housing programmes of a number of large English cities over the same period. In cities like Birmingham, Liverpool, Manchester and Leeds, housing was never far from the top of the local political agenda. As reconstruction cleared the acute shortages of the immediate post-war years, and housing priorities shifted to slum clearance, councillors still found that they were besieged with requests for help with urgent housing cases.[61] The importance of housing issues locally meant that the council leader or the Housing Committee chairman needed to be a powerful figure capable of facing down trouble and demanding prompt action from officials. Given the continuing pressure for more housing throughout the first post-war decade, it was inevitable that in most cities the principle measure of housing success was the number of dwellings built. John Braddock in Liverpool, Karl Cohen in Leeds and, north of the border, David Gibson in Glasgow, all politically ambitious to build more housing, justified an emphasis on production as serving the best interests of their constituents. Inevitably, the emphasis on production favoured a no-nonsense approach to housing which shocked many of those who believed in the value of design:

> The most prominent councillors were just blustering, coarse heavy men who were extremely ambitious – 60 per cent proof personal ambition, to get knighthoods or hold the Mayor's mace! The key officers were the professional engineers, used to top-down command socialism – gross men marching paternalistically over the landscape.[62]

Birmingham

Birmingham's approach to housing during the first post-war decade is typical of many other large industrial cities and reflects the shifting priorities of production and design.[63] During the war, Birmingham had lost around 5,000 houses as a result of bombing and ended the war with a housing shortage which left at least 51,000 unfit dwellings still in use and around 17,000 families living in rooms or shared houses. The city's wartime plans had envisaged building a target of 5,000 dwellings in the first year after the war and a programme to provide between 15,000 and 20,000 houses for immediate need.[64] This housing was to continue the city's garden suburb policy of the pre-war years, which had been given added prominence in the war-time debates on rebuilding by the Bourneville Trust's study *When We Build Again*.[65] In the suburbs, plans for Tile Cross Estate and West Heath Estate, ready in 1946, were to carry on the best of the garden suburb tradition while avoiding the inflexible symmetries and the monotony of the pre-war estates. For the central areas, Herbert Manzoni, the City Engineer, proposed to continue slum clearance measures planned before the war. Having extraordinarily persuaded the government to allow the city to use the 1944 Town and Country Planning Act to acquire areas of bomb-damaged property and land for slum clearance, Manzoni started to draw up plans for building flats in the Duddleston and Nechells areas along lines approved by the City Council in 1943.[66]

Initially Manzoni and the Public Works Department had envisaged the extensive use of non-traditional housing on suburban estates, but shortages of material and delays in delivery curtailed this plan. Instead the council embarked on a twin policy of traditionally built housing of conventional appearance complemented by several thousand temporary bungalows to meet the growing short-term demand.[67] Despite the priority given to the production of housing, the two principal results of these policies were, first, to slow the rate of building so that the housing lists grew longer and, second, to create estates that again attracted widespread criticism for their monotony. By mid-1948 the housing programme was lagging far behind the city's plans and the achievements of other cities: only 2,000 houses had been built since the war, and waiting lists were growing rapidly.[68] As the local elections approached, 65,000 households were on the city's waiting lists.

In the elections in 1949, the Conservatives took control of the council after a campaign which had been highly critical of Labour's housing record. To increase the rate of house building, the new council transferred responsibility to a new House Building Committee (HBC) under the autocratic chairmanship of Sir Charles Burman, who swept away the city's relationship with local contractors and struck new agreements with national builders, most prominently with Wimpey. Using non-traditional construction, especially no-fines concrete construction, Wimpey, Wates and Laing were to make a real improvement in the rate of building: in 1951 the number of houses built was 3,555, 75 per cent above the previous year, itself already double the level of the late 1940s. Production rose to a peak of 4,817 in 1954. But despite these successes, this form of building could not be sustained. Already by 1950 the city authorities had come to the conclusion that any continuation of low-density estates would consume the city's entire stock of housing land and that finding land for housing would be critical to the future of the housing programme. This led to renewed pressure for a change of policy to building more densely. With the land purchased for clearance in the central areas only slowly becoming cleared for redevelopment, the council decided that the only way to provide housing was to build blocks of flats. As a result the city increased the proportion of dwellings that were six- and eight-storey blocks of flats to 28 per cent of all approvals in 1955. The flats built as a result of this policy include the massive steel-framed and masonry-clad blocks in Duddleston and Nechells and the six- and eight-storey no-fines blocks built by Wimpey.

The HBC's position in the early 1950s marked the high tide of support for production. With the return to power of Labour in 1952 there was renewed concern about the quality of the city's housing. When Herbert Bradbeer, leader of the Labour group, took over the HBC he pressed for the appointment of a City Architect to take over the design and production of housing, a challenge to the wisdom of concentrating responsibility for the city's housing in the hands of the City Engineer. In the following year Birmingham appointed its first City Architect, A.G. Sheppard Fidler, in the hope of improving the quality of design.[69] Although he was not to lead an independent Architect's Department until 1954, Fidler was able to build up a sizeable staff and to start the painful process of persuading the city to take an interest in the design of housing. He continued the policy of advocating flats not just for central sites but for the suburbs as well, though these were to be built to new standards. In place of the old alternatives of cottage estates or six- and eight-storey blocks, Fidler advocated a new policy of mixed development combining flats and cottages planned, according to the *Housing Manual*'s orthodoxy, on neighbourhood lines.

Despite his position, Fidler found it difficult to change Birmingham's attitudes, and he remained shocked by the coarse indifference to architectural issues:

When I went to Birmingham, you could have called it Wimpey Town or Wates Town. The Deputy City Engineer came into my office the very first day I arrived, shoved all these plans on my desk, and said, 'Carry on with these!' He was letting contracts as fast as he could go, didn't know what he was doing, just putting up as many Wimpey Y-shaped blocks as he could! This rather shattered me, because we'd had very careful schemes prepared at Crawley, with very great interest on the part of the Development Corporation, whereas in Birmingham the House Building Committee could hardly care about the design as long as the numbers were kept up … There was very little quality about these 'mud pies', but I either had to let it run and hope to bring in changes – which is what I did – or go to the Council and say 'Stop everything for two years while I change things!' Then I'd have been out, not them![70]

Despite Fidler's distaste for what he called Manzoni's 'mud pies', the no-fines flats then being built by Wimpey, it took time to transform the quality of housing design.[71] Soon, however, Fidler was able to introduce three new policies to improve quality. First, he ensured that the Architect's Department would be responsible for the design of the housing built by the national contractors with whom the city was already working. Second, he demanded the replacement of the six- and eight-storey blocks of flats with mixed development – with the mix of housing determined by the nature of the individual site. Finally, he called for the appointment of a landscape architect to improve the planning and planting of housing sites, an innovation that took a number of Birmingham councillors by surprise. The changes he introduced were slow to take effect, and for some time the appearance of the two-storey housing built by the city remained

conventional, the flats utilitarian. Fidler's designs continued to be constrained by external forces and practices established before he arrived: under Burman and Manzoni the design of multi-storey flats had been negotiated with a number of national contractors in order to bring down costs and construction times in terms that suited the contractor. Still beset by pressure to increase the volume of production and by disagreements with Manzoni and the Department of Public Works over responsibility for housing layout, Fidler had yet to win a free design hand for housing.[72] But at last in 1954, with a separate department and independence from Manzoni, Fidler was able to secure some of the changes he wanted. The improvements in the quality of design are already visible in the proposals for the suburban flats at Rubery and the Hankey Farm Estate, which were selected for exhibition at the Royal Academy and published by the *Review* in 1954 for its annual Preview (Figure 10.9).[73] The overall impression of Fidler's flats may be ponderous: each is six storeys high but built of load-bearing brickwork; and in contrast to the clarity and simplicity of the LCC's elevations, those at Rubery and Hankey Farm use brick both for the main structure and for the thin infill panels and share the same complex pattern of fenestration. Set beside the tower blocks being built by the LCC at Alton

i   ii

10.9 The changing face of housing in Birmingham – blocks of flats built under Manzoni contrasted with the first estate developed by A.G. Sheppard Fidler: (i) no-fines flats built by Wimpey on the Marston Green Estate; (ii) Sheppard Fidler's design for flats at Rubery

East and Alton West around the same time, perhaps Fidler's achievements are best understood in terms of the improvement these flats represented over the quality of the blocks built by Wimpey and Wates, as such they are an important step to modernising the design of the city's housing programme. But even these achievements were short-lived. The new equilibrium between design and production struck by Fidler and Bradbeer in the HBC was not to last for long. The arrival at the end of the 1950s of Harry Watton, as the new leader of the Labour group, saw the end of Bradbeer's influence, a revived commitment to production and, with it, a new indifference to design.

Coventry

Production values were not necessarily at odds with innovation and good design. The housing built under Donald Gibson, City Architect at Coventry, provides a useful counter-example of a city which was less subject than most to the alternation of policies so evident during the first postwar decade in Birmingham and at the LCC.[74] Gibson enjoyed from the start the great advantage of the backing of leading figures in the Labour group that controlled the city. George Hodgkinson, the mayor during the mid-1940s, was remembered by Percy Johnson-Marshall as a convert to town planning, eagerly reading Lewis Mumford's *Culture of Cities*. Henry Watson, chairman of the Housing Committee, was a founder member of the CISPH and an enthusiastic but not uncritical supporter of non-traditional construction. With their backing Gibson had every opportunity to develop a new approach to the design of Coventry's housing. The city's position as an important test case for modernist reconstruction rests on the rebuilding of the city centre, but the extent of Gibson's activities there was not at the expense of work elsewhere in the city. Gibson was keen to experiment, and with his reputation as a forward-looking modernist he was able to attract able and enthusiastic staff to try new ideas in housing and schools.[75]

At the end of the war Coventry confronted the same problems facing other Midlands cities. As a result of the war-time losses the shortage of housing, bad before the war, became more acute. The waiting list, which stood at just over 7,000 in 1945, had more than doubled by 1948, and in the early winter months there were reports of between 500 and 1,000 squatters in properties scattered around the city.[76] The difficulty facing Gibson and the Housing Committee was the shortage of building labour for local authority housing, as men were attracted by higher wages to engineering or to working on war-damage repairs in the private sector.

With permanent housing production down to only 340 dwellings eighteen months after the end of the war, Gibson urged his committee to consider experimenting with new forms of house building, something that he had tried during the war.[77] To absorb the most acute housing need while new permanent housing was being built, Gibson called for a large allocation of temporary bungalows, of which Coventry was allocated 2,117.[78] This at least bought time to set in hand the programme of permanent housing which Gibson was negotiating, and by December he had secured the further promise of an allocation of 20,000 BISF houses. But even retaining the relatively unskilled labour required for their construction proved impossible, and with only 25 per cent of the labour force necessary to undertake the work, Coventry's allocation was directed elsewhere. Eventually the city would build only 506 of the original 20,000 BISF houses. With the annual rate of house building until 1952 running between a low of 380 and maximum of 860, Gibson had to explore other ways of building housing. By 1949 he was beginning to negotiate a contract with Wimpey for no-fines houses and in the autumn of 1950 agreement had been reached. The result, in production terms alone, was a success: by 1952 production of permanent new housing, encouraged by the incentive payments favoured by the new Conservative government, had risen to 1,380, and by 1956 it topped 2,000.[79]

i   ii

10.10 The Tile Hill Estate, Coventry, exemplifies the translation into practice of many of the ideas set out in *The Housing Manual 1949*: (i) a mixed development in no-fines concrete; (ii) a view of the neighbourhood centre showing the eleven-storey flats and the shops with maisonettes above

Gibson and his team were more successful than Manzoni in their use of no-fines construction, and they combined a high volume of building with a sympathetic approach to current housing ideas. The Tile Hill Estate on the western edge of the city centre best represents their achievement (Figure 10.10).[80] It is a suburban mixed-development neighbourhood planned around a centre which houses a number of shops with maisonettes above, including a newsagent and a fish and chip shop, and even a modern church designed by Basil Spence. Three eleven-storey blocks of flats mark its location and provide a focal point for the estate's two- and four-storey housing. This housing is arranged on principle used in Radburn, New Jersey: from one side there is access to the neighbourhood centre by a sequence of pedestrian ways; on the other there are car courts giving onto a distributor road that leads to the neighbourhood centre in one direction and the city centre in the other. At Tile Hill, the arrangement of the linked green spaces of the footpaths, the planting and the existing trees, together with the sense of the centre marked by the eleven-storey towers, avoids the monotony and the trite formal layouts of so many early post-war estates. The form of the individual dwelling is typically colour-washed no-fines concrete, but this is contrasted with occasional blocks built of brick; both are detailed with a sensitivity reminiscent of Gibberd's best work, whether in Hackney or Harlow.

The layout and design of Coventry's post-war neighbourhoods like Tile Hill or Monks Park – awarded a MOHLG Housing Medal in 1950 – represent a successful realisation, with limited resources, of the recommendations of the *Dudley Report* and the *Housing Manual 1949*. Architecturally, they are a modest reflection of the *Architectural Review*'s hopes for an English modernism and have the simple unaffected quality and the quiet conviction of a modern vernacular. Contemporaries recognised these qualities: Rigby Childs generously praises the layout and design of the city's estates in his survey of the reconstruction of blitzed cities in the *Architects' Journal*, singling out Tile Hill as 'second to none in the whole of England'.[81]

Other authorities

Both Birmingham and Coventry had City Architects to design their housing, but what of the housing built by that large majority of authorities that had no in-house architect and relied instead on the services of private practice or architects working for the Borough Engineer? For many local authorities the most straightforward way to obtain designs for housing was to seek the service of private practitioners, a practice favoured by the London boroughs. This too was the arrangement chosen by many of the smaller, rural authorities. Sometimes the results were highly, if unassumingly, successful. Housing built for

i   ii

10.11 'Routine functionalism' in housing: (i) flats on the Charlton Estate (1947–49) designed in the office of C.H. Jennings, Borough Engineer, Greenwich; (ii) flats at Poplar (1949) designed in the office of the Borough Engineer, J. Rankin

Loddon Rural District Council by Tayler and Green grew out of a long-term collaboration between architects and the council. Here the chairman of the Housing Committee, E. Hastings, had the commitment to design and quality, and the perseverance and political skills, to retain Tayler and Green's services.[82] In authorities like these it was just as important as in a large urban authority to have a key advocate or a group who would stand up for design and quality. For rural authorities the need for ever more housing at ever lower costs might be on a smaller scale but was no less acute than in Coventry or Finsbury.

Housing authorities that employed private firms were a minority. Most preferred to maintain the degree of control over costs and design, and the coordination between departments, that came with keeping design in-house. This would be left to the architects – or more commonly the architectural assistants or surveyors – working for the authority's engineer, surveyor or public works department. Housing built in this way might occasionally match the quality of designs by an independent Architect's Department; occasionally, like the flats at Southgate by Walthamstow's Engineer or those designed by Poplar's Engineer's Department, they were illustrated in mainstream architectural journals (Figure 10.11).[83]

For the majority of authorities, however, the task of designing housing was not so much a question of designing flats or something novel; it was largely a question of adapting the designs and layouts of the inter-war years to the changed conditions of the post-war years, to the new standards and layouts suggested by the *Housing Manuals*, and to the new forms of construction that might help keep production levels high at a time of shortages of traditional skills and materials. This was the case in Cambridge. The new cottage estates at Arbury, Ditton Fields or Trumpington laid out and designed by architects working under City Engineer C. Cresswell in the late 1940s and early 1950s differed only in detail from those built two decades before.[84] Planned as neighbourhoods with a token row of shops, a few flats and, perhaps, a pub, they were provided with primary schools and eventually with secondary schools. In contrast to the layout of their pre-war forebears, there was now provision for car-parking. Perhaps layouts are less formal than those of the inter-war years; some have large green spaces, a common around which the houses are grouped. A number of houses are of non-traditional construction, and some of those built during the late 1940s were planned to the generous space standards recommended by the Dudley Committee. But the designs for these new cottage estates are remote from the influence of the ideas circulating in the architectural press. On the evidence of estates like these, the norm of British housing for much of the post-war decade, it would be easy to assume that architectural thinking had changed little since the 1920s.[85]

The public sector and modern architecture

After a decade of building dominated by the public sector, how had the activities of the different housing and education authorities affected the fortunes of modern architecture? School building was generally judged a success with teachers and with the public. Strong and effective leadership given by the architects and administrators at the Ministry of Education was part of the reason; the wealth of architectural skills available to the education authorities played a role too, as did the general political agreement on the need to preserve the essential continuity of the post-war school building programme. The result was an architecture which was distinctive and modern. In the mid-1950s the *Architects' Journal* was praising school building as the best example of an emerging modern vernacular: 'In the development of the modern school architecture ... we can see at work the process whereby architectural style is created.' For Richards, school architecture exemplified the way in which the values of modern architecture were finding widespread acceptance:

> [These schools] are by different architects, and in different parts of the country, yet they have a clear family resemblance ... indicating that, in school building at least, a recognisable but flexible idiom is at last emerging, in which architects can work unselfconsciously and as a matter of course. That is surely the beginning of all good architecture.[86]

But with housing the picture is more complex. The great majority of the 1,500 housing authorities, in villages and towns across the country, built little and what they did build was only slightly different from the cottage housing they had been building before the war, updated to keep abreast of the recommendations of the *Housing Manual* and, perhaps, where traditional skills and materials were short, built using one of the new systems of non-traditional construction. Overall the appearance, the urban landscape of small towns and villages, remained broadly unchanged, though occasionally a New Town like Harlow might build a tower block as a focus to one of the new neighbourhoods.

But in many larger cities there was ready evidence by the mid-1950s of the emergence of a new order, a new urban and suburban landscape, as tower and slab blocks of flats and maisonettes first started to appear. These new forms of housing were forced upon authorities as they struggled to maintain housing programmes despite the shortage of land. Authorities like Birmingham and Liverpool were forced to innovate, and to take up new ideas on the design of flats. Architects in some authorities might start from scratch, others might draw on foreign experience, but most turned to ideas closer to home, to the ideas developed by the designers working for other British authorities like the LCC or the London boroughs, where the value of design was recognised. In place of the old block dwellings of the 1930s large cities now started to build towers and slabs as part of mixed-development schemes, adapting – sometimes crudely – the point blocks of Alton East or the Unité-inspired maisonette blocks of Alton West. By the mid-1950s large authorities up and down the country were building housing, sometimes in the form of isolated blocks or towers, sometimes as whole neighbourhoods with a mix of different types of dwellings, focused on a small centre made up of a few shops, a primary school, perhaps a secondary school that looked radically different from the past. Already local authorities were beginning to build the form of modern urban and suburban landscape that was to become widespread over the next fifteen years.

The fortunes of modern architecture in the hands of the public sector architects of the first post-war decade were mixed. As the volume of local authority building declined, the prospect of building by the private sector grew. By 1955 it was not just private house building that was increasing, the overall volume of building – offices, shops, town centres – was growing too. The long-awaited ending of all controls on building in 1954 heralded the day when private clients and commercial interest could build freely again. Would the patronage of the private sector now do more than the public sector to advance the fortunes of the new architecture?

Notes

2 A systematic survey of the working practices of the profession, *The Architect and his Office*, London, RIBA, 1962, completed in 1960 but drawing on data for the 1950s, provides an overall impression of how architects and architectural assistants worked in both the public and the private sector. Section 2 contains much of the comparison between the size of offices in the two sectors.

2 R. Furneaux Jordan, 'LCC, New Standards in Official Architecture', *AR*, Nov. 1956, pp. 303–24.

3 E. Layton, *Building by Local Authorities*, London, George Allen & Unwin, 1961, ch. 4.

4 A. Sutcliffe and R. Smith, *History of Birmingham. Vol III: Birmingham 1939–1970*, Oxford, Oxford University Press, 1974, pp. 430–3.

5 'Cambridge, New Town Centre Plan', *AJ*, 27.3.1963, p. 650.

6 Layton, *Building by Local Authorities*, ch. 4.

7 The proportion of architects in different grades is taken from the 1960 survey (note 1 above); the estimated number of architects in each category assumes that the position in 1957 was broadly the same as it was in 1960.

8 Layton, *Building by Local Authorities*, ch. 4.

9 *Ibid.*, ch. 5; Layton's discussion of the use of private architects is revealing, implying that they were used principally as a stop-gap to meet the pressure of work on the local authority's own staff. However, this was not always the case. The LCC had long used a panel of private architects, particularly for school work, despite the size of the council's own resources, and fully recognised the value of the stimulus to design provided by outside architects; *ibid.*, p. 175–6.

10 *Ibid.*, p. 184–6.

11 The Ministry of Education pioneered a number of developments that were to be taken up by other ministries, particularly by the Ministry of Housing and Local Government. The example of MOE's Development Group was not followed by MOHLG until 1957, and MOE's elemental analysis of building costs set an example that was gradually taken up by other ministries. MOHLG did not introduce the Housing Cost Yardsticks until nearly 20 years after MOE's analysis.

12 For a fuller discussion of the work of A&B Branch and the Development Group, and the role of Stirrat Johnson-Marshall, see A. Saint, *Towards a Social Architecture: The Role of School Building in Post-War England*, London, Yale University Press, 1987, ch. 5.

13 The Building Bulletins were to influence the design of educational buildings across the country. Eleven titles had been published by 1955.

14 S. Maclure, *Educational Development and School Building: Aspects of Public Policy 1945–73*, Harlow, Longman, 1984, pp. 16–37.

15 Ministry of Education, *Cost Study*, Building Bulletin 4, 1951.

16 St Crispin's, Wokingham, and its structural system were described at length in *AJ*, 8.1.1953, pp. 42–4; 12.3.1953, pp. 342–7; 28.5.1953, pp. 671–8.

17 Ministry of Education, *New Secondary Schools*, Building Bulletin 2, 1955, p. 2.

18 R. Llewelyn Davies and J. Weeks, 'The Hertfordshire Achievement', *AR*, Jun. 1952, pp. 367–72.

19 The Development Group's work at Belper is described in *AJ*, 15.12.1955, pp. 797–814, 823–4, and in *OAP*, Jan. 1956, pp. 40–2.

20 The development of the BAC system at Limbrick Wood, Coventry is described in *JRIBA*, Oct. 1952, pp. 446–9, and *OAP*, Nov. 1952, pp. 524–5.

21 Lyng Hall Comprehensive School was published (with the Finmore Park School also of Coventry) in *AJ*, 28.2.1957, pp. 321–9.

22 The use of the Laingspan system for the Arnold Grammar School is described in *OAP*, Oct. 1959, pp. 449–54.

23 The use of the Intergrid structural system is described in *AJ*, 8.7.1954, pp. 53–6.

24 The Worthing project is described in *AJ*, 4.8.1955, pp. 145–64. A&B Branch's judgement is reported in Saint, *Towards a Social Architecture*, p. 149.

25 Enthusiastic contemporaries include J.M. Richards, who regularly commented on the quality of modern school design in his review 'Buildings of the Year' in the *Architects' Journal*, and John Summerson, in his introduction to the Arts Council's 1956 exhibition 'Ten Years of British Architecture'. For a recent appreciation see Saint, *Towards a Social Architecture*, ch. 9.

26 The general enthusiasm in educational circles for the new schools was exemplified by regular articles in *Education*, a weekly journal widely read by teachers and educationalists: 'School Building in Hertfordshire', 28.12.1955, pp. 867–8; 'Hertfordshire Century of Post-War Schools', 28.1.1955, pp. 185–

6; 'Post-War Progress in Essex', 26.8.1955, pp. 311–20; 'Fifty Post-War Schools in Derbyshire', 27.5.1955, pp. 999–1007.

27 'Triennale – Hardware or Humanity', *AJ*, 4.8.1960, p. 162, and, for an Italian view, '1960 Milano, sezione della Gran Bretagna alla XII Triennale, Italia, Scuola Elementare', *Casabella*, 245, Nov. 1960, p. 31.

28 Saint, *Towards a Social Architecture*, ch. 3, and G.A.N. Lowndes *The Silent Social Revolution*, London, 1969, ch. XVI.

29 For a discussion of attitudes to school building in the inter-war years see F. Clay, *Modern School Buildings*, 3rd edn, London, Batsford, 1929, and M. Seaborne and R. Lowe, *The English School, its Architecture and Organization. Vol II: 1870–1970*, London, Routledge & Kegan Paul, 1977, chs 8 and 9.

30 Ministry of Education, *New Primary Schools*, Building Bulletin 1, 1949, p. 2.

31 'Britain Builds for Education', *OAP*, 16, 1953, pp. 119–50.

32 Tulse Hill Comprehensive School is described in *AJ*, 29.11.1956, p. 765, and *OAP*, Sep. 1955, pp. 477–9. Other LCC comprehensives, less densely developed, include Catford Comprehensive, *AJ*, 25.8.1955, pp. 249–64; Mayfield Comprehensive, *AJ*, 2.8.1956, pp. 163–78; Blackheath Comprehensive, *AJ*, 23.9.1954, pp. 371–7.

33 J.M. Richards, 'Buildings of the Year: 1954' *AJ*, 20.1.1955, p. 89.

34 For a general discussion of the programme of cost reduction see Maclure, *Educational Development*, pp. 67–73, and especially the chart of the reduction in the allowance per place (p. 140) and the associated tables (pp. 86–7).

35 Ways of cutting costs explored by Hertfordshire and tried by A&B Branch also included the design in house and the bulk ordering of special fittings and furniture. With the establishment of the large consortia of local education authorities in the late 1950s, the idea of bulk ordering was greatly extended; Saint, *Towards a Social Architecture*, pp. 80–6, 120, 157–83.

36 R.B. White, *Prefabrication: A History of its Development in Great Britain*, London, HMSO, 1965, pp. 247–9; M. Bowley, *The British Building Industry: Four Studies in Response and Resistance to Change*, Cambridge, Cambridge University Press, 1966, p. 274.

37 *Ibid.*, pp. 276–83.

38 For a survey of non-traditional forms of school construction see White, *Prefabrication*, ch. 4, especially pp. 250–4.

39 G.N. Hill, 'Low Cost Schools in Lancashire', *JRIBA*, May 1955, pp. 286–9.

40 'Post-war Building in Northamptonshire', *OAP*, Apr. 1957, pp. 185–8.

The values of different stategies for cutting school building costs, and the importance of arranging multi-use of the hall for dining and circulation as well as other uses, were discussed in the Ministry of Education, *New Secondary Schools*. The arguments couched in terms of secondary schools were equally applicable to primary schools.

42 Taking the 1949 figure as 100%, the area per place had fallen to 77% in 1950, to 69% in 1951 and down to 62% by 1953. Maclure, *Educational Developments*, p. 140.

43 Layton, *Building by Local Authorities*, ch. 2.

44 By 1949 the immediate post-war difficulties of coordinating and controlling the housing programmes of the different local authorities, which had done so much to frustrate the smooth running of the housing drive, were largely resolved. But the administration of housing remained split across more departments than that of school building.

45 J.B. Cullingworth, *Housing and Local Government*, London, George Allen & Unwin, 1966, p. 61.

46 *Ibid.*, p. 117.

47 Birmingham was able to benefit substantially by demanding that the MOHLG allow it exceptionally to use the expensive site subsidy to build multi-storey blocks on cheap farmland, M. Glendinning and S. Muthesius, *Tower Block: Modern Public Housing in England, Scotland, Wales and Northern Ireland*, London, Yale University Press, 1994, p. 179.

48 Ministry of Housing and Local Government, *The Density of Residential Areas*, London, HMSO, 1952.

49 *Housing Manual 1949* and its Scottish equivalent, *Planning our New Homes*, London, HMSO, 1944, were less dogmatic and provided more inspiration in the form of photographs than earlier manuals.

50 Ministry of Housing and Local Government, *Design in Town and Country*, London, HMSO, 1953, p. iii; see also Central Housing Advisory Committee, *The Appearance of Housing Estates*, London, HMSO, 1949.

51 E. Sharp, *The Ministry of Housing and Local Government*, New Whitehall Series no. 14, London, George Allen & Unwin, 1969, ch. IV.

52 *Ibid.*, pp. 82–3.

53 An MOHLG development group was formed by A.W. Cleeve Barr after he left the LCC, having worked on the Alton East and Picton St estates; A.W. Cleeve Barr, *Public Authority Housing*, London, Batsford, 1958; For a discussion of this development group see P. Dunleavy, *The Politics of Mass Housing in Britain 1945–1975*, Oxford, Clarendon, ch. 4.

54 The LCC published no account of its housing work during the 1950s, though it is covered in a number of publications, e.g. Furneaux-Jordan, 'LCC, New Standards', and *Home Sweet Home: Housing Designed*

by the LCC and the GLC Architects 1888–1975, London, Academy Editions, 1976.

55 Even the LCC's lesser-known estates were generously covered in the professional press. The Picton Street Estate may have attracted interest because of its novel form of construction, but it alone was the subject of over 20 articles. The coverage of LCC estates is indicated in Glendinning and Muthesius, *Tower Block*, Gazetteer II, pp. 373–4.

56 Furneaux-Jordan, 'LCC, New Standards'; also, the personal recollections of the author working in one of the less glamorous housing sections during the summer of 1962.

57 *Home Sweet Home*, p. 56–7.

58 *Ibid.*, pp. 44–5.

59 Glendinning and Muthesius, *Tower Block*, p. 105.

60 See e.g. Andrew Saint's opinion of Colin Lucas's response, as leader of one of the LCC housing sections, to the need to meet production and cost targets: 'Colin Lucas would crumple up memos about money and throw them out of the window, if he didn't like them', Glendinning and Muthesius, *Tower Block*, p. 265.

61 K. Newton, *Second City Politics: Democratic Processes and Decision Making in Birmingham*, Oxford, Clarendon Press, 1976, pp. 194–203.

62 Glendinning and Muthesius, *Tower Block*, p. 166.

63 Newton, *Second City Politics*, pp. 200–2; Sutcliffe and Smith, *History of Birmingham*, pp. 232–4.

64 This brief account of Birmingham's housing relies heavily on Sutcliffe and Smith, *History of Birmingham*, especially chs 4 and 7.

65 Bourneville Village Trust, *When We Build Again*, London, George Allen & Unwin, 1941, pp. 83–90; A.G. Sheppard Fidler, 'Post-War Housing in Birmingham', *Town Planning Review*, Apr. 1955, pp. 25–47.

66 Sutcliffe and Smith, *History of Birmingham*, pp. 224–5; Glendinning and Muthesius, *Tower Block*, p. 25; Sir H.J. Manzoni, 'Redevelopment of Blighted Areas in Birmingham', *OAP*, Mar. 1955, pp. 128–32.

67 Sutcliffe and Smith, *History of Birmingham*, pp. 226–7.

68 Birmingham was building less than half the number of houses per 1,000 of population compared with similar cities, *ibid.*, p. 228.

69 On Sheppard Fidler see Glendinning and Muthesius, *Tower Block*, pp. 166–8; Sutcliffe and Smith, *History of Birmingham*, pp. 429–37; *ABN*, Aug. 1954, p. 303.

70 Glendinning and Muthesius, *Tower Block*, p. 167.

71 Typical of the no-fines blocks were the six-storey blocks at Tile Cross, Marston Green, built by Wimpey in 1951–53; 'Six Storey Flats at Birmingham', *OAP*, May 1953, pp. 245–7.

72 Sutcliffe and Smith, *History of Birmingham*, pp. 430–3.

73 'Architecture at the Royal Academy', *OAP*, Jun. 1953, p. 282; 'Preview', *AR*, Jan. 1954, pp. 62–3.

74 For a discussion of the development of Coventry during this period see: N. Tiratsoo, *Reconstruction, Affluence and Labour Politics: Coventry 1945–60*, London, Routledge, 1990, chs 4, 6 and 8; 'Coventry Rebuilds', *AD*, Dec. 1958, pp. 473–503; D. Rigby Childs and D.A.C.A. Boyne, 'Coventry', *AJ*, 8.10.1953, pp. 428–58.

75 D. Rigby Childs and D.A.C.A. Boyne, 'Coventry Architectural and Planning Department', *AJ*, 8.10.1953, pp. 435–6, and P. Johnson-Marshall, *Rebuilding Cities*, Edinburgh, Edinburgh University Press, 1966, pp. 225–6. Gibson's encouragement of non-traditional building generally and for ARCON in particular is covered in 'Techniques/Manufacturer Cooperation III', *AR*, Jul. 1957, pp. 201–4.

76 Tiratsoo, *Reconstruction, Affluence*, p. 34.

77 CISPH, one of the committees campaigning for the application of volume production methods to housing, was founded in Coventry with Gibson as one of its members, and he encouraged Coventry to investigate different forms of non-traditional housing: 'Coventry I: Wartime', *AJ*, 24.4.1941, pp. 273–6; *ABN*, 1.10.1943, pp. 6–11.

78 Coventry's housing problems in the immediate post-war years are discussed in Tiratsoo, *Reconstruction, Affluence*, ch. 4.

79 D. Rigby Childs, 'Rebuilding Bombed Cities', *AJ*, 8.7.1954, p. 46 (table 10).

80 D. Rigby Childs and D.A.C.A Boyne, 'Tile Hill Housing Estate', *AJ*, 8.10.1953, pp. 444–5.

81 *Ibid.*, p. 443.

82 The point is well made by I. Nairn, 'Rural Housing: Post-War Work by Tayler and Green', *AR*, Oct. 1958, pp. 226–36, and in E. Harwood and A. Powers, *Tayler and Green*, London, Prince of Wales Institute, 1998, pp. 43–70.

83 L. Brett, 'Towards an Architecture: Post-War Flats in Britain', *AR*, Nov. 1949, p. 319; J.M. Richards, 'The Next Step?', *AR*, Mar. 1950, p. 171.

84 The early post-war estates in Cambridge are described in N. Pevsner, *Cambridgeshire*, Harmondsworth, Penguin Books, 1970, pp. 252–3, and N. Taylor and P. Booth, *A Guide to Cambridge New Architecture*, London, Leonard Hill, 1972, pp. 22–4.

85 See e.g. the winners of the Ministry of Housing's annual prize for housing illustrated in *Official Architecture and Planning* in the late 1940s and early 1950s.

86 J.M. Richards, 'Buildings of the Year: 1955', *AJ*, 19.1.1956, p. 107.

11 The revival of private and commercial practice

By the early 1950s the economy was beginning to brighten, and the pace of building to accelerate. Housing and schools were still a priority but other types of buildings could now be built as well. Private enterprise, encouraged by the Conservative government, joined with local authorities to rebuild the shops, the offices, the cinemas, the commercial centres of cities that an increasingly affluent society now demanded. By the mid-1950s a second phase of reconstruction, concentrated on the opportunities for developing war-damaged city centres, was well under way. The terms of the debate began to shift from post-war reconstruction to talk of modernising Britain and keeping up to date with America.[1]

This new phase of reconstruction offered unprecedented opportunities for architects and, potentially, for the development of modern architecture. The rebuilding of city centres and the return to commercial building meant the design and construction of a range of building types that had not been built since the beginning of the war. Work for private practices expanded as developers and commercial clients started to build again. In January 1955 the *Architectural Review* celebrated the new freedom enjoyed by architects:

> Since the war architects have been struggling to advance their art under the handicap of an outlook no broader than that afforded by a prison cell with three walls

labelled schools, housing and factories and the fourth just allowing a glimpse of a few more glamorous enterprises. Architecture is eagerly shaking itself free of the restrictions that have shackled it for so long.[2]

Barely two years earlier, J.M. Richards had bemoaned the irksome limitations on practice and the restricted range of commissions available.[3] But with the deregulation of building these limitations were gone, and with the publication for the first time in January 1954 of what was to become the *Review*'s annual Preview, there was an expression of optimism about architectural possibilities to come.[4]

Much of what was built was of uneven quality. The *Builder*'s yearly selection of the architectural submissions to the Royal Academy show designs that reflect a cautious use of the forms of modern architecture and show that the stripped classicism and the variants of pre-war modernism which had dominated the exhibition during the late 1940s were giving way in the early 1950s to designs that bore the influence of the debate since the war.[5] Champions of the modernist cause viewed this growing interest in modern architecture with mixed feelings, seeing it as a dilution of the modernist canon on the one hand and as a diffusion of modernist ideas – a broadening of the appeal of modern architecture – on the other. In 1950 Richards had characterised popular forms of modern architecture in two ways: first, as 'formalism', a 'premature stylisation of modern architecture, an attempt on the basis of certain elements characteristic of modern technique to anticipate the evolution of a (true) decorative and idiom'; and second, as 'routine functionalism', an approach that had become the 'unquestioned idiom of the ordinary architect, usurping the pattern-book of the Georgian routine of twenty years before'.[6] Five years later, in 1955, Richards welcomed the wealth of experimentation evident in the projects chosen for the *Review*'s special Preview edition.[7] Both this and the Academy exhibition illustrate the extent to which the ideas of the modern movement had spread throughout the profession. Although the projects chosen for the annual Preview and the Royal Academy exhibition represent an elite selection, not the general run of practice, they were also not the work of the avant-garde. They were for the most part designs by the leaders of the profession. It was they who from the mid-1950s were to constitute the mainstream modernists. It was their work that was to establish modern architecture in Britain.

The changing face of private practice

Thumbing through the pages of the architectural press to catch the flavour of contemporary practice, there are evident changes in the circumstances of practice, but many aspects of professional life carried on much as they had in the 1930s (Figure 11.1). Most private firms in the late 1940s and early 1950s resumed work again in the manner they had been using before the war. Meeting the demands of the post-war school building programme or developing a new approach to the design of the flat called for invention, but in commercial practice the pressure for change, at least initially, seemed less, and the acceptance of continuity more willing.

One reason for this initial continuity of pre-war ideas was the survival through to the late 1940s and early 1950s of so many of the pre-war firms and so much of the rank and file of the profession: in 1955 75 per cent of the profession was over 40 years old.[8] The war had brought some change. A small number of architects had been killed in the bombing or on active service.[9] Older leading members of the profession had died, Reggie Blomfield in 1942 and Lutyens in 1944. But other senior figures of the 1930s remained in practice through into the 1950s: Giles Gilbert Scott and Charles Holden, active after the war, lived on until 1960. The composition of the

i

ii

11.1 The post-war work of established practices: (i) T.P. Bennett and Son, flats at Highgate (1946–49); (ii) Lanchester and Lodge, Geology and Mineralogy Building, Oxford (1947–49)

profession that faced the challenges of reconstruction in 1945 was substantially as it had been in 1939, six years earlier.

New recruits were slow to arrive, but by the mid-1950s the profession was changing. Those whose training had been interrupted by the start of the war were able to qualify before 1945 – some, for example, took the RIBA examinations in prisoner of war camps.[10] Although student numbers increased immediately after the war, it was not until the very end of the 1940s that students who had started or resumed their studies after the war entered practice in any number. By the early 1950s around 900 new associate members of the RIBA were being elected every year.[11] It would be several years before these new recruits would have much impact, but by 1953 around 33 per cent of the profession had been registered for only seven years or less. Here was a demographic basis for the shift in architectural attitudes and the growing sympathy for the new architecture.

For architects already qualified there was no lack of work.[12] The local authorities grappled with a shortage of architects and staff as they prepared plans for housing and schools. War-damage repairs were a steady source of employment for many private firms into the 1950s. Much of this work was dreary, made so by the bureaucratic complications of dealing with the forms and procedures of the War Damage Commission.[13] However, high-profile practitioners like Giles Gilbert Scott, Albert Richardson, or Edward Maufe, welcomed the chance to repair and restore buildings of historical interest as an alternative to more utilitarian forms of reconstruction. Scott, for example, was engaged in rebuilding the House of Commons; Maufe was employed around the Inns of Court, rebuilding at Gray's Inn and Middle Temple; Richardson restored Wren's St James's, Piccadilly, and Hawksmoor's St Alphege's, Greenwich.

Before the 1950s commissions for new private and commercial work were few and far between. Firms were frequently compelled to look for work in fields in which they had little previous experience. Many found work with local authorities. Firms that had barely touched local authority housing work were now glad to get what they could: Farquarson and Macmorran were building working-class flats in Poplar and Hampstead; Joseph Emberton was building housing for Finsbury; even Albert Richardson was designing council flats at Blackheath.

Some new commissions were available in the late 1940s. Industry continued to build new factory buildings, power stations and other forms of plant essential to the reconstruction of the economy. Universities, too, frantic to accommodate the post-war surge in student numbers, were granted building permits on the grounds of national priority. Oxford and Cambridge sought established practitioners like Maufe, Richardson, Scott or Lanchester and Lodge. Other universities were more adventurous and hired modernists like Easton and Robertson.[14]

Another source of work was building abroad, particularly in areas of the British Empire like Africa and the Caribbean which were short of architectural skills. This course of action was urged on a number of occasions by the president and other senior figures of the RIBA, and work abroad attracted both well established and younger, more progressive architects.[15] Louis de Soissons worked in Southern Rhodesia and South Africa; Adams, Holden and Pearson worked in Malta; Oliver Hill in Rhodesia; Lanchester and Lodge designed a palace for the Maharajah of Jodhpur. Young modernists also found opportunities to build in India and Africa: Maxwell Fry and Jane Drew collaborated on Chandigarh with Le Corbusier and worked in Ibadan, Nigeria.[16]

One example of an established modernist practice whose work carried through from the pre- to the post-war years was Easton and Robertson (Figure 11.2). Howard Robertson, trained in 1908–12 at the Paris Ecole des Beaux Arts, and John Murray Easton, articled in Aberdeen, founded their partnership in 1919, having first met while working in Le Touquet before World War I.[17] Both were Royal Gold Medallists. Robertson received the Royal Gold Medal in 1949, principally for pre-war work that

i

ii

iii

11.2 The work of Easton and Robertson, the face of established modernist practice in the late 1930s and '40s: (i) Royal Horticultural Hall, Westminster (1927–29); (ii) British Pavilion, New York World's Fair (1939); (iii) Loughton Underground Station, Loughton, Essex (1940–42)

included national exhibition buildings at the 1925 Paris Exposition des Arts Décoratifs, in Johannesburg in 1936, the Paris Exhibition in 1937, and the New York World's Fair in 1939. He designed hotels, offices, cinemas and shops in a style that reflected the modern architecture of inter-war Sweden and Holland, though he was just as likely to design houses in a more classical manner. Easton, winner of the Royal Gold Medal in 1955, was credited with the practice's most recognisably modern buildings: the Royal Horticultural Society's Hall, Westminster; Sadler's Wells Theatre; the London Underground station at Loughton; and a residential block for Gonville and Caius College, Cambridge. In the post-war years the practice built a

number of school and university buildings: Easton continued to work at Cambridge and started to design hospitals for the new National Health Service. Robertson was responsible for the Faculty of Letters at Reading, the Library at Newcastle, the Secondary Technical School and the Technical College at Hatfield for Hertfordshire County Council, as well as commercial buildings, including a new printing works at Debden for the Bank of England. Their work exemplifies the 'routine functionalism' and modern 'formalism' of mainstream practice.

Robertson's modernist reputation was strengthened by his achievements as teacher and writer. He was a regular contributor to the *Builder* (Easton was architectural editor of *The*

Architect and Building News) and author of *Modern Architectural Design* (1932) and *Architecture Arising* (1944). He began teaching at the Architectural Association in 1919 and became principal in 1920. Working closely with Frank Yerbury, Secretary of the AA at the time, Robertson encouraged enthusiasm for the new architectural ideas sweeping across Europe during the 1920s and 1930s, and was familiar with the latest US architecture. Born in Salt Lake City to an American mother and British father, Robertson kept up with the American students, Raymond Hood, Clarence Stein and Albert Kahn, whom he had met during his time at the Beaux Arts. Travelling with Yerbury, Robertson also became acquainted with leading Scandinavian architects such as Østberg and Tengbom as well as young European modernists like Dudok, Lurçat and Le Corbusier.

The Cambridge University Engineering Building is representative of the practice's post-war university work. Perhaps to the critical sensibilities of the 1950s the gentle curve of its main facade and the use of brick might represent a New Humanist softening of pre-war modernism (Figure 11.3).[18] But mainstream modern architecture was already beginning to differentiate cladding, brickwork and frame, and the Engineering Building's predominantly brick elevations are at odds with the elegant steel frame designed by the Head of Department using plastic theory. The detailing is confusedly eclectic, with references both to stripped classicism of the 1930s and to the contemporary Festival of Britain. Though Richards approved of the building, in comparison with other recent buildings in Cambridge and Oxford, it remains in essence a design of the 1930s, untroubled by the terms of the current debate.[19] Robertson would not have wished his buildings to be judged by the values of the architectural avant-garde, which he had long distrusted as extreme and partisan. He would have been more comfortable with contemporary judgement of his work as representing an unassuming, non-dogmatic modernism rightly rewarded with the Royal Gold Medal. These were the terms in which he was elected to

11.3 Easton and Robertson's Department of Engineering, Cambridge University (1950–52)

the presidency of the RIBA for 1952–53. To most members of the profession Robertson was the successful face of established British modernism.[20]

Younger firms began to appear from the mid-1950s, brought into being by the opportunities in the private sector, exemplified by the huge expansion of university building, which in turn encouraged architectural innovation on an unparalleled scale.[21] Not necessarily part of the avant-garde, although often sympathetic to it, these younger firms may not have played much of a role in the debate on modern architecture, but their buildings reflected the new ideas and the core issues that were being discussed. Reyner

i   ii

11.4 Examples of the work of 'mainstream' modernist practices: (i) secondary school at Herne Bay, Kent (1953–55) by Lyons, Israel and Ellis; (ii) rubber factory at Brynmawr, Architects' Co-Partnership (1947–51)

Banham characterised them collectively as 'routine' or 'mainstream' modernism (Figure 11.4).[22] Typical were those whose work appeared in the *Review*'s Previews or was selected for the Arts Council's first exhibition of architecture, '45–55: Ten Years of British Architecture'.[23] Many practices, like Yorke, Rosenberg and Mardall, Richard Sheppard and Partners, or Lyons, Israel and Ellis, began by working for the public sector and found opportunities in the early 1950s to diversify and work for a wider range of clients. Young partnerships like Powell and Moya and Chamberlin, Powell and Bon were able to build on competition success in housing and then branch out into the design of schools and university buildings. The civic universities, expanding as fast as Oxford and Cambridge, provided opportunities for new practice. Gollins, Melvin and Ward, winners in 1952 of the competition for the expansion of Sheffield University, set up a thriving partnership on the strength of this success. The following year they designed the Colleges of Technology and Commerce in Sheffield and, after the design of an office building in Manchester, went on to build office buildings in London and elsewhere.[24] With industrial buildings, too, young firms were soon to establish a national reputation. Prominent among them was the Architects' Co-Partnership, a practice formed by eleven graduates of the Architectural Association in 1939. In 1946

they won national recognition and a stream of new commissions with the success and the structural daring of their design, in conjunction with Ove Arup, for a rubber factory in Brynmawr in South Wales.[25]

By the mid-1950s a new, emergent modern architecture establishment was regularly published in the press – notably in the *Review*'s Preview – and was well represented in the RIBA (Figure 11.5). Frederick Gibberd, who rose to post-war prominence as a housing architect with his work in Hackney and Poplar and as the planner of Harlow, began in the early 1950s to work for private clients.[26] In 1953 he exhibited designs for the control tower and the passenger terminal – the first of a number of buildings – at London's Heathrow Airport. In 1954 Gibberd designed buildings for a steelworks in Scunthorpe. The same year saw him working on the civic centre for Doncaster, a number of office and educational buildings in London and elsewhere in England, and the replanning of the area around St Pancras in London. The rise of Gibberd's practice was not unique. Basil Spence, barely known before his success in the Coventry Cathedral competition – and then principally for his exhibition pavilion on the South Bank and two local authority housing schemes in Dunbar and Sunbury – had by the mid-1950s launched a practice in both London and Edinburgh. In addition to three more churches built in

i   ii

11.5 Work of the new modernist establishment: (i) the control building at London Airport by Frederick Gibberd and Partners (1951–55); (ii) housing at Sunbury-on-Thames by Basil Spence and Partners (1950–52)

Coventry, Spence won a reputation as a designer of schools in London, Sheffield and Kilsyth and university buildings in Durham, Edinburgh, Liverpool and Southampton.[27]

The revival of private practice and the formation of new firms still left untouched some basic characteristics of the profession. One of the most enduring distinctions was between design-led practices and commercial firms. As the economy grew stronger and property developers scrambled for a share of the action, commercial firms also experienced a revival of activity. Those that had survived during the lean years of the 1940s on war-damage repairs and whatever else they could glean now found eager takers for their ability to pack a site with the maximum permissible floor space and their willingness to overlook architectural niceties.[28] These firms were as different from the design-led but successful partnerships like Easton and Robertson, and as committed to the raw values of production, as their opposite numbers in the public sector. As redevelopment got under way in London and provincial centres like Bristol and Birmingham, maximising the client's financial return, minimising construction times and negotiating the way through planning regulations were the skills sought by commercial clients. Old-established partnerships like T.P. Bennett and Son; Lewis Solomon, Kaye and Partners; Trehearne and Norman Preston and Partners; and Howard Souster and Fairburn could deliver these

requirements.[29] As the office boom of the late 1950s accelerated, the ability of young firms like Richard Seifert or Fitzroy Robinson to match or better these skills lead to the rise of a new generation of commercial firms.[30]

Another characteristic of the profession that survived the war was the distinction between those firms with a national reputation, generally and increasingly based in London, and the tradition of local practice. Local practice served the general needs of the cathedral and university cities, county towns and regional centres like Birmingham, Bristol, Liverpool and Newcastle. A few firms based outside London, for example Cruikshank and Seward of Manchester, or Percy Thomas and Partners of Cardiff, might achieve national recognition. But as the articles in the architectural press on the cities which hosted the RIBA conference reveal, the strength of regionally based firms was their rootedness in the local professional and commercial community.[31] For the reconstruction of provincial city centres it was the weight of community values and opinions, the pull of local patronage and politics, that counterbalanced national policies and priorities and the predominantly national and metropolitan debate on architecture conducted in the architectural press.

The 1950s saw real changes in the profession. By the end of the decade a number of enlightened commercial clients, and thus a number of commercial firms, were acknowledging the value of good modern design, spurred by impressive new buildings in Manhattan like Lever House or the Seagram Building. Perhaps, too, the sense of provincial isolation was breaking down as the number of those trained in practice and admitted as licentiates of the RIBA declined, and as young school-trained architects entered local practice, keeping up their magazine subscriptions to stay in touch with architectural developments elsewhere. But any review of the spread of work in private practice during the early 1950s must balance the work of nationally known private firms, increasingly the stars of the profession and dominating the national debate, with the workaday world of commercial architecture and the tenor of general practice in provincial cities.

Commercial architecture in the City of London

The City of London stands as the first example of commercial reconstruction in a major central area. It was here that rebuilding first began, not in Coventry, Bristol or Birmingham, the three cities selected as 'test case cities' by the Ministry of Town and Country Planning on the grounds of the severity of the damage they had suffered.[32] The need to safeguard the position of the City as the centre of international finance, the government's own need for offices, as well as the comprehensive scale of the damage suffered during the Blitz, all ensured that development in the City was given first priority.[33] The task differed from that of rebuilding the centre of any other city – the range of buildings was limited almost exclusively to office buildings – but the extent of the task and the interplay between town planning decisions and architectural design in shaping the whole anticipated developments elsewhere.

The City's plans for rebuilding had not started well. In 1944, F.J. Forty, the City Engineer, published a plan widely dismissed as 'unimaginative and reactionary'.[34] In July 1945, the report, attacked in the press and opposed by the Royal Fine Arts Committee, was rejected by the Minister of Town and Country Planning, W.S.

Morrison, who directed the City to appoint planning consultants to draw up a new plan. As a result Charles Holden and William Holford were selected. Their complementary skills were well suited to the City's needs. Holden's long record of pre-war practice and City connections appealed to the caution of the City, faced with rebuilding and restructuring under a Labour government, while Holford, fresh from the new Ministry of Town and Country Planning, brought an intimate understanding of the latest planning techniques the ministry had been devising for just such an undertaking.[35]

Within six months of their appointment Holden and Holford submitted an interim report which by July 1946 had won the broad support of the City's Court of Common Council.[36] The tenor of the report was hardly radical, focusing on the City as a financial and commercial centre and largely ignoring the links with the rest of London. In the face of Abercrombie's plea in the County of London Plan for decentralisation of employment away from the centre of London, Holden and Holford proposed to maintain the pre-war concentration of activity within the City: the area of office floorspace was to be held at the 1939 level, and even the daytime working population was to be kept at only 6 per cent below the pre-war peak of 500,000. But there was progress: in order to improve conditions within the City, particularly daylighting, the provision of open space and the circulation of traffic, while maintaining the pre-war level of floor space, Holden and Holford proposed, for new buildings, a reduction in site coverage linked to a corresponding increase in height. They also argued for a greater range of commercial uses, for markets, shops and accommodation for the book trade and printing, to complement the predominance of office space. Their report also drew attention to the importance for the City as a whole of the design and the setting of the City churches, most important of all St Paul's. The cathedral was not only to be given an enlarged precinct from which traffic was to be excluded, but also to be opened up to views from the river and vistas across the City through control of the height and massing of new buildings. Equally welcome was Holden and Holford's attitude to motor traffic. Their schemes, which took account of the County of London Plan's proposals for traffic, were markedly less ambitious than those of Forty. They envisaged only a strengthening of east–west routes to the north and the south sides of the City and a limited section of new road to ease the flow of north–south traffic.

Despite concern about the proposed road alterations the City's Improvements and Town Planning Committee expressed a general sympathy for the report, and by July 1947 Holden and Holford submitted their final report.[37] In its final version the plan was broadly similar to that set out in the interim report, although there were fewer new roads or road improvements. Apart from the redesign of the precinct around St Paul's, the principle difference in the second report was the willingness to spell out the way in which the bulk of new building was to be controlled. In contrast to the pre-war blanket limitation on the height of buildings, massing was now to be regulated both by enforcing minimum daylighting standards, through the use of the new daylight protractors developed by the BRS during the war, and to be regulated by limiting the density of development through the use of a predetermined 'plot ratio', the ratio of floor space of a building to its site area and by enforcing minimum daylight standards.[38] Such a system of controls had been developed between 1944 and 1947 by Holford, Stephenson, Kennedy and the research team in the Technical Section of the Ministry of Town and Country Planning. Drawing on Allen and Crompton's work on the use of daylight protractors at the Building Research Station, the team had established controls of density that would give freedom for designers to depart from the conventional type of pre-war building along the corridor street with light-wells behind, without compromising standards of daylighting.[39] The form of development envisaged by the Technical Section of the Ministry of Town and Country Planning and described in *The Handbook for the*

Redevelopment of Central Areas of 1947 was directly applicable to the City of London Plan.[40]

With the plot ratio for the city as a whole set at 5:1 and with a higher ratio still of 5:5:1 for the area around Bank, the response from the City was again favourable. Faced with the loss of its traditional independent planning powers as a result of the 1947 Town and Country Planning Act, and thus required to submit the Holden and Holford plans to the LCC for approval, the City set aside its reservations on the proposed limitations on the bulk of buildings and wholeheartedly adopted the proposals as its own. When the plan was presented at a public inquiry in February 1948 there was outright hostility from property owners who foresaw the curtailment of their redevelopment profits by the new massing restrictions: there were over 330 objections to the plan. But the results of the public inquiry were a triumph for Holden and Holford and the City of London. Under cross-examination Holford proved most effective in defending the plan, and the pressure to start rebuilding caused a number of objectors to withdraw. In 1951, Morrison, Minister of Town and Country Planning, approved the declaratory order for all but 40 acres of the area proposed in the plan. Property owners, too, accepted the provisions of the plan in the interest of rapid rebuilding, and by the time the declaratory order was made, planning permission for over 4.5 million square feet of new development had already been granted.

Conceived in the spirit of the new planning techniques, Holden and Holford's proposals for the City of London Plan were of considerable sophistication. The new system of controls made it possible, if the developer so desired, to build with greater freedom than before, allowing a shift from the old pre-war street-frontage office buildings to office blocks conceived as slabs surrounded by open space or even as free-standing towers in the manner of the centre of Le Corbusier's *Ville Radieuse*. For the architect the challenge was to find a vocabulary that would suit these new forms. With the dissolving of the corridor street, facades based on classical conventions were more difficult to handle. Holden's pre-war buildings, such as the London Transport headquarters and the London University Senate House, showed how stripped classicism might be used for the new slab blocks. But as blocks became taller designers were more willing to abandon heavy masonry facades for the explicit acknowledgement of the structural frame that was now common to new office buildings.[41]

At first, redevelopment in the City was slow, held back by government's unwillingness to award building licences. But from 1949 developers were able to start building under the provisions of the government's London-wide 'lessor scheme' (Figure 11.6).[42] This scheme was established because the shortage of office space and demand for accommodation by government departments prompted the granting of licences for buildings which would be leased to the departments at a fixed rate of interest, typically 8 per cent. This had the advantage for government of reducing public expenditure and of guaranteeing for the developer a certain, if modest, return. However, overseen by the Ministry of Works, which was committed to saving public expenditure rather than securing good architecture, the lessor scheme had the predictable result of encouraging developers to build as cheaply as possible.

The first lessor scheme blocks completed in 1949, two undistinguished stripped-classicism buildings on Theobald's Road, Belfort House and Lacon House by Major A.S. Ash, were roundly criticised in the press for their dreariness.[43] The first lessor block in the City, Atlantic House, designed by T.P. Bennett and Son and finished in 1951, was also attacked for its architectural blandness.[44] Conceived as a massive symmetrical composition facing onto Holborn Viaduct, of which only the first phase was built, Atlantic House was built as a steel frame clad in red brick. Stylistically it was rooted in the 1930s, caught between pre-war commercial modernism and stripped classicism. The balance of window to masonry might well suggest a load-bearing brick structure, but for the long horizontals of the windows with thin masonry mullions overlooking Holborn Viaduct. In contrast to the ponderous formality of the main facade, the court elevations looked utilitarian and grim, barely relieved by small low-relief panels of sculpted stone.

The design of the other early lessor block, the building on New Change facing the east end of St Paul's, was even more regressive. A progressive scheme for the site designed by Sir John Burnet, Tait and Partners, of free-standing blocks at right angles to the street – in place of the old convention of City office building along

i

ii

11.6 Early examples of the 'lessor scheme' blocks built in the City of London: (i) Atlantic House by T.P. Bennett and Son (1946–49); (ii) New Change House by Victor Heal and Smith (1952–58)

the street line with an internal courtyard – had been offered first.[45] But the design was rejected by the City authorities for failing to show due deference to St Paul's. In its place Victor Heal, Baker's successor as architect to the Bank of England, conceived a block which reverted to the old conventions and slavishly followed Holden's guidelines on cornice, string course and the detailing of buildings around St Paul's.[46] The result was a huge mass camouflaged with Neo-Georgian elevations, lifelessly – if correctly – detailed, but quite unequal to the task of giving architectural coherence to a building of such size.

The shortcomings of the lessor scheme system, the regulation of elevations and massing within the immediate context of St Paul's and the innate conservatism of many City institutions may go some way to explain the lack of architectural distinction of these buildings. However, the quality of specially commissioned buildings elsewhere in the City was not necessarily higher. Terrence Heysham's massive symmetrical design for Lloyd's, exhibited at the Royal Academy in 1952, is a reminder of the reactionary stylistic preferences of many City clients for a representative building.[47]

By the start of the 1950s the architecture of the City was criticised in the architectural press as undistinguished, as so many opportunities for reconstruction thrown away.[48] J.M. Richards' denunciation of contemporary City of London architecture could be dismissed as the pronouncements of a disaffected elitist. But the enthusiastic responses by radio critics and the general press to his attacks suggest that Richards' views were widely shared.[49] Even government was critical. Sir David Eccles, Minister of Works, was quite prepared to use a speech at the Mansion House to upbraid the City, traditionally favoured by Conservative governments, for the poor quality of its architecture: 'I fear that unless swift and effective action is taken, we shall see fat and familiar, mediocre and characterless neo-Georgian architecture rising from Hitler's ruins to betray the confident spirit of the new reign.'[50]

Why was the architecture so uninspired? The Corporation of the City of London might have had a reputation for being old-fashioned, even anachronistic, but it had done as much as it could to secure the best results for reconstruction. After the debacle of Forty's plan, the City had taken steps to secure Holford, whose experience with the Ministry of Town and Country Planning made him one of the best-qualified planners to be had at the time. Moreover, where the City had direct powers of patronage it had not stooped to cronyism or the old-boy network. It had used a competition to select an architect for the design of the Golden Lane housing estate in preference to employing an established commercial firm. Further, it had stayed with Chamberlin, Powell and Bon, the unknown partnership that had won. When faced again with the need to choose an architect for the rebuilding of London Wall, the City had retained the same practice. Where it could, the City Corporation backed progressive architecture. It was not itself responsible for the dismal architectural standard of so much new building in the City.

Above all, it was the developers and the companies responsible for commissioning the new buildings who determined the architecture of the City (Figure 11.7).[51] Initially at least, their preferences were generally for some form of simplified classicism, whether because it was the conventional style known to be acceptable to

11.7 The City's traditional architectural preferences in the 1950s: Bracken House for the *Financial Times* by Albert Richardson (1955–59)

City clients and their tenants or, as fragmentary evidence suggests, because of personal preference.[52] For the developer seeking to wring the maximum return from a lessor block or a speculatively financed office building, the job of the architect was to build as cheaply and as quickly as possible. Some larger developers employed their own in-house architects. Typical of these was W.H. Rogers, architect to the City of London Real Property Company and designer of a succession of bland Neo-Georgian blocks.[53] More commonly, developers turned to the commercial firms that had specialised in this kind of work before the war: Trehearne and Norman Preston and Partners, T.P. Bennett and Son, Howard, Souster and Fairburn, Solomon and Partners, Joseph and Partners, or Wills and Hamp.

Not all office buildings were built by developers as a speculative venture. Companies like the Financial Times, Lloyd's or Lever Brothers were building on their own account. Here the main consideration was to secure a design that would represent the company rather than turn a profit, though before the late 1950s no City client had chosen a design like Lever House or the Seagram Building in New York that consciously used architecture to convey an image of innovation and modernism. Generally, the choice of architect, at least in the early 1950s, might be no more progressive than the choices made by speculative developers, but the quality of both design and construction was generally higher. As submissions to the Royal Academy suggest, companies favoured classical designs that conveyed stability, responsibility, security. Occasionally, however, the language of classicism could be used inventively and forcefully. Bracken House by Richardson was regarded by modernists and classicists alike as a 'serious and sincere building, a real attempt to adapt and extend eighteenth century language to modern conditions'.[54] In contrast to the dull austerity of his earlier Chancery Lane Safe Deposit building, Bracken House shows how a simplified classicism could be adapted to the Financial Times's distinctive brief, with the printing house placed between the two blocks of offices. The quality of the building is to be found, too, in the sense of presence created by Richardson's detailing and the handling of materials. The dark brick and the sombre bronze of the windows work well with the robust composition of the facades – the base (expressive of the continuity with the printing house), the giant order, the strong cornice and the crowning attic. No other stripped-classical office building in the City could match its vigour.[55]

By New Year 1952, even the *Architects' Journal* – which had led the attack on the lessor blocks – was ready to concede that a number of new developments were less regressive than those built so far.[56] The first major development in a recognisably modern idiom was Bucklersbury House, whose design by Owen Campbell-Jones was approved by the planning authorities in 1953, an event trumpeted by the *Architects' Journal* as the first breach in the City's instinctive preference for classicism and Portland stone (Figure 11.8).[57] Commissioned by Aynsley Bridgland, a self-made man with a clear preference for classical buildings and sharp dislike of modern architecture, Campbell-Jones's initial scheme was an exercise in monumental classicism conceived to please his client. This was rejected by the LCC planners, who wanted a building on the site that did not simply hug the street line and thus condemn most of the occupants to look into internal courts and light-wells. After four years of difficult four-cornered negotiations between the LCC, Royal Fine Arts Commission, developer and architect, Bridgland was finally persuaded to accept the modern building that won the approval of the LCC's planners.

The end product is a bland and bulky building with no clear relationship to the surrounding streets or adequate indication of the points of entry. Iain Nairn described it as a building with neither vices nor virtues: 'This mass of building has a lot of storeys, a lot of windows, freedom from pointlessly applied period detail, freedom from obvious gracelessness, freedom from aesthetic megalomania. It is the null point of architecture.'[58] But it is easy to forget how radical the building seemed in the City in 1953. The straightforward use of reinforced concrete frame and the glazed wall, frankly treated as infill with metal windows and stone panels, was untried in the early 1950s and anticipated the rapid proliferation of curtain walling and glazed-walled office buildings from 1955 onwards. The sense of excitement at seeing modern architecture in the City was real. A symbolic victory had been won, a victory over the architectural dressing-up of City building, a more honest architectural statement than cladding a frame with brick or Portland stone, only to deny the frame behind.

Bucklersbury House did not mark the end of the City's predilection for classicism, stripped or otherwise. In the vicinity of the Guildhall and St Paul's a deferential and cautious classicism remained the norm. Thus Sir John Burnet, Tait and Partners, who were simultaneously submitting a modern scheme for the competition for offices on the Gaiety site, Aldwych, were

designing a block on Gresham Street in which the frame was clad with stone and the windows were placed to read like openings in a masonry structure, the whole capped with a cornice, a dutiful echo of classicism. Blocks of this kind, designed with only the most anodyne and dilute references to classicism, continued to be built long after the mid-1950s.

By the mid-1950s, however, as the boom in speculative office building accelerated, the attraction of stripped classicism was closely challenged by the growing popularity of a simplified, if crude, modernism in the manner of Bucklersbury House. This reversal in the fortunes of architectural style marks the recognition by developers firstly that the financial institutions for whom the new office blocks were being built were prepared to rent or lease modern buildings, and secondly that modern buildings could be built both more

11.8 The 'breakthrough' to a modern architecture in the City: Bucklersbury House by Campbell-Jones and Sons (1953–58)

i

ii

11.9 Commercial modernism in the City: (i) Fountain House, by W.H. Rogers with Howard Robertson as consulting architect (1954–58); (ii) Saracen's Head Yard; (iii) two blocks designed by Howard Souster and Fairbairn for the City of London Property Co, 1955, at Minories

iii

cheaply and more quickly, thus more profitably, than blocks styled in the classical manner. This change is evident, for example, in the design of buildings commissioned by the well-established City developer the City of London Real Property Company Ltd. In 1955 the company was able to secure an increase in the size of a site it was developing on Fenchurch Street and took this opportunity to abandon a conventional classical scheme for a modern design, Fountain House, using the same in-house architect, W.H. Rogers, but now with Howard Robertson as design consultant – a change of heart, explained Edmund Howard, the managing director, to take advantage of the extra floor area offered by the City's planning controls on the larger site (Figure 11.9).[59] Fountain House became not only the first City office building to try the tower and podium format already established in New York City, but also one of the first blocks with an all-glass curtain wall. Yet set beside the sheer elegance of Gordon Bunshaft's Lever House of 1952, Fountain House appears clumsy: the clarity of contrast between tower and podium is compromised by the four-storey block that encloses the rear of the site, and the podium hugs

i   ii

11.10 'Mainstream' modernist office buildings of the mid-1950s in London: (i) offices for the National Dock Labour Board by Frederick Gibberd and Partners (1952–56); (ii) Electrin House, New Cavendish Street, by Gollins Melvin Ward (1953–56)

the line of the street, creating, at street level, the traditional sense of narrowness and constraint of City lanes. Nor does the curtain wall, clamped between the vertical elements of the frame, match its US predecessor. But Fountain House was a measure of things to come. It illustrates the impact of the LCC's new building controls and technical innovations like curtain walling, both of which would do much to shape the form of office building over the next decade.

A measure of the exploitation of this vocabulary by commercial firms and its more considered use by more committed modernists is revealed by comparing Bucklersbury House or Fountain House with two buildings outside the City, Frederick Gibberd and Partners' National Dock Labour Board offices on the Albert Embankment and Gollins, Melvin and Ward's Electrin House in New Cavendish Street (Figure 11.10).[60] Both blocks suggest a debt to developments in the

United States and how much British designers still had to learn from leading US practices like Skidmore Ownings and Merrill: in both, the ground floor is compromised and overly complicated, both lack the steady refinement and rigour of the best contemporary US architecture. But overall both blocks display a directness and clarity in the handling of the composition of the block as a whole, in the relationship between the structural logic and architectural form and in the finesse of the detailing, that their commercial contemporaries had yet to achieve.

Commercial practice was itself increasingly keen to exploit these ideas. By the end of 1955, a number of the large commercial firms were happy to display their new-found modernist credentials. Howard, Souster and Fairbairn exhibited two blocks at the Royal Academy designed for the City of London Real Property Company which typify this new direction (Figure 11.9).

One, 28–35 Minories, used a curtain wall – without any interruption of the curtain by structure as at Fountain House – to clad a reinforced-concrete frame. The other, at Saracen's Head Yard, uses a structural frame, fully revealed at ground level, that is clad on the upper floors in brick in which are set large areas of glazing framed in a concrete surround.[61] While the latter, neither wholeheartedly resolved as a frame nor a masonry building, courted confusion, both were part of a growing number of office blocks that gave the impression of the modernising of the City – and, now that licensing was over, of the West End as well.[62] The office block for the Atomic Energy Authority on Lower Regent Street by Trehearne and Norman, Preston and Partners, the office buildings by T.P. Bennett and Son on the Albert Embankment, in Jermyn Street and on the corner of Southampton Row, and Monsanto House on Victoria Street by Sir John Burnet, Tait and Partners were no advance on Bucklersbury House or Fountain House, but serve as further evidence of the general swing by developers to 'routine' modernism and the adoption by the large commercial firms of the basic elements of the architectural vocabulary of modernism.

The reconstruction of provincial city centres

Rebuilding the City of London as a succession of office blocks was simple compared with the larger, more complex task of rebuilding a city centre; even in the City the reconstruction of the architecturally sensitive area of non-office building around St Paul's had not yet begun ten years after the end of the war.[63] What had been achieved in the City by the mid-1950s was atypical, favoured in its timetable and in its resources. Set close to the heart of the profession, the City could afford, if it chose to employ it, the best professional advice. It is not surprising that some of the first examples of the new routine modernism should appear here early on. But what of the experience of rebuilding away from this privileged location? What happened to the dream of reconstruction in the smaller cities and towns less favoured with resources?

In the City the overriding priority had been to re-establish as rapidly as possible the position of London as the financial centre of Europe, a goal shared by developers and the local authority. In most cities the collaboration between the local authority, armed initially with only limited planning powers, and private commercial interests, which generally provided capital for redevelopment, was not straightforward.[64] The legal basis for city-centre reconstruction was the Town and Country Planning Act 1944, but the powers that it provided were limited, as were the areas, of Blitz rather than blight, to which it was applicable. Reconstruction in most cities was a struggle between local government and local commercial interests, between local interests and representatives of national government, and finally, at national level, between the interests of the Treasury in limiting the costs of reconstruction and the hopes of Ministry of Town and Country Planning, or after 1951 the Minsitry of Housing and Local Government charged with overseeing the rebuilding of the cities. Moreover, even this simple characterisation overlooks the problems generated by disagreements and tensions at local level between local authority officers – between City Architects and City Engineers – or between local and central branches within the same government department, between the Ministry of Town and Country Planning's regional planning officer and those in the ministry in London.

At the heart of these difficulties lay the problem of costing and paying for reconstruction. While central government undertook to finance reconstruction in the short term, the 1944 Act was drawn up on the assumption that in most circumstances replanning and rebuilding should be capable of paying for itself. This forced local authorities to make hard choices. Given the limited time for which the exchequer grant was available, even for blitzed areas, local authorities needed to judge their ambitions for reconstruction against the revenues that their proposals would produce: would the areas of open space and greenery at the heart of so many plans for reconstruction be economically viable? City councils were asked to choose, for example, between modest schemes that might pay for themselves and more ambitious proposals that would necessarily involve attracting the capital of outside developers. Moreover, local authorities inevitably found that they also needed to balance the costs of city-centre reconstruction against other priorities, like housing and schools, and the political costs of increasing the rates. Those seeking to define and defend the public interest often found themselves at odds with those who saw the city as a commercial centre in which to make money. In cities with a Labour council and Conservative backing for commercial interests, conflict was frequent. As a counterweight to the atypical experience of reconstruction in the City of London, the examples of Bristol and Coventry provide an understanding of the complexities of rebuilding British cities and the difficulties faced by many cities as they struggled to meet the public's hopes of reconstruction.

Rebuilding the centre of Bristol

In the period immediately after the war, when the role of the 'expert' still carried weight, the City of London was fortunate to have a planner like Holford who commanded the respect of the City Corporation and could speak on equal terms with senior officials and even with Lewis Silkin, the Minister of Town and Country Planning. Bristol lacked this advantage, and the making of its plans was much less straightforward.[65] Not only did Bristol refuse to engage an outside expert on planning matters, but responsibility for drawing up a plan was divided between the City Engineer, Marston Webb, and the city's first City Architect, Nelson Meredith. Appointed in 1938 and very much the junior of the two, Meredith disagreed fundamentally with the priorities to be embodied in the plan. Equally important were the disagreements over the strategy for rebuilding the city centre throughout the post-war decade between the local authority, controlled by Labour, and the city's business and commercial interests, represented by the Citizens' Party and the Bristol

Retailers Council. Complicated by these disagreements, the debate on the rebuilding of Bristol was conducted in essentially local terms by architects and the other professionals who moved in circles dominated by the life of the city. Those responsible for planning and rebuilding in the city were aware of the national debate on reconstruction and the ideas being discussed in the architectural press, but there was scant opportunity to engage with these issues. Local firms were dominated by senior partners whose architectural attitudes had been set before the war. They were unlikely to jeopardise a relationship with an established client to pursue what seemed like nothing more than a passing London fashion.

Preparing visitors for the 1950 RIBA conference in Bristol, Lance Wright, a regular contributor to the *Architects' Journal* and familiar with Bristol, sketched in the world of the Bristol architect sharply but sympathetically, emphasising the smallness of the circles in which the architects and their clients moved:

> The architect draws his client to himself by means of the figure he cuts in the social life of his city. He is always moving in a very small and, by London standards, intimate society. Everybody knows everybody else, and most of those who have the misfortune to need an architect are on the lookout, not for someone dashing who will make their commission the raw material of experiment, but for someone distinctly conventional and reassuring.[66]

The character of much Bristol building, Wright argued, reflected the nature of the Bristol client: 'It is quite easy to think of "the Bristol client" as a single person because the social life he leads begets great unanimity.'[67] Bristol citizens were not philistines. Far from dismissing architecture as 'stuff and nonsense', Wright wrote, the notional Bristol client had an exaggerated and almost embarrassing respect for architecture but very little idea of what it meant. Accustomed to operating in local professional circles, it was only natural for him to look to local architects for guidance.

Wright's description has an element of caricature; Bristol clients and their architects were not all as parochial as he implies. Vincent Harris, Sir Percy Thomas and Sir Giles Gilbert Scott were working in the centre; Nelson Meredith was well known in official architectural circles; Eric Ross's buildings for BAC were illustrated in the *Review* and the *Builder*; and small companies like Frenchay Products Ltd were prepared to bring in young architects like Leonard Manasseh and Partners, known for their work at the Festival of Britain, to design a small but crisply detailed curtain-walled office building at Kingswood. But like any good caricature, Wright's portrait had a sound basis in truth. With the exception of buildings by in-house architects working for national chain stores like Marks and Spencer, Woolworths or Burton's, the great majority of buildings in central Bristol were designed locally. There were no competitions, no equivalent to Coventry Cathedral, to attract talent into Bristol from outside.

Social life for many Bristol architects was comfortably organised around the meetings, outings and the occasional balls of the Bristol Society of Architects (BSA). To complement this social scene, professional and aesthetic interests were catered for by a number of societies, the most important of which were the BSA, which celebrated its centenary in 1950 with an exhibition of its members past and present, and the Bristol Savages, a select and flourishing artists' club. This convened regularly to discuss architecture and the arts in the Wigwam, 'a raftered hall built in the courtyard of an old city mansion called Red Lodge, and hung with Waterloo helmets, assegais, buffaloes' horns and all the trophies which an acquisitive past membership could bequest'.[68] Many members of both societies were supporters of the Civic Society and the Council for the Preservation of Ancient Bristol, and both the BSA and the Savages formed the core opposition to the City Engineer's pre-war proposals for road building in the city centre and post-war plans for reconstruction. With many

local architects trained at the Bristol School of Architecture and then articled in the city, the Bristol School of Architecture under Gordon Hake exercised a considerable influence on the local profession. The school might be characterised by Wright as 'intellectually relaxed', but at least it did provide a setting for lectures and discussions and a forum for debating the larger architectural issues of the moment.

Even before the bombing raids of late 1940 and early 1941 that devastated the centre of the city, Bristol had been ambitiously preparing the redevelopment of areas in the city.[69] In 1935 the City Council agreed that College Green should be redeveloped to provide a new civic centre to the grandiose, simplified classical designs of Vincent Harris. By September 1939 the council announced four other schemes covering 16 acres within the city and a further 78 beyond. Responsibility for these schemes was already an issue of contention. Although Abercrombie and B.F. Brueton, the city's Executive Planning Officer, had published a regional survey and plan in 1930, responsibility for planning in the city rested directly with Marston Webb, whose first priority was not town planning but speeding up the flow of traffic around the city.[70] His success, in the face of strong opposition from the Civic Society, the Council for the Preservation of Ancient Bristol, the BSA and the Savages, in forcing a main traffic artery diagonally across Queen Square, one of Bristol's grandest squares, was to colour relations between the City Engineer and the local architectural community throughout the period of post-war reconstruction.

The heavy raiding that began in November 1940 laid waste to much of Bristol's historical heart. Key buildings like St Mary Redcliffe, Quakers Friars and John Wesley's Chapel survived, but large areas of the centre were devastated, including the central shopping area around Wine Street and Castle Street.[71] The need for large-scale reconstruction was inevitable. After further raids in the spring of 1941, the city centre had been so badly damaged that Bristol was selected, along with Coventry and Birmingham, as one of the Ministry of Works and Planning's test case cities to be used to develop the planning powers necessary for post-war reconstruction. As in his dealings with Coventry, Lord Reith urged Bristol City Council to 'replan boldly' without being hobbled by the constraints of cost.[72]

Spurred on by encouragement from central government, the Labour-controlled council was keen to start the process of planning for reconstruction but uncertain how to proceed, not least because of concern about the costs of rebuilding and doubts about whether these costs would be met by central government. The council's eagerness to rebuild was initially matched by the enthusiasm of other interests in the city. From the spring of 1941, a special advisory committee had been formed by small traders, builders, architects, the Bristol Property Owners' Association and the Multiple Shops Federation and was to become the voice of professional and commercial interests throughout the debate on reconstruction.[73]

In the summer of 1941, as the proposals for reconstruction took shape, the consensus of the spring drained away. Disagreement between the council and the city's commercial interests was fuelled by two areas of dispute. First was the city's unwillingness to consult the local interest groups and the property owners who would be directly affected by reconstruction, a dispute further exacerbated by the city's refusal to allow any representation of these interests on the committee centrally responsible for replanning. Second was the mounting opposition during 1942 from commercial interests to the city's plans to shift the commercial centre northwards from its original location along Wine Street to the site of the present centre around Broadmead. This opposition, though vociferous, remained politically ineffective, and in February 1944 the City Engineer presented extensive proposals to the City Council for rebuilding the centre. These envisaged a new commercial centre at Broadmead, complete with a new cultural forum and an education precinct, all enclosed within an inner ring road. Six hundred acres were identified as necessary for reconstruction and included in the declaratory order required by the 1944 Town and Country Planning Act.[74]

Though the public responded favourably to signs that the council was preparing for reconstruction, the commercial reaction to proposals for the shopping centre was lukewarm and the city's business community soon rallied support for their objections. To head off its critics, the city's Planning and Reconstruction Committee agreed minor modifications to the plan. Potentially more important were the critical recommendations made by an advisory panel from the ministry, which urged the city to reduce the scale of its plans for rebuilding. The city declined to heed this advice, and the plan which was put before the council in July 1945, though slightly less ambitious than that of the previous year, remained unchanged in principle. In this form the city's plans for reconstruction won popular endorsement at the municipal elections in November 1945, though it is significant that all parties gave housing priority over rebuilding the city centre.[75]

In March 1946 Bristol submitted proposals to the Ministry of Town and Country Planning for approval, only the second city to do so. With 771 acres included in the declaratory order, the plan had changed little since the previous year, despite unwavering opposition from the Bristol Retailers Council and other professional and commercial interests. Notwithstanding enthusiastic endorsement by Holford at the ministry, and a hint in discussions with Silkin that the Bristol plan might be adopted without a public inquiry, the city's hopes of successful approval for the plan were dashed. Pressed by the Treasury to limit the scale and speed of reconstruction, the ministry refused to grant approval to the plan as presented. The earlier concern outlined by the ministry's advisory panel about the large size of the plan was reflected in the ministry's cautious view that 66 per cent of the land which the city sought to purchase by compulsory powers was not covered by the provisions of the 1944 Act. Another meeting in February 1947 between the ministry and a deputation from the city depressed the council's hopes still further by attacking the proposed new shopping centre and demanding further cuts in the scale of the plan to meet Treasury-enforced guidelines on the costs of reconstruction. In April 1948, when the city authorities submitted new plans, they finally admitted defeat and drastically pruned their proposals so that only 19 acres were requested for the Broadmead centre. But even this was judged too large by the ministry. On a ruling that 'only land for essential and immediate need should be purchased', the ministry finally conceded permission for the compulsory purchase of no more than four acres. After an inquiry approved these new minimal plans in April 1949, it took a further eight months, until December 1949, before the first steel allocation was agreed and the projected shopping centre could finally start to be built.[76]

Bristol's plan was an ambitious attempt to make a new city centre. But the four acres finally approved were all that could be earmarked for rebuilding until the submission of a revised city development plan in 1952 under the more generous provisions of the 1947 Town and Country Planning Act. The 1952 plan confirmed the key elements of the proposals already agreed and reaffirmed the city's commitment to building the Broadmead shopping centre. It zoned land for new office development and created separate precincts for the expansion of the university and the hospitals. Prepared by the City Engineer, the plan placed greater emphasis on the provision of new and improved roads to ease the flow of the growing volume of traffic. Its principal feature was an inner ring road, much of it dual carriageway, drawn tight around the centre. The provision of new housing, still an important issue in local politics in the early 1950s, was directed to the outskirts, to the forty-six new neighbourhoods at Lawrence Weston and Henbury to the North, and to Heathcliffe and Stockwood to the South.

The city's failure to secure approval for its grand plan to rebuild the city centre undermined the hopes of reconstruction raised during the war and robbed Bristol of any architectural opportunities that large-scale rebuilding might have brought. The few architectural opportunities presented by the plan, above all the design of the new Broadmead shopping centre, were not exploited

as they might have been. As part of the proposals submitted to the ministry in 1946, Meredith produced a schematic design for the Broadmead Centre in the Beaux Arts manner (Figure 11.11).[77] Painfully adjusted to accommodate two of the

i

ii

iii

11.11 Meredith's 1946 plans for Bristol's new Broadmead shopping centre: (i) aerial view of the centre looking north-west; (ii) sketch of the heart of the centre; (iii) the new shopping centre surrounding the historic Quakers Friars

most important remaining historic buildings, Quakers Friars and John Wycliffe's house, the shopping centre would have sat like the imposed creation of an alien culture in the tight grain of what was left of the centre, sadly lacking the vitality and animation of old Bristol streets like Wine Street.

In other areas of the city Meredith had made positive contributions to the preservation of the Bristol streetscape. He had been responsible, with the Council for the Preservation of Ancient Bristol, for retaining the Greyhound Hotel and the restoration of the Lower Arcade. But his proposals for the Broadmead Centre are quite at odds with his interest in old Bristol: the bird's-eye perspective, an uncomfortable cross between a zoning diagram in three dimensions and an architectural sketch, emphasises the large monotonous areas of flat roofs. The detailed treatment of the intersection at the heart of the new centre shows a brutally scraped classicism, animated by an arcade and cantilevered canopy on the main axes of the centre. The drawing of the square designed to contain Quakers Friars and John Wycliffe's house shows the irreconcilable collision of the scale of the new centre with the domestic scale of the two historic buildings. The version of the plan finally approved retained only the central area of the shopping centre, a drastically truncated version of the original proposal.

Meredith's hopes of retaining architectural control of even this small central area of shopping foundered on the determination of each shop to produce its own design (Figure 11.12). At the heart of the new centre, Meredith designed a shop front for Swears and Wells, a lacklustre scheme of pre-war modernist character with a steel frame clad in polished stone. But any hope of sustaining even the pallid order which he proposed for the rest of the centre was undermined by the frontages of the adjacent national stores designed by in-house architects.[78] Woolworths sported a flashy facade of 1930s commercial moderne by H. Winbourne. On the opposite side Montague Burton was given a stripped classical facade by N. Martin, its staff architect, as was Marks and Spencer by James M. Monro and Son. The only frontage worthy of architectural attention was the facade of the Dolcis store by Ellis E. Somake, again a staff architect, but working for a company that valued architectural design and had established a national reputation for innovative design. Working within the same overall height as the other shops on the south side of Broadmead, Somake used the freedom offered by a reinforced concrete frame to create a bold recession from the street at ground and first-floor level, fully glazing the entrance and displaying the columns of the frame within. The result rivals the best modern shops built in the West End of London.

Aside from Broadmead and the completion of the Civic Centre in College Green, there was little building in the centre of Bristol before 1955. Developers and shopkeepers, like those in other provincial cities, had to wait longer for building licences than their counterparts in London. The principle exception was a nine-storey office block, built under the lessor scheme, the appropriately named Gaunt House designed by Alec French and Partners.[79] Built as a steel frame clad in Bath stone with small panels of flattened sculptural detail, this block trod the fine line between the stripped classicism of, say, Holden's London University Senate House and the commercial modernism of Emberton's Olympia to produce what the *Architects' Journal* judged 'typical of the rather heavy, cautious modernity of the better post-war office building'.[80] Just beyond the centre the university had built a few new buildings, typical of which was the Veterinary School, a bland brick building with a pitched roof and metal windows designed by Oatley and Brentall, the practice whose partner Sir George Oatley had designed the heroic gothic University Tower. But otherwise the city centre had little to show for a decade of reconstruction.

After the high hopes of the early 1940s this lack of achievement was dispiriting. But it was not atypical. Other cities, like Canterbury, Southampton and Exeter, that had suffered

i

ii

iii

iv

11.12 The architecture of reconstruction in Bristol: (i) Meredith's design for Swears and Wells; (ii) new premises for Montague Burton Ltd by N. Martin; (iii) a night view of the Dolcis shoe shop by Ellis E. Somake; (iv) Gaunt House by Alec French and Partners (1950–52)

damage found rebuilding their centres just as slow. Without the economic priority accorded to the City of London, they had to join the other cities, all with projects, in the long queue for resources. But what of Coventry? Would the special circumstances of its destruction enable it to rebuild more quickly and more comprehensively than other cities?

Rebuilding the centre of Coventry

Many of the difficulties that beset the rebuilding of Bristol can be recognised as Coventry set about the same tasks.[81] There was the same tension between the city and central government over the scale of the proposals for reconstruction and, as in Bristol, the Ministry of Town and Country Planning was ever pressing for a reduction in the acreage to be included in the declaratory order. The timetable of rebuilding was painfully slow, again a reflection of the determination of the Treasury to rein in the costs of reconstruction. At Coventry too there were the same differences of approach between the City Engineer, E.H. Ford, and the City Architect, Donald Gibson, and the same political divisions between a Labour-controlled council pressing ahead to realise a vision of a new city and the more conservative community of business and commercial interests.

But for all these similarities the situation in Coventry was different in important ways. More so than Bristol or any other provincial city, Coventry was identified nationally as the city whose centre had been devastated by bombing. The fact that it was the first city outside London to be badly blitzed, the concentration of damage, the loss of life, the burning of the cathedral, all combined to capture the nation's imagination so that it came to represent the war suffering of towns and cities across the country. It was natural therefore that the reconstruction of Coventry should take on a special significance: if reconstruction were to be a success it had to be successful in Coventry. Reith's encouragement to the city 'to plan boldly and comprehensively' and 'at this stage to [not] worry about finance of local boundaries' reflects central government's willingness, in 1941 at least, to recognise the unique position of Coventry and its significance for the hopes of reconstruction nationally.[82]

Coventry was also more fortunate than most cities in the quality of the advice it received from its young City Architect.[83] Appointed City Architect and Planning Officer (jointly with the City Engineer) in 1938 at the age of 30, Gibson was regarded as one of the most progressive city architects before the war. Trained at the Manchester School of Architecture, Gibson worked briefly in the United States before lecturing for a short time at the Liverpool School of Architecture, an institution that emphasised links between social policy and architecture and town planning. It was at Liverpool too that he was first to meet Percy Johnson-Marshall, with whom he was later to work at Coventry, and his brother Stirrat. From Liverpool Gibson moved to the Building Research Station, where he worked with Stirrat Johnson-Marshall, before deciding to change direction. In 1937 he opted for a career in official architecture, accepting a post as deputy county architect at the Isle of Ely.

Gibson never played an active part in the national debate on architecture and took no part in either of the two English meetings of CIAM, though the design for the centre of Coventry was presented at the debate entitled 'Heart of the City' at the congress in Hoddesdon in 1951. As a designer he was closer to pre-war modernists like Dudok and members of the older generation of Swedish modernists like Tengbom and to the formal planning of the Liverpool School than to the Continental avant-garde. But he did share many of the ideals of the new architecture. He saw architecture and planning as inseparably linked and, like Le Corbusier, regarded the architect as the natural authority for the structuring and design of the city. Gibson shared too the conviction of the importance of the new methods of construction and new materials, an interest strengthened by his work at the BRS. Both during and after the war he engaged in the debate on prefabrication, encouraging experimentation in Coventry with new forms of construction for both housing and schools.

His most important contribution at Coventry was the leadership he brought to the department, his role as 'umbrella man' for the department and staff, and his ability to inspire individuals and the exchange of ideas.[84] In contrast to the hierarchical way of working to be found in most Architect's Departments, the Coventry office was arranged in loose groups, each of which was given responsibility for a project from start to finish, and where all new projects were discussed openly in a manner more like a school of architecture than an official Architect's Department. Collaboration within the office was complemented and stimulated by occasional competitions, run like the *esquisse* competitions of the Beaux Arts, for the design of small-scale projects such as street furniture, with the winner carrying the project through to realisation. Percy Johnson-Marshall, who joined the Coventry Architect's Office in 1938 as Gibson's first assistant, remembered the sense of opportunity for change that Gibson created around him:

> A few of us went to help start the new office, and we went bursting with ideas; ideas about prefabrication in building, about new kinds of housing layout, about carrying good design into every detail of the townscape, and about making the whole city a collective work of art.[85]

Crucial to Gibson's achievement as City Architect was his positive relationship with the council. From the start of his appointment before the war both architect and council shared the conviction that architecture and planning could transform the city to make good the effect of the years of neglect on the part of the Conservative and Liberal coalition which had governed Coventry during the 1920s and 1930s. Then, reductions in rates and limiting the city's expenditure had been the benchmark of success.[86] In sharp contrast, the new Labour council wanted both to provide the libraries, concert halls, picture galleries and other public buildings that the city had been denied for so long and to ensure that the provision of housing, schools and other facilities kept pace with Coventry's rapidly growing population. Central to the council's support for Gibson and his proposals was George Hodgkinson, variously councillor, alderman, mayor and chairman of the Planning Committee, and a key figure in the local Labour party throughout Gibson's period at Coventry.[87] Hodgkinson's belief in the importance of

architecture and planning for the transformation of the city, spurred by his reading of US architectural critic Lewis Mumford, Le Corbusier and others, matched that of Gibson.[88] He was crucial to ensuring Gibson's advantage in any conflict with E.H. Ford, the Chamber of Commerce or those who favoured rebuilding the city as quickly as possible on the existing pattern of ownership – a view of reconstruction derided by Hodgkinson as no better than 'a wash and brush up'.[89]

The war overtook Gibson's early plans, but working furiously Gibson, Johnson-Marshall and their wives were able to mount an exhibition of these first proposals in June 1940.[90] The presentation of the model, accompanied by a series of public lectures given by leading planners like Thomas Sharp and William Holford, sparked local interest in planning and stirred a sense of expectation. These proposals anticipated in broad outline the form of the plans for the city centre finally submitted after the war: a new pedestrianised shopping centre aligned on the spire of the old cathedral, leading to a modernised Broadgate, in turn leading on to a cathedral close containing the still (in June 1940) undamaged cathedral and Holy Trinity Church. Immediately to the south the planners envisaged a civic centre containing the most important new public buildings for the city: law courts, library, museum, college, health centre and swimming pool. Planned independently of the street lines as pavilions set in open space, in the manner of Le Corbusier's 1922 City of Tomorrow, the buildings were to enclose green and paved spaces which would connect north to Pool Meadow, the major green space for the heart of the city, all to be protected from through traffic by a surrounding ring road. The plan may have proposed a radical rebuilding of the centre, but Gibson and his team argued that they were nevertheless retaining the established order of the centre of the city as urged in Mumford's *The Culture of Cities* (1938).[91]

This first exhibition ensured a surge of interest in Gibson's proposals in the immediate aftermath of the November 1940 raid that devastated the city centre (Figure 11.13). In December the

 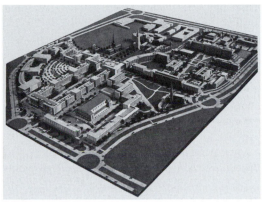

i ii

11.13 The evolution of Gibson's proposals for the centre of Coventry: (i) the pre-Blitz proposals for a new civic centre exhibited in May 1940; (ii) the first post-Blitz proposals published in April 1941

city established a City Reconstruction Committee to set in hand the process of replanning and rebuilding, and by February 1941 the committee was in a position to consider two distinct plans for rebuilding submitted separately by the city's joint planning officers. In contrast to Gibson's ambitious proposals, the plans from the City Engineer were based on the notion that rebuilding should proceed as quickly as possible to preserve the commercial life of the city centre and that little change to the status quo was needed, other than adjustments to the road network to meet the demands of the growing volume of traffic passing through the centre. In the spring of 1941, encouraged by their meeting with Lord Reith, the City Reconstruction Committee recommended the adoption of Gibson's plan as the starting point for the city's reconstruction.[92]

The adoption of Gibson's plans by the council was followed by a long period of disagreement and negotiation between the council and local commercial interests on the one hand, and the council and the newly formed Ministry of Town and Country Planning on the other. The objections from the city's shopkeepers are readily understood: Gibson's plans, drawn up unofficially in late 1939 and early 1940, had been prepared without any of the consultation required for the preparation of an official plan. Adopted

by the Labour council before the process of consultation began, it took no account of the views of the Coventry Chamber of Commerce, which spoke for the city's shopkeepers and other commercial interests. Over the next three years, the local retailers remained fiercely opposed not only to the form of the pedestrian precinct – cut off, in their opinion, from traffic and thus from shoppers – but also to the advantages that the tenants of the centre, the large shops and chain stores, would have over shops located elsewhere in Coventry.

The ministry was equally opposed to the scale of Gibson's plans, though for other reasons. Both ministry's regional planning officer and more senior officers in the ministry's head office in London were troubled by the extent and thus the expense of the city's plans and further distressed by the failure of the city to consult with local commercial interests. Nor did a visit by a ministry team in the summer of 1943 do anything to resolve these concerns. On both counts the council insisted on standing by its City Architect and his plan.

By February 1944, however, the situation was improving. The city started to consult the Chamber of Commerce, and Gibson helped by signalling his willingness to reconsider his proposals. In November, Gibson publicly pledged his readiness to look again at the plan and redesign the shopping centre if required. At last, by May 1945, the city and the Chamber of Commerce had agreed, at Holford's urging, to reduce the size of the shopping centre to a fifth of the total shopping frontage in the city and to the introduction of a north–south road bisecting the precinct at right angles to provide additional access for shoppers.

In October 1945, to celebrate the ending of the war and to publicise the city's plans for reconstruction, the city opened an exhibition, 'Coventry of the Future'. The plan, viewed by an estimated one in four of the city's population, was widely acclaimed.[93] Keen to take advantage of this surge of popular support, Mayor Hodgkinson pressed Lewis Silkin for swift approval of the city's plans. But Silkin responded with a warning of the shortage of resources nationally and a reminder of the need to adjust the priorities of reconstruction to the resources available locally, a restatement of the ministry's concerns over the scale of the city's proposals and a reminder as well of the acute shortage of housing in the area.

Nevertheless, six months later the city still wished to press forward with the plan, its resolve strengthened by the renewed success of Labour in the local elections. In February 1946 the city applied under the provisions of the Town and Country Planning Act 1944 for a declaratory order for 452 acres. By the summer, anxious to get reconstruction under way, the city took symbolic action. It commissioned a statue of Lady Godiva from Sir William Reid Dick to be placed on the Broadgate garden and laid a levelling stone at the centre of Broadgate as part of that year's victory celebrations. Yet despite pressure from the council, delays and doubts persisted: the ministry remained reluctant to agree the city's plan, and when the public inquiry on the plan opened in June there were misgivings about its scale and the extent to which the costs of rebuilding would be met by central government. At long last, however, in the spring of 1947 the plan emerged successfully from the inquiry with the Chamber of Commerce's backing. The

minister's confirmation of the order, issued in May, was for only 274 rather than the 452 acres requested by the city, but still sufficient to realise the most important elements of Gibson's plan.[94] One year later in May 1948, the city invited Princess Elizabeth to open Broadgate Gardens and, with this fanfare of publicity, embarked on the building of the five central blocks of the shopping precinct, all on land already owned by the city and therefore not subject to the delays of compulsory purchase. Finally, in May 1949, the minister approved the bulk of the city's central area plan and, two months later, the city's plans for the whole area within the ring road. Almost nine years after the first presentation, the council's proposals for reconstruction were finally approved.[95]

By comparison with other cities, Coventry had been quick to secure approval for its plan, but this was only the first hurdle. The progress of reconstruction was to remain slow as the city struggled to find the workforce and materials for housing. In October 1953, the *Architects' Journal* wrote that no single building in the centre had been completely finished.[96] Yet comparison with Bristol showed how much had been achieved.[97] The blocks around Broadgate were still under construction, but there was already sufficient progress to give some impression of the final appearance of the upper precinct of the shopping centre. With the pedestrian spaces and the first-floor arcades completed, the essential elements of the centre were beginning to emerge.

What were the architectural qualities of Coventry's new centre? Gibson and Johnson-Marshall's first proposals, the 1940 model for the civic centre, were schematic in the extreme: the bulk of the new accommodation was to be concentrated in two curved linear blocks which enclosed the centre's outdoor spaces. But at this stage Gibson's principal concern was to inspire enthusiasm for the idea of replanning; the architecture of the shopping centre would have to wait. By the following spring the scale of the replanning proposals had expanded to include the shopping centre, now necessary to replace

i

iii

ii

iv

11.14 The architecture of Broadgate and the new shopping precinct: (i) view looking westwards across Broadgate in the early 1960s; (ii) Broadgate House in the early 1950s; (iii) aerial view of the shopping centre in 1959; (iv) Owen Owen department store from Broadgate

the blitzed shopping streets, and a remodelling of the civic area. Twenty years later, Johnson-Marshall was to claim Gropius and Le Corbusier as the source of inspiration, but certain elements of the design share another parentage: the axial arrangement of the shopping centre, aligned on the spire of the cathedral, looks to the Liverpool School's interpretation of the Beaux Arts, and to Sweden and America for its layout and to the brick modernism of the 1930s for its architecture.[98]

It was not until 1945 that a new model was made. This showed the new north–south road cutting across the precinct, but Gibson remained as non-committal as ever about the architecture of the new centre. His proposals remained essentially illustrative. With pressure on the Architect's Department to build housing and schools for the city's new suburban estates at Canley,

Monks Park and Tile Hill, plans for the central area had to wait.[99] Only with the confirmation of the declamatory order in 1947 would Gibson finally find time to finalise the design of the new shopping centre.

Broadgate House and the upper precinct, the initial stage of this redevelopment finished by the end of 1953, illustrate best the way that Gibson hoped to rebuild the city centre as a whole (Figure 11.14).[100] Compared with contemporary interest in Picturesque town planning, the new centre gives an overriding impression of formality. This is heightened by the contrast between the haphazard texture of old Coventry, with its tangle of workshops, housing and shops, and the rigidly diagrammatic composition of the new centre. The design of Broadgate, intended as the heart of the rebuilt city, illustrates the problem of reconciling the new centre with the fabric of the existing city and at the same time meeting the demands of the City Engineer. The central garden is cut off, separated by a road from the shopping centre, an ornamental roundabout engulfed, then as now, by the traffic channelled through the city. Within the shopping centre the formality of Gibson's design is more successful. Walking from the west along the central axis, the shopper passes under the pedestrian bridge into the animation of the upper precinct. This is enclosed on either side by shops, upper-level galleries and balconies, and contained to the east by the two brick pavilions of Broadgate House, which frame the view of the cathedral spire beyond. In contrast to Broadgate, the precinct, with its flowering cherry trees, works well as an urban square where people can sit and talk, aware of but untroubled by the bustle of passing shoppers.

Inevitably the design of Broadgate House and the shopping precinct is subservient to Gibson's layout of the centre as a whole. The different blocks of the shopping centre share the same framed structural system but are treated differently: in the pavilions on Broadgate, they are treated as buildings of load-bearing brickwork; in the shops flanking the precinct, as frame buildings generously glazed. This variety owes nothing to the informality of the New Empiricism. Instead, the different treatments are determined by the need to articulate and order the design for the centre as a whole. The brick pavilions, for example, are used to mark the entrance to the upper precinct from Broadgate and to signal the break between the upper and lower precinct. Within, the continuous nature of the space of the different blocks is at odds with their external treatment: the offices overlooking the precinct enjoy floor-to-ceiling glazing, those in the brick pavilions peer through smaller windows punched in a masonry wall. Nowhere is the lack of architectural coherence more obvious than in the bridging section of Broadgate House facing north across Broadgate: rendered blockwork balancing uncomfortably on a fully glazed wall spans Hertford Street to find support from the brick clocktower. Contemporary critics were kind in their assessments. Rigby Childs praised it as 'not in any way ponderous', and thought the use of 'native materials … and of interesting, almost picturesque shapes and massing give a "friendly" look to the building group'.[101] Richards dutifully allowed that Broadgate was 'so far' the most 'impressive piece of civic planning that has been achieved in any of our bombed cities'.[102]

By early 1954, Gibson's just finished Broadgate House was complemented by the 'mainstream modernism' of the Owen Owen department store, designed by the private firm Helberg and Harris, rather than the city's Architect's Department.[103] With its great glazed facade to the sales floors behind contrasting with the travertine and brick clad offices, the building has more in common with contemporary commercial architecture in London than with Gibson's design. Richards used the Owen Owen store to introduce his selection of buildings of the year for 1954, but damned it with faint praise: 'if not a brilliant piece of architecture, it handles contemporary idiom in a workmanlike way'.[104]

Whatever the failings of the architecture of the individual buildings, the design for the centre of Coventry deserves to be appreciated, as Gibson and his team intended, for the effect of the whole. At the time – it precedes the centres of Stevenage and Harlow – Coventry was the only example of modern architecture used to create the public space of a city centre outside London. The overall impression may be dull and seemly, of unpolished modernism owing more to the 1930s than the 1950s. Dick's statue of Lady Godiva is pre-war in feeling but, here and there, touches like the lamp-standards and the decorative metalwork of the balustrades, reveal its contemporaneity with the Festival of Britain, but the architecture of the centre has little to do with the New Empiricism and the *Review*. It is closer to pre-war modernism, to the architecture of Holden's underground stations or to Dudok's Hilversum Town Hall.

Despite its lack of critical acclaim, the architecture of the centre did not fail the promise of reconstruction. It answered the vision of 1941. Designed in outline long before the war was over, and caught in the endless tussle between central and local government, between Labour council and commercial interests, its principal failing in the eyes of those who judged it in the mid-1950s was that it had been overtaken by the changing nature of modern architecture.

The developments in the City of London, Bristol and Coventry convey something of the difficult experiences of reconstruction of British city centres by the mid-1950s. Five years later the process of rebuilding was much further advanced. In Coventry and Bristol bomb-site car parks had been closed and built over, as they had in cities like Exeter, Hull, Canterbury, Southampton and Plymouth. The changes, restricted to a few key cities before 1955, were now widespread. The methods used to redevelop Bristol and Coventry, the partnership of public and private investment and the forms of development, tried tentatively in the late 1940s and early 1950s, were now increasingly familiar. After five years of economic prosperity, the centres of British cities were already beginning to look very different from the way they had looked before the war. These changes were a product of the late 1940s and the early 1950s. Just as the new flats, mixed developments and neighbourhood centres were starting to change the suburbs, so the new everyday landscape of the city centres of the 1960s was already beginning to take shape by the mid-1950s. The mainstream modern office blocks in the City of London, the new pedestrian shopping centre in Coventry, the rebuilt shopping streets in towns like Bristol, built at the end of the first post-war decade, were a measure of things to come.

Notes

1   For a general account of the transformation of the economy see G.D.N. Worswick and P.H. Ady (eds), *The British Economy in the Nineteen Fifties*, Oxford, Clarendon Press, 1962. For the impact of these changes on British society in the mid-1950s see P. Clarke, *Hope and Glory: 1900–1990*, London, Allen Lane, 1996, ch. 8.

2   'Preview', *AR*, Jan. 1955, p. 5.

3   J.M. Richards, 'Buildings of the Year 1952', *AJ*, 15.1.1953, p. 89.

4   'Preview', *AR*, Jan. 1954, p. 13.

6   Compare, for example, a selection of the work exhibited at the Royal Academy for 1949 and 1950 – *Builder*, 6.5.1949, pp. 553–62; 20.5.1949, p. 626; 5.5.1950, pp. 580–2; 12.5.1950, pp. 589–93; 19.5.1950, p. 680 – with those for 1954 and 1955 – *Builder*, 7.5.1954, pp. 797–807; 14.5.1954, pp. 843–50; 6.5.1955, pp. 745–52; 13.5.1955, pp. 791–2.

7   J.M. Richards, 'The Next Step?', *AR*, Mar. 1950, pp. 17–71.

'Preview', *AR*, Jan., 1955, p. 5–7.

8   I. Bowen, 'Focus on You', *AJ*, 15.10.1955, p. 469.

9   The RIBA recorded monthly the death of those killed during the war; by VJ Day 201 members of the institute had been killed, *JRIBA*, Jun. 1947, p. 400.

10   During the war the *JRIBA* recorded the progress through the institute's external examinations of those in prisoner of war camps. See e.g. the exhibition of work by those held in Oflag 79, 'Target for Tomorrow', which was based on Ralph Tubbs' 'Living Cities' exhibition, *JRIBA*, May 1945, p. 195.

11   This figure is calculated from the record over each year of elections to associate and licentiate members of the RIBA. In 1949–50, the number of those elected was 896 (compared with a pre-war figure of around 650); in 1952–53 it had risen to 1,375; finally, in 1954–55 it had fallen back to 978. Further evidence comes from a series of short articles on the profession, 'Focus on You', by Ian Bowen in *AJ*: 9.4.1953, p. 550; 26.3.1953, p. 390; 2.4.1953, p. 420; 23.4.1953, p. 515.

12   For a discussion of the changing numbers of job vacancies and unemployed architects see Bowen, 'Focus on You', *AJ*, 30.4.1953, p. 94; 21.5.1953, p. 634.

13   Howard Robertson recalled the trials of war-damage repairs in *Builder*, 1.6.1962, p. 1121.

14   J.M. Richards, 'Recent Building in Oxford and Cambridge', *AR*, Aug. 1952, pp. 73–9.

15   'The Architect and the Economic Crisis', *JRIBA*, Apr. 1948, p. 235; see also 'Prospects for British Architects in the Empire', *AD*, Aug. 1948, pp. 178–81.

16   The *Architects' Journal*'s annual January survey 'Architecture Abroad' regularly reported the work of British architects; see also 'Recent Planning Developments in the Colonies', *JRIBA*, Feb. 1948, pp. 140–8.

17   Howard Robertson published an account of his life and practice, 'Obbligato to Architecture', in the *Builder* in 12 parts between April and June 1962. Robertson's work was reviewed in the *Review* when he was president of the RIBA: R. Banham, 'Howard Robertson', *AR*, Sep. 1953, pp. 161–8. Easton's life

and professional achievements were briefly summarised in the citation for the Royal Gold Medal for Architecture, *JRIBA*, Jan. 1955, pp. 295–6.

18 'Engineering Department, Cambridge', *AJ*, 22.1.1953, pp. 129–32.

19 Richards, 'Buildings of the Year 1952', pp. 101–2.

20 However, Robertson's reputation was to be damaged in the late 1950s by his design for the Shell Building, which appeared to younger architects as a betrayal of the modernist cause; 'Obligato to Architecture', *Builder*, 22.6.1962, pp. 1278–80.

21 A measure of the scale of the universities' building programme can be inferred from the rate at which student numbers increased: between 1939, when university building ceased, and 1954/55 student numbers rose from 50,000 to 82,000; *Higher Education*, Report of the Committee under the chairmanship of Lord Robbins, London, HMSO, 1963, p. 14–15.

22 R. Banham, *The New Brutalism: Ethic or Aesthetic?*, London, Architectural Press, 1966, p. 41.

23 *45–55: Ten Years of British Architecture*, exhib. cat., Arts Council, London, 1956; this was later published as a book, T. Dannat (ed.) *Modern Architecture in Britain*, London, Batsford, 1959.

24 Their work diversified to include a range of non-educational buildings: the Seamen's House in Erith, a curtain-walled office block in New Cavendish Street and, by the end of the 1950s, Castrol House on the Euston Road, one of the most assured of British interpretations of current US office building practice.

25 'Factory at Brynmawr', *AJ*, 20.3.1952, pp. 363–74; V. Penny, *Built for a Better Future: The Brynmawr Rubber Factory*, Oxford, White Cockade, 1994.

26 By the end of the 1950s Gibberd was working as a planner architect in a number of cities, as well as an architect with a varied practice which included industrial, airport, hospital and office buildings like the National Dock Labour Board building on the Albert Embankment in London.

27 By the end of the 1950s Spence was making a name for himself as an architect with a wide variety of work in addition to the exhibition and religious buildings: housing, schools, university buildings and medical buildings; B. Edwards, *Basil Spence 1907–1976*, Edinburgh, Rutland Press, 1995.

28 The role of the architect in property development is discussed in O. Marriott, *The Property Boom*, London, Hamish Hamilton, 1967, ch. 3.

29 *Ibid.*, p. 27.

30 Richard Seifert published plans for a large office development on Fetter Lane in London in 1955; Fitzroy Robinson launched his commercial practice in 1956.

31 Each year the *Architects' Journal* devoted a special number to describing the architectural qualities of the town chosen for the RIBA's annual conference; most of these special numbers included a description of the work of local practices. In addition, D. Rigby Childs and D.A.C.A. Boyne wrote a series of articles the *Architects' Journal* on the reconstruction of cities that had been badly bombed: Bristol (2.10.1952, pp. 396–405), Canterbury (24.4.1952, pp. 505–30), Coventry (8.10.1953, pp. 428–58) and Southampton (4.5.1953, pp. 480–508).

32 The three test surveys of blitzed cities were presented to the Interdepartmental Committee of Officials on Reconstruction in February 1941, and the results were incorporated in Reith's draft Town and Country (Reconstruction) Bill, submitted to the Cabinet's Committee on Reconstruction Problems in November 1941, just before Reith's dismissal.

33 The reconstruction of the City after WWII is discussed in G.E. Cherry and L. Penny, *Holford, a Study in Architecture, Planning and Civic Design*, London, Mansell, 1986, chs 6–9; Marriott, *Property Boom*, ch. 6; S. Humphries and J. Taylor, *The Making of Modern London 1945–85*, London, Sidgwick & Jackson, 1986, ch. 3; S. Bradley and N. Pevsner, *The Buildings of England. London 1: The City of London*, Harmondsworth, Penguin Books, pp. 125–41.

34 'The City of London Plan', *Town and Country Planning*, Autumn 1947, p. 137.

35 For a discussion of Holford's role in the rebuilding of the City see Cherry and Penny, *Holford*, chs 8 and 9.

36 'The City of London', *AJ*, 18.7.1946, pp. 43–54.

37 'Reconstruction in the City of London', *AJ*, 22.5.1947, pp. 425–41.

38 See, for example, Ministry of Works, *The Lighting of Buildings*, Post-war Building Studies No. 12, London, HMSO, 1944, and W. Allen and D. Crompton, 'A form of control of Building Development in Terms of Daylighting', *JRIBA*, August 1947, pp. 491–9.

39 The system of controls on building form and daylighting for the City of London Plan is spelt out in paragraph 6 of '30 Year Plan for the Reconstruction of the City of London', *AJ*, 22.5.1947, pp. 432–3.

40 Ministry of Town and Country Planning, *Advisory Handbook on the Redevelopment of Central Areas*, London, HMSO, 1947.

41 For a measure of the growing awareness of the need to elaborate a new approach for the cladding of the ubiquitous structural frame, see e.g. F. Gibberd, 'Expression in Modern Architecture', *JRIBA*, Jan. 1952, pp. 79–87, an article that was also published shortly afterwards in *AJ*, 24.2.1952, pp. 118–24.

42 The scheme is described in Marriott, *Property Boom*, pp. 50–1, and by J.M. Richards, 'The New London Office Buildings: The Lessor Scheme Critically Examined', *AJ*, 30.3.1950, pp. 394–8.

43 *Ibid.*, pp. 397–8.

44 'Atlantic House', *Builder*, 27.5.1949, pp. 649–52; J.M. Richards, 'Rebuilding the City', *AR*, Jun. 1954, pp. 379–81.

45 'Astragal', *AJ*, 19.3.1953, p. 357.

46 J.M. Richards, 'City Rebuilding: 2', *AR*, Sep. 1954, pp. 145–7.

47 'Astragal', *AJ*, 13.3.1952, p. 573.

48 This attack was voiced most forcefully by J.M. Richards. His first article, 'The New London Office Blocks', appeared in the *Architects' Journal* in March 1950 and was followed by others in April 1950 and February 1952. Richards also used his position as architectural correspondent of *The Times* and appearances on the BBC Third Programme's 'The Critics' to keep up the attack. He wrote three articles under the title 'Rebuilding The City' (*AR*, Jun. 1954, pp. 379–85; Sep. 1954, pp. 145–7; Dec. 1954, pp. 355–7).

49 Richards' attack received support from liberal papers, if not from those that traditionally supported the City, e.g. L. Brett, 'Business and Beauty', *Observer*, 25.5.1952, p. 8, and N. Gosley, 'The Big Battalions', *Observer*, 8.6.1952, p. 8.

50 'Astragal', *AJ*, 28.1.1954, p. 66.

51 At least this was J.M. Richards' view of developments in the City: 'The New Patrons', *AR*, Oct. 1955, pp. 215–18. But developers like Ravenseft were quick to blame the local authority: 'Aesthetically we had no control. The local authority always dictated … The local authority took the credit when the buildings were praised and the developers were blamed if the building was attacked', Marriott, *Property Boom*, pp. 63–4.

52 Marriott, *Property Boom*, pp. 50–1, describes Bridgland, the developer behind the building of Bucklersbury House, as typical of many City builders: a reactionary who disliked modern architecture and wanted a classical design but was forced to compromise by the LCC in order to secure permission to develop the site he had acquired with such difficulty. Owen Campbell-Jones, feted in the architectural press for his design, had served his apprenticeship in commercial architecture: after the AA, he had worked in the family firm, a practice with predominantly banking and financial clients; 'Men of the Year', *AJ*, 21.1.1954, p. 74.

53 'Astragal', *AJ*, 19.1.1956, pp. 79–80.

54 I. Nairn, *Modern Buildings in London*, London, London Transport, 1964, p. 2.

55 'Astragal', *AJ*, 6.5.1954, p. 537.

56 Bridewell Place by Trehearne and Norman, Preston and Partners, completed in 1951, was greeted as evidence of more enlightened patronage, *AJ*, 9.8.1951, pp. 167–9.

57 'Astragal', *AJ*, 10.9.1953, pp. 275, 278–9.

58 Nairn, *Modern Buildings*, p. 1.

59 'Astragal', *AJ*, 19.1.1956, p. 80.

60 The National Dock Labour Board offices are described in *AJ*, 18.10.1956, pp. 561–74, and Electrin House is discussed in *AR*, Oct. 1956, pp. 232–3.

61 'New City Buildings', *Builder*, 8.7.1955, p. 45.

62 I. McCullum, 'West End Offices', *AR*, Oct. 1956, pp. 225–6.

63 For an account of the development of the area around St Paul's during the 1950s see Cherry and Penny, *Holford*, ch. 9.

64 For a discussion of the provisions of both the 1944 and the 1947 Town and Country Planning Acts see J.B. Cullingworth, *Reconstruction and Land Use Planning 1939–47*, London, HMSO, 1975, especially chs IV and VIII.

65 For a general account of the reconstruction of Bristol see D. Punter, *Design Control in Bristol 1940–1990*, Bristol, Redcliffe, 1990; J. Hasegawa, *Replanning the Blitzed City Centre*, Buckingham, Open University Press, 1992, ch. 6; D. Rigby Childs and D.A.C.A. Boyne, 'Bristol', *AJ*, 2.10.1952, pp. 396–405.

66 L. Wright, 'The Architect in Bristol', *AJ*, 1.6.1950, p. 658.

67 *Ibid*., p. 659.

68 *Ibid*., p. 660.

69 C.W.F. Dening, 'Bristol, Past Present and Future', *OAP*, Jan. 1947, pp. 23–37.

70 The city's Executive Planning Officer and the City Architect both worked under Webb on planning matters, though the former reported directly to the city's Planning and Public Works Committee. For a discussion of pre-war planning in Bristol see Hasegawa, *Replanning the Blitzed City Centre*, pp. 17–19.

71 Dening, 'Bristol', pp. 23–7.

72 'Town Planning: Local Test Surveys Made', *The Times*, 9.4.1941, p. 2.

73 Hasegawa, *Replanning the Blitzed City Centre*, pp. 70–1.

74 'The Redevelopment of Bristol', *OAP*, Sep. 1953, pp. 427–34.

75 Hasegawa, *Replanning the Blitzed City Centre*, pp. 87–8.

76 Punter, *Design Control*, pp. 32–3; J. Nelson Meredith, 'Post-War Municipal Development in Bristol', *OAP*, May 1950, pp. 257–65.

77 Dening, 'Bristol'; Punter, *Design Control*, pp. 34–9.

78 *Ibid*.; Rigby Childs and Boyne, 'Bristol', pp. 396–400.

79 *Ibid*., p. 401.

80 *Ibid*., p. 394.

81 For a general discussion of the reconstruction of the centre of Coventry see: T. Mason and N. Tiratsoo, 'People, Politics and Planning: the Reconstruction of Coventry's Civic Centre, 1940–53', in J.M. Dieffendorf (ed.), *Rebuilding Europe's Bombed*

Cities, London, Macmillan, 1990, pp. 94–113; Hasegawa, *Replanning the Blitzed City Centre*, ch. 4; N. Tiratsoo, *Reconstruction, Affluence and Labour Politics: Coventry 1945–60*, London, Routledge, 1990; N. Bethune, *Bold and Comprehensive: Modern Public Architecture in Coventry 1937–1960*, dissertation, Cambridge University Department of Architecture, 1999; G. Hodgkinson, *Sent to Coventry*, Bletchley, Robert Maxwell, 1970; F. Carr, 'Municipal Socialism: Labour's Rise to Power', and B. Lancaster and T. Mason, 'Society and Politics in 20th Century Coventry', both in B. Lancaster and T. Mason (eds), *Life and Labour in a 20th Century City: The Experience of Coventry*, Warwick, Cryfield Press (no date).

82 J. Reith, *Into the Wind*, London, Hodder & Stoughton, 1949, p. 424.

83 Gibson's achievements are summarised in the obituary by Fred Pooley in the *Guardian*, 7.1.1992, and by William Allen in *JRIBA*, Sept 1992, p. 69.

84 P. Johnson-Marshall, *Rebuilding Cities*, Edinburgh, Edinburgh University Press, 1966, p. 292; P. Johnson-Marshall, 'Coventry: Test Case for Planning', *OAP*, May 1958, pp. 225–6.

85 *Ibid.*, p. 225.

86 Mason and Tiratsoo, 'People, Politics and Planning', pp. 94–6.

87 Hasegawa, *Replanning the Blitzed City Centre*, chs 4 and 7; see also Hodgkinson, *Sent to Coventry*, chs 11 and 12.

88 Johnson-Marshall, *Rebuilding Cities*, p. 295.

89 *Ibid.*, pp. 170–1; Gibson described Ford's proposals as rebuilding the city 'around the old drains', *ibid.*, p. 171.

90 *Ibid.*, pp. 292–5.

91 *Ibid.*, p. 295.

92 Hasegawa, *Replanning the Blitzed City Centre*, pp. 32–3.

93 'The New Coventry', *Coventry Evening Telegraph*, 8.10.1945, p. 7.

94 Tiratsoo, 'People, Politics and Planning', p. 107.

95 *Ibid.*, pp. 108–10.

96 Rigby Childs and Boyne, 'Coventry', p. 442.

97 D. Rigby Childs, 'A Comparison of Progress in Rebuilding Bombed Cities', *AJ*, 8.7.1954, pp. 41–52.

98 Johnson-Marshall, 'Coventry: Test Case', p. 225.

99 The urgent need for housing, and schools, for workers in the car-building industry demanded that housing take priority over other forms of building, including the city centre.

100 Rigby Childs and Boyne, 'Coventry', pp. 436–9; 'Reconstruction of Coventry', *Builder*, 19.11.1948, pp. 590–2; 'Coventry Rebuilds', *AD*, Dec 1958, pp. 483–9.

101 Rigby Childs and Boyne, 'Coventry', p. 430.

102 J.M. Richards, 'Buildings of the Year: 1954', *AJ*, 20.1.1955, p. 86.

103 'Owen Owen Department Store, Broadgate, Coventry', *Builder*, 12.11.1954, pp. 774–9.

104 Richards, 'Buildings of the Year: 1954', p. 85.

12 Conclusion

By 1955 the terms in which the new architecture was to develop for the next ten years had been largely set. The New Brutalists had built little, but were already sketching out the ideas through into the 1960s. The widespread enthusiasm for the New Empiricism encouraged by the *Architectural Review* was still running strong. The Hertfordshire achievement in schools, encouraged by the Ministry of Education, looked forward to the schools that were to be built by the Consortium of Local Authority Schools' Programmes from 1956 on into the late 1960s. The new curtain-walled office blocks rising in city centres across the country were as representative of the 'mainstream modernism' identified by Reyner Banham as the new technical colleges, hospitals and university buildings that appeared every January for the next decade in the *Review*'s Preview of forthcoming architecture.

But if the basic characteristics of modern architecture had been set for the next ten years or so, the world in which they were being built was changing. After 1955, the language of reconstruction gives way to talk of modernisation. Ten years after the end of the war, building proposals, decisions and actions no longer took the war and its consequences as a starting point. People talked instead of bringing Britain up to date, of the need to look forward to the second half of the twentieth century, even of the beginnings of a new Elizabethan age. Discussion of rebuilding gave way to the need to keep up with the United States or at least ahead of Europe.

The passing of the old talk of reconstruction, with its emphasis on collectively building a New Britain, marked a major shift in values. The Conservatives had come to power in 1951, and initially much remained as it had been. Tory policies on education and health, at least in broad outline, varied little the course set by Labour. But in areas such as the management of the economy change was brisker. The belief that the state had a fundamental role to play in building a New Britain – one of the central tenets of post-war reconstruction – now gave way to the belief that modernisation could best be achieved by liberating the creative forces of private enterprise. As the economy prospered and the constraints and regulations of the post-war command economy were cast aside, the opportunities for private enterprise boomed. As we have seen, the deregulation of the building industry allowed developers to start building the new shops, offices, cinemas and other commercial buildings that a buoyant economy demanded.

Nowhere was this change more visible than in housing. During the reconstruction years housing had been the central priority for the state's national building programme, but no longer. At the Conservative Party conference in 1951 Harold Macmillan, the Minister of Housing, had promised to unleash the energy of private enterprise to build 300,000 houses a year.[1] By 1953 he could claim to have reached this magic target, though only with the massive contribution of the local authorities, who had finished nearly four times as many houses in that year as private enterprise.[2] But thereafter local authority plans for general-needs housing were cut short. Private enterprise was to house the nation. These changes were enacted by the Housing Act 1956: general house building was to be the province of private enterprise, the local authorities were henceforth to concentrate their efforts on slum clearance. Housing starts already agreed might carry on for a year or two, and Labour-controlled authorities like the LCC might be able to sustain the momentum of their housing programmes to the end of the 1950s, but these were the exceptions to the rule.

Freed from government restraint, private enterprise launched a boom of new building. If the new spec-built housing estates in the suburbs were one obvious image of change, bright new commercial developments in city centres were another. The frenzy of speculative office building in the City of London in the late 1950s or city-centre developments such as the Bull Ring in Birmingham were a reminder of the fundamentally different way in which British cities were being built from the mid-1950s.

What had been achieved architecturally before the passing of the reconstruction years? Whatever the views of the critics, the people in whose name reconstruction was undertaken seemed at ease with what was being built. The new architecture appeared to win public acceptance and, occasionally, interest or even approval. Evidence of public support is anecdotal and fragmentary and generally focused on the merits of the individual building. More persuasive is the absence of the kind of opposition that modern architecture faced in the 1930s. Introducing the exhibition '45–55: Ten Years of British Architecture' in 1956, John Summerson (admittedly a critic with a sympathy for modern architecture) drew attention to the new status of modern architecture:

Few would think that label worth applying now; the expression is obsolescent and may perhaps be said already to have become an historical term appropriate to the 1930s. The 'modern movement' implied movement within a state of affairs alien to the ideas by which the movement

was inspired and that state of affairs no longer exists. Which is simply to say that a generation has passed. There is no Sir Reginald Blomfield now to castigate 'modernismus'; and the movement itself is very respectably old, its still acknowledged leaders bemedalled veterans.[3]

Despite their new powers, planning officers and their committees, ever sensitive to public opinion, seemed to acquiesce in the new architecture. Perhaps the very fact that modern buildings were being built across the country is itself evidence of a kind of its broad acceptability. For certain types of buildings, exemplified most prominently by the debate about the design of Coventry Cathedral, public taste might favour traditional architectural values. But for the vast mass of building, for houses, schools and commercial building, modern architecture appears to have been acceptable. Sources of information such as Margaret Willis's survey of the views of tenants moving to the housing built by the LCC in the 1950s or the attitudes of those settling in the first New Towns like Stevenage and Harlow suggest the pleasure that most people felt with their new homes.[4] But with fitted kitchens and modern bathrooms, it was the quality of the accommodation rather than the architecture for itself that scored most highly.

More clear cut is the evidence of the public's reaction to the architectural qualities of key modern buildings or events. Public reaction to the Festival of Britain is well documented.[5] The festival may have failed to command the interest of the international avant-garde, but it did have an impact on the British public. It was heavily publicised and widely discussed. Though the Beaverbrook papers, the *Daily Express* and *Evening Standard*, were hostile before it opened (and praised it thereafter), national newspapers like the *News Chronicle*, *Manchester Guardian* and *Observer* gave it extensive coverage. So too did the BBC: during the festival's five months 2,700 programmes were devoted to it.[6] Not only did people hear and read about it, they went in huge numbers to see it. By the time the lights went off at the end of September, over 8.5 million people had visited it.

What did they think? Gallup's poll of popular reaction showed that of those who had heard something of it – but not necessarily visited it – 58 per cent had formed a favourable impression and only 15 per cent were opposed. Those who had visited it were more enthusiastic still. Of course there were those like Evelyn Waugh or Albert Richardson who knew what they liked (and what they didn't) and knew that they did not like the festival. Richardson inveighed against it as 'a monumental piece of imbecility and iniquity'.[7] But for every one who spoke against, there were more who spoke for. Contemporaries and those looking back 25 years later judged the festival 'a knockout'. Whatever the reasons, as a release from austerity, as a promise of what a new and more prosperous Britain might be like, the public seemed to take the festival to its heart.

In retrospect the festival seems to have marked a turning point in the public's view of modern architecture. In 1951, day-to-day familiarity with modern architecture was still to come. That the glimpses into a modern world offered by the South Bank were associated with the colour, the music, the floodlighting of the festival helped people to accept the unfamiliar. People were willing to consider the new architectural forms and ideas because they were linked to the buzz and the fun of the festival. Above all, the festival helped to make the Modern Movement accessible to a larger public than had enjoyed it so far. It did much to start that process of democratisation that was to transform the status of modern architecture from the activity of a small avant-garde coterie that it had been before the war into something that was widely accepted.

But how did the champions of the new architecture see the achievement of the reconstruction years? In 1957, looking back over a decade of reconstruction, J.M. Richards was scathing in his condemnation of the results, not just in Britain but across Europe. Contrasting the hopes and the sense of opportunity with which people had looked forward to reconstruction with the dreary reality, he concluded 'that confusion is still with us and that the general standard of design and building was no better than it had been before', prompting the subtitle of the article, 'What has happened to the Modern Movement?'[8]

Richards agreed that the Western European countries could boast a small number of handsome modern buildings, such as Le Corbusier's Unité d'Habitation in Marseilles or Callini's railway station in Rome, the work of the architectural vanguard. But he was clear that the standard of the 'ordinary level of building' lagged far behind and that, in looking for an index of architectural progress, this, rather than the work of the leading elite, was the standard to judge. Britain was no exception. The Royal Festival Hall, the housing and schools of the LCC, the prefabricated Hertfordshire schools, the housing of Powell and Moya, the recently finished school at Hunstanton, these buildings might command respect, but the majority of buildings built since 1945 represented so many lost opportunities, in Richards' view:

The only phenomenon that has emerged since the war is a meanly finished utility commercial style of no distinction whatsoever, employed by development companies for the rebuilding of city sites often of such importance that in other countries it would be regarded as a matter of public pride that they were rebuilt worthily. In Britain nobody cares. These pages are concerned especially with the opportunities presented by wartime destruction, and it is saddening that it is in the blitzed cities that the failure of British architecture to show decision, enterprise or taste is most apparent.[9]

Richards' judgement on the fortunes of reconstruction since the war was harsh. He explained the timidity and the lack of architectural invention in a number of ways: the failure to modernise and mechanise the building industry, thus encouraging – as in spec-built housing – the persistence of outmoded ways of building; the failure to treat the rebuilding of bombed cities as anything more than a series of isolated, individual buildings. But above all he was saddened that so much work was entrusted to the older generation of commercial and official architects, thus perpetuating the architectural attitudes of the pre-war years, and by the very limited skills with which the ideas of the new architecture were being applied. He was cast down not by the failure of modern architecture to take root in post-war Britain, but by the depressing quality of the majority of modern buildings that had been built since the war. For Richards, editor of the *Review* and an influential spokesman for the new architecture, the gap between the buildings illustrated in the architectural press and the 'ordinary standard of building' was all too evident.

Was Richards' judgement a fair assessment of the practice of reconstruction or just another expression of the enduring disdain of the architectural vanguard for ways of thinking not its own? The judgement that he made is essentially stylistic. It is framed in terms of the vanguard's formal preoccupations. Inevitably Richards fails to acknowledge much of what had been done by way of reconstruction in the name of modern architecture, understood in broad, inclusive terms.

But how would an inclusive view of modern architecture weigh the achievements of the reconstruction years? The extraordinary circumstances created by the war, the scale of destruction, the shortages of resources, of labour and materials, had forced architects and the building industry to think of new ways of doing things. The war, and conditions during the following decade, had been the mother of invention and innovation. Equally important, these same circumstances had forced society to determine its priorities in a way that was impossible in peacetime: planning for reconstruction demanded a serious reconciliation of the nation's ideals with its resources in a way that conventional peacetime politics could not. The terms in which the priorities were set by the national building programme – the housing drive, the exploration

of non-traditional ways of building, the preparation for post-war school building – did begin to liberate the profession's collective imagination from the grip of the time-honoured procedures and practices of the past. The systematisation of research and enquiry orchestrated across the whole building industry and the related professions by the Directorate of Post-War Building was unparalleled. Equally heroic was the meshing of plans for post-war building with the creation of a coherent framework of national planning, an achievement of real intellectual and political courage.

Of course the results were mixed. The crippling shortages of resources during the early years of reconstruction created the bitter suspicion that the plans had been wrongly made, that faith in the ability of the state to match scarce resources to society's priorities was misplaced. Examples of failure and difficulty are legion. The housing drive, the nation's top priority in the years immediately after the war, was beset by problems: housing completions in London remained pitifully slow even five years after the war; the local authorities refused to believe in the solidity of non-traditionally built houses; the cost of some temporary bungalows rose so fast as to prohibit their production. But these set-backs must not blind us to the successes: the raising of standards in housing and schools even during a period of acute need; the successful development of new ways of building, especially in schools; the introduction of new ways of controlling the density of urban developments; the design and construction of the New Towns like Harlow and Stevenage, to highlight but a few of the decade's brighter achievements.

The war and reconstruction changed the practice of architecture in many ways. Perhaps practice in out-of-the-way rural areas might still be recognisably the same in 1955 as it had been before the war, but this would have been the exception. For most architects the decade of reconstruction saw a sweeping transformation of professional life. Many more architects were now engaged in public service, whether as employees of a local or central government or as private architects working on publicly funded commissions New materials and new methods of construction were changing the way that buildings were built. Planners now presumed to determine in advance the type and the volume of development allowed for every site in a way unthinkable before the war.

For the most part these changes had little immediate bearing on the appearance of buildings. Stylistically, the profession resumed in 1945 where it left off in 1939. Three-quarters of the profession were over 40 years old in 1953, thus many had trained in the 1920s, some before World War I. Unsurprisingly, many of the architects of the late 1940s took the forms of modern architecture in the 1930s as the starting point for new designs. But the nature and the scale of the changes affecting architecture and the building industry were eventually to affect attitudes to architectural form. The advent of lightweight steel-frame structures, used so successfully in schools but also in other building types like factories, is but one prominent example. New policies, for example the official encouragement of mixed development in housing or the planners' demand for higher residential densities within green belts, encouraged architects to think afresh about the design of housing. Innovation was fostered too by the changing demands of society, as set out in the Ministry of Health's *Housing Manuals* or the Ministry of Education's Building Bulletins.

Innovation also came from the avant-garde. And architectural practice drew on these ideas. Most architects responded sympathetically to the *Review*'s call for a New Humanism in architecture and shared its frank admiration for the work of Swedish architects like Asplund or Backström and Reinius. The small change of stylistic imitation is another measure of the exchanges between the elite and general practice. The proliferation of details such as rough stone walls, hexagonal paving slabs, wavy-edged canopies and decorative metal balcony surrounds during the decade after 1951 represent the stylistic fallout from the Festival of Britain and serve as a reminder of its influence. But more important were the major contributions of the architectural vanguard in developing new architectural types. British architects old and young made the pilgrimage to Marseilles to visit the Unité, but it needed the LCC, with its Development Group and its ability to attract designers of the highest ability, to show how the Unité could be 'translated' for British use. The slab blocks at Roehampton – Bill Howell's 'Marseilles pups' – were affordable interpretations of Le Corbusier's great prototype and retained some quality of the original. Projects like these, extensively discussed in the architectural press and tried out in vanguard buildings, were readily known to the profession as a whole. Formal innovation by the avant-garde was not ignored by practice – the widespread popularity of LCC-inspired point and slab blocks is a measure of the general interest in these new types – even if the absorption of new ideas into routine practice was gradual and uneven.

Richards' assessment of reconstruction reflects the contested relationship between architectural practice and the architectural vanguard. The post-war decade did see, as Richards had hoped, reconstruction with 'a standard of architecture deserving the adjective modern', albeit not on the terms of the avant-garde. The transformation in architectural values was more fundamental. The exceptional demands of the war and the opportunities it created had forced change on the way architecture was practised. The establishment of modern architecture as the mainstream style grew out of the expectations and hopes for a New Britain and the failures and successes of reconstruction.

Notes

1 K. Jefferys, *Retreat from New Jerusalem: British Politics 1951–64*, Basingstoke, Macmillan Press, 1997, ch. 1.

2 For housing production figures by local authorities and private enterprise see J.R. Short, *Housing in Britain: The Post-War Experience*, London, Methuen, 1982.

3 J. Summerson, *45–55: Ten Years of British Architecture*, exhib. cat., London, Arts Council, 1956, p. 6.

4 Margaret Willis, 'Living in High Flats', *JRIBA*, Mar. 1955, pp. 203–4.

5 M. Banham and A. Forty, *A Tonic to the Nation*, London, Thames & Hudson, 1976, ch. 8; M. Frayn, 'Festival', in M. Sissons and P. French (eds), *The Age of Austerity: 1945–1951*, London, Hodder & Stoughton, 1963.

6 *Ibid.*, p. 324.

7 *Ibid.*, p. 316.

8 J.M. Richards, 'Europe Rebuilt: 1946–56', *AR*, Mar. 1951, p. 159.

9 *Ibid.*, p. 170.

Index